# Computers and Technology in a Changing Society

**Deborah Morley**

**Contributing Author Charles S. Parker**

THOMSON COURSE TECHNOLOGY™

Australia • Canada • Mexico • Singapore • Spain • United Kingdom • United States • Japan

THOMSON
COURSE TECHNOLOGY

**Computers and Technology in a Changing Society**
is published by Course Technology.

**Managing Editor:**
Rachel Crapser

**Senior Product Manager:**
Kathy Finnegan

**Technology Product Manager:**
Amanda Young Shelton

**Product Manager:**
Karen Stevens

**Associate Product Manager**
Brianna Germain

**Editorial Assistant:**
Emilie Perreault

**Marketing Manager:**
Rachel Valente

**Developmental Editor:**
Pam Conrad

**Associate Production Manager:**
Jennifer Goguen

**Composition:**
GEX Publishing Services

**Text Designer:**
Abby Scholz

**Cover Designer:**
Abby Scholz



Printed in the United States of America

1 2 3 4 5 6 7 8 9 BM 07 06 05 04 03

For more information, contact Course Technology, 25 Thomson Place, Boston, Massachusetts, 02210.

Or find us on the World Wide Web at:
www.course.com



ISBN 0-619-16201-5

# PREFACE

**When it comes to technology, the only constant is evolution.** *Computers and Technology in a Changing Society* presents an integrated, well balanced look at the issues and concepts of a constantly-changing, computer-oriented society. The first thing you will notice is the engaging writing style and easy to navigate layout. In every chapter, the focus is not only on the uses and benefits of computer technology, but the risks and the flip-side of issues as well. Each chapter's learning tools help the reader master important concepts and the numerous marginal notations direct students to tutorials, resources, and video clips on the robust **Online Companion** site. You will even find boxed features throughout the book, called Trends In, A Closer Look At, or How To—each providing a more in-depth focus on how emerging technologies will impact our lives. Examples include everything from how to send encrypted e-mail messages, to trends in fingerprint identification scanning, to a closer look at digital copy protection.

## KEY FEATURES

### Clear & Simple Writing Style

The down-to-earth writing style makes the subject matter easy to understand and easy to translate to everyday life situations. Technical concepts that could be daunting to a reader are made simple through well organized explanations and well laid-out images.

### Timely, Comprehensive Coverage

Accommodating a wide range of teaching preferences, the book and companion Web site provide comprehensive coverage of traditional topics while also covering accurate, up to-the-minute societal issues such as safeguarding your privacy, protecting your computer from theft and viruses, protecting against identify theft and online fraud, intellectual property rights, equal access to technology, and other timely social issues.

### Learning Tools

**1. Outline, Objectives, and Overview:** Each chapter starts with an outline of the major topics covered, a list of student learning objectives, and a chapter overview. These added tools not only help instructors put the subject matter into perspective, but they also demystify the chapter for students.

**2. Chapter Boxes:** In each chapter, a **Trends In…** box provides students with a look at a new or upcoming development in the world of computers. The **A Closer Look At…** box explains and discusses a particular technology or issue, and the **How To…** box, which is presented on a two page spread, provides hands on instruction for how to do a specific computer task related to the chapter material.

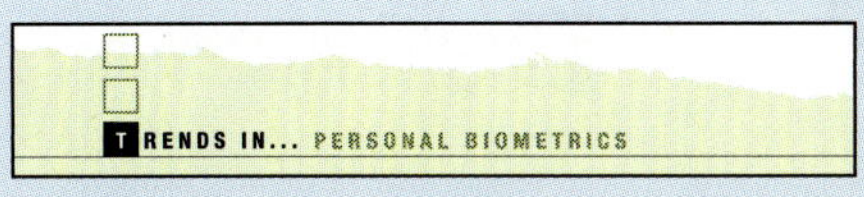

**3. Online Tutorials and Online Resources:** Each chapter contains several Online Tutorials and Online Resources, which are clearly called out in the margins within each chapter. The Online Resources provide students with a collection of relevant links located on the Online Companion site. The Online Tutorials provide students with short, topical PowerPoint presentations accessed from the Online Companion site.

**4. Illustrations and Photographs:** Current, full-color photographs and illustrations appear throughout the book to demonstrate important concepts. Figures and screen shots are carefully annotated to convey important information.

**5. Boldfaced Key Terms:** Important terms appear in boldface type as they are introduced in the chapter. These terms appear and are defined in the end-of-text Glossary.

**6. Summary and Key Terms:** A concise, section-by-section summary of the main points in the chapter. Boldfaced key terms in the chapter also appear in boldface type in the summary. A matching exercise of selected key terms helps students test their retention of the chapter material.

**7. Balancing Act:** A culminating exercise located at the end of each chapter that consists of a short essay examining the pros and cons of a particular technology-oriented issue, followed by discussion questions designed to promote interesting class discussions or thoughtful student opinion papers.

**8. Self-Quiz and Projects:** An end-of-chapter **Self-Quiz** (with the answers at the end of the text) consists of true-false and completion questions and allows students to test themselves on what they have just read. End-of-chapter **Projects** require students to extend their knowledge by doing research beyond merely reading the book and to form opinions about timely and potentially controversial issues. These Projects are organized into five types: Your Opinion, Independent Research, Hands On, Group Presentation, and Video Viewpoint. The Video Viewpoint project instructs students to watch a TechTV news clip (located on the Online Companion site) and then express their viewpoint on the issue detailed in the video either in class, via an online discussion group or class chat room, or in a written paper, depending on their instructor's directions.

**9. Glossary and Index:** A Glossary at the end of the book defines all boldfaced key terms in the text with a page reference indicating where the term is discussed. The Index contains page references for key terms, as well as other important, but non-boldfaced, words.

## STUDENT AND INSTRUCTOR SUPPORT MATERIALS

*Computers and Technology in a Changing Society* comes with a complete package of support materials for instructors and students. The package includes a comprehensive Online Companion site, a CD-ROM Instructor's Resource Kit, and a full-content online course.

## THE ONLINE COMPANION SITE

Providing media-rich support for students, the Online Companion site is located at:

*http://www.course.com/morley2003*

Once online, you will find:

- **Online Tutorials**—Links to short PowerPoint presentations covering additional, relevant material related to the concepts in the chapter.
- **Online Resources**—Links to Web sites with more in-depth information on a given topic.
- **Online Videos**—Links to TechTV news clips that students watch as part of the Video ViewPoint end-of-chapter project, to prepare for a class discussion or written opinion paper.

**ONLINE TUTORIAL**

For an online look at significant events in the history of computers, go to www.course.com/morley2003/ch1

**ONLINE RESOURCES**

For links to information about computer certification programs, go to www.course.com/morley2003/ch1

**ONLINE VIDEO**

To view the High Tech Climbing video clip, go to www.course.com/morley2003/ch1

### Instructor's Resource Kit CD-ROM

All of the Instructor's Resources that come with this book are provided to the instructor on a single CD-ROM that includes an Electronic Instructor's Manual, ExamView Testbank, and PowerPoint Presentations. Please note that these materials are also available online at *www.course.com*.

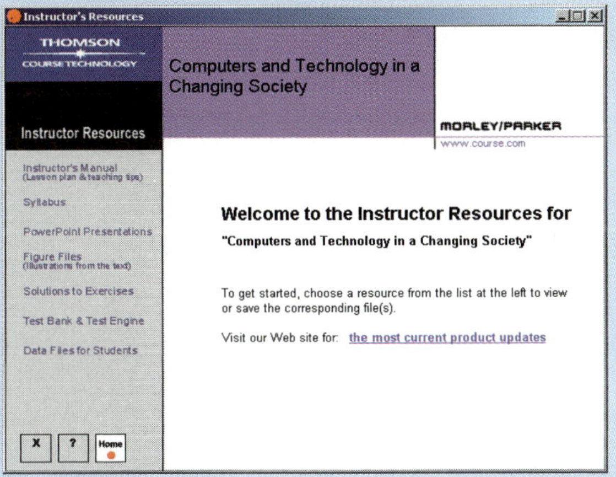


### Electronic Instructor's Manual

The Instructor's Manual is written to provide instructors with practical suggestions for enhancing classroom presentations. For each of the 8 chapters of the text, the Instructor's Manual provides:

- Chapter Objectives and complete, three-level Chapter Outline
- Key Terms with their definitions
- Lecture Notes and Teaching Tips
- Quick Quizzes
- Discussion Questions
- Classroom Activities
- Projects to Assign

### ExamView Testbank

ExamView is a powerful software testing package that allows you to not only create and administer traditional paper and LAN-based tests, but also Web-deliverable exams. Each testbank contains 100–150 questions per chapter, and is made up of Multiple Choice, True/False, Modified True/False, Completion, Short Answer, and Essay questions.

### PowerPoint Presentations

These PowerPoint Presentations, containing key points and illustrations from each chapter, offer a visual enhancement to your lecture, and we are excited to be able to offer them to you. Because they are in PowerPoint format, you can use them as they are, or modify them for your own use to have the perfect online or in-class presentation. They can also be printed for classroom distribution.

### Online Learning

Interested in online learning? You can enhance your course with rich online content for use through MyCourse 2.0, WebCT, and Blackboard. We are proud to present the *Computers and Technology in a Changing Society* Online Course in all three of these online learning platforms. This course provides students with lecture notes, practice tests, and additional projects. To learn more about our online learning solutions, visit www.course.com/onlinecontent.

## ACKNOWLEDGMENTS

I'd like to thank the following reviewers for their assistance during the creation and development of this text. Their time and efforts are greatly appreciated and the book benefited significantly from their expertise, helpful suggestions, and honest feedback.

Wade Graves, Grayson County College

Tamara Griffin, University of Arkansas Community College at Batesville

Charles Haynes, University of British Columbia

Randy Marak, Hill College

Mary Muldoon, Nova Southeastern University

Karen O'Brock, Nova Southeastern University

Pat Ormond, Utah Valley State College

Laurie Patterson, University of North Carolina at Wilmington

I am also very grateful to the people on the Course team—their professionalism, attention to detail, and enormous enthusiasm made working with them a pleasure. In particular, Rachel Crapser, Amanda Young Shelton, and Pam Conrad were instrumental in developing the concept and structure of this book. Pam, Amanda, and Jennifer Goguen were invaluable during the writing, rewriting, and production of this book—the balanced content and the accuracy of the book are a direct result of their untiring efforts. Thanks also to Abby Scholz for her great book design; Harold Johnson for his corrections and suggestions while copyediting the book; Abby Reip and Bonnie McLellan for their photo research; Rachel Lucas for her video research; Anne Leuthold at TechTV for helping us secure the Online Video clips; nSight for the development of the Online Companion; Brianna Germain for managing the Instructor's Resources package and Online Companion; Emilie Perreault for all of the work that she has done; and Rachel Valente for her efforts on marketing this text. I am very appreciative of Becky Holmes, RiverStones Learning and Paul Griffin for their work on the Instructor's Manual, ExamView Testbank, and PowerPoint Presentations. I am also very grateful to the numerous organizations that were kind enough to supply information and photographs for this text.

Finally, I would like to thank my family—Dennis, Nick, and Anne—whose patience and support made this book possible.

**Deborah Morley**

I sincerely hope you find this book interesting, informative, and enjoyable to read. If you have any suggestions for improvement, comments, or corrections that you'd like to be considered for future editions, please send them to deborah.morley@course.com

# BRIEF CONTENTS

# CONTENTS

# 36 Chapter 2—A Closer Look at Hardware and Software



**CHAPTER BOXES**

# 72 CHAPTER 3—A QUICK TOUR OF CYBERSPACE



**CHAPTER BOXES**

## 114 CHAPTER 4—COMPUTERS AND SECURITY



**CHAPTER BOXES**

## 158 Chapter 5—Computers and Privacy



**CHAPTER BOXES**

## 194 CHAPTER 6—ETHICS AND INTELLECTUAL PROPERTY RIGHTS



**CHAPTER BOXES**

# 258 CHAPTER 8—EMERGING TECHNOLOGIES

# ONLINE COMPANION

**As part of your fully integrated learning experience, we've created a multimedia-enhanced Web site at www.course.com/morley2003 where you will find:**

## Online Videos

Provide links to TechTV news clips. Available to you as part of your Video ViewPoint project.

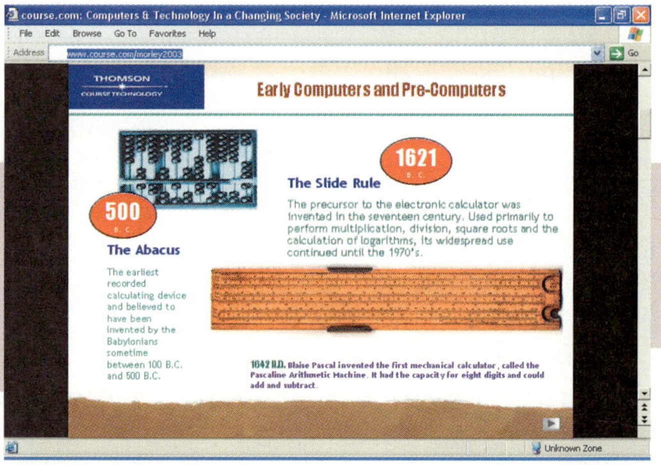


## Online Tutorials

Designed to extend your learning experience beyond the text, these brief PowerPoint presentations provide bonus material on specific topics related to each chapter.

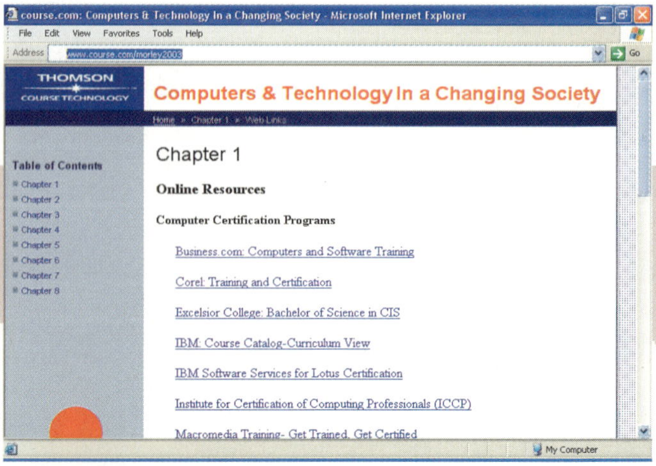


## Online Resources

Designed to provide you with more in-depth information on particular topics from the book, these resources are collections of links to informative Web sites.

# INTRODUCTION TO COMPUTERS AND TECHNOLOGY

## OUTLINE



## OBJECTIVES

**After completing this chapter, you will be able to:**

- Explain why it's essential to learn about computers today.
- Discuss several ways computers are integrated into our lives.
- Define a computer and describe its primary operations.
- List some important milestones in computer evolution.
- Identify the major parts of a personal computer, including input, processing, output, storage, and communications hardware.
- Contrast the difference between operating system software and application software, and list several examples of each.
- Describe the purpose of a network and what the Internet is.
- List the five basic types of computers, giving at least one example of each type of computer and stating what that computer might be used for.
- Provide an overview of the social impact of computers, including some benefits and risks related to their prominence in our society.

# CHAPTER 1

## OVERVIEW

Though computers have been in existence for several decades, it has only been during the last few years that computers and technology have had a significant impact on our daily lives. They have drastically changed the way we look up information, shop, pay bills, manage our investments, order supplies, keep track of inventory, prepare business presentations, plan trips, take exams, communicate with others, and more. Experts call this trend *pervasive computing*, in which few aspects of daily life remain untouched by computers and computer technology.

Not surprisingly, there are tremendous benefits of having such a computer-oriented society. But there are potential shortcomings, as well. Exploring today's computers and technologies and the various social issues surrounding them is what this book is all about.

Chapter 1 provides an overview of what computers are and how they are used. To help give you a firmer foundation for understanding and discussing the issues covered throughout the book, Chapter 2 explains the various components of a computer in more detail and Chapter 3 provides you with an introduction to the Internet and World Wide Web. Chapter 4 through Chapter 7 discuss the various important issues that arise from today's computers and technology, such as security, privacy, ethics, intellectual property rights, health, access, and the environment. The closing chapter, Chapter 8, looks at artificial intelligence, virtual reality, robotics, and other emerging technologies that may affect us in the future.

# COMPUTERS IN YOUR LIFE

As you probably already have noticed, computers are virtually everywhere. Many people's daily activities rely a great deal on a computer or a device using related technology, such as a cell phone or pager. Computer use is frequently required on the job, and home computer use—for productivity and communications purposes, as well as for entertainment and education—is growing. In addition, it is not unusual to have to use some type of computer for many consumer applications today, such as ATM machines or bridal registry systems. In fact, special-purpose, *embedded computers* are commonly found in watches, televisions, telephones, fax machines, kitchen appliances, exercise equipment, and many other everyday devices. As computers become embedded into more and more devices and as people increasingly depend on technology for their everyday activities, computers will become even more entrenched in our society. This trend of pervasive computing—also called *ubiquitous computing*—goes beyond traditional *general-purpose* computer use. Instead, this trend foreshadows a future where practically any device can contain embedded computer technology to give it additional functions or to enable it to communicate with other devices on an on-going basis.

## Why Learn About Computers?

Because computers are so prominent in our society and will become even more so in the future, it is to everyone's advantage to be able to use a computer. In addition, even though it is possible to use a computer without knowing what the various components are called and how they work, just as with a car or other important tool, it is a good idea to understand what a computer is and how it works. For example, knowing something about cars can help you to make wise purchases and save money on repairs. Likewise, knowing something about computers can help you buy the right one for your needs, get the most efficient use out of it, and give you a much higher level of comfort and confidence along the way. Therefore, basic *computer literacy*—knowing about and understanding computers and their uses—is an essential skill today for everyone.

## How Are Computers Used Today?

From the general-purpose computers that many of us use every day at home, school, and work; to the point-of-sale systems used to check us out at the grocery store or restaurant; to the complex computer systems used to diagnose our medical problems; computer use abounds. The next few sections discuss in more detail how computers are used at home, in education, in the workplace, and on the go in our society.

### At Home

Home computing has increased dramatically over the last few years as computers and Internet access have become less expensive and more consumer activities have become available. Use of the Internet at home to exchange e-mail, shop, download music and software, research products, pay bills, manage investments, play games, and so forth has grown exponentially. It is now estimated that over half of all U.S. households have a computer at home, and the vast majority of those individuals (over 40% of all Americans) have home Internet access. Most of this access is through a personal computer, though some users choose instead to use a dedicated *Internet appliance*—an easy-to-use device designed for specific Internet tasks, such as accessing the World Wide Web or checking e-mail.

Another growing use of computers at home is in the home office. With the ability to communicate with others via e-mail, fax, telephone, and other methods, more and more people are doing some type of work at home. From taking work home in the evening, to *telecommuting* part-time or full-time, to working entirely from home as a consultant or other self-employed individual, home computing for work purposes is increasing rapidly.

It is also becoming possible to have a *smart home* in which household tasks (such as watering the lawn, turning on and off the air conditioning, making coffee, monitoring the security of the home and grounds, and managing Internet access) can be controlled by a main home computer. *Smart appliances*—traditional appliances with some type of computer or communications technology built in—are expected to be even more prominent in the future.

Figure 1-1 provides several examples of computer use in the home.

### In Education

Today's children could definitely be called the computing generation. Unlike baby boomers who may have been introduced to computers at college or on the job, and older Americans who may never have used a computer until after retirement, if at all, today's young people have been brought up with computing technology. From video games to computers at school and home, most children and teens today have been exposed to computers and related technology all their lives. In fact, a recent report from the U.S. Census Bureau stated that approximately 65% of U.S. children live in a home with a computer, and about 90% use a computer at school. According to the study, while the *digital divide* (the gap between those who have access to technology and those who don't) still exists, "schools level the playing field by giving computer access to children who have none at home." Though the amount of computer use varies from school to school, many elementary and most secondary schools now have computers either in the classroom or in a computer lab. Most of these schools are also connected to the Internet, thanks in part to groups such as the nonprofit NetDay which has helped to wire over 75,000 classrooms across the U.S. for Internet access.

With the increased availability of computers and Internet access in elementary schools, the emphasis on computer use has evolved from straight drill-and-practice programs to using the computer as an overall student-based learning tool. Today, students use multimedia programs to enhance learning; productivity software—such as word processors and presentation programs—for creative writing and preparing class presentations; and the Internet for research. Many teachers use a computer to create lesson plans, as well as to submit required school information, such as attendance and grade reports.

**FIGURE 1-1**

**Computer use at home**

**^ Communications and other Internet tasks**

Many households today have access to the Internet and e-mail through either a home PC or an Internet appliance (as shown here).

**^ Home office**

Many people today use a computer to work from home on a part-time or full-time basis.

**> Education and entertainment**

For both children and adults alike, computers and the Internet offer a host of educational and entertainment activities.

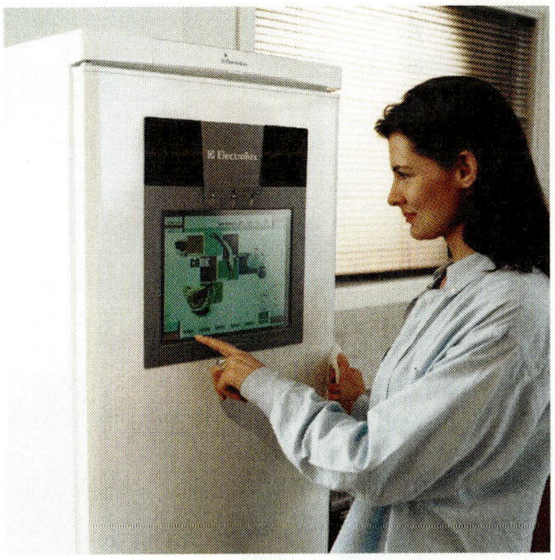

**^ Smart homes and appliances**

Smart homes use a computer or similar device to facilitate home networking and to control household appliances, security, and media systems. Smart appliances (such as the smart refrigerator shown here) are regular appliances with some type of computer technology built in.

At many high schools and most colleges and universities, computer use is much more integrated into daily classroom life than in elementary schools. Computers are commonly found in classrooms, computer labs, residence halls, and libraries. Students may be expected to use the Internet for research, to prepare computer-based papers and classroom presentations, and to access online course materials. In fact some institutions—primarily colleges and universities—require all students to have a computer.

In addition to their uses for homework and other supplemental tasks, computers facilitate *distance learning*—a fast-growing alternative to traditional classroom learning where students participate from remote locations, instead of at the educational institution. Distance learning students can do coursework and participate in class discussions from home, work, or wherever they happen to be at the moment, which gives these students greater flexibility to schedule class time around their personal, family, and work commitments. Distance learning also allows students to take courses when they are not physically located near an educational institution.

Figure 1-2 shows several examples of computer use in education.

### In the Workplace

Though computers have been used in the workplace for years, their role is continually evolving. Originally just a research tool for computer experts and scientists, and then a productivity tool for office workers, the computer today is used by all types of employees in all types of businesses—from the CEO of a multinational corporation, to the check-out clerk at the grocery store, to a traveling sales professional. The computer has become a universal tool for decision making, productivity, and communications (see Figure 1-3). One of the fastest growing new uses for workplace computing is in the service industry, where service professionals such as waiters, auto technicians, and delivery people are now using computers to record customer information, prepare bills, and store authorizing customer signatures.

**ONLINE RESOURCES**

For links to information about computer certification programs, go to www.course.com/morley2003/ch1

**FIGURE 1-2**

**Computer use in education**

**^ Elementary classrooms**

Many elementary school students today have access to a computer in the classroom or school computer lab.

**< High school and college classrooms**

The computer is used in many high school and colleges classrooms today as a learning tool and presentation tool; in addition, it is commonly used by instructors for preparing lessons and filing reports.

**< Other campus locations**

Most high school and college students have access to a computer and the Internet in a campus computer lab or library.

**< Distance learning**

Many students do homework and take online classes at home or wherever they happen to be at the moment.

### On the Go

In addition to being found in the home, at school, and in the workplace, most people encounter and use all types of computers in day-to-day life—from using an ATM machine to deposit or withdraw money from their bank account, to entering desired workout data into the smart treadmill or stationary bike at the local gym, to using a portable navigation system while traveling or hiking. As they become more and more integrated in our society, computers are becoming less visible and more easy to use. For example, *kiosks*—small self-service booths providing information or other services to the public—often include a computer with a screen that users touch with a finger to select options and request information. Kiosks are commonly found in hotels, conference centers, retail stores, and other public locations to allow individuals to look up information or purchase products. Some special types of kiosks even allow people to download specific information (such as sporting event statistics or programs for cultural events or trade shows) wirelessly to their handheld computers.

For Internet access while on the go, computers are increasingly being found in a wide variety of public locations, such as libraries, airports, health clubs, coffee houses, hotel rooms, taxis, and restaurants. In addition, computing technology and Internet capabilities are starting to be built into a wide range of everyday devices, such as cell phones, pagers, exercise equipment, digital photo frames, cars, and more. Figure 1-4 shows some examples of computers encountered in everyday life.

**FIGURE 1-3**

**Computer use in the workplace**

**^ Personal productivity**

Many business professionals today use a work computer to prepare budgets, reports, and other documents; exchange e-mail and otherwise communicate with others; maintain schedules, appointments, and contact information; and perform research and other tasks on the Internet.

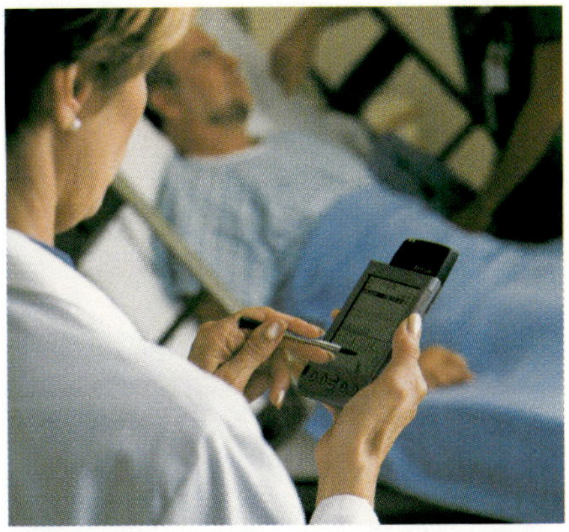

**^ Communications**

Handheld computers are commonly used by employees who need to record data while away from their desks, or who need to access data located on the Internet or company network when they are out of the office.

**^ Presentations**

Computers are commonly used today to create and give business presentations to both large and small audiences.

**^ Customer service**

Service professionals frequently use computers to record orders, prepare bills, and store authorizing customer signatures.

## WHAT IS A COMPUTER?

A **computer** can be defined as a programmable electronic device that accepts data, performs operations on the data, presents the results, and can store the data or results as needed. Being *programmable*, a computer will do whatever the instructions—called the *program*—tell it to do. As new programs are run on the computer, it becomes capable of performing new tasks.

**FIGURE 1-4**

**Computer use in everyday activities**

**Electronic signature**

It is becoming increasingly common to be asked to sign electronically for purchases, deliveries, service orders, and more on a computer or digital input device; an electronic signature is immediately available for proof of delivery and other applications.

**Consumer accessories**

Smart accessories, like the digital frame shown here that can display multiple photos and receive new photos over a standard telephone line, are becoming more and more common.

**Self-service kiosks**

Computerized kiosks are widely available to view conference or bridal registry information, create greeting cards, print photographs, order products or services, and more.

**GPS applications**

Global positioning capabilities enable cars, GPS receivers, handheld computers, and some cell phones to show users their exact geographical location, usually for navigational purposes.

The four operations described in this definition are more technically referred to as *input, processing, output,* and *storage.* These four primary operations of a computer can be defined as follows:

- **Input**—entering data into the computer
- **Processing**—performing operations on the data
- **Output**—presenting the results
- **Storage**—saving data, programs, or output for future use

For example, let's assume that we have a computer that has been programmed to add two numbers. As shown in Figure 1-5, *input* occurs when data (in this example the numbers 2 and 5) are entered into the computer; *processing* takes place when the computer program adds those two numbers; and *output* happens when the sum of 7 is displayed on the monitor. If at any time the data, program, or output was saved for future use, that would be *storage.*

For an additional example, let's look at a supermarket bar-code reader to see how it fits our definition of a computer. First, the grocery item being purchased is passed over the bar-code reader—*input.* Next, the description and price of the item are looked up—*processing.* Finally, the item description and price are displayed on the cash register and printed on the receipt—*output*; and the inventory, ordering, and sales records are updated—*storage.*

This progression of input, processing, output, and storage is sometimes referred to as the *information processing cycle.* In addition to these four main computer operations, today's computers also typically perform communications functions, such as retrieving data from the Internet or other network, or sending a file or e-mail message to another computer. Therefore, **communications**—technically an input or output operation, depending on which direction the information is flowing—is beginning to be thought of as a fifth primary computer operation.

## Computers Then and Now

The computer, in the form we recognize today, is a fairly recent invention. In fact, personal computers have only been around since the 1970s. But the basic ideas of computing and calculating are very old, going back thousands of years. The history of computers is often referred to in terms of *generations,* with each new generation characterized by a major technological development. The next few sections take a look at early calculating devices and the different computer generations.

**ONLINE TUTORIAL**

For an online look at significant events in the history of computers, go to www.course.com/morley2003/ch1

### Pre-Computers and Early Computers (before Approximately 1945)

Ancient civilizations demonstrated a desire to count and compute, as illustrated by archeological finds such as notched bones, knotted twine, and hieroglyphics. The *abacus* is considered by many to be the earliest recorded calculating device. Believed to have been invented by the Babylonians sometime between 500 B.C. and 100 B.C., it and similar types of counting boards were used solely for counting.

FIGURE 1-5

Input, processing, and output

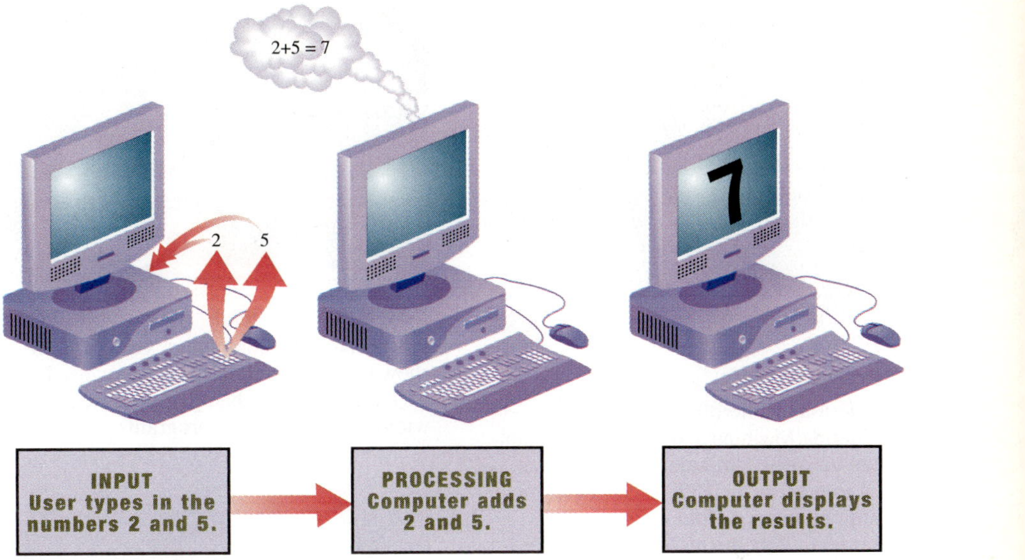


Other early computing devices include the *slide rule*, the *mechanical calculator*, and Dr. Herman Hollerith's *Punch Card Tabulating Machine and Sorter*. This device (see Figure 1-6) was the first electromechanical machine that could read *punch cards*—special cards with holes punched in them to represent data. Hollerith's machine was used to process the 1890 U.S. Census data and was able to complete the task in two and a half years, instead of the decade it usually took to process the data manually.

### First Generation (Approximately 1946–1957)

*First-generation* computers were powered by *vacuum tubes* and were enormous, often taking up entire rooms. The vacuum tubes—glass tubes that look similar to large cylindrical light bulbs—needed replacing constantly, required a great deal of electricity, and generated a lot of heat. These computers could only solve one problem at a time, and needed to be physically rewired to be reprogrammed. Usually paper punch cards and paper tape were used for input, and output was printed on paper.

Two of the most significant examples of first generation computers were *ENIAC* and *UNIVAC*. ENIAC (shown in Figure 1-6) was the world's first large-scale, general-purpose computer and was developed for the U.S. Army. UNIVAC was the first computer to be mass produced for general commercial use and was used to analyze votes in the 1952 U.S. presidential election. Interestingly, its correct prediction of an Eisenhower victory only 45 minutes after the polls closed wasn't publicly aired because the results weren't trusted.

### Second Generation (Approximately 1958–1963)

The *second generation* of computers began when the *transistor* started to replace the vacuum tube. Transistors—devices made of semiconductor material that can act like switches to open or close electronic circuits—allowed computers to be physically smaller, more powerful, cheaper, more energy-efficient, and more reliable than before. Typically data was input on punch cards and magnetic tape, output was on punch cards and paper printouts, and magnetic tape and disks were used for storage (see Figure 1-6). *Programming languages* (such as *FORTRAN* and *COBOL*) were also developed and implemented during this generation.

### Third Generation (Approximately 1964–1970)

The replacement of the transistor with *integrated circuits (ICs)* marked the beginning of the *third generation* of computers. Integrated circuits incorporate many transistors and electronic circuits on a single tiny silicon *chip*, allowing computers to be even

**FIGURE 1-6**

**A brief look at computer generations**

**^ Pre-computers**

Dr. Herman Hollerith's Punch Card Tabulating Machine and Sorter is an example of an early computing device. It was used to process the 1890 U.S. Census in about one-quarter of the time usually required to tally the results by hand.

**^ First generation**

First-generation computers, such as ENIAC shown here, were large and bulky, used vacuum tubes, and had to be physically wired and reset to run programs.

**^ Second generation**

Second-generation computers, such as the IBM System/360 shown here, used transistors instead of vacuum tubes so they were physically smaller, faster, and more reliable than earlier computers.

**^ Third generation**

The integrated circuit marked the beginning of the third generation of computers. These chips allowed the introduction of smaller computers, such as the DEC PDP-8 shown here, which was the first commercially successful minicomputer.

**> Fourth generation**

Fourth-generation computers (such as the original IBM PC shown here) are based on microprocessors. Most of today's computers fall into this category.

smaller and more reliable than in earlier generations. Instead of punch cards and paper printouts, keyboards and monitors began to be used for input and output; magnetic disks were typically used for storage. The introduction of the computer operating system during this generation meant that operators no longer had to reset relays and wiring manually. An example of a third-generation computer is shown in Figure 1-6.

### Fourth Generation (Approximately 1971–present)

The ability to place an increasing number of transistors on a single chip led to the invention of the *microprocessor* in 1971, which ushered in the *fourth generation* of computers. In essence, a microprocessor contains the core processing capabilities of an entire computer on one single chip. The original IBM PC (see Figure 1-6) and Apple Macintosh, and most of today's modern computers, fall into this category. Computers in this generation typically use a keyboard and mouse for input; a monitor and printer for output; and magnetic disks and optical discs for storage. This generation also witnessed the development of computer networks and the Internet.

### Fifth Generation (Now and the Future)

Though some people believe that the *fifth generation* of computing has not yet begun, most think it is in its infancy stage. This generation has no precise classification and some experts disagree with one another about its definition, but one common opinion is that fifth generation computers will be based on *artificial intelligence*, where computers can think, reason, and learn. Voice recognition will likely be a primary means of input, and computers may be constructed differently than they are today, such as in the form of optical computers that can compute at the speed of light.

## Hardware

A computer can be divided into two parts: *hardware* and *software.* **Hardware** includes all of the physical parts of the computer, such as the keyboard, screen, printer, and so forth. Hardware can be *internal* (located inside the main box or *system unit* of the computer) or *external* (outside of the system unit). External pieces of hardware plug into connectors called *ports* located on the exterior of the system unit, unless they are wireless devices.

There is hardware associated with each of the five computer operations discussed earlier (input, processing, output, storage, and communications). Hardware that can be found in each of these categories is briefly discussed next and illustrated in Figure 1-7. **Software**—the instructions or programs used in conjunction with a computer—is discussed in a later section. Both hardware and software are covered in more detail in Chapter 2.

### Input Devices

An *input device* is any piece of equipment that is used to input data into the computer. The most common input devices today are the *keyboard* and *mouse* (shown in Figure 1-7). Other possibilities include *image* and *bar-code scanners, joysticks, touch screens, digital cameras, electronic pens, fingerprint readers, smart card readers,* and *microphones*. For a look at how fingerprint readers are becoming more common for everyday activities, see the Trends In box.

### Processing Devices

The main *processing device* for a computer system is the *central processing unit (CPU).* The CPU is a chip located inside the system unit that performs the calculations and comparisons needed for processing, and also controls the computer's operations. For these reasons, the CPU is often considered the "brain" of the computer. Also involved in processing are various types of *memory*—temporary holding places where the computer can store data and instructions when it is working with them.

**FIGURE 1-7**

**Typical hardware found in a computer system**

## TRENDS IN... PERSONAL BIOMETRICS

### Everyday Uses for Fingerprint Scanners

*Biometrics* is the study of unique, measurable biological characteristics, such as fingerprints, irises, faces, hands, voices, and so forth. *Biometric devices* are used to authenticate an individual's identity through the use of a biometric characteristic. These types of devices have been used in recent years for granting access to secured facilities, and authenticating that the person using some type of access card (ATM card, student body card, corporate ID card, etc.) is really the authorized individual. These devices are even used to try to locate terrorists and criminals in airports and other public locations.

One of the fastest growing areas of biometrics is the use of the *fingerprint scanner.* Instead of using time cards, ID cards, or PIN numbers, employees at many organizations clock in and out of work using their fingerprints, which completely eliminates the possibility of "buddy punching," where one employee punches another employee in or out. It is also becoming increasingly common for work computers to require a quick fingerprint scan to access the computer and the company network. And at least one company has developed a fingerprint identification system for cars that allows consumers to enter and start their vehicle using only their fingerprint, or "finger image" as some companies prefer to call it.

One of the newest consumer applications—in the test marketing stage by several companies at the time this book was written, and likely to be available in the very near future—is the use of fingerprint scanners to buy goods and services at restaurants, grocery stores, video stores, warehouse stores, and other types of retail establishments. One of the leading companies in this area is Indivos Corporation. Their *Pay By Touch* fingerprint payment service—whose 2002 test locations included some California McDonald's, Blockbuster, and Walgreens stores—uses a standard credit card point-of-sale reader with a small fingerprint scanner attached (see Figure 1-8). All consumers who would like the option of paying with this method simply enroll in the program by scanning in their fingerprint, entering their appropriate contact information, and adding the desired payment options (such as credit card or checking account information). Then, to pay for goods and services in the future, customers need only touch their finger to the fingerprint scanner, select the desired payment method from a list, and they're good to go.

While fingerprint payment systems are convenient for consumers, reduce fraudulent transactions for merchants, and move customers through checkout lines faster, there are skeptics. Some individuals, worried about privacy and security, will likely never enter their fingerprint into a payment database. And though information entered into one brand of system (such as Indivos or their competitor Biometric Access) is available at any other retailer using the same system, until one standard or clear winner in this market emerges, incompatibility between rival systems may become a frustration for consumers. But consumer reaction so far seems to be positive. In one Indivos pilot test, 65% of the 3,000 consumers offered the service were willing to enroll.

To try to eliminate privacy and security concerns, Indivos has an extensive privacy policy that states, among other things, that the company will not sell, share, or rent consumers' information to others, except as needed to provide the Indivos payment service; the biometric information gathered will not be used to uniquely identify users across other databases; and consumers can modify or delete their information at any time. Whether consumers will trust fingerprint payment systems when they are widely introduced remains to be seen, but the outlook appears promising.

**FIGURE 1-8**

**Fingerprint payment systems allow consumers to quickly pay for goods and services.**

### Output Devices

An *output device* accepts processed material from the computer and presents it to the user, most of the time on paper (via a *printer)* or on the computer screen or *monitor,* as shown in Figure 1-7. Other possible output devices are *speakers*, *headphones*, and *data projectors* (which project computer images onto a projection screen).

### Storage Devices

*Storage devices* include a variety of types of *drives* and other types of hardware used to access data stored on *storage media,* such as *removable disks, CD discs,* or *DVD discs.*

The storage hardware featured in Figure 1-7 include a *hard drive*, a *floppy disk drive*, a *CD* or *DVD drive*, removable disks, and CD or DVD discs. Storage devices are used whenever data, programs, or output need to be saved for future use.

### Communications Devices

In addition to the traditional hardware already discussed, most computers today also have some type of *communications device* to allow the user to communicate with others, such as over the Internet or through a school or company *network*. The most common type of communications hardware is the *modem.* A variety of modems are available for the various types of possible connections, such as via telephone line, cable, or satellite.

## Software

The term *software* refers to the programs or instructions used to tell the hardware in a computer system what to do. Software is generally purchased on disk or CD, though many programs can be downloaded from the Internet instead. A newer alternative is running programs via the Internet without installing them on your computer. Instead, the programs are located on computers belonging to *application service providers (ASPs)* who typically charge a fee for their use.

Computers use two basic types of software: an *operating system* and *application software*. In addition, specific types of application software—such as *programming, markup,* or *scripting languages*—can be used to create customized applications.

### Operating Systems

The **operating system** is the main program in a collection of software—sometimes referred to as *systems software*—that allows a computer to operate. The operating system starts up the computer and controls its operation, such as setting up new hardware and allowing users to run other types of software and manage their documents on the computer. Without an operating system, a computer can't function at all. Common operating systems are *Windows* (see Figure 1-9) and *Mac OS.*

### Application Software

**Application software** consists of programs designed to perform specific tasks or applications, such as computing bank-account interest, preparing bills, creating letters, preparing budgets, managing inventory and customer databases, playing games, scheduling airline flights, viewing *Web pages*, recording or playing CDs, and sending e-mail. The application programs illustrated in Figure 1-10 are sometimes referred to as *productivity software,* since they help people be more efficient in performing daily tasks and activities.

**FIGURE 1-9**

**The Microsoft Windows operating system**

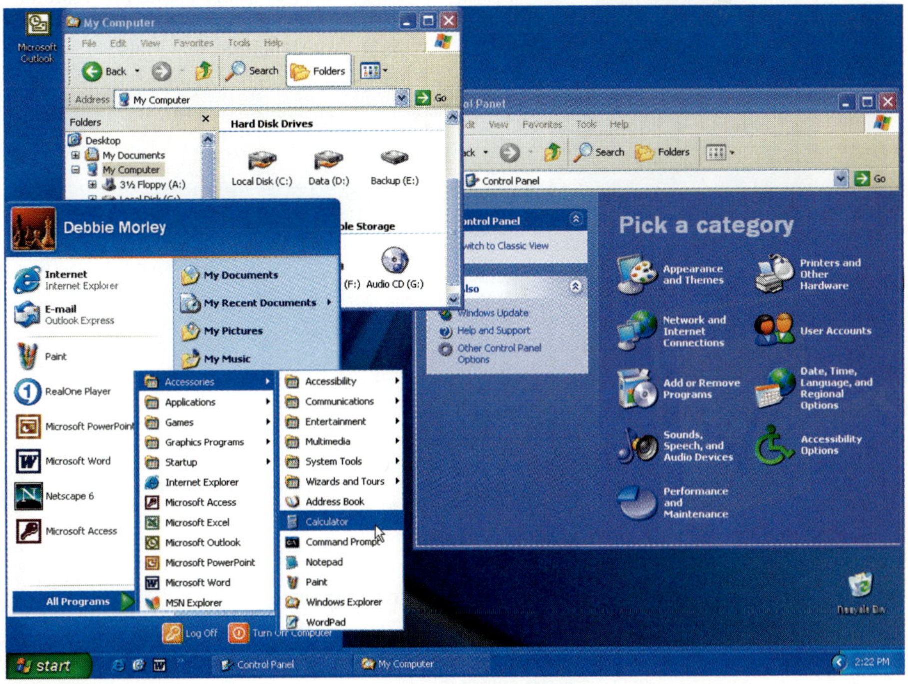

## FIGURE 1-10

**Various types of application software**

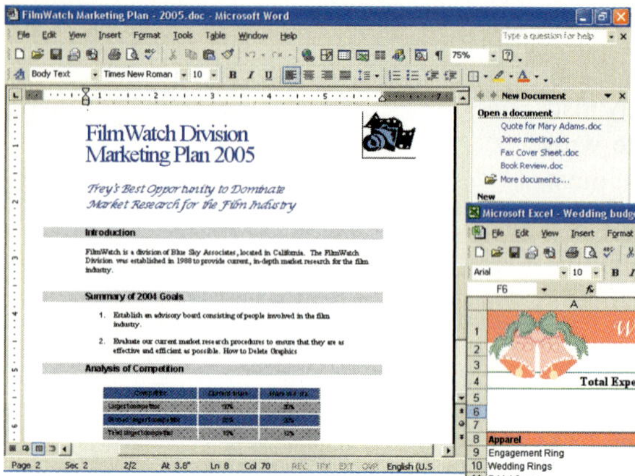

### Word processing programs

Word processing programs are used to create written documents, such as reports, letters, and memos.

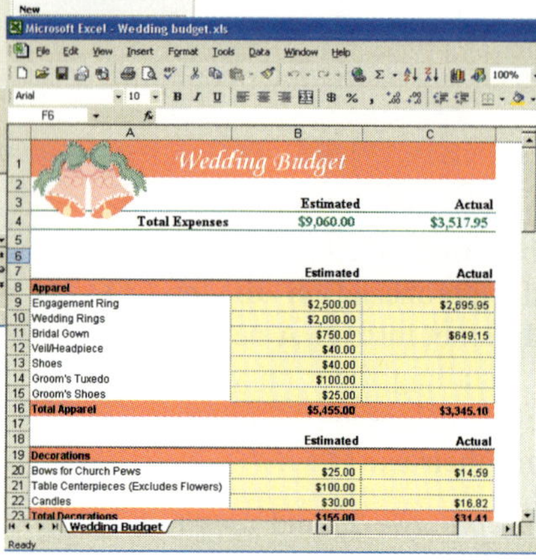

### Spreadsheet programs

Spreadsheet programs are used to create documents containing lots of numbers and computations, such as budgets, expense reports, invoices, and financial statements.

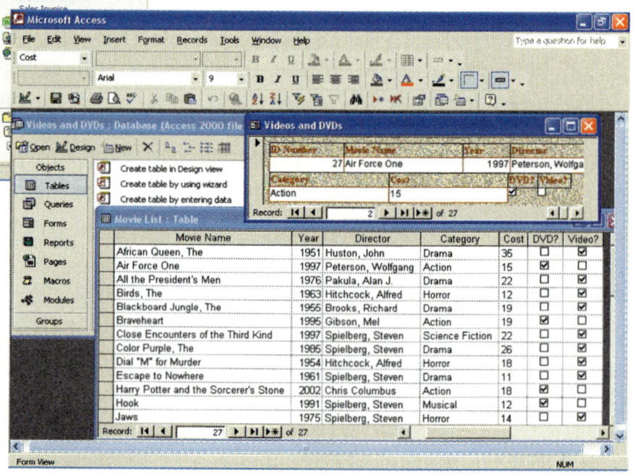

### Database programs

Database management programs allow users to create and access large collections of data, such as for customers, employees, inventory, and more.

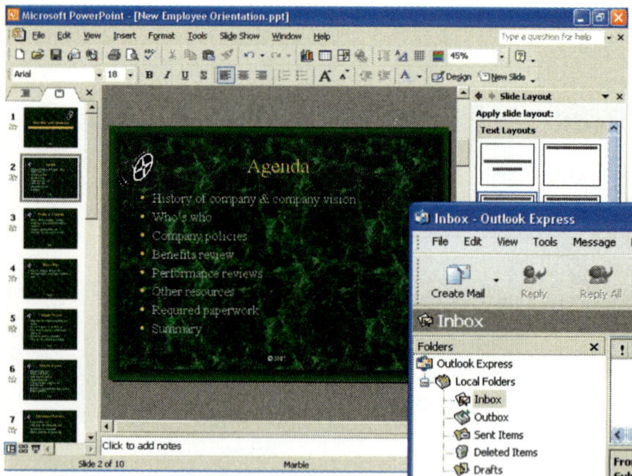

### Presentation programs

Presentation programs allow the user to easily create professional-looking slide shows and other presentation materials.

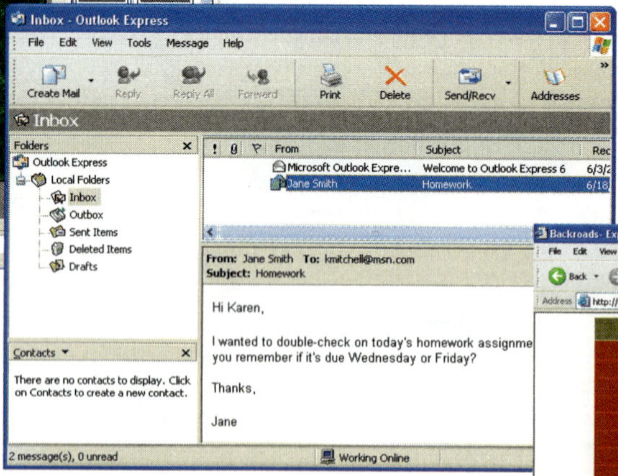

### E-mail programs

E-mail programs are used to compose, send, receive, and manage electronic messages sent over the Internet or a private network.

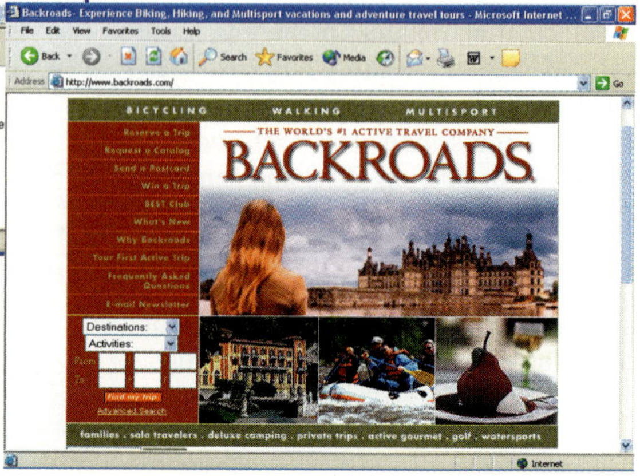

### Web browser programs

Web browser programs allow users to view Web pages and other information located on the Internet.

Application programs are commonly sold either as individual programs or as a *software suite,* which is a group of programs designed to be used in conjunction with one another (see Figure 1-11). Common software suites include *Microsoft Office, Microsoft Works, Corel WordPerfect Office, Lotus SmartSuite,* and *Sun StarOffice*.

**FIGURE 1-11**

**Software programs are available as individual programs (left) or as part of a software suite (right).**

### Programming, Markup, and Scripting Languages

A *programming language* is a set of rules used to write computer programs. Most often used by professional *programmers,* programming languages allow businesses and individuals to create or modify custom applications. For example, a business might use a programming language to create a customized inventory system or order-entry system.

Like computers, the development of programming languages is described in terms of generations. The earliest programming languages were *machine language* and *assembly language,* called *first-* and *second-generation languages,* respectively. These *low-level languages* were very difficult to use and were *machine dependent,* so programs could only be run on the computer for which they were created. Then came *third-generation programming languages*, such as *BASIC, COBOL, Pascal, FORTRAN, C, C++, Java,* and *Visual Basic* (see Figure 1-12), which are still widely used today. Newer *fourth-generation languages (4GLs)* are typically closer to a natural language (such as English, Spanish, or Chinese) than third-generation languages, and are much easier to use. Fourth-generation languages are commonly used to pull information out of databases. For example, the following fourth-generation programming statement is used to find all records in a database that have the last name of "Hancock":

```
FIND ALL RECORDS WHERE LAST_NAME = "HANCOCK"
```

While programming languages can also be used to create some elements of a Web page, *markup languages* are more commonly used for overall Web page development. Markup languages—such as *Hypertext Markup Language (HTML)*—indicate where text, images, hyperlinks, and other elements on a Web page should be displayed and how they should look by the use of special codes called *tags* that are inserted in the appropriate locations in the Web page document. For example, the HMTL tag <B> indicates where bolded text should start, </B> indicates where bolded text should stop, and the <IMG> tag contains information about an image file that is to be displayed at a specific location on the Web page.

When interactivity and dynamic content (such as having a description or menu pop up when the user points to a button) is needed on a Web page, a *scripting language* is often used. These languages—such as *JavaScript* and *VBScript*—enable Web developers to include small sets of instructions, or *scripts,* within the page's HTML code. As shown in Figure 1-12, neither the markup tags nor the scripting code is visible to users unless they request to see it. For more complex applications, a programming language (such as Java) or a program designed for creating multimedia Internet applications (such as *Flash)* can be used.

## FIGURE 1-12

**Programming, markup, and scripting languages**

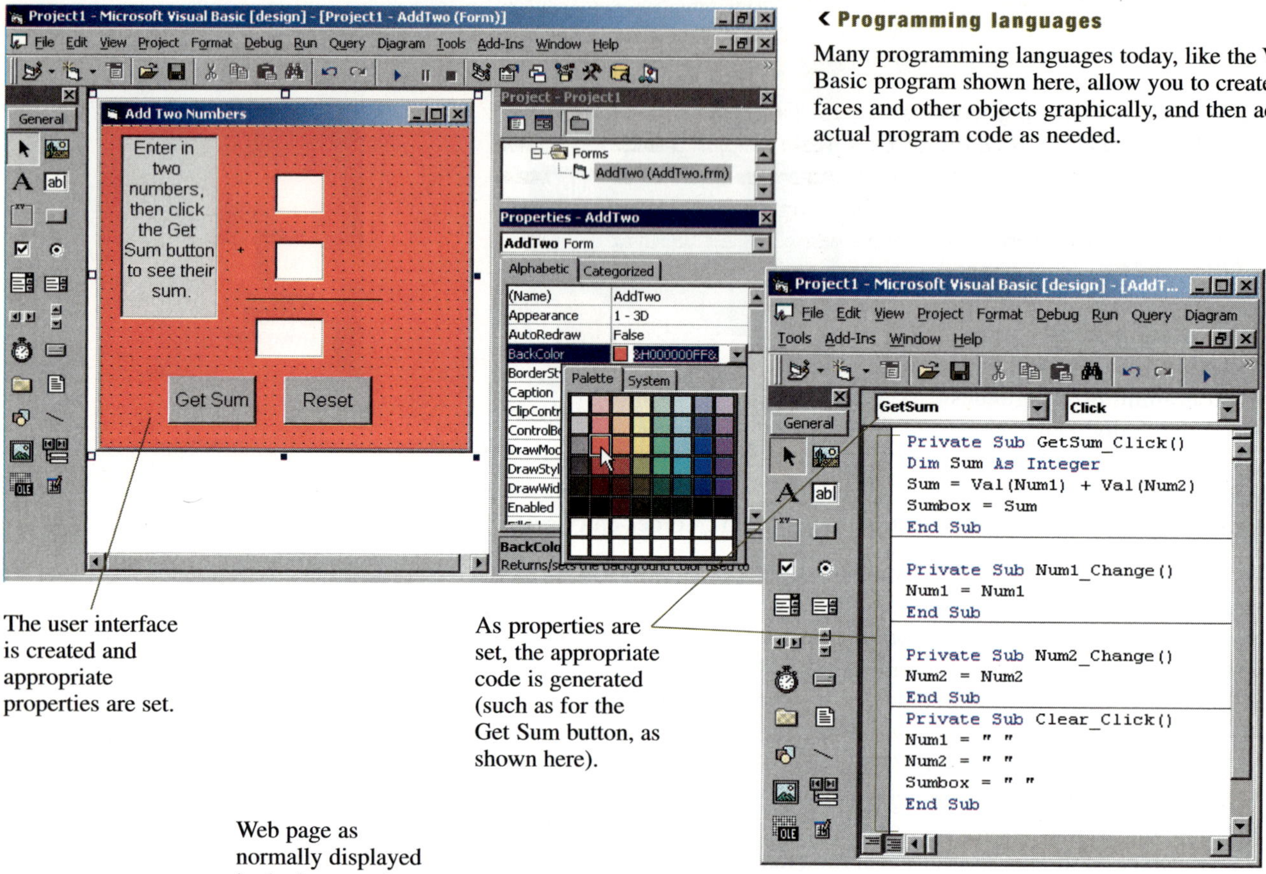


**‹ Programming languages**

Many programming languages today, like the Visual Basic program shown here, allow you to create user interfaces and other objects graphically, and then add or edit actual program code as needed.

The user interface is created and appropriate properties are set.

As properties are set, the appropriate code is generated (such as for the Get Sum button, as shown here).

Web page as normally displayed in the browser (no code is visible).

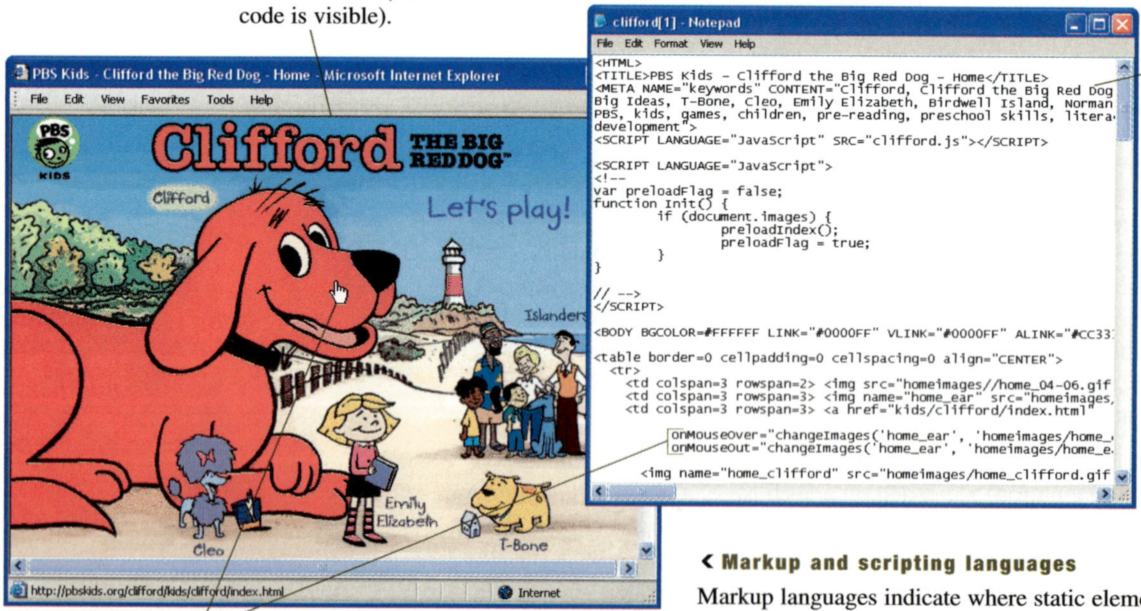


The underlying HTML code specifies keywords to be used with search sites, text and background colors, how text is laid out, what hyperlinks are linked to, where images are displayed, etc.

The underlying JavaScript code causes the character's name to light up when the user points to a character on the page.

**‹ Markup and scripting languages**

Markup languages indicate where static elements on a Web page (text, images, etc.) should be displayed and how they should look. Scripting languages can be used to add interactivity and dynamic content.

## Computer Networks and the Internet

A **computer network** ties computers together so that users can share hardware, software, and data, as well as electronically communicate with each other (see Figure 1-13). As illustrated in this figure, many networks use a *network server* to manage the data flowing through the network devices.

Computer networks exist in many sizes and types. For instance, a home network might connect two computers inside the home to share a single printer and Internet connection. A small office network of five or six computers might be used to enable workers to share an expensive printer, access the company database, and get on the Internet. A large corporate network might connect all of the offices or retail stores in the corporation, creating a network that spans several cities or states. Networks that cover a small geographical area (such as a room or building) are called *local area networks* or *LANs*. Larger networks designed for a city or town are sometimes referred to as *metropolitan area networks (MANs);* networks covering an even larger area are called *wide area networks (WANs).*

**FIGURE 1-13**

Example of a computer network

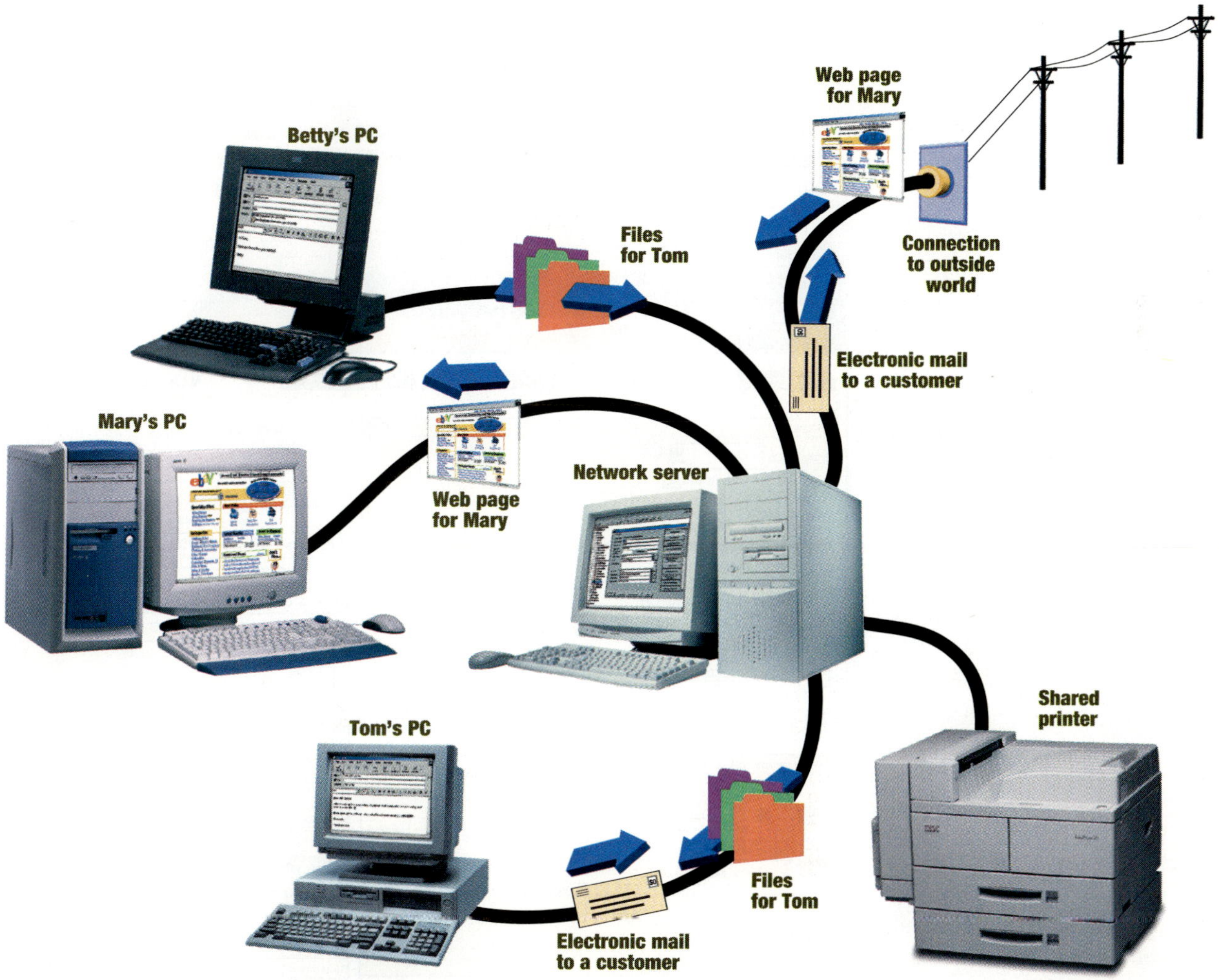

## Information Provider for the Campus and Community

The word *portal* means an entrance; in computer context, it is used to refer to a Web page that is designed as an entrance—or starting point—to the Internet or other network resources. Common consumer *Web portals* include Yahoo!, MSN, Excite, Bolt, and Lycos. These sites usually offer links and searching capabilities to locate Web information; they also allow easy access to news, entertainment, shopping, e-mail, and more.

A growing trend on college campuses today is the *college portal*—a gateway to a vast collection of resources for students, faculty, alumni, and other members of the campus community. One of the most complete and innovative college portals is Gettysburg College's *CNAV* (for *C*ollege *Nav*igation) system (see Figure 1-14).

Begun in 1995, CNAV evolved over the years from a simple collection of Web pages to a powerful information system capable of distributing a wide variety of highly customized, college-related information to many different groups of individuals. For example, students regularly use the CNAV system to get information about campus events and other activities that meet their personal interests; view the course catalog, their grades, and transcripts; access and update their personal and financial information, or access personal information about other students; communicate with students and faculty; schedule appointments; access course materials; and so forth. Faculty members use CNAV to perform such tasks as viewing and updating course information; accessing and updating student progress reports; viewing text or photo rosters for their classes; accessing student and budget information; posting grades and assignments; and e-mailing students. Alumni use CNAV to view their transcripts, learn about campus events, access class bulletin boards, locate other alumni, post resumes and social event notices, and more. Parents can use the CNAV system to obtain general college information as well as—with student permission—view transcripts, schedules, and financial records. Community members can use CNAV to view information about clubs, lectures, concerts, volunteer opportunities, sporting events, movies, plays, concerts, and other events open to the general public.

Because many college portals are tied into databases containing sensitive information about students and the college, their implementation can raise a host of privacy and security questions. If outsiders are allowed access to such a system, is there a higher risk of security and privacy breaches? How do you protect confidential records? Who should decide what personal information about individuals should be available to others over the network?

Since CNAV's development began, privacy and security have been very important considerations for Gettysburg College. To protect the system from misuse, several levels of security are in place. For example, the system resides on a secure server and access to CNAV is restricted to account holders only. Student accounts are automatically created, but parents, alumni, and other outsiders need to apply for their accounts and have their IDs and addresses verified. In addition, students need to OK their parents' accounts before an account will be issued to them.

**FIGURE 1-14**

**College portals, such as this one at Gettysburg College, allow customized access to college information. The screen shown here is the standard starting page for students; the starting page for faculty, parents, alumni, or others would look different.**

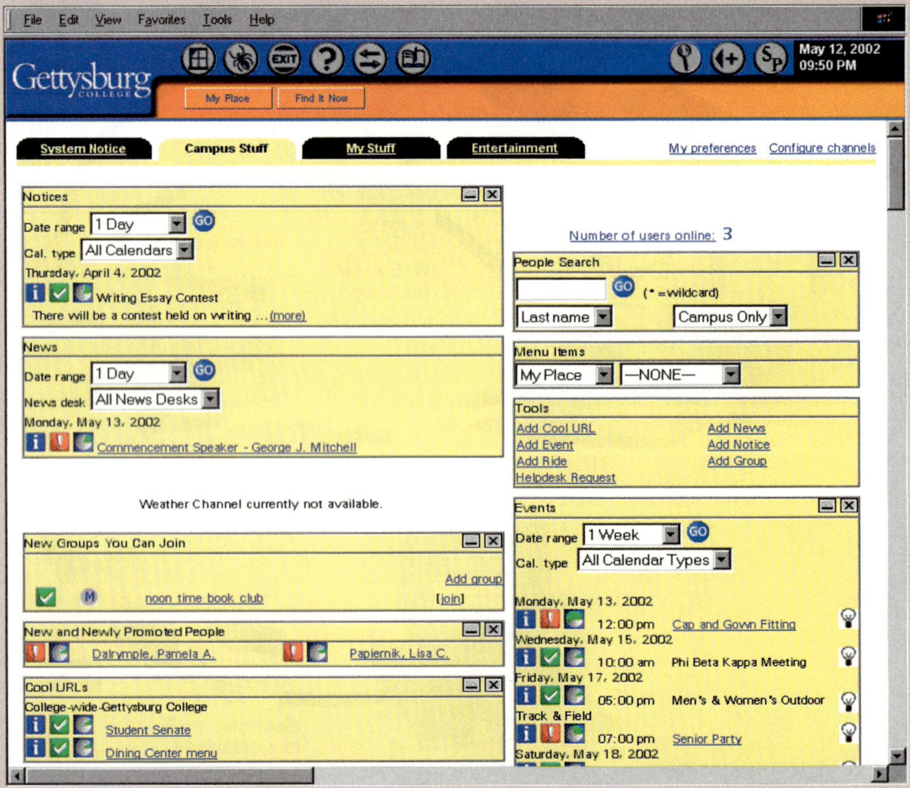

To protect student privacy even further, each student has complete control regarding what personal information (photo, campus address, campus phone, home address, class schedule, and so on) is available through the system and which users are authorized to view each piece of information. For example, one student may grant all students access to his or her photo and e-mail address, deny outsiders access to any personal information, and give his or her parents access to all information including transcripts. Another student may allow everyone access to all personal information, but deny his or her parents access to grades and transcripts. For a further level of control, the college can globally turn on and off access to a particular piece of information as needed. They can also hide all information about an individual, if appropriate for safety or other reasons. Hesitant to censor any information, the college has only done this two or three times during the entire life of the system, such as following the death of a student out of respect and consideration for the student's family.

Giving the students control of who can access their personal information and having a highly secure system resolves many of the privacy concerns associated with a college portal, but other problems can emerge as the system grows and needs change. For these reasons, the potential impact of adding a new type of information or retrieval ability should be carefully evaluated prior to its implementation. For example, before adding the ability to post and retrieve grades online, the college should consider when that information should be available through the portal. Even though the system may be capable of allowing students access to their grades as soon as they are posted, whether or not that is the best thing to do needs to be considered. For instance, will knowing their final grade in one course affect the students' ability to concentrate on finals not yet taken? Will students who get their grades back earlier than others tie up instructor time that might be better spent helping students who still have to take their final exam? Also, if students have the ability to correct their contact information or upload a more current photo, are there checks in place so that erroneous or inappropriate updates cannot be made?

With proper planning and a great deal of input from all possible users of a college portal, the vast majority of potential problems and controversies involving such a system can be avoided as any concerns are dealt with before the system is implemented. Provided that adequate security and privacy controls remain in place as both technology and hackers' abilities to break into remote systems improve, college portals such as CNAV should remain useful tools for the college community. They can save students and faculty time, increase the enjoyment of the campus experience, and provide an information bridge to parents, alumni, and prospective students.

The **Internet** is the largest and most well known computer network in the world. It is technically a network of networks, since it is comprised of thousands of networks that can all access each other via the main *backbone* infrastructure of the Internet. Typically, individual users connect to the Internet through their *Internet service provider (ISP).* ISP computers are continually connected to the Internet, so once users connect to their ISPs, they have access to the entire Internet. In other words, ISPs provide an *onramp* to the Internet for their subscribers. Connecting to the Internet is discussed in more detail in Chapter 3.

There is a vast abundance of information and resources available through the Internet, such as news, games, files, product information, government publications, shopping, music downloads, maps, and much, much more. Figure 1-15 illustrates just a few of these possibilities. Many Internet resources are in the form of Web pages and are accessed using a *Web browser*—a special program designed to view Web pages. To access a Web page, its *Internet address* can be typed into the appropriate location on the Web browser screen. Alternately, special text or images (called *hyperlinks)* that are linked to other Web pages can be clicked to display the corresponding Web page. Using the Internet and a Web browser are explained in more detail in Chapter 3.

For a look at the way many colleges are providing specific access to college Web pages and other resources through a *college portal,* see the Closer Look box.

**FIGURE 1-15**

**Common Internet activities (shown top to bottom, left to right) include reading news, mapping locations, searching for information, and shopping online.**

## BASIC TYPES OF COMPUTERS

The types of computers available today vary widely from ones small enough to fit in your pocket that do a limited number of tasks, to powerful desktop computers used for home and business, to the super-powerful computers used to control the country's defense systems. Computer systems are generally classified in one of four categories, based on size, capability, and price: small, or *microcomputers* (also called *personal computers)*; medium-sized, or *midrange servers*; large, or *mainframe computers*; and super-powerful *supercomputers*. An emerging fifth category on the small end of this continuum is *mobile communications devices*. In practice, classifying a computer into one of these five categories is not always easy or straightforward. For example, the Apple G4 is marketed as a very high-end personal computer, but its speed and processing power cause it to be classified sometimes as a supercomputer. In addition, technology changes too fast to have precisely defined categories. Instead, these five categories are commonly used to refer to a group of computers designed for similar purposes.

## Mobile Communications Devices

A **mobile communications device** is loosely defined as a very small device—usually based on a wireless phone, pager, or similar communications device (see Figure 1-16)—that has some type of computing or Internet capability built in. If the device is based on a wireless phone, it is sometimes referred to as a *smart phone;* if it based on a pager, it can be called a *smart pager*. Generally speaking, the computing capabilities of these devices at the present time are fairly limited. They are primarily designed to access the Web and e-mail wirelessly, in addition to their regular communications capabilities. Because of their small screen and keyboards (if the device contains a keyboard at all), today's mobile communications devices are most appropriate for individuals wanting constant e-mail and messaging ability—as well as occasional updates on stock prices, weather, directions, and other timely information—rather than general Web browsing.

**FIGURE 1-16**

**Mobile communications devices include Web-enabled phones (top) and pagers (bottom).**

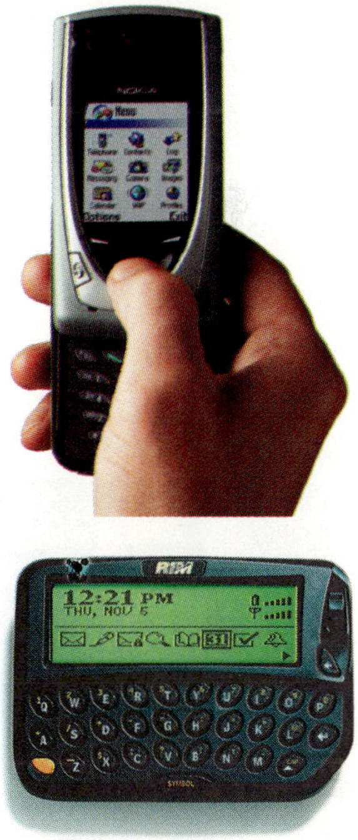


## Personal Computers

**Personal computers**, also called **PCs** or **microcomputers**, are computers designed to be used by one person at a time. They are typically small enough to fit on a desktop, inside a briefcase, or even inside a shirt pocket. PCs are widely used in homes, small businesses, and large businesses alike. They are also commonly connected together to form networks.

### Desktop and Portable PCs

Conventional PCs are often referred to as **desktop computers** because the complete system (system unit, monitor, keyboard, and mouse) fits on or under a desk. As shown in Figure 1-17, a desktop PC can have a *desktop case,* where the monitor sits on top of the system unit which in turn is located on the desk's surface, or a *tower case* that is typically placed on the floor. *All-in-one* desktop PCs incorporate the monitor and system unit into a single package.

Desktop computers usually conform to one of two standards: *PC compatible* or *Macintosh.* PC compatibles (sometimes referred to as *Windows PCs* or *IBM-compatible PCs)* evolved from the original IBM PC—the first PC widely accepted for business use—and are by far the most common type of desktop PC used today. In general, PC-compatible hardware and software are compatible with all brands of PC-compatible systems, such as those made by IBM, Dell, Hewlett-Packard, NEC, and Gateway, and typically run the Windows operating system. The Macintosh is made by Apple, uses the Mac OS operating system, and is traditionally the computer of choice for artists, designers, and others who require advanced graphics capabilities. Though some hardware and software are available in both Mac OS and PC-compatible versions, typically they are not interchangeable. Deciding between these two platforms typically depends on what the computer will be used for and if there are any other PCs, such as a school or office computer, with which it needs to be compatible.

Desktop computers typically cost between $500 and $2,000. The How To box at the end of this chapter discusses some strategies for selecting a PC and illustrates how to set up a desktop computer.

Smaller **portable PCs** are designed to be carried around easily, such as in a carrying case, briefcase, purse, or pocket, depending on their size. Some portable computers are even designed to be *wearable,* for workers who need computer access but don't have their hands free. Several different types of portable PCs are illustrated in Figure 1-17.

**ONLINE RESOURCES**

For links to information about personal computers, go to www.course.com/morley2003/ch1

**FIGURE 1-17**

**Personal computers (PCs) can come in a variety of sizes, shapes, and colors.**

**‹ Desktop computers**

Desktop PCs can come with a (clockwise from top left) tower, desktop, or all-in-one case.

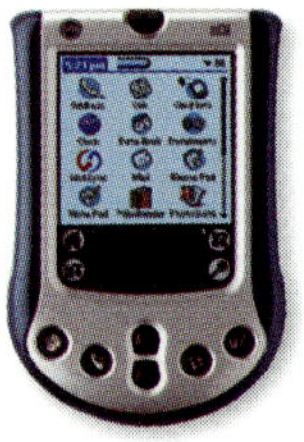

**‹ Portable computers**

Portable PCs include (left to right) notebook, handheld, and tablet PCs.

**Notebook computers** (sometimes called *laptops*) are fully-functioning computers that open to reveal a screen and keyboard. **Tablet computers** are of similar size, but they don't fold shut. They also typically don't include a keyboard—the screen is touched with a finger or special pen instead. **Handheld** (sometimes called *pocket)* **computers** are about the size of a paperback book or pocket calculator and are held in one hand while entering data with the other. Many handheld PCs don't have a keyboard; instead—like tablet PCs—the screen is touched with a finger or special pen. Sometimes handheld PCs are referred to as *personal digital assistants*, or *PDAs,* since they provide personal organizer functions such as a calendar, appointment book, and address book, as well as messaging, electronic mail, and other communications functions. Notebook and tablet PCs usually conform to either the PC-compatible or Macintosh standards; handheld computers typically use a portable version of Windows or an alternate operating system, such as *Palm OS* for *Palm PCs* and compatible devices.

With the increasing use of portable computers, sharing information and synchronizing data between a portable computer and a primary desktop computer at home or in the office is becoming an important consideration. There are a variety of options, depending on the types of computers being used. Some handheld PCs come with a cradle that attaches via a cable to the user's primary PC. After inserting the handheld PC into the cradle, the data on the two PCs can be updated. Other portable PCs come with infrared capabilities that allow you to "beam" data from that device to your primary PC. Emerging wireless networking technologies can enable portable and desktop PCs to be in communication with each other and to synchronize data whenever they are within a particular range.

**ONLINE TUTORIAL**

For an online look at how to set up a PC and troubleshooting tips, go to www.course.com/morley2003/ch1

Though desktop PCs are the norm for stationary home and office setups and are less expensive than comparable notebooks, portable computers are absolutely essential for many workers, such as salespeople who need to make presentations or take orders from clients off-site, agents who need to collect data at remote locations, and managers who need computing and communication resources as they travel. Today's notebooks are powerful enough that they can even be used as an individual's sole computer, if desired.

Notebook computers typically cost between $1,000 and $2,500; tablet PCs usually run between $1,000 and $2,000; and handheld PCs are normally between $100 and $500.

### Network Computers, Thin Clients, and Internet Appliances

Most personal computers sold today are sold as *stand-alone*, self-sufficient units that are equipped with all the necessary hardware and software to operate independently. In other words, they can perform input, processing, output, and storage without being connected to a network, though they can be networked if desired. In contrast, a device that must be connected to a network to perform processing or storage tasks is referred to as a *dumb terminal.* In-between a PC and dumb terminal in terms of capability are devices that can perform a limited amount of independent processing, but are designed to be used with a network. Two examples of these are *network computers* and *Internet appliances.*

**Network computers (NCs)**—more commonly called **thin clients** today—are designed to be used in conjunction with a company network (see Figure 1-18). Instead of using their own local disk drives for storage, these computers typically access software and store data on a network's storage devices.

In addition to the advantage of costing less than stand-alone PCs, thin clients give the businesses that utilize them the added benefit of easy upgrades to software programs. Since software is stored on the network, changing or upgrading software involves updating only the software located on the network's hard drive, not on each individual device. Disadvantages of using thin clients include having limited or no local storage and not being able to function as a stand-alone computer when the network isn't working. Despite the disadvantages, the low price of network computers/thin clients has made them a growing sector of the desktop computer market.

Network computers designed primarily for accessing Web pages and exchanging e-mail are called **Internet appliances** (also referred to as *information appliances* or *Web pads).* As shown in Figure 1-18, these devices can be designed specifically for just e-mail exchange, or they can allow both e-mail and Web browsing. Most of these devices are intended to be located in the kitchen or other convenient location. They can be set up to log on to the Internet automatically on a regular basis to download new e-mail. Internet appliances usually have no function other than Internet access, have limited local storage, and may not be able to be connected to a printer—they cannot be used as general-purpose PCs because of their limited capabilities. Though many Internet appliances have been discontinued shortly after their release, most experts view this as a still-growing area for consumer use—especially for individuals who don't want or need a conventional home PC.

**FIGURE 1-18**

**Network computers and Internet appliances are designed to be used only with company networks or the Internet.**

**^ Network computers**

Network computers (also called thin clients) are small, inexpensive computers with limited local storage that are designed to run software and store data on a network.

**^ Internet appliances**

Internet appliances allow users easy access to e-mail and the Web or just e-mail (as shown here) depending on the type of device used.

## Midrange Servers

**Midrange servers**—called *minicomputers* or *minis* in past years—are medium-sized computers used to host programs and data for small networks. Typically larger and more powerful than a desktop PC, the midrange server is usually located in a closet or other out-of-the way place. Users connect to the server through a local area network, using their regular PC, a network computer, or a terminal consisting of just a monitor and keyboard (as in Figure 1-19). Midrange servers are commonly used in small-to-medium sized businesses, such as medical or dental offices.

**FIGURE 1-19**

**Midrange servers are used to host data and programs on a small network and are typically stored in a nearby closet or other out-of-the way place.**

FIGURE 1-20

Mainframe computers are frequently used by large businesses, schools, and hospitals to maintain records and other types of shared data.

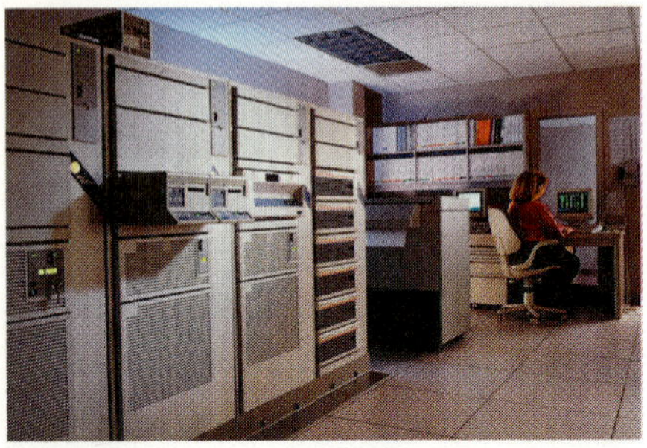

FIGURE 1-21

Supercomputers are used for specialized situations where immense processing speed is required.

### Mainframe Computers

The **mainframe computer** (see Figure 1-20) is the standard choice for most large organizations, such as hospitals, universities, large businesses, banks, and government offices, which need to manage large amounts of centralized data. Larger, more expensive, and more powerful than midrange servers, mainframes usually operate 24 hours a day, serving thousands of users connected to the mainframe via a PC, a network computer, or a terminal, similar to midrange server users. During regular business hours, a mainframe runs multiple programs as needed to meet the different needs of its wide variety of users. At night, it commonly performs large processing tasks, such as payroll and billing. Today's mainframes are sometimes referred to as *high-end servers* or *enterprise-class servers*.

### Supercomputers

Some applications require extraordinary speed and processing capabilities—for example, sending astronauts into space, controlling missile guidance systems, forecasting weather, exploring for oil, and assisting with some kinds of scientific research. **Supercomputers**—the most powerful and most expensive type of computer available—were developed to fill this need. Some new supercomputing applications include hosting extremely complex Web sites and decision-support systems for corporate executives. Future applications will likely include three-dimensional applications, such as 3D medical scans, 3D architectural modeling, and holograms. Unlike mainframe computers, supercomputers generally run one program at a time, as fast as possible.

Conventional supercomputers can cost several million dollars each. Over the past few years, it has become more common to build less-expensive supercomputers by connecting hundreds of smaller computers—typically high-end personal computers or midrange servers—into a *cluster* that acts as a single computer. The computers in the cluster often contain several CPUs each and are dedicated to running cluster jobs. The resulting supercomputer is often referred to as a *massively parallel processor (MPP)*. For example, one of the fastest supercomputers in the world, NEC's Earth Simulator (shown in Figure 1-21), contains a total of 640 computers containing 8 CPUs each for a combined total of 5,120 CPUs. It cost approximately $400 million, can perform about 40 trillion calculations per second, requires the floor space of four tennis courts, and is used primarily to simulate various global environmental phenomena such as global warming, the El Niño effect, and atmospheric and marine pollution, as well as to predict environmental changes on Earth.

## COMPUTERS, TECHNOLOGY, AND SOCIETY

The vast improvements in technology over the past decade have had a distinct impact on the way we live today. At both home and work, computers impact our lives. They have become indispensable tools in our homes and businesses, and related technological advancements have changed the way our everyday items—cars, microwaves, coffee makers, exercise bikes, telephones, and more—look and behave. In fact, we may use a computer or computerized device without even realizing that a computer is involved. As our computers and everyday devices become smarter, they tend to do their normal jobs faster, better, and more reliably, as well

**Computer networks** are used to connect individual computers and related devices so that users can share hardware, software, and data as well as communicate with one another. Many networks use a *network server* to host common files and programs and to manage the traffic on the network.

The **Internet** is the largest and most well known computer network in the world and is typically accessed through an *Internet service provider (ISP).* There is a vast amount of information available through the Internet, typically located on *Web pages*. Web pages are viewed with a *Web browser* and can be brought up by typing their appropriate *Internet address* or by clicking on a *hyperlink* on the currently-displayed Web page.

**CHAPTER OBJECTIVE 7**

Describe the purpose of a network and what the Internet is.

## Basic Types of Computers

Small computers used by individuals at home or work are called **microcomputers** or **personal computers** (**PCs**). Most PCs today are either **desktop computers** (with a *desktop, tower,* or *all-in-one case*) or **portable PCs** (**notebook**, **tablet**, or **handheld computers**) and typically conform to either the *PC-compatible* or *Macintosh* standard. **Network computers** (also called **NCs** and **thin clients**) are designed solely to access a network and usually use the network for storage, programs, and processing, instead of using local hardware. A type of network computer called an **Internet appliance** is designed specifically for accessing the Internet and e-mail.

**Mobile communications devices** are usually based on a cell phone or pager and are commonly used for accessing Web page data and e-mail, in addition to their regular phone or pager functions. Mobile communications devices are used by individuals to maintain communications with the office while on the road, as well as for quick checks of weather forecasts, stock prices, flight information, and other Internet resources available for that particular device.

Medium-sized computers, or **midrange servers,** are used in small- to medium-sized businesses to host data and programs that can be accessed by the company network. The large computers used by most large businesses and organizations to perform the information processing necessary for day-to-day operations are called **mainframe computers.** The very largest, most powerful computers, which typically run one application at a time, are classified as **supercomputers.**

**CHAPTER OBJECTIVE 8**

List the five basic types of computers, giving at least one example of each type of computer and stating what that computer might be used for.

## Computers, Technology, and Society

Computers and devices based on related technology have become indispensable tools for modern life, making ordinary tasks easier and quicker than ever before and helping make today's worker more productive than ever. However, their growing use has also created potential problems, ranging from health concerns to personal security and privacy issues to ethical dilemmas.

**CHAPTER OBJECTIVE 9**

Provide an overview of the social impact of computers, including some benefits and risks related to their prominence in our society.

# BALANCING ACT

## NEW TECHNOLOGY: BENEFITS VS. RISKS

As we've seen throughout this chapter, new technology adds convenience to our lives, helps many employees become more productive, and can increase the length and quality of our lives. So, is a new technological advancement always a good thing? Possibly not.

There is usually a good side and bad side to each new technological improvement. Agricultural advancements help farmers grow more food more economically, but many people are concerned that heavy pesticide use and genetic engineering of crops and animals is dangerous to our health. Nuclear energy gives us a very clean source for needed power, but it also has the possibility of tremendous destruction. The Internet allows us to obtain information very quickly and efficiently and communicate with others at our convenience, but it also permits unscrupulous individuals to find out private information about others and commit fraud in ways that are easier than ever before.

Before forming an opinion about a new technology or deciding whether or not to incorporate that technology into your home or workplace, it is worth taking the time to ask yourself a few questions. What benefits does this new advancement offer me? Does it bring any potential risks to my health, privacy, or security? If so, what can I do to minimize these risks? Is it compatible with any related existing technology I currently use? What changes will I need to make to my current situation to take full advantage of the new technology? If I don't use this new technology, will I be at a disadvantage? If so, in what ways? Though chances are most of the time you will decide new technology is a good thing and the benefits outweigh the potential risks, it is always good to make an informed decision.

### YOUR TURN

Think of a technology, product, or service that you use and like (desktop PCs, handheld PCs, distance learning, online shopping, ATM machines, e-mail, electronic signature devices for deliveries and credit card purchases, music CDs, DVD players, etc.), and then answer the following questions.

1. What are the benefits that you get from this product or service?
2. If this product or service did not exist, how would your life be different?
3. What type of data about you, if any, is collected by using this product or service? Should the government or other organizations have access to this data?
4. Are there any potential risks to you from using this product or service? If so, what are they?
5. If the government decided that your selected product or service was too risky to be used, should they be able to ban it?
6. Are there any circumstances in which you believe the government has the right or obligation to ban a technology, product, or service? If so, what are they?

## KEY TERMS

**Instructions:** Match each key term on the left with the definition on the right that best describes it.

**a. computer**

**b. computer network**

**c. handheld computer**

**d. hardware**

**e. input**

**f. Internet**

**g. mainframe computer**

**h. microcomputer**

**i. midrange server**

**j. mobile communications device**

**k. notebook computer**

**l. operating system**

**m. output**

**n. personal computer (PC)**

**o. portable PC**

**p. processing**

**q. software**

**r. storage**

**s. supercomputer**

**t. thin client**

**1.** ______ A collection of computers and devices that are connected together to share hardware, software, and data, as well as to communicate electronically with one another.

**2.** ______ A computer designed to be used by one person at a time; also called a microcomputer.

**3.** ______ A computer used in large organizations (such as hospitals, large businesses, and colleges) that need to manage large amounts of centralized data.

**4.** ______ A fully-functioning portable PC that opens to reveal a screen and keyboard.

**5.** ______ A medium-sized computer used to host programs and data for a small network.

**6.** ______ A PC, often without local storage capabilities, designed to be used in conjunction with a company network.

**7.** ______ A portable PC about the size of a paperback book or pocket calculator.

**8.** ______ A programmable electronic device that accepts data input, performs operations on that data, presents the results, and can store the data or results, as needed.

**9.** ______ A very small device, usually based on a wireless phone or pager, that has some type of computing or Internet capability built in.

**10.** ______ Another name for personal computer or PC.

**11.** ______ Performing operations on data that have been input into a computer to convert that input to output.

**12.** ______ Presenting the results of processing; can also refer to the results themselves.

**13.** ______ Saving data, programs, or output for future use.

**14.** ______ A small personal computer, such as notebook, tablet, and handheld PC, designed to be carried around easily.

**15.** ______ The fastest, most expensive, and most powerful type of computer.

**16.** ______ The instructions, also called computer programs, that are used to tell a computer what it should do.

**17.** ______ The largest and most well known computer network, linking millions of computers all over the world.

**18.** ______ The physical parts of a computer system, such as the keyboard, monitor, printer, and so forth.

**19.** ______ The process of entering data into a computer; can also refer to the data themselves.

**20.** ______ The software program that enables a computer to operate.

# ✓ SELF-QUIZ

Answers for the self-quiz appear at the end of the book.

## True/False

**Instructions:** Circle **T** if the statement is true or **F** if the statement is false.

**T F 1.** Software includes all the physical equipment in a computer system.

**T F 2.** The mouse is a common input device.

**T F 3.** A computer can run without an operating system if it has good application software.

**T F 4.** Web pages are displayed using a Web browser program.

**T F 5.** One of the most common types of home computer is the midrange server.

## Completion

**Instructions:** Supply the missing words to complete the following statements.

**6.** ____________ is the computer operation where data is entered into the computer.

**7.** Devices such as a removable disk or DVD drive would be classified as ____________ devices.

**8.** First-generation computers were powered by ____________.

**9.** A(n) ____________ language is used to write computer programs, whereas a(n) ____________ language is most often used to create Web pages.

**10.** To share hardware, software, and data easily, as well as communicate electronically with each other, users need to connect their PCs to a(n) ____________.

**11.** With PCs that have a(n) ____________ case, the system unit is typically located on the floor.

**12.** Another name for microcomputer is ____________.

**13.** A(n) ____________ computer is a portable, fully-functioning computer that unfolds to reveal a screen and keyboard.

**14.** A version of a desktop PC that usually doesn't have local storage or processing capabilities since it is designed to be used in conjunction with the company network is called a(n) ____________.

**15.** The most powerful computers in the world are referred to as ____________.

# PROJECTS

YOUR OPINION

## 1. Cash, Credit Card, or Fingerprint?

The chapter Trends In box discussed using biometric devices to pay for goods and services. This new type of payment method raises some concerns about privacy and security, which are probably not much different than the concerns raised when credit cards were first introduced. For example: Could the goods and services I buy become public knowledge? Could someone else make charges on my account? However, this new payment method also raises new and potentially frightening questions, such as: Once my fingerprints are in electronic format, could they be mixed up accidentally with someone else's fingerprints? Could someone trade my fingerprint image for another in a crime database to make it appear that I'm a criminal? Could my fingerprint image be used to make fraudulent purchases, as well as for voting and other applications that may soon use biometric identification? Some characteristics of biometric systems make them more secure than credit cards or cash—fingerprints can't be lost or used by another person, for example. Other characteristics of these systems may raise grave new concerns.

For this project, consider the questions asked above and write a short essay expressing your opinion about the security of paying by cash, credit card, and fingerprint today. Would you be willing to use a fingerprint payment system? Do you think such systems will be well received by consumers? List any additional pros and cons of these systems not covered in the Trends In box or this project's instructions. Provide a concluding paragraph stating other possible uses for biometric ID systems and indicate whether or not you believe these systems would be useful. Submit your opinion on this issue to your instructor in the form of a short paper, not more than two pages in length.

INDEPENDENT RESEARCH

## 2. Online Education

The amount of distance learning available through the Internet and World Wide Web has exploded in the last couple of years, from originally being able to take an occasional course online a few years ago to now being able to complete an entire college degree online.

For this project, look into the online education options available at your college or university and at least two other institutions of higher learning. Compare and contrast the programs in general, including such information as whether or not the institution is accredited, the type of courses available online, whether or not an entire certificate or degree can be earned online, and the required fees. After you have completed your general research, select one online course that interests you and research it more closely. Find out how the course works in an online format, including whether or not any face-to-face class time is required, whether assignments and exams are submitted online, which programs or *plug-ins* (programs that give extra capabilities to a Web browser) are required, and other class requirements. Summarize your findings in a two- to three-page paper. Be sure to include your opinion as to whether or not you would be interested in taking an online course and why.

HANDS-ON

### 3. Buying a New PC

New PCs are widely available directly from manufacturers, as well as in retail, computer, electronic, and warehouse stores. Some stores carry just standard configurations as set up by the manufacturers; others allow you to customize a system.

For this project, assume that you are in the market for a PC for your personal use. Make a list of your hardware and software requirements (refer to the chapter How To box, if needed), being as specific as possible. By researching ads in the newspaper, manufacturer Web sites, or systems for sale at local stores, find three systems that meet your minimum requirements. Prepare a one-page comparison chart, listing each requirement and how each system meets or exceeds it. Also include any additional features each system has, and information regarding the brand, price, delivery time, shipping, sales tax, and warranty terms for each system. On your comparison sheet, mark the system that you would prefer to buy and write one paragraph explaining why. Turn in your comparison sheet and summary to your instructor, stapled to copies of the printed ads, specifications printed from Web sites, or other written documentation that you collected during this project.

### 4. Software Search

Just as with toys, movies, and music, the price of a software package can vary tremendously, based on where you buy it, sales, rebates, and more. Though most packages claim a manufacturer's suggested retail price, it is almost always possible to beat that price—sometimes by a huge amount—with careful shopping.

For this project, select one software program that you might be interested in buying and research it. Either by reading the program specifications in a retail store or over the Internet, determine the minimum hardware and software requirements (processor type and speed, amount of free hard drive space, amount of memory, operating system, etc.) for your chosen program. By checking in person, over the phone, or via the Internet, locate a minimum of five quotes for the program. Be sure to check availability and estimated delivery time, and include any sales tax and shipping charges. If any of the online vendors have the option to download the software, instead of sending a physical package, be sure to record that information as well. Prepare a one-page summary of your research and submit it to your instructor. Be sure to include a recommendation of where you think it would be best to buy your chosen product and why.

GROUP PRESENTATION

### 5. Super Supercomputers

Supercomputers today are being used for amazing things. From controlling satellites and missiles, to oil exploration, to mapping weather and environmental changes, to pulling information out of large consumer databases, supercomputer use is growing.

For this project, form a group to research one specific application where a supercomputer is being used. Which computer is it? How large and powerful is the computer? How much did it cost? Is it a cluster or just a single supercomputer unit? What is it being used for? Could it be done with a less powerful computer? Share your findings with the class in the form of a short presentation. The presentation should not exceed 10 minutes and should make use of one or more presentation aids such as the chalkboard, handouts, overhead transparencies, or a computer-based slide presentation (your instructor may provide additional requirements). Your group may also be asked to submit a summary of the presentation to your instructor.

### 6. Computer Use on the Job

Most jobs today—from an administrative assistant, to the CEO of a multinational corporation, to the check-out clerk at the grocery store—require some level of computer skills.

For this project, form a group to explore the computing requirements for one job that the typical student in your group should be qualified for after graduating from college. Research that position to determine the minimal computer skills needed at the entry level, plus any additional skills that would give an applicant an advantage. If there is a management position or other possiblity for advancement that an individual in this position would eventually want to attain, find out if there are any other computer skills that would be needed for advancement. Share your findings with the class in the form of a short presentation. The presentation should not exceed 10 minutes and should make use of one or more presentation aids such as the chalkboard, handouts, overhead transparencies, or a computer-based slide presentation (your instructor may provide additional requirements). Your group may also be asked to submit a summary of the presentation to your instructor.

### 7. High Tech Climbing

**VIDEO VIEWPOINT**

The number of technological devices and gadgets for sportspeople has increased in recent years. The accompanying video clip features professional mountain climber Ed Viesturs who brings a variety of high-tech gear (such as a notebook computer, digital video camera, satellite phone, solar panels to recharge the equipment, and an all-in-one digital barometer, thermometer, altimeter, and wind gauge) on his climbs.

After watching the video, think about the impact of technology on sporting and recreational activities. Viesturs' ability to get updated weather reports on his satellite phone as he is climbing unarguably keeps him safer, but is there a chance that this type of technology may endanger others? Could high-tech gadgets lead individuals into participating in potentially dangerous activities—such as mountain climbing and long-distance sailing and kayaking—that require expert knowledge, physical strength, and special skills to perform successfully? Could high-tech gadgets give individuals who are not properly prepared for an activity enough of a false sense of security so that they participate in the activity anyway assuming that their technological devices will protect them? If so, does society have a responsibility to rescue these individuals if something goes wrong? Will even experienced sportspeople rely too much on technology and ignore their good sense? Viesturs says he's not counting on his phone or digital altimeter to get him up or off the mountain; instead he wants to rely on his own experience and instincts. But do others feel the same way?

**ONLINE VIDEO**

To view the High Tech Climbing video clip, go to www.course.com/morley2003/ch1

**Express your viewpoint:** What is the impact of high-tech sporting gadgets on personal safety?

Use the video clip and the questions previously asked as the foundation for your response. Your instructor will direct you to be prepared to discuss your position (either in class, via an online class discussion group, or in a class chat room), or to write a short paper stating and supporting your viewpoint on the issue. You may also be asked to do research and provide resources to support your point of view on this issue.

# A CLOSER LOOK AT HARDWARE AND SOFTWARE

## OUTLINE



## OBJECTIVES

**After completing this chapter, you will be able to:**

- Understand the difference between data and information, as well as how data and programs are represented to a computer.
- Identify several types of input devices and explain their functions.
- Explain the functions of the primary hardware components found inside the system unit, namely the motherboard, the CPU, and memory.
- List several output devices and explain their functions.
- State the difference between storage and memory, as well as between a storage device and a storage medium.
- Name several storage devices and media and explain under what circumstances they are typically used.
- Describe the purpose of communications hardware.
- Understand how several basic software tasks are performed, such as how to start a program and how to use toolbar buttons or menus to issue commands.

# CHAPTER 2

## OVERVIEW

When you think of a computer system, you probably picture hardware—a desktop PC or notebook computer, or maybe a new PDA. But a computer system involves more than just hardware. There's the data that is input into the computer to begin the information processing cycle. And, as you already know from Chapter 1, computers also need software in order to function. It is the software that tells the hardware what to do and when to do it.

This chapter opens with a discussion of data, how it differs from information, and how it is represented to a computer. Next, we take a closer look at the different pieces of hardware that can make up a computer system. Since it isn't possible to mention all the various hardware products available today, a sampling of the most common pieces of hardware used for input, processing, output, storage, and communications are described in this chapter. Though a complete discussion of software is beyond the scope of this book, the chapter concludes with a brief look at some basic software concepts and operations.

The basic hardware and software concepts and terminology covered in this chapter are important for all computer users to understand. These concepts will also provide you with a solid foundation for discussing the important societal issues featured throughout this text. While most of you reading this chapter will apply the principles discussed in this chapter to conventional personal computer systems—such as desktop and notebook PCs—keep in mind that these principles apply to virtually all types of computers and related devices, from smart appliances to supercomputers.

# DATA, INFORMATION, AND DATA REPRESENTATION

So far we've used the term *data* to describe what is input into the computer. Now we need to look at the difference between data and *information* and how data needs to be represented to the computer in order for it to be recognized, processed, and stored.

## Data vs. Information

**Data** is essentially raw, unorganized facts. Almost any kind of fact or set of facts can become computer data—the words in a letter to a friend, the text and pictures in a book, the numbers in a monthly budget, a photograph, or the facts stored in a set of employee records. Data can exist in many forms, such as text, graphics, audio, and video. When data is processed into a meaningful form, it becomes **information**.

## Bits, Bytes, and Coding Systems

The computers we have discussed so far in this book (mobile communications devices, PCs, midrange servers, mainframes, and supercomputers) are all *digital computers*. Digital computers—the norm today—can understand only two conditions, usually thought of as *off* and *on* and represented by the digits 0 and 1. Consequently, all data we input into a computer must be in digital form (0s and 1s) for it to be processed and stored. Fortunately for us, the computer takes care of translating our input into 0s and 1s as it is being entered into the computer. After processing the data in digital form, the computer translates and presents the output to us in a form we can understand.

### Bits

The 0s and 1s used with digital devices can be represented in a variety of ways, such as with an open or closed circuit, the absence or presence of an electronic charge, the absence or presence of a magnetic spot or depression on a storage medium, and so on. Regardless of their physical representation, these 0s and 1s are commonly referred to as *bits*, a computing term derived from the phrase *binary digits (*binary means *two*). The input you enter from the keyboard, the software program you use to play your MP3 files, and the term paper stored on your PC are all groups of bits.

### Bytes

Eight bits are collectively referred to as a **byte**. It is important to be familiar with this concept because "byte" terminology is frequently used in a variety of computer contexts. For example, document size and storage capacity are measured in bytes, based on the amount of data contained in the document or that can be stored on the storage medium. Since one byte holds only a very small amount of data, prefixes are commonly used with the term *byte*. A **kilobyte (KB)** is equal to 1,024 bytes, but is usually thought of as approximately 1,000 bytes. A **megabyte (MB)** is about 1 million bytes; a **gigabyte (GB)** is about 1 billion bytes; and a **terabyte (TB)** is about 1 trillion bytes. Therefore, 2 KB is about 2,000 bytes and 10 MB is approximately 10 million bytes.

### Coding Systems

To represent numbers and perform math computations using only 0s and 1s, computers use the *binary numbering system*. Instead of the 10 symbols (0–9) used in the *decimal numbering system*, the binary numbering system has just two symbols—0 and 1. Representing numbers using the binary numbering system works similarly to the decimal numbering system, except the columns have different place values. For example, the first column is the *ones* column (for $2^0$), the second column is the *twos* column ($2^1$), the third column is the *fours* column ($2^2$), and so on. Therefore, though 101 represents "one hundred one" in decimal notation, it equals "five" ($1 \times 2^2 + 0 \times 2^1 + 1 \times 2^0$ or $4 + 0 + 1$) using the binary numbering system.

To represent text-based data, special binary coding systems (namely, *ASCII* and *Unicode*) were developed. These codes represent all characters that can appear in text data—including numeric characters, alphabetic characters, and special characters such as the period (.) and dollar sign ($). ASCII (*A*merican *S*tandard *C*ode for *I*nformation *I*nterchange) normally represents each character as a unique combination of eight bits (a string of eight 0s and 1s); that is, it is an 8-bit code that can represent up to 256 ($2^8$) unique characters. Some examples of ASCII representation are shown in Figure 2-1.

Unicode is a newer code, now being used widely for Web pages and in recent software programs, such as Windows XP, Mac OS X, Netscape, and Internet Explorer. Unlike ASCII, which is limited to just the Latin alphabet, Unicode is a universal coding system that can be used regardless of the language or alphabet being used. It is a longer code (32 bits per character is common), so there are enough unique combinations to represent all the written characters for most alphabets used around the world (English, Chinese, Greek, Russian, etc.), as well as thousands of mathematical and technical symbols. The biggest advantage of using Unicode is that it can be used worldwide with consistent and unambiguous results.

**FIGURE 2-1**

**Examples from the ASCII code**

| Character | ASCII Code |
|---|---|
| 0 | 00110000 |
| 1 | 00110001 |
| 2 | 00110010 |
| 3 | 00110011 |
| 4 | 00110100 |
| 5 | 00110101 |
| A | 01000001 |
| B | 01000010 |
| C | 01000011 |
| D | 01000100 |
| E | 01000101 |
| F | 01000110 |
| + | 00101011 |
| ! | 00100001 |
| # | 00100011 |

# INPUT HARDWARE

*Input* is the process of entering data into a computer. An **input device** is any piece of hardware that is used to perform data input.

**ONLINE RESOURCES**

For links to information about input devices, go to www.course.com/morley2003/ch2

## Keyboards

Most PCs are designed to be used with a **keyboard** (a typical desktop PC keyboard layout is shown in Figure 2-2). All notebook and some handheld PCs have built-in keyboards, but they are usually smaller with fewer keys, and the keys are typically placed closer together than on a conventional desktop keyboard. The majority of handheld PCs and mobile communications devices don't include a keyboard at all. They usually rely on *pen input*, but there are several types of special keyboards that can be used with these devices. As shown in Figure 2-3, some of these keyboards resemble conventional keyboards, but fold up and so are extremely portable. Others—sometimes called *thumb pads*—slip over the bottom of a handheld PC and are pressed with your thumbs instead of your fingers. Portable PCs can also be used with a full-sized keyboard, if the proper connector is built into the PC.

## Pointing Devices

In addition to a keyboard, most PCs also have some type of **pointing device**. Unlike keyboards, which are used to enter characters at the *insertion point* (sometimes called *cursor*) location, pointing devices are used to move an onscreen pointer—usually an arrow. Once that pointer is pointing to the desired object on the screen, the object can be selected or otherwise manipulated. The two most common pointing devices are the *mouse* and the *electronic pen*.

**FIGURE 2-2**

**The keyboard is the primary input device for many computers.**

**FIGURE 2-3**

**For easier data entry, portable keyboards can be used with handheld PCs, smart phones, and other portable devices.**

**Foldable keyboard**

**Slip-on thumbpad**

### The Mouse

A **mouse** rests on your desk or other flat surface and is moved with your hand in the appropriate direction. As the mouse moves, an onscreen pointer—usually called the *mouse pointer*—moves correspondingly. When the mouse pointer is pointing to the appropriate object on the screen, the buttons on top of the mouse are used to select it. Older *mechanical mice* have a ball exposed on the bottom surface of the mouse to control the pointer movement; newer *optical mice* (such as the one in Figure 2-4) are completely sealed and track movements with light instead of a ball. While mechanical mice are usually used in conjunction with a protective *mouse pad* and require regular cleanings to operate properly, optical mice typically don't. Mice are commonly used to start programs; open, move around, and edit documents; draw or edit images; and more. Some of the most common mouse operations are listed in Figure 2-4.

### Electronic Pens

An **electronic pen** can be used instead of a mouse to select objects, draw, or write electronically on the screen. There are two main types of electronic pens. A *light pen* is usually connected to the computer with a cable and senses marks or other indicators through a light-sensitive cell in its tip (see Figure 2-5). A *stylus* is a cordless electronic pen that looks similar to a ballpoint pen and is commonly used with handheld PCs, tablet PCs, and *graphics tablets* (flat, rectangular tablets that automatically transfer what is drawn on them to their connected PCs). As shown in Figure 2-5, some desktop PCs accept electronic pen input, as well.

Though their capabilities depend on the type of computer and software being used, electronic pens can typically be used to issue commands to the PC, such as selecting options from a menu. In addition, some pen-based devices can accept handwritten text and sketches as graphical images; PCs with *handwriting recognition* capabilities can accept handwritten text as editable text input. Just as with *speech recognition*—where the computer accepts spoken input—handwriting recognition usually requires some training for the PC to adjust to the particular style of the user, and the input is not always interpreted correctly.

For a look at how pen-based handheld PCs are being used in the medical field, see the Closer Look box.

**FIGURE 2-4**

**A mouse and its operations**

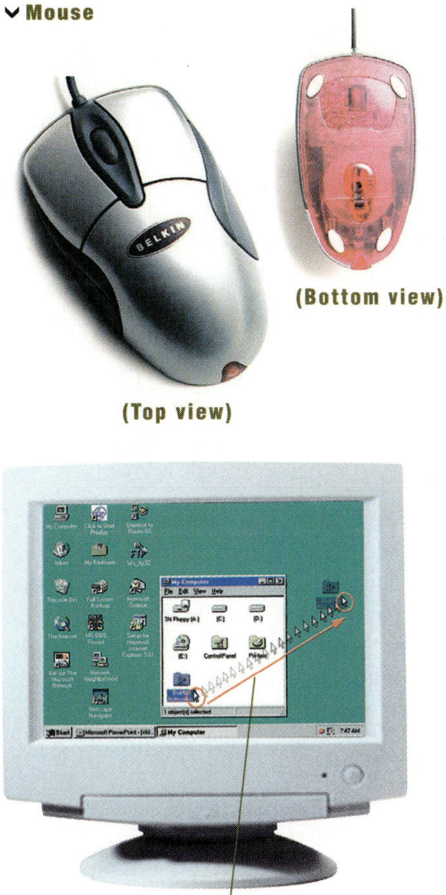


**MOUSE OPERATIONS (Right-handed; can be reversed for left-handed users.)**

**POINT**
Move the mouse until the mouse pointer is at the desired location on the screen.

**CLICK**
Press and release the left mouse button.

**RIGHT-CLICK**
Press and release the right mouse button.

**DOUBLE CLICK**
Press and release the left mouse button twice, in rapid succession.

**DRAG AND DROP**
When the mouse pointer is over the appropriate object, press and hold down the left mouse button, drag the object to the proper location on the screen, then release the mouse button.

**SCROLL WHEEL/BUTTON**
If your mouse has a wheel or button on top of it, use it to scroll through the displayed document.

**FIGURE 2-5**

**Examples of electronic pen use**

Light pen

Handheld PC

Desktop PC

## A CLOSER LOOK AT... WIRED DOCTORS

Recent studies predict that by the end of 2003, between 75 and 85 percent of all doctors will use pen-based handheld PCs for tasks such as writing electronic prescriptions, recording patient charges, and maintaining electronic charts. Additional handheld PC applications geared toward improving patient care and saving physicians time include appointment schedulers, medical calculators, drug encyclopedias, diagnostic software, and medical reference programs. Ideally, handheld PCs can help doctors diagnose, prescribe, enter billing information, order lab tests, and update the patient's chart all while in the exam room (see Figure 2-6).

**FIGURE 2-6**

**Handheld PCs with appropriate software can be used to assist physicians with routine tasks.**

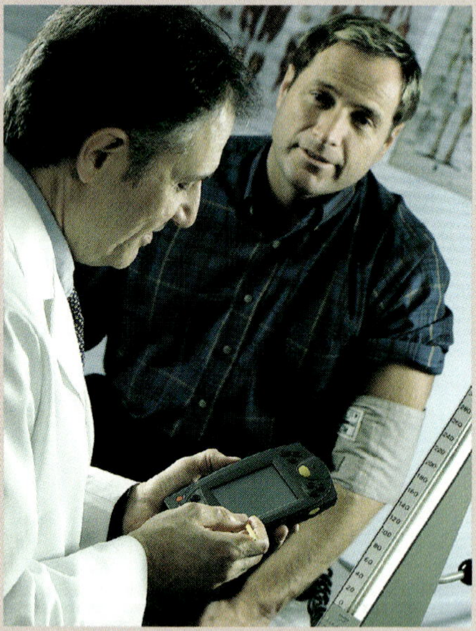

Plus they can be used to check the patient's record automatically for such things as previous symptoms, allergies, drug interactions, and insurance coverage limitations to help the physician plan the appropriate treatment. Assuming the handheld PC is connected to a wireless network, this information can be transferred automatically to the main computer system for the practice or hospital, and prescriptions can be sent electronically to the appropriate pharmacy. A Harvard study found that using electronic prescriptions reduced errors—which can be expensive, time-consuming, and potentially dangerous—by 55 percent.

Other related intriguing possibilities include medical professionals receiving information about a patient's current health via some type of health monitor and the Web. For example, some home asthma and blood pressure monitors can upload readings to a Web site whenever the patient uses them so a medical professional can read the results and determine if any change in treatment is needed. New monitors for implanted devices (such as the defibrillators and pacemakers used with cardiac patients) can transmit data over the Internet, as well.

For closer monitoring of critical hospital patients, some systems can transmit clinical data—such as heart rate, respiration, blood pressure, and even photographs of the patient—on a continual basis. For example, Miami Children's Hospital uses Palm PCs and a continuous monitoring system to allow physicians to check on children before and after surgery at any time of the day or night. For ambulatory patients, there are even portable monitoring systems that are worn under clothes and send continuous physiological data to attached PDAs while the patients perform normal everyday activities. The data is then downloaded to the physician's computer and is analyzed using special software to give the doctor a more thorough understanding of patients' health. These systems can be used for diagnostic purposes—such as when physicians were deciding whether or not Vice President Dick Cheney needed an implanted cardiac device—or for follow-up care.

Handheld PC use in the medical community is growing rapidly and is likely to explode in the near future. The portability of PDAs versus charts and reference books, the ability to transfer information electronically to the appropriate locations, and instant ongoing access to the latest medical news and information all help to make handheld PCs a beneficial tool for doctors. In fact, many medical schools today—such as the one at Stanford University—are incorporating the use of handheld PCs into their curriculum.

Critics of handheld PC use by medical professionals are concerned about the private information stored on these handheld PCs being transmitted over the airwaves, such as to pharmacies and the main computer systems at physician offices and hospitals. To address this concern, developers of handheld PC medical software typically build encryption methods into the software and recommend the use of secure Web servers to protect patient privacy.

### Other Pointing Devices

In addition to the mouse and electronic pen, there are other types of pointing devices. A few of the most common are illustrated in Figure 2-7.

- *Trackball*—a device that looks like an upside-down mechanical mouse with the ball on the top. The ball is rotated with the thumb, hand, or finger to move the onscreen pointer.
- *Pointing stick*—a pencil-eraser-shaped device found in the middle of many notebook keyboards; works similarly to a trackball, except the thumb or finger pushes the stick instead of rolling a ball.
- *Touchpad*—a rectangular pad across which a fingertip or thumb slides to move the onscreen pointer. It can be a standalone device or built into a notebook PC or keyboard.
- *Touch screen*—a special computer screen that the user touches to select commands or options, used in settings where people may not be comfortable using a keyboard or mouse (such as consumer kiosks), as well as in places where using a keyboard or mouse is impractical.
- *Joystick* and *game pad*—gear sticks or game controller-shaped devices frequently used with computer games.

**FIGURE 2-7**

**Other pointing devices**

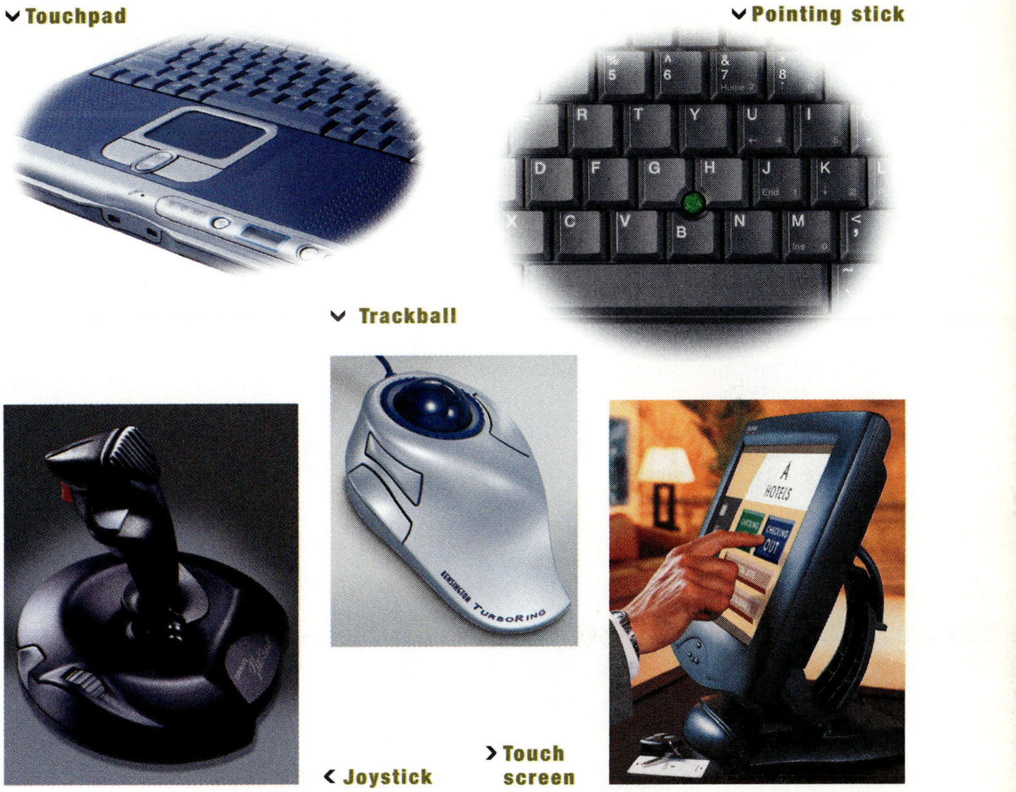


## Scanners and Digital Cameras

When input already exists in printed form, it is almost always more efficient to capture the data directly from that *source document*, if possible, instead of reentering the data manually. *Scanners* capture data from a source document and convert it into input that a computer can understand. When objects exist in real life, *digital cameras* can capture them as digital photographs, which is a format computers can understand.

### Scanners

Scanners, some of which are illustrated in Figure 2-8, come in a variety of types and are used for a variety of purposes.

**FIGURE 2-8**

**Scanners transform printed data into a form the computer can recognize.**

**> Optical scanners**

Flatbed scanners (right) can be used to input printed documents into the computer; handheld scanners (below) can be used to capture small amounts of text and images.

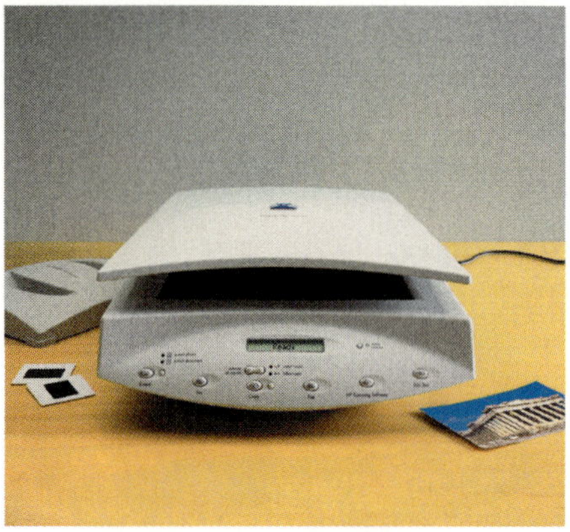

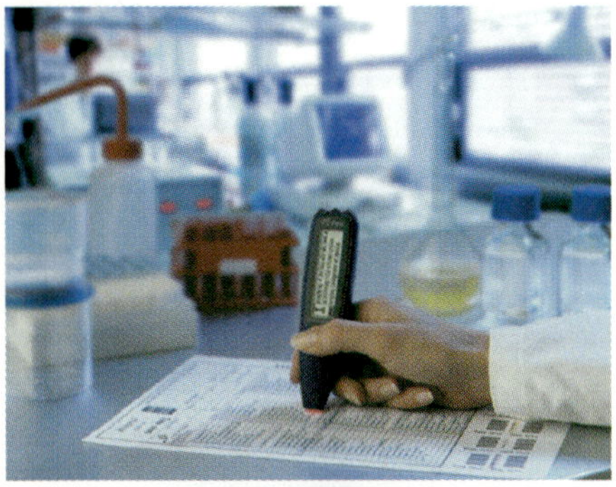

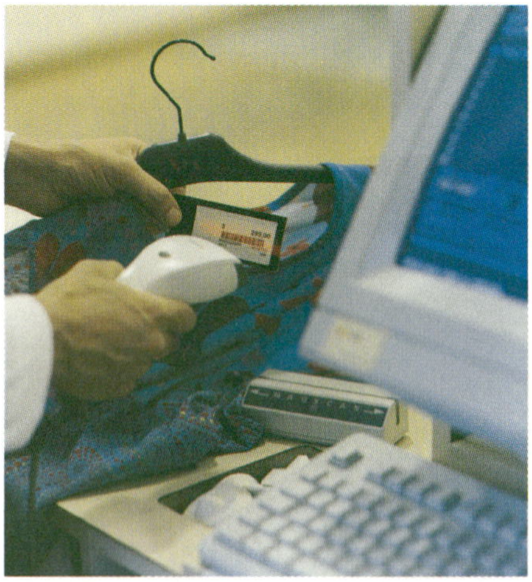

**^ Bar code scanners**

Bar code scanners can be handheld (above) or stationary (left).

An *optical scanner*—usually just called a **scanner**—captures the image of a flat object (printed document, photograph, drawing, etc.) in digital form and transfers that data to a PC. The most common type of optical scanner is the *flatbed scanner;* other configurations, such as a *handheld scanner*, are also available. If *optical character recognition (OCR)* software is used in conjunction with a scanner, scanned text can be recognized by the computer as text that can be edited. Otherwise, the entire document (including text and graphics) is input as a single image that can be modified, inserted into other documents, or printed just as you would any other graphical image, but any text in that image cannot be edited.

**Bar code scanners** can be handheld or stationary and read *bar codes*—images that represent data with bars of varying widths. The most familiar bar code is the *UPC (universal product code)* commonly found on packaged goods in supermarkets. Businesses and organizations, such as clothing stores, package delivery services, video stores, libraries, and law enforcement agencies, can also create and use custom bar codes to fulfill their unique needs, such as labeling merchandise, tracking packages, checking in and out media, marking evidence, and so forth. The chapter Trends In box discusses a new type of bar code—the *smart bar code*.

*Optical mark readers*—such as the Scantron readers commonly found on college and university campuses—input data from special forms to score or tally exams, questionnaires, ballots, and so forth. The marks are usually made with a pencil and consist of bubbling in small circles or other shapes. When these devices are connected to a computer, the responses can be input automatically into the appropriate program (such as exam scores being transferred to a grade book program).

## TRENDS IN... SMART BAR CODES

It's been almost 30 years since the first bar-coded item—a ten-pack of Wrigley's chewing gum—was scanned. Since then, bar codes have appeared on all kinds of items, from products and packages, to file folders and evidence bags, to receipts and airline tickets. Bar codes help all kinds of businesses and organizations keep track of their inventory and otherwise organize important data.

Now the bar code is getting smart.

New advances in radio communications have led to the development of *radio frequency identification*, or *RFID*. RFID relies on tiny chips and radio antennas that store and transmit data located in an *RFID tag*. These tags can be attached permanently to products, product packaging, or product labels—printed antennas make them thin enough to be glued onto items—and can store much more data than the typical bar code.

RFID applications used in recent years include tracking inventory pallets in warehouses and huge shipping containers in transit. Consumer applications include special key fobs or wands that allow customers to pay for gas or fast food by waving the wand close to a special reader (the purchase amount is automatically deducted from a checking account or charged to a credit card, depending on each customer's preferences when he or she signed up for the system). An increasing number of highways in the U.S. use RFID tags on cars for automatic toll collection. Singapore has gone a step further by using them to charge different toll prices at different times of the day to encourage drivers to stay off busy roads during busy times.

Until recently, however, RFID systems have been too expensive to use as bar code replacements. Currently costing about 5 to 7 cents each, they can be used on an increasing number of products, but are still too expensive to put on a soda can, pack of gum, or other low-price item. Many experts predict that once the cost reaches 1 cent or less apiece, they will be a viable bar code replacement for all products.

The advantages of using RFID-based product labels, which contain a unique identifying product code referred to as an *electronic product code* or *EPC*, include the ability to store much more data than a UPC code and to update that information during the life of the product. For example, when a container of orange juice is packaged, the code might contain the expiration date and grower and grove information, in addition to regular manufacturer and product size data. The code would then be updated with data regarding its shipment, and then would alert the store when the product is purchased or if it expires on the shelf. During the purchase, the tags would allow consumers to check out all their products at one time just by pushing their carts through a special walk-through scanner, since a group of RFID tags can be read at one time. At home, EPCs could be used in conjunction with a smart fridge to keep an up-to-the-minute inventory of the contents of the refrigerator, as well as to inform the consumer when it's getting close to a product's expiration date. Finally, when the empty container is thrown out, the code could be used to add the item to an electronic shopping list or to help ensure the container is recycled properly. In conjunction with the Internet, EPCs can also automatically bring up menu suggestions, recipes, and other useful information related to a particular product.

Currently being tested by a number of manufacturers and retailers (see Figure 2-9), RFID seems very promising. Procter & Gamble estimates the technology could massively cut inventory costs. Prada, the Italian luxury goods designer, is using RFID tags to try to increase sales. When each EPC-marked product is brought into the dressing room, the RFID chip causes a video to play showing models wearing the item and the designer suggesting the appropriate accessories needed to complete the ensemble.

**FIGURE 2-9**

**Smart RFID tags are expected eventually to replace conventional bar codes.**

Despite all its advantages, privacy advocates are concerned about a global use of EPCs because they can allow stores (and any one else with an appropriate scanner) to know where you bought your clothes and any other items you have with you that contain a permanent RFID tag. And with the need to minimize the cost of such tags, many are skeptical about the inclusion of any form of privacy protection. The European Central Bank's plan to install RFID chips in Euro bills by 2005, supposedly to reduce counterfeit bills and track money following a kidnapping or other crime, has increased privacy advocates' objections to this technology. Possible solutions include allowing consumers to deactivate a tag after purchase (similar to deactivating the anti-theft device in a library book or rented video during checkout) or to delete information from the tags.

FIGURE 2-10

A digital camera

**Previews**

Most digital cameras let you display and erase images while shooting.

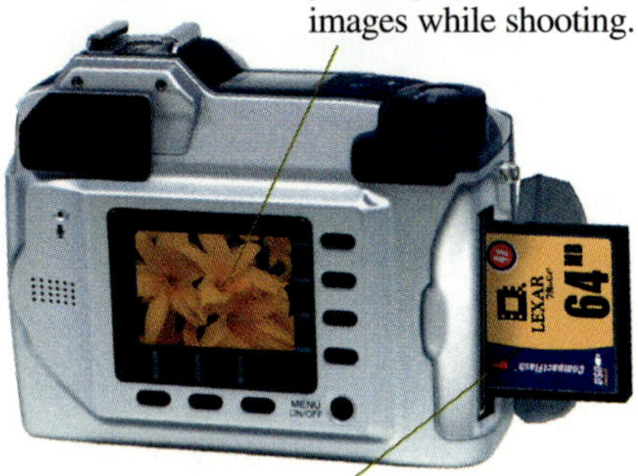


**Storage media**

Digital cameras store images on reusable storage media, such as disks or flash memory cards.

### Digital Cameras

**Digital cameras** work much like regular cameras, but instead of recording images on film they record them on some type of digital storage media. Most of the time, the storage medium is removable, such as disks or *flash memory cards*. *Digital still cameras* (such the one shown in Figure 2-10) take individual still photographs. As soon as they are taken, photographs can be viewed, transferred to a PC, or printed (either the storage medium is inserted into the PC or printer, or the images are transferred to the PC by connecting the camera to the PC with a cable). *Digital video cameras* include *digital camcorders* and small *PC video cameras*. Digital camcorders are used by both consumers and professionals and record video images on digital media. PC video cameras—commonly called *PC cams*—are designed to transmit video images over the Internet, such as during a *videoconference* or *video phone call*. Digital video cameras can also be used to broadcast images continually to a Web page, such as the cameras frequently found in zoo animal exhibits, on top of mountains, or other locations of interest to the general public. In this type of application, the video camera is referred to as a *Web cam*.

## Other Input Devices

Other input devices include microphones (used for voice-input, such as to issue commands to the computer, dictate documents, or record vocal input); *MIDI*—*m*usical *i*nstrument *d*igital *i*nterface—devices, such as keyboards with piano-type keys instead of alphanumeric keys that are used to input musical compositions; *modems* (to input data from other PCs via a company network or the Internet), and *adaptive input devices* (such as Braille keyboards and pointing devices controlled with the foot or breaths of air) designed for visually-impaired users or users with limited physical mobility. Many input devices come in modified versions for other special needs, such as wireless mice and keyboards for a more flexible work environment, and *ergonomic keyboards* for users concerned about wrist injuries.

# PROCESSING HARDWARE AND OTHER HARDWARE INSIDE THE SYSTEM UNIT

The **system unit** is the main case of a computer. For desktop computers, the system unit is usually a separate piece of hardware that sits either on the desk underneath the monitor (for *desktop-style PCs*) or on the floor (for *tower-style PCs*). The system unit for portable PCs and all-in-one desktop PCs is combined with the computer screen to form a single piece of hardware. Hardware found within the system unit includes the *motherboard,* the *central processing unit (CPU),* and *memory modules*. The system unit also houses other devices, such as the disk drives used for storage, the power supply, and cooling fans. The inside of a system unit for a typical PC is shown in Figure 2-11.

## The Motherboard

A *circuit board* is a thin board containing *chips*—very small pieces of silicon or other semiconducting material onto which *integrated circuits* are embedded—and other electronic components. The main circuit board inside the system unit is called the **motherboard** or *system board*. As shown in Figure 2-11, the motherboard has a variety of chips and boards attached to it; in fact, all devices used with a computer need to be connected in one way or another to the motherboard. Typically, *external* devices (such as monitors and printers) connect to the motherboard by plugging into a special

**FIGURE 2-11**

Inside a PC's system unit

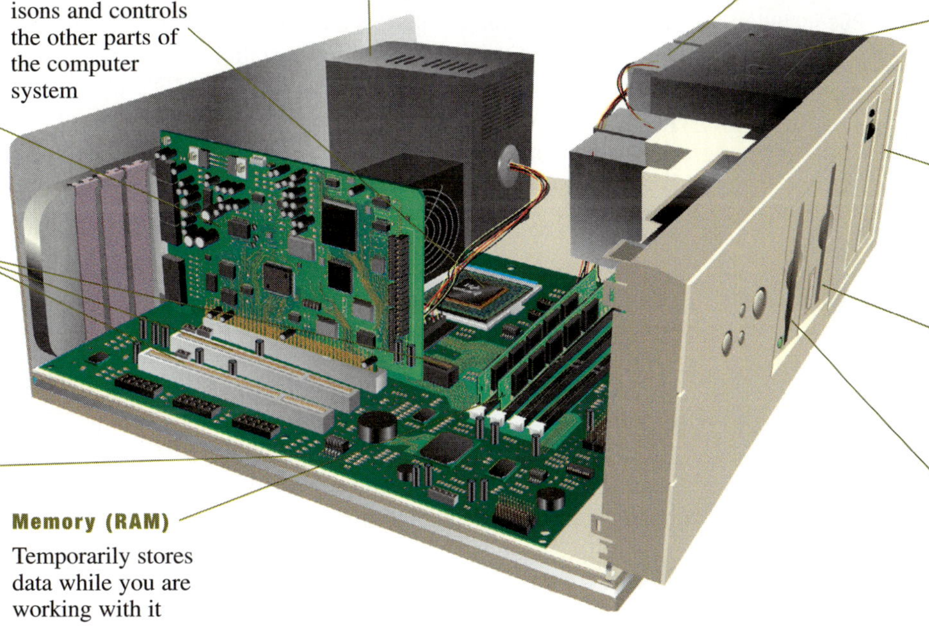


connector (called a *port*) exposed through the exterior of the system unit case (see Figure 2-12). The port is either connected directly to the motherboard, or is connected through an *expansion card* plugged into an *expansion slot* on the motherboard.

## The Central Processing Unit (CPU)

The **central processing unit (CPU)** consists of a variety of circuitry and components contained in a single unit that is plugged directly into the motherboard. The CPU—also called the **microprocessor** (when talking about PCs) or the *processor*—does the vast majority of the processing for a computer.

The CPU has two principle parts. The *arithmetic/logic unit (ALU)* is the section of the CPU that performs arithmetic (addition, subtraction, multiplication, and division) and logical operations (such as comparing two pieces of data to see if they are equal or determining if a specific condition is true or false). In other words, it's the part of the CPU that

**FIGURE 2-12**

Ports are used to connect all external devices.

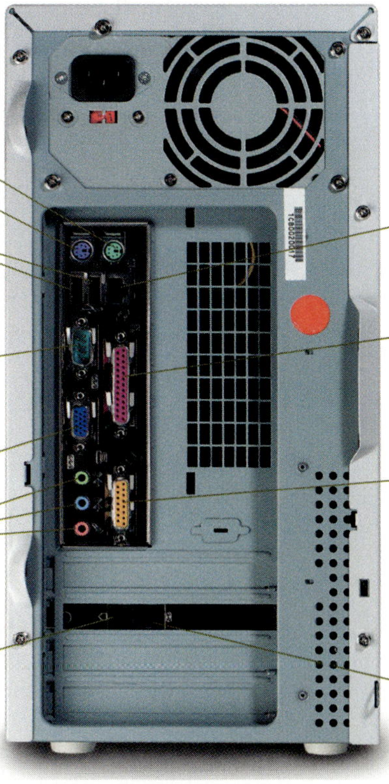

computes. The *control unit* coordinates and controls the computer's operations, such as retrieving instructions, decoding them, and passing them on to the ALU for execution.

Most PCs made today typically use CPUs manufactured by Intel or Advanced Micro Devices (AMD) (see Figure 2-13). CPUs commonly used with desktop PCs include the Intel *Celeron* and *Pentium 4,* and the AMD *Athlon, Athlon XP*, and *Duron*. Typically, portable computers use either desktop PC chips or similar chips designed for portable PC use; powerful work-stations and servers use more powerful processors, such as Intel's *Xeon* and *Itanium 2,* AMD's *Opteron*, and Sun's *UltraSPARC* processors. Apple Macintosh computers use the *PowerPC* chip—a CPU that was developed through a cooperative effort by Apple, Motorola, and IBM. The most recent PowerPC chip is the *G4*.

**FIGURE 2-13**

**Common CPUs for desktop PCs include the Intel Pentium 4 and AMD Athlon XP.**

In addition to being classified by name, CPUs also come in a variety of *processing speeds*, also known as *clock speeds*. Clock speed indicates how many ticks of the *system clock*—the internal clock for a computer that synchronizes all its operations—occur each second. It is a measurement of the speed at which a processor executes instructions; the faster the clock speed, the more instructions the CPU can execute per second. Clock speed is rated in *megahertz (MHz)* or *gigahertz (GHz);* that is, millions or billions of ticks per second, respectively. CPUs for the earliest PCs ran at less than 5 MHz; today's CPUs run at more than 2,000 MHz (2 GHz). Though processing speed is an important factor in computer performance, other factors (such as the amount of memory and the speed of peripheral devices) greatly affect performance, as well.

## Memory

**Memory** refers to chip-based storage used by the computer. When someone uses the term *memory* in reference to computers, they are usually referring to **random access memory** or **RAM**. RAM consists of a group of chips where data and programs are temporarily stored while they are being used. It is *volatile,* which means that the data placed there is removed when it is no longer needed. In addition, all data in RAM is erased when the power to the PC is turned off. RAM chips are typically mounted onto small circuit boards (called *memory modules*) that are plugged into the motherboard.

RAM capacity is measured in bytes. Most desktop PCs sold today have at least 128 megabytes (MB) of RAM and have room to add additional memory modules, if needed. It is important for a PC to have enough RAM to run the needed applications (minimum RAM requirements are almost always stated on a software program's packaging), as well as to work efficiently (more RAM allows more programs to be opened at one time).

Though less commonly discussed than RAM, there are other types of computer memory that are essential to a computer including *cache memory, registers, ROM,* and *flash memory*.

*Cache memory* is a special group of fast memory chips located inside or close to the CPU chip. It is used to speed up processing by storing the most frequently and recently used data and instructions. *Internal cache* is built right into the CPU chip; *external cache* is located close to, but not inside, the CPU. Level numbers indicate the distance between a particular cache and the CPU: *Level 1* is closest (virtually always internal cache), *Level 2* (usually internal cache) is the next closest, and *Level 3* (appearing now in newer computers as external cache) would be even further away.

*Registers* are another type of high-speed memory built into the CPU. They temporarily store each program instruction and piece of data just before they are processed by the CPU. Generally, the more data the register can contain at one time—usually 32 bits, though the newer 64-bit processors such as the Itanium and Opteron use 64-bit registers—the faster the CPU is. Most CPUs contain several registers.

*ROM* (for *read-only memory*) consists of nonvolatile memory chips mounted onto the motherboard into which data or programs have been permanently stored; data stored in ROM is retrieved by the computer when it is needed. Unlike RAM, whatever is stored in ROM cannot be changed or erased (which is why ROM is called *read-only*). For example, a PC's *BIOS* or *basic input/output system*—the sequence of instructions the PC follows when it is started up—has traditionally been stored in ROM.

*Flash memory* (sometimes called *flash RAM*) is a type of nonvolatile memory that can be erased and reprogrammed when needed. Flash memory has begun to replace ROM for system information, such as a PC's BIOS information. By storing the information in flash memory instead of in ROM, it can be updated as needed. Flash memory chips also are used in memory cards and other media used for storage.

## OUTPUT HARDWARE

Output hardware consists of all the devices that are used to produce the results of processing—usually on the computer screen, on paper, or as audio output. Hardware that produces output are called **output devices**.

### Monitors and Other Display Devices

A **display device—**the most common form of output device—presents output visually, typically on some type of computer screen. With desktop PCs, the computer screen is more formally called a **monitor**. With notebook computers, handheld PCs, and other devices where the screen is built into the unit, the term **display screen** may be used instead. Display screens are also built into *e-books* (small book-sized devices that are used to display electronic versions of books) and digital picture frames. A *data projector* is a display device that projects computer output onto a wall or projection screen for a large group presentation.

The traditional type of monitor for desktop PCs is the *CRT* monitor (see Figure 2-14). CRTs use *cathode-ray tube* technology to display images, similar to conventional televisions, so they are large, bulky, and heavy. Thinner and lighter *flat-panel displays* form images using a different technology, such as *liquid crystal* or *gas plasma*. Flat-panel displays are almost always used on portable computers and mobile communications devices. As shown in Figure 2-15, flat panel displays are also available for desktop PCs. Though more expensive than CRTs, advantages such as taking up less desk space and consuming less power have resulted in a huge increase of flat-panel usage for desktop systems.

**FIGURE 2-14**

**CRT monitors are commonly used with desktop PCs.**

Regardless of the technology used, the screen of a display device is divided into a fine grid of small areas or dots called **pixels** (from the phrase "picture elements"), as illustrated in Figure 2-16. The number of pixels used determines the *screen resolution,* which affects the size of the elements displayed on the screen. When a high resolution is selected, such as 1,024 pixels horizontally by 768 pixels vertically (written as 1,024 × 768 and read as 1,024 by 768), more data can fit on the screen, but everything will be displayed smaller than with a lower resolution, such as 640 × 480 or 800 × 600 (refer again to Figure 2-16). *Dot pitch,* which indicates how tightly the pixels are packed together, affects the quality of the image—a smaller dot pitch results in a better, sharper image. Common dot pitch for monitors today ranges from .25 to .28 millimeters. Unlike screen resolution, the dot pitch for a display device cannot be changed by users.

**FIGURE 2-15**

Examples of flat-panel displays

**FIGURE 2-16**

A higher screen resolution (measured in pixels) displays everything smaller than a lower screen resolution.

Monitor size is measured diagonally from corner to corner, similar to the way TV screens are measured. It is important to realize, however, that the actual viewing area is usually smaller than the stated monitor size. For example, one 17-inch monitor might have a *viewable image size* (*vis*) of 16 inches, while another 17-inch monitor might have a viewable image size of 15.7 inches. Though 0.3 inches may not sound like much of a difference in size, small size variations can be noticeable and are important to keep in mind when comparing the quality and price of two monitors.

## Printers

Instead of the temporary, ever-changing *soft-copy* output that a monitor produces, **printers** produce *hard copy*; that is, a permanent copy of the output on paper. Most desktop PCs are connected to a printer; portable PCs can use printers as well.

Though older *dot-matrix printers* are *impact printers*—printers that have a print mechanism that actually strikes the paper—most printers today are nonimpact. Impact printers are primarily used today for producing multipart forms, such as invoices and credit-card receipts. Both impact and nonimpact printers form images with dots, similar to the way monitors display images with pixels. Because of this, printers are very versatile and can print text in virtually any size, as well as print photos and other graphical images. Whether the printer uses dots of ink or flecks of toner powder or some other print method, printer quality is typically measured in *dots per inch (dpi)*. The two most common types of printers used today are *ink-jet printers* and *laser printers*.

### Ink-Jet Printers

**Ink-jet printers** form images by spraying tiny drops of ink onto the page (see Figure 2-17). Because they are relatively inexpensive, have reasonable-quality output, and can print in color, ink-jet printers are often the printer of choice for home use. With the use of special photo paper, many ink-jet printers can also print respectable-looking photographs. At around $100 or less for a simple home printer, ink-jet printers are affordable, though the cost of the replaceable *ink cartridges* can add up, especially if you do a lot of color printing.

**FIGURE 2-17**

How an ink-jet printer works

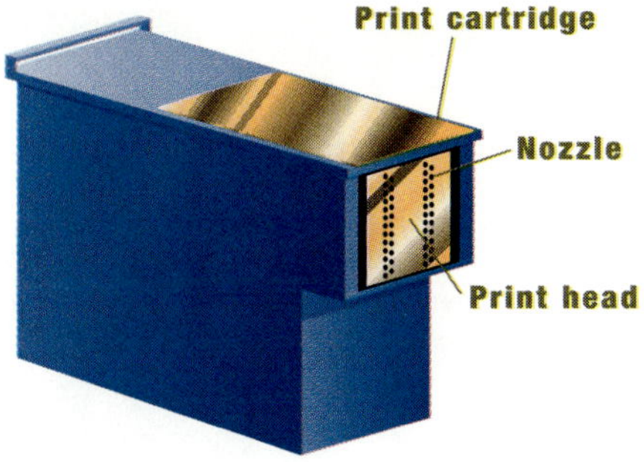


**How ink-jet printing works**

Ink-jet printers create colors by mixing different combinations of four colors of ink—magenta, cyan, yellow, and black. The different colors can be in one or multiple cartridges. Each cartridge is made up of some 50 ink-filled firing chambers, each attached to a nozzle smaller than a human hair. To print images, the appropriate color ink is ejected through the appropriate nozzles.

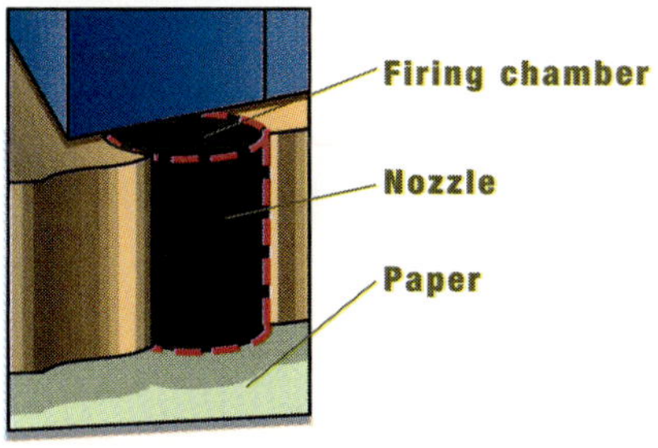


**1.** An electric current flows along the bottom of a firing chamber. This makes the ink boil and a steam bubble forms.

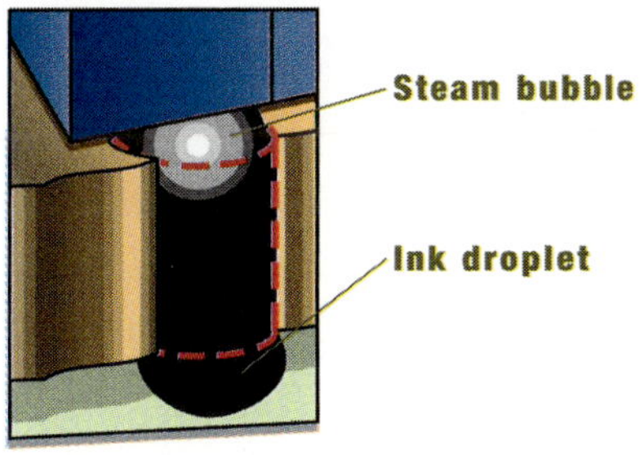


**2.** As a bubble expands, it pushes ink through the nozzle. The pressure of the bubble forces an ink droplet to be ejected onto the paper.

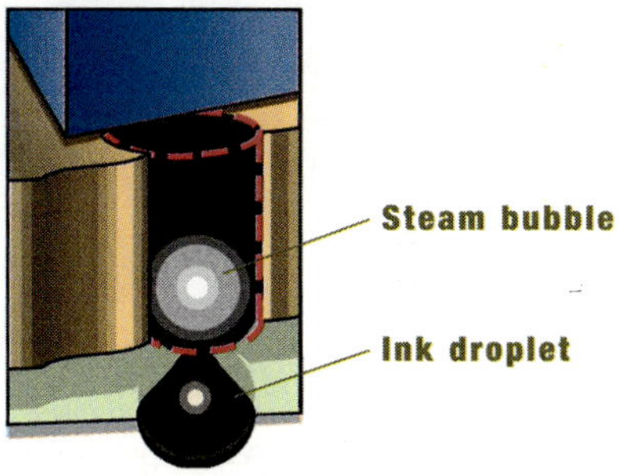


**3.** The volume of ink deposited is about one millionth that of a drop of water from an eyedropper. A typical character is formed by a 20-by-20 array of drops.

### Laser Printers

**Laser printers** are the standard for business documents. To print a document, the laser printer first uses a laser beam to charge the appropriate locations on a drum to form the page's image, and then ink toner powder is released from a *toner cartridge* and sticks to the drum. The toner is transferred to a piece of paper when the paper is rolled over the drum, and then a heating unit fuses the toner powder to the paper to permanently form the image (see Figure 2-18). Most laser printers use just black toner powder, similar to photocopying machines, though relatively expensive color laser printers are available. Laser printers typically print faster and have better quality output than ink-jet printers. In addition to personal laser printers, faster and more expensive *network laser printers* are available for shared office use.

## Other Output Devices

Other types of output devices include *speakers, headphones,* and *headsets* for voice and music output, as well as specialty printers to produce labels, bar codes, photos, large documents, etc. Communications devices, such as *fax/modems,* can be used to output documents from your PC to another computer or to a fax machine. A *multifunction device* (sometimes called an *all-in-one device*) is a single piece of hardware that incorporates the functions of several devices, such as printing, scanning, copying, and faxing, into one unit.

**ONLINE TUTORIAL**

For an online look at a variety of printers available for specialty applications for businesses and consumers, go to www.course.com/morley2003/ch2

**FIGURE 2-18**

**How a laser printer works**

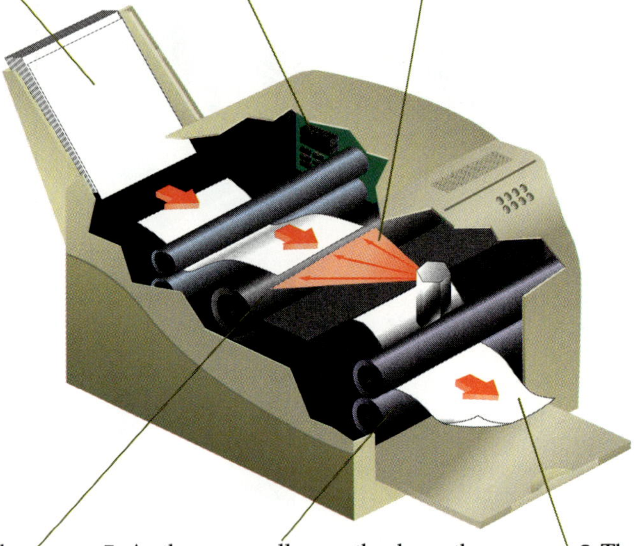

^ **Network laser printer**

^ **Personal laser printer**

# STORAGE HARDWARE

Because data in RAM is stored only temporarily, storage hardware is needed anytime you want to save a document for future use. There are several important characteristics of *storage systems* and many forms a storage system can take.

## Storage System Characteristics

All storage systems consist of a *storage device* and a *storage medium*, typically use *magnetic* or *optical* technology, and are either *removable* or *fixed* systems.

### Storage Medium vs. Storage Device

There are two parts to any storage system: a **storage medium** and a **storage device**. The storage medium is where the data is actually stored (such as a *floppy disk* or *CD*); a storage medium is inserted into the appropriate storage device (such as a *floppy drive* or *CD drive*) to be read from or written to. Usually the storage device and medium are two separate pieces of hardware, although with some systems—such as a *hard drive*—the two parts are permanently sealed together to form one piece of hardware.

Storage devices can be *internal* (located inside the system unit), *external* (plugged into an external port on the system unit), or *remote* (located on another computer, such as a network server). Regardless of how they are connected to the computer, letters of the alphabet and/or names are assigned to each storage device, so the devices can be identified when they need to be used (see Figure 2-19).

### Magnetic Disks vs. Optical Discs

On some storage media, such as floppy disks, data is stored *magnetically* (with the 0s and 1s being represented with different magnetic alignments). The magnetization can be changed, so the data on magnetic disks can be erased and overwritten as needed. Other storage media (such as CDs and *DVDs*) store data *optically* using laser beams. On some optical media, the laser burns permanent depressions into the surface of the media, so the data cannot be erased or rewritten. With *rewritable* optical media, the laser just changes the reflectivity of the media, which can be changed back again to erase the data. Some storage systems use a combination of magnetic and optical technology.

Magnetic storage media are typically referred to as *disks;* optical media are called *discs.*

**FIGURE 2-19**

**How a PC's storage devices might be identified**

### Removable Media vs. Fixed Media

In many types of storage systems, although the storage device is always connected to the computer, the storage medium used with that device can be inserted and removed. Floppy disks, CDs, and DVDs are examples of *removable media.* Hard drives are typically *fixed-media* systems.

## Floppy Disks

Over the years, most PCs have been set up to use a **floppy disk**—sometimes called a *diskette* or *disk*—to fulfill removable storage needs. Floppy disks are made out of flexible plastic protected by a hard plastic cover (see Figure 2-20). To use a floppy disk, it must first be inserted into a **floppy drive** (with the label area facing up and closest to the user). When it is completely inserted, the disk clicks into place and can be rotated within its plastic cover. While the disk spins, a *read/write head* can *read* (retrieve) data from or *write* (store) data onto the actual surface of the disk.

The surface of a floppy disk is organized into circular rings called *tracks*, and pie-shaped *sectors*. On most PC systems, the smallest storage area on a disk is a *cluster*—the part of a track that crosses a specific number (always two or more) of adjoining sectors (refer to Figure 2-21). Tracks, sectors, and clusters are numbered so that the computer can keep track of where data is stored. The PC keeps a directory—called the *file allocation table* or *FAT*—of where each document (called a *file*) is physically stored and what *filename* the user has assigned to it. When the user requests a document (always by filename), the computer uses the FAT to retrieve it. Most floppy disks in use today measure 3½ inches in diameter and can store 1.44 MB

FIGURE 2-20

A floppy disk

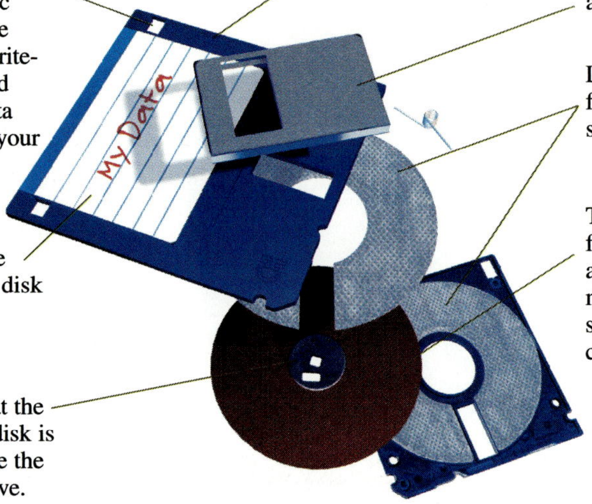


FIGURE 2-21

Magnetic disks (such as floppy disks) are organized into tracks, sectors, and clusters.

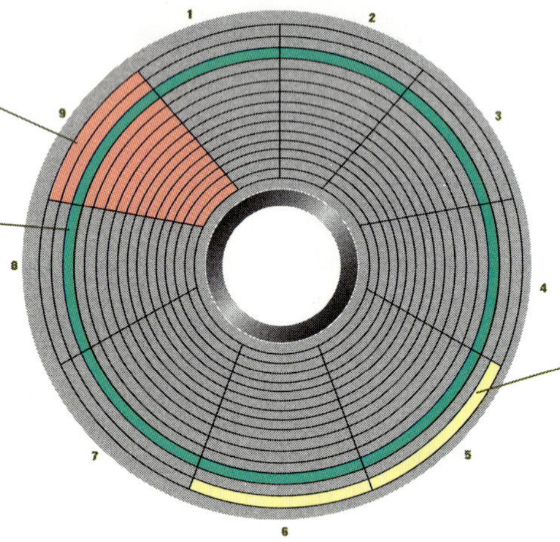


of data. When larger amounts of data need to be stored or transported, higher-capacity removable storage media—such as CDs, DVDs, and high-capacity magnetic disks—can be used.

## CDs and DVDs

Because **CDs (compact discs)** and **DVDs (digital versatile discs)** are optical discs, a laser beam is used to record data onto and read data from them. When data is recorded onto a CD or DVD disc, a high-intensity laser either permanently burns tiny depressions into the disc's surface or temporarily changes the reflectivity of the disc's surface, depending on whether or not the disc can be erased and reused. Regardless of how they are formed, these altered spots on the discs are called *pits.* The pits and areas that aren't changed (called *lands)* represent the data's 0s and 1s. The data is read by a lower-intensity laser beam, based on the reflection of light from the disc, as illustrated in the top part of Figure 2-22. To keep data organized, optical discs are divided into sectors, but use a single spiral track beginning at the center of the disc, instead of a series of concentric tracks like magnetic disks.

One of the biggest advantages of CDs and DVDs is their large capacity—typically 650 MB per CD and 4.7 GB per DVD, though double-sided DVDs currently hold 9.4 GB and are expected eventually to reach 17 GB. Another advantage is that optical discs are expected to last longer and be more durable than magnetic media, though the discs should be handled carefully and stored in a protective *jewel case* when not in use to prevent scratches and fingerprints on the recorded surface of the disc that can affect its performance. There are a variety of types of CDs and DVDs; some are shown in Figure 2-22.

### Read-Only Discs: CD-ROMs and DVD-ROMs

*CD-ROM* and *DVD-ROM discs* are *read-only* storage media and come prerecorded with commercial products, such as software programs, clip-art and other types of graphics collections, and product demos. The data on a CD-ROM or DVD-ROM cannot be erased, changed, or added to. CD-ROM and DVD-ROM discs are designed to be read by *CD-ROM* and *DVD-ROM* drives, respectively. CD-ROM drives can usually also play audio CDs. DVD-ROM drives can typically play CD-ROM discs, audio CDs, DVD-ROM discs, and DVD movies.

### Recordable Discs: CD-Rs and DVD-Rs

*Recordable discs* can be written on, but the discs cannot be erased and reused. *CD-R* and *DVD-R discs* are the most common types of recordable optical storage media. CD-R and DVD-R discs are inserted into recordable optical storage devices (*CD-R drives* and *DVD-R drives*, respectively) to be written on. Once recorded, CD-Rs can be read by most types of CD and DVD drives, and DVD-R discs can be read by most DVD drives. Recordable CDs are commonly used for backing up files, sending large files to others, and creating custom music CDs from downloaded files or CDs the user already owns. DVD-Rs can be used for similar purposes when more storage space is needed, as well as for storing home movies and other video applications since video requires a tremendous amount of storage space.

### Rewritable Discs: CD-RW and DVD+RW

The newer *rewritable discs* can be recorded on, erased, and overwritten just like a magnetic disk. Two of the most common types of rewritable optical media are *CD-RW* and *DVD+RW discs.* CD-RW discs are written to using a *CD-RW drive* and can be read by most CD and DVD drives, although they may not be compatible with some older CD-ROM drives. DVD+RW discs are recorded using a *DVD+RW drive* and can be read by most DVD drives. It is important to realize that recordable DVDs have not yet reached a single standard, so there are competing formats (such as *DVD-RAM* and *DVD-RW)* that are not necessarily compatible with each other or with all DVD+RW devices. Some double-sided recordable DVDs may also need to be inserted into a special cartridge to be accessed, which limits the types of drives in which they can be used.

### Miniature Discs

While most optical discs are the standard 4 ¾-inch size, *mini optical discs* are available, such as 3-inch CD-R discs that can hold 185 MB and are read with standard CD and DVD drives, and the quarter-size *DataPlay digital media* disc that can hold 500 MB, but can only be read by a DataPlay-compatible device. Mini discs are used most often to transport data (particularly music and photos) from one computer or device to another; they can also be purchased with prerecorded music, games, e-books, and more. It is becoming increasingly common for mobile communications devices (cell phones, handheld PCs, digital music players, etc.) to support a type of miniature optical disc format.

**FIGURE 2-22**

**Optical discs**

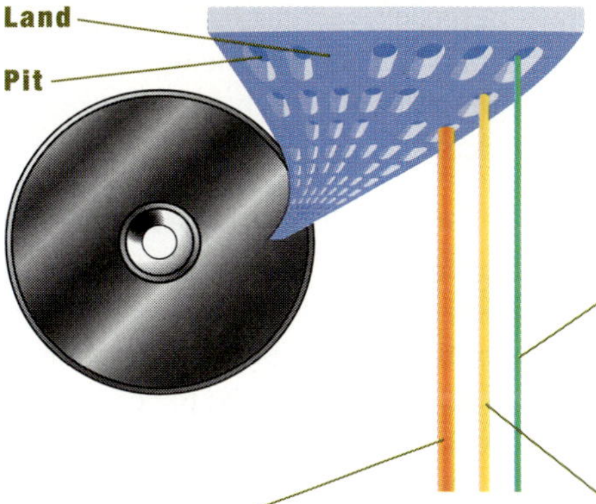


DVD discs can store more data than CDs because the pits are smaller and placed more closely together. Some DVDs also use multiple layers and record both sides of the disc to increase storage capacity.

**Reading data**

A low intensity laser beam reads the disc. It can tell the binary 1s from the binary 0s because light is reflected from nonburned surfaces—called *lands*—but not from the darkened *pits*.

**Writing data**

When programs or data are written onto the disc at the factory, a high intensity laser beam burns the surface to inscribe them.

**Rewriting data**

If the disc is rewriteable, a lower powered laser converts pits to their original state, allowing the disc to be rewritten.

**^ CDs**

CDs are available in read-only, recordable, and rewritable (as shown here) formats and typically hold 650 MB.

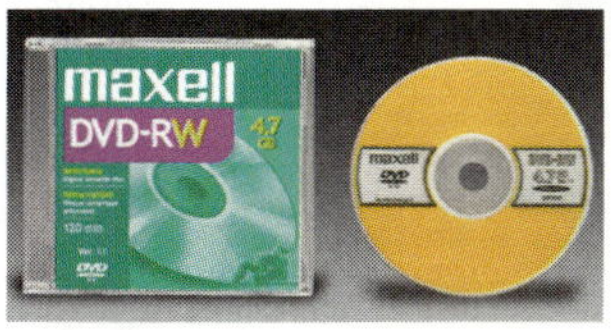


**^ DVDs**

Because they are now available in read-only, recordable, and rewritable (as shown here) formats and typically hold between 4.2 and 9.4 GB, DVDs are expected to eventually replace CDs.

**^ Mini optical discs**

Mini optical discs, such as the 500 MB DataPlay disc shown here, are frequently used with portable PCs and mobile devices.

## Other Removable Media

There are a variety of other types of removable media that can be used for specialized purposes, such as backing up data, exchanging data with others, and transporting data between portable devices and a PC. The most common types of removable storage media are high-capacity removable disks and *flash memory media. Smart cards* are another possibility for certain applications.

**ONLINE RESOURCES**

For links to information about removable storage media, go to www.course.com/morley2003/ch2

### High-Capacity Removable Disks

Before recordable CDs became available, the primary means of exchanging large files with others was by using high-capacity removable disks (see Figure 2-23). Though some of these systems have a large installed base and are still widely used at the present time, that may not be the case in the future as recordable optical disc technology improves. Most of these systems are *proprietary;* that is, the media can only be used in one specific type of storage device. High-capacity removable disks include:

- *Zip disks*—hold 100, 250, or 750 MB of data and are used only in *Zip drives.* Though proprietary, there is a huge installed base of Zip drives, so Zip disks are considered to be a fairly standard medium.
- *SuperDisks*—hold 120 or 240 MB of data and can be used only in *SuperDisk* (also called *laser servo* or *LS) drives.* Although a SuperDisk cannot be used in a floppy drive, a conventional floppy disk can be used in a SuperDisk drive.
- *Peerless disks*—a replacement for the popular high-capacity *Jaz disk*, Peerless disks can hold 10 or 20 GB of data.

**FIGURE 2-23**

**A high-capacity (250 MB) removable disk and drive**

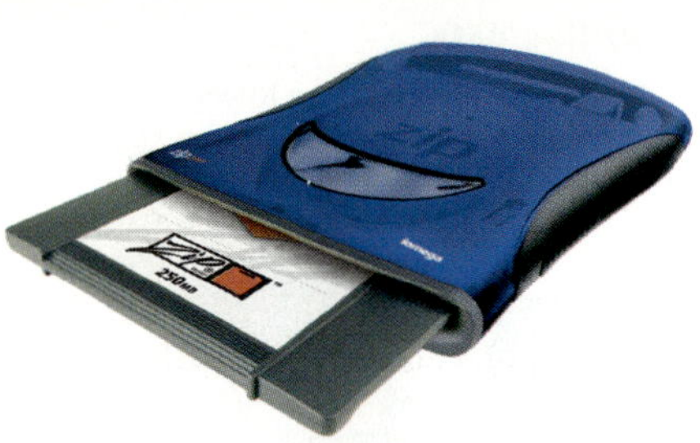

### Flash Memory Media

Unlike magnetic and optical storage systems whose drives have moving parts, **flash memory** storage systems use nonmoving chips and circuitry. Because flash memory devices and media are typically very small, use much less power than conventional drives, and are very resistant to shock and vibration since they have no moving parts, they are especially appropriate for use with notebook computers, digital cameras, handheld PCs, digital music players, smart phones, and other types of portable devices. Today, flash memory is found in the form of rewritable sticks, cards, or drives (see Figure 2-24).

- *Flash memory sticks* are about the size of a stick of gum and hold from 4 to 128 MB each. Memory sticks are commonly used with digital music players, digital cameras, PCs, printers, and other devices via a *memory stick port*, either built directly into the device or into a mouse, external adapter, or other peripheral device.
- *Flash memory cards* come in a variety of formats, such as cards that plug into a notebook computer's *PC card* port, as well as the *CompactFlash, SmartMedia, Secure Digital (SD)*, and *MultiMedia Card (MMC)* formats frequently built into handheld PCs, digital cameras, and mobile communications devices. Common storage capacities for flash memory card media are from 2 to 1 GB.
- *Flash memory drives* contain the storage media and device in a single self-contained unit. For example, miniature portable flash memory drives can be carried on a keychain and plugged into any computer's USB port to be instantly recognized as an additional drive; they are available in sizes from about 16 to 128 MB.

### Smart Cards

A **smart card** is a credit-card-sized piece of plastic that contains some computer circuitry, typically a processor, memory, and storage (see Figure 2-25). Though the storage capacity of a smart card is fairly small—usually from a few kilobytes to a few megabytes—it can be used to hold specific pieces of information that may need to be updated periodically. For example, a smart card can store a prepaid amount of digital cash for purchases using a smart card-enabled vending machine or PC; can hold identification data for accessing facilities or computer networks; or can store an individual's medical history and insurance information for fast treatment and hospital admission in an emergency. Many debit and credit cards today are beginning to include smart card capabilities, as well.

**FIGURE 2-24**

**Common forms of flash memory media**

**Memory sticks**

Are used with special memory stick ports built into PCs, mobile devices, and peripheral devices.

**Memory drives**

Can be full-sized, but are more commonly portable devices, such as the one shown here that connects to a PC's USB port and can be carried on a key chain.

**Memory cards**

Are available in a variety of formats. External readers are available; some readers and ports built into devices accept more than one type of card.

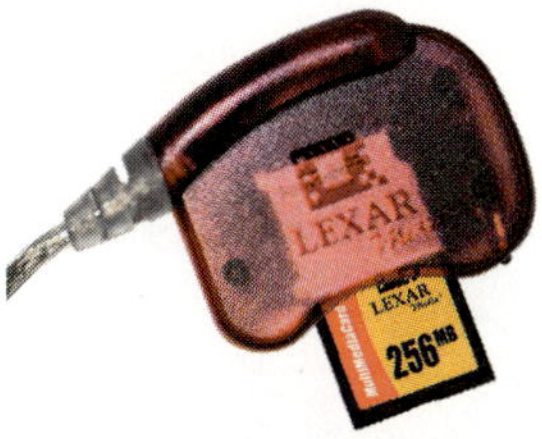

## Hard Drives

With the exception of computers designed to use only network storage devices (such as network computers and some Internet appliances), virtually all PCs come with a **hard drive** that is used to store most programs and data. Similar to floppy drives, hard drives store data magnetically; their disks are organized into tracks, sectors, and clusters; and they use read/write heads to store and retrieve data. However, the disks used with a hard drive are made out of metal and are permanently sealed inside the hard drive; one drive may contain a stack of several *hard disks* (see Figure 2-26). Hard drives are fixed-media systems where the storage media (the hard disks) are not removable from the storage device (the hard drive).

Hard drives are faster than removable-media systems and can store a great deal more data. The capacity of a typical hard drive for today's desktop PCs ranges from 40 to 160 GB.

For users who need to transport, archive, or secure large amounts of data, *portable hard drives*—drives that can be transported from PC to PC—are available (see Figure 2-27). Portable drives designed for notebook PCs typically plug into a PC's PC card port. Drives designed to connect to a computer's *USB* or *Firewire* port can be used with any computer that has that type of port. Portable hard drives are frequently used in exceptionally secure facilities—such as government and research labs—where all hard drives must remain locked up when they are not in use.

**FIGURE 2-25**

**A smart card**

## Remote Storage Systems

*Remote storage* refers to using a storage device that is not directly a part of your PC system; instead, it is accessed through a local network or the Internet. Using remote storage devices and media works very similarly to using *local storage* (the storage devices and media that belong to your PC); you just need to select the appropriate remote storage device (typically a hard drive attached to a network server) and then you can store data on or retrieve data from it. When the remote device is accessed through a local network, it is sometimes referred to as *network storage;* the term *online storage* most commonly refers to storage accessed via the Internet. Individuals and businesses can use online storage Web sites to transfer files between two computers, to share files with others, and for backup in case of a fire or other disaster. For some Internet appliances, network computers, and mobile communications devices with little or no local storage capabilities, online storage is especially important.

### Choosing among Storage Alternatives

With so many different storage alternatives available, it's a good idea to give some thought to which devices and media are most appropriate for your personal situation. In general, most users today need a hard drive (for storing programs and data), some type of CD or DVD drive (for installing programs, backing up files, and sharing files with others), and a floppy drive (for sharing small files with others and booting up your PC if your hard drive malfunctions). Some users may also choose to include an additional drive for a particular type of high-capacity removable media, such as Zip disks or Peerless disks, if they only need to use the disks in their PC or a PC they know has a drive compatible with that medium. Users who plan to transfer music, digital photos, and other multimedia data on a regular basis between several different devices, such as a PC, digital camera, handheld PC, and printer, may want to select and use the flash memory media that is most compatible with the devices they are using.

**FIGURE 2-26**

Inside a hard drive

**Access mechanism**

The access mechanism moves the read/write heads in and out together between the hard disk surfaces to access required data.

**Sealed drive**

The hard disks and the drive mechanism are hermetically sealed inside a case to keep them free from contamination.

**Hard disks**

There are usually several hard disk surfaces on which to store data. Most hard drives store data on both sides of each disk.

**Mounting shaft**

The mounting shaft spins the disks at a speed of several thousand revolutions per minute while the computer is turned on.

**Read/write heads**

There is a read/write head for each disk surface. On most systems, the heads move in and out together and will be positioned on the same track and sector on each disk.

**FIGURE 2-27**

Portable hard drives

**^ PC card drives**

Notebook PCs can use portable hard drives that plug into the PCs PC card slot.

**^ USB and Firewire drives**

Both desktop and notebook PCs can use portable hard drives that plug into the PC's USB port. Some drives come in Firewire versions, as well.

## COMMUNICATIONS HARDWARE

To enable communications with others over a network or the Internet, most computers today include *communications hardware.* Common **communications devices** are *network adapter cards* (to connect to a network via a wired or wireless network connection) and *modems* (to connect to the Internet via a telephone, cable, satellite, or similar connection). The various options for connecting to the Internet are discussed in more detail in Chapter 3.

Though features and capabilities vary from program to program, most software today uses similar basic features and operations. While covering how to use specific software programs is beyond the scope of this book, an understanding of basic software concepts and operations is an important part of becoming familiar with computers. In addition, an understanding of these concepts and operations will help prepare you to use a PC to complete class assignments, perform research for chapter projects, and do the Internet activities that accompany this book.

**ONLINE TUTORIAL**

For an online look at basic document-handling and file management operations, go to www.course.com/morley2003/ch2

## What Are Files and Folders?

Anything (a document, program, digital photograph, song, etc.) stored on a storage medium is called a **file**. When the item is first saved, the user gives it a **filename** and that filename is used whenever the file needs to be retrieved, updated, or otherwise accessed. To keep files organized, related documents can be stored inside **folders**, as shown in Figure 2-28. Folders can contain both documents and other folders, and documents can be moved from folder to folder as needed. (The chapter How To box discusses file management in more detail.) Whenever a user saves a file, he or she specifies both the drive to be used and the folder in which the file should be stored.

**FIGURE 2-28**

**Files can be stored within folders on a storage medium to keep them organized and easy to find.**

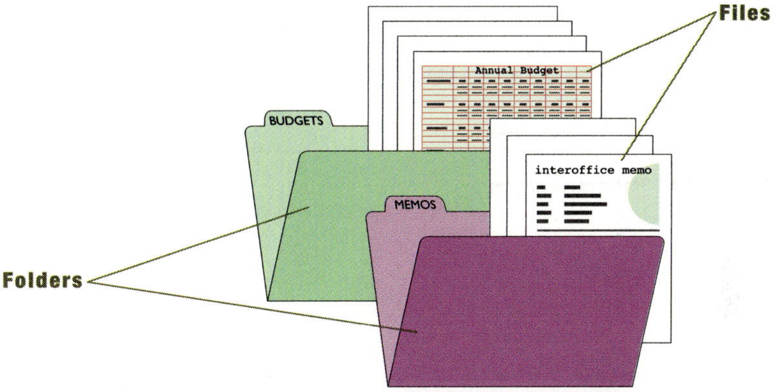


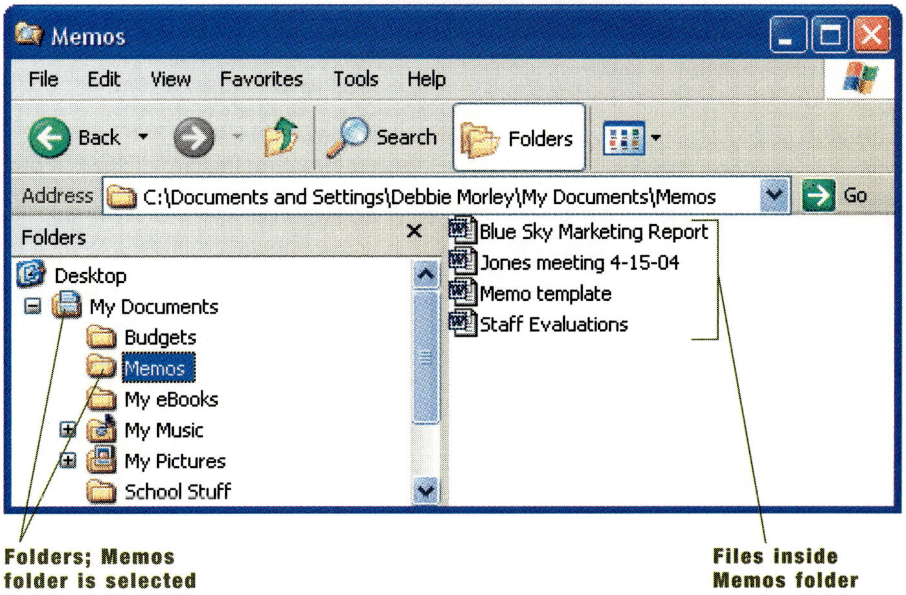


## Starting a Program

Once a computer has been powered up and the *boot process* has been completed, programs can be opened using the commands appropriate for that PC's operating system. For example, to start a program in the Windows environment, any of the following mouse operations can be used (refer to Figure 2-29):

- Click the appropriate *taskbar toolbar icon*, if one exists for the desired program.
- Click the appropriate *desktop icon*, if one exists for the desired program and the icon looks like a *hyperlink* (it is underlined and the mouse pointer turns into a pointing hand when the icon is pointed to).
- Double-click the appropriate desktop icon, if one exists for the desired program and the icon doesn't look like a hyperlink.

**FIGURE 2-29**

**Starting a program on a Windows PC**

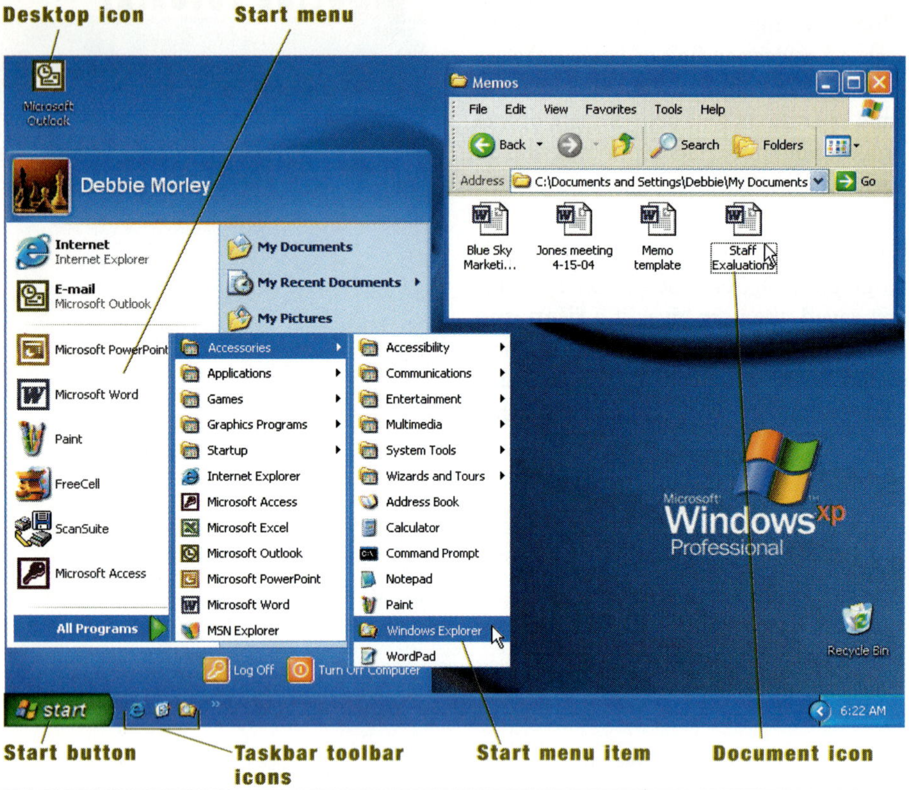


- Click the *Start button* and then select the desired program from the *Start menu*, resting the mouse pointer on any item containing an arrow ▶ to the right of it to reveal a submenu containing more choices.
- In a file management program, double-click a document icon to open the document in the associated program (right-click the document instead to choose the program in which it should be opened).

## The User Interface

All software programs have a *user interface* that allows a user to interact with the program. The user interface for most software programs today includes a variety of icons, buttons, and other objects that can be clicked to issue commands to the program. For example, the programs shown in Figure 2-30 contain the following objects:

- *Icons*—located on the desktop or within windows and used to open documents, folders, or programs.
- *Menus* and *toolbar buttons*—used to issue commands such as to print, save, and spell-check a document. As shown in Figure 2-30, when you click a menu name on a program's *menu bar*, the appropriate menu is displayed, and pointing to a toolbar button identifies its function.
- *Command buttons*—used to authorize or cancel the options on *dialog boxes* that are displayed when more information is needed from the user about a command that was issued.
- *Sizing buttons*—small buttons located at the top right corner of each window used to minimize, restore or maximize, and close that window.
- *Hyperlinks*—linked text or images located on the desktop, a Web page, or a program option that are clicked to display information or to select that option.
- *Scroll bars*—used to scroll up, down, left, or right through a document that is larger than the window in which it is displayed.
- *Taskbar buttons*—used to select which window is the *active window;* that is, the program on which commands will be executed. The active window appears on top of all other windows and has a different colored *title bar* (the top strip of the window).

**ONLINE RESOURCES**

For links to tutorials and other resources for common application programs, go to www.course.com/morley2003/ch2

## Common Software Commands

While some commands are specific for a particular program, many—such as opening a document, saving it, changing the format of the document, and printing it—are fairly universal. Some of the more common software commands are described in Figure 2-31, with examples of the toolbar buttons used to perform the operations in Windows applications. In general, the commands to perform these operations are the same or very similar in most software programs; programs within a *software suite* (such as *Microsoft Office* or *Corel WordPerfect Office)* use identical commands whenever possible.

**FIGURE 2-30**

**Icons, buttons, menus, and other objects can be used to issue commands to the computer.**

**FIGURE 2-31**

**Many software programs have similar basic document-handling operations and commands.**

| | | | |
|---|---|---|---|
| Start a new document. | | Undo the last change made to the document. | |
| Open a document. | | Zoom in or out on the current document. | 75% |
| Save the current document. | | Change the font face of the current word, selected text, or text to be entered next. | Times New Roman |
| Print the current document. | | Change the font size of the current word, selected text, or text to be entered next. | 12 |
| Spell-check the current document. | | Bold the current word, selected text, or text to be entered next. | B |
| Move the selected text or image to the clipboard. | | Italicize the current word, selected text, or text to be entered next. | I |
| Copy the selected text or image to the clipboard. | | Underline the current word, selected text, or text to be entered next. | U |
| Paste the contents of the clipboard to the current location in the current document. | | Close the current document, window, or program. | X |

**File management** is the term used to describe the process of organizing and maintaining your files. It includes looking at what is stored on a particular storage medium, copying files from one location to another, renaming files, deleting files, and so forth. Every operating system includes some file management capabilities. For example, Windows file management typically takes place in either *Windows Explorer* or *My Computer* (accessible through either a desktop icon or the Start menu). Although these two programs are initially set up to work slightly differently, their options can be changed and either program can be used to perform basic file management tasks.

### Seeing the Files Stored on a Disk

Once your file management program is open, to see the files and folders stored on your floppy disk, hard drive, or any other storage medium, click the appropriate letter or name for that medium (some programs or setups may require you to double-click instead). To look inside a folder, double-click the folder (see Figure 2-32). To open a file, double-click it.

In the Windows Explorer program shown in Figure 2-32, clicking a drive or folder icon in the left pane displays its contents in the right pane (the folder list in the left pane is usually hidden in My Computer). A plus sign (+) in front of a folder or drive indicates that there are *subfolders* inside the folder or drive that are currently not listed; a minus sign (-) indicates that all subfolders are displayed (clicking a plus or minus sign or double-clicking the folder toggles between exposing and hiding the subfolders). Folders without any subfolders inside have neither a plus nor minus sign next to them.

The desired drive and folder can also be selected using the Address toolbar usually located just below the Standard toolbar. Clicking the Back button on the Standard toolbar redisplays what you were looking at previously; the Up toolbar button can be used to close a folder and move you up one level in the hierarchy of that drive. To create a new folder under the

**FIGURE 2-32**

**The Windows Explorer program can be used to see the contents of your PC.**

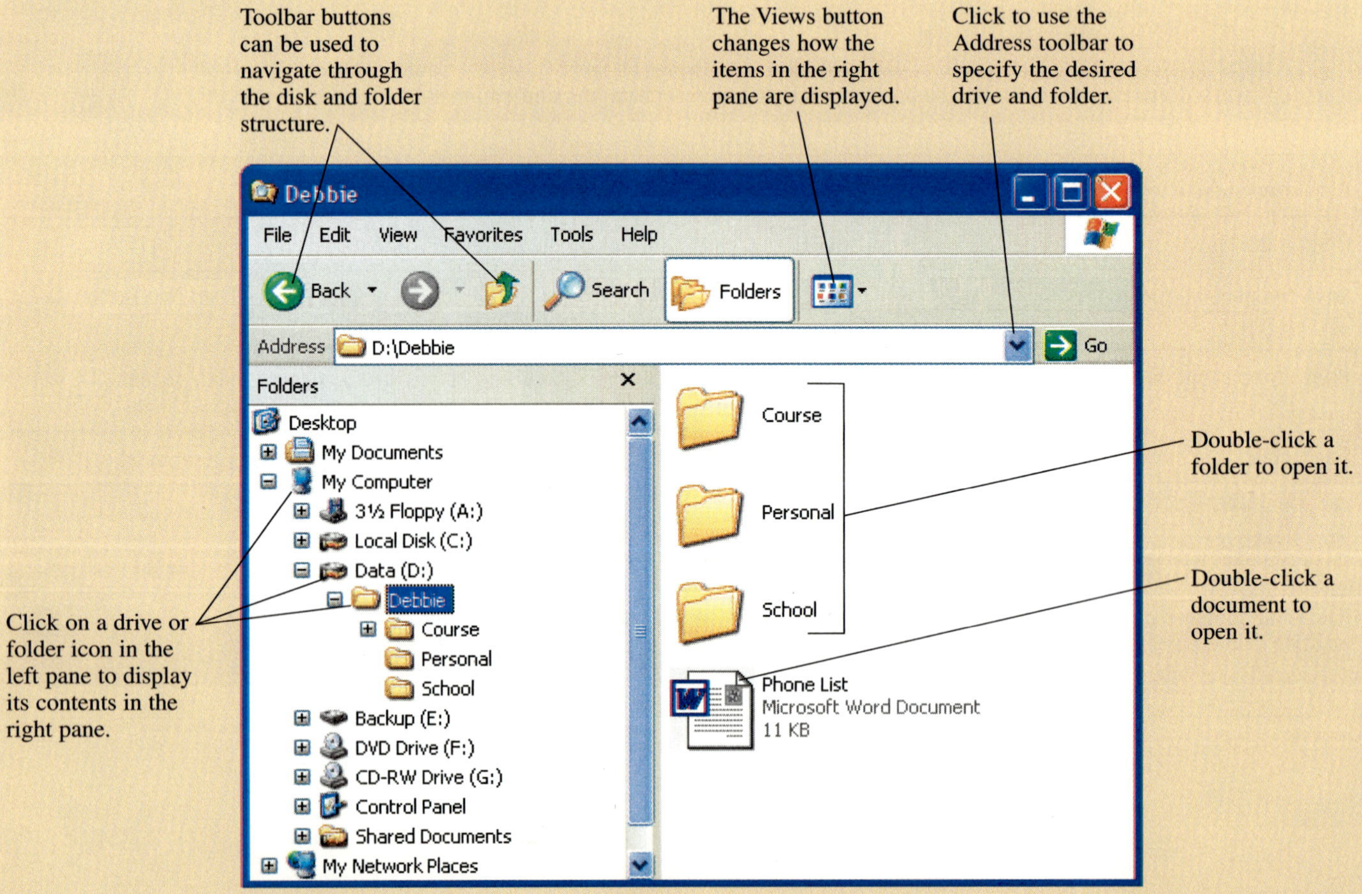

current location, select *New* and then *Folder* from the File menu, and then enter the desired folder name while the default name *New Folder* is highlighted.

### Copying, Moving, Renaming, and Deleting Files and Folders

To copy or move a file, follow the steps listed next. (To copy or move an entire folder, use the same procedure, but select the folder instead of a file.)

1. Open the drive and folder where the file is located.
2. Select the desired file.
3. Select *Copy* from the Edit menu to copy the file to a temporary storage area called the *clipboard.* (If you want to move the file instead of copying it, select *Cut* instead of *Copy,* as in Figure 2-33).
4. Open the drive and folder where you want the file to go, and then select *Paste* from the Edit menu to transfer the item from the clipboard to the new location.

To change the name of a file or folder:

1. Open the drive and folder where the item to be renamed is located.
2. Select the appropriate item.
3. Either choose *Rename* from the Edit menu or click a second time on the filename or folder name.
4. When the name is highlighted, either type the new file or folder name or click the highlighted name to remove the highlighting and display an insertion point, and then edit the name.

To delete a file or folder:

1. Open the drive and folder where the item to be deleted is located.
2. Select the appropriate item and press the Delete key on the keyboard.
3. At the Confirm File/Folder Delete dialog box, select *Yes* to delete the file or folder.

Deleting a folder will delete all the files and folders contained within that folder.

To cancel the deletion of a file or folder, select *No* at the Confirm File/Folder Delete dialog box. To retrieve a file or folder accidentally deleted from your PC's hard drive, open your PC's *Recycle Bin* and *restore* the file to its original location. (Files and folders deleted from a removable disk cannot be restored in this manner.)

### Copying, Moving, or Deleting More Than One File or Folder at a Time

You can copy, move, or delete more than one item at a time by selecting all of the items before invoking the appropriate command—all of the selected items will then be copied, moved, or deleted together.

- To select a group of contiguous files, click the first file in the group and *Shift+click* (hold the Shift key down while clicking the mouse) on the last item.
- To select more than one noncontiguous file, click the first file and then *Ctrl+click* each additional file.

**FIGURE 2-33**

**File management programs allow you to move and copy files and folders easily.**

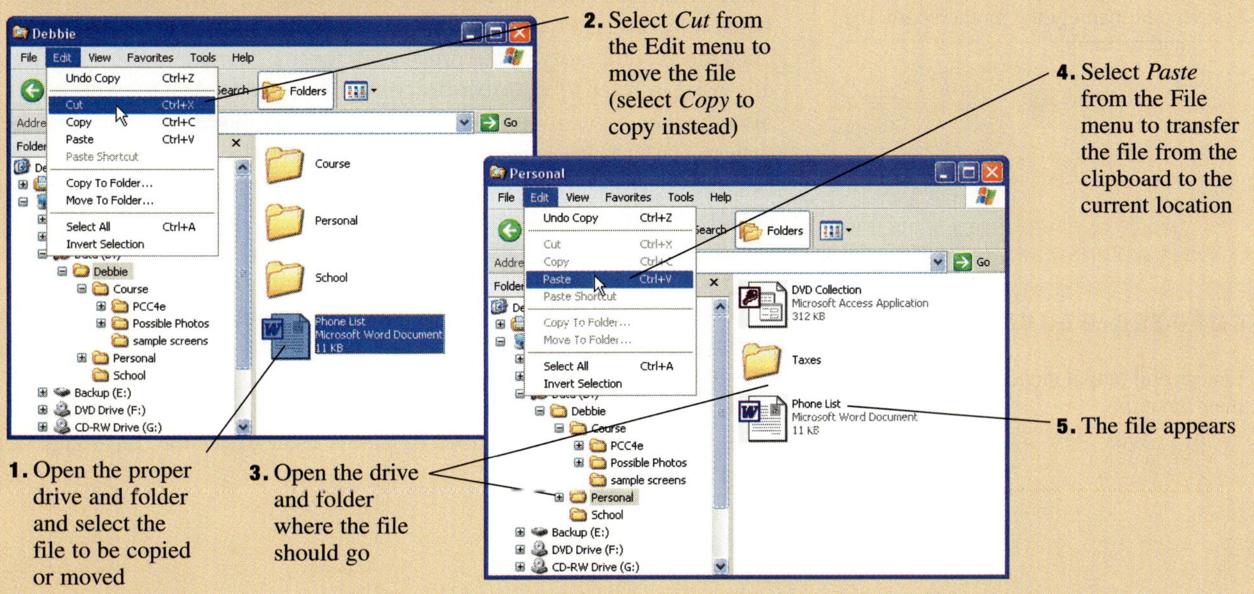

## SUMMARY

**CHAPTER OBJECTIVE 1**

Understand the difference between data and information, as well as how data and programs are represented to a computer.

### Data, Information, and Data Representation

**Data** is the term used for raw facts, before they are organized into meaningful **information**. To process data into information, computers need to convert data input into strings of 0s and 1s. The individual 0s and 1s are called *bits*; when 8 bits are used together, it is called a **byte**. A **kilobyte (KB)** equals 1,024 bytes; a **megabyte (MB)** is about 1 million bytes; a **gigabyte (GB)** is about 1 billion bytes; and a **terabyte (TB)** is about 1 trillion bytes. To represent numbers and do mathematical operations, computers use the *binary numbering system*; for representing characters, coding systems such as *ASCII* and *Unicode* can be used.

**CHAPTER OBJECTIVE 2**

Identify several types of input devices and explain their functions.

### Input Hardware

An **input device** is any piece of hardware that is used to input data into a computer. The two most common input devices are the **keyboard** and **mouse**. While a keyboard is designed to enter input by pressing keys, a mouse is a **pointing device** that is used to select objects and commands on the screen. Another type of pointing device used with portable PCs and mobile communications devices is the **electronic pen** (the cordless type used with portable PCs is called a *stylus*). Other possible devices include the *trackball*, *pointing stick*, *touchpad*, *touch screen*, and *joystick*.

To input already printed data, *optical scanners*—usually just called **scanners**—can be used. Special types of scanning devices include **bar code scanners** (used to read bar codes on consumer products and other objects) and *optical mark readers* (used to input exam or other data from special forms). **Digital cameras** work much like regular cameras but record images digitally on some type of storage medium instead of recording images on film. Microphones, *MIDI devices*, *adaptive devices*, and *ergonomic keyboards* can be used for input, as well.

**CHAPTER OBJECTIVE 3**

Explain the functions of the primary hardware components found inside the system unit, namely the motherboard, the CPU, and memory.

### Processing Hardware and Other Hardware Inside the System Unit

Processing hardware is located within the **system unit,** along with other important components. The **motherboard** is the main circuit board inside the system unit that all hardware attached to the computer must somehow be connected to, usually via *ports*. The **central processing unit (CPU)**—also called a **microprocessor** when referring to PCs—is a chip-based component attached to the motherboard that does the vast majority of the processing for the computer. The term **memory** is usually used to refer to **random access memory (RAM)**—groups of chips that are also attached to the motherboard and provide temporary storage for the PC to use. All data in RAM is erased when the power to the computer goes off. Less commonly referred-to types of memory include *cache memory*, *registers*, *read-only memory (ROM)*, and *flash memory*.

**CHAPTER OBJECTIVE 4**

List several output devices and explain their functions.

### Output Hardware

**Output devices** present the result of processing to the user, usually in the form of a **display device**—also called a **monitor**—or a **printer**. The common types of monitors are *CRTs* (the traditional desktop PC monitor) and *flat-panel displays* (used with portable PCs, as well as newer desktop systems). Monitors form images using **pixels**, and the number of pixels used to display an image determines the *screen resolution*.

Though older printers—such as *dot-matrix printers*—are *impact printers* that actually strike the paper to form images, today's newer printers are *nonimpact*. The most widely-used printers today are **ink-jet printers** (used in homes and for inexpensive color printouts) and **laser printers** (the standard for business documents). Other output devices include *speakers*, *headphones*, *fax/modems*, specialty printers, and *multifunction devices.*

## Storage Hardware

Because data is stored in memory (RAM) only temporarily, storage hardware is needed whenever a document should be saved for future use. Storage systems contain two parts: a **storage medium** (onto which data is stored) and a **storage device** (which reads from and writes to the medium). Most storage systems use *magnetic* or *optical* technology and can either be *removable-* or *fixed-media systems.*

**CHAPTER OBJECTIVE 5**

State the difference between storage and memory, as well as between a storage device and a storage medium.

**CHAPTER OBJECTIVE 6**

Name several storage devices and media and explain under what circumstances they are typically used.

Magnetic storage devices include removable **floppy disks**, which are written to and read using a **floppy drive**, and **hard drives**, which contain one or more *hard disks* permanently sealed inside the drive. To transfer large files, high capacity removable storage media, such as *Zip disks*, *SuperDisks*, and *Peerless disks* can be used; portable hard drives can be quickly switched between computers or locked up for security purposes. Magnetic disks are divided into *tracks*, *sectors*, and *clusters* so the computer can keep track of where each file is stored.

*Optical discs* include **CDs (compact discs)** and **DVDs (digital versatile discs)**. Both CDs and DVDs are available in *read-only*, *recordable*, and *rewritable* formats. The main difference between CDs and DVDs is storage capacity—DVDs hold significantly more data.

Some storage systems use **flash memory** media, such as sticks, cards, or drives, which use chips instead of moving parts. Other storage media include **smart cards** that contain small amounts of data (such as digital cash or personal data) for a variety of purposes, and *remote storage* (storage accessed through the Internet or other network).

Compatibility is important when selecting which storage devices to use. Most users will want a hard drive, an optical (CD or DVD) drive, and a floppy drive. Other devices can be added as needed.

## Communications Hardware

*Communications hardware*, namely *network adapters* and *modems*, are used to communicate with others over a network or the Internet.

**CHAPTER OBJECTIVE 7**

Describe the purpose of communications hardware.

## Software Basics

Though features and capabilities vary from program to program, most software today use a similar basic *user interface*, features, and operations. Anything stored on a storage medium (such as a document, program, or image) is called a **file** and is given an identifying **filename** by the user. To keep files organized, related documents can be stored inside **folders**. The process of organizing and maintaining files on storage media is called **file management**. Software programs are typically started using a desktop icon or the operating system's main menu, such as the Windows *Start menu.* Once open, most programs have a variety of objects—*menus*, *toolbar buttons*, *dialog boxes*, and more—that enable users to issue commands to the program.

**CHAPTER OBJECTIVE 8**

Understand how several basic software tasks are performed, such as how to start a program and how to use toolbar buttons or menus to issue commands.

## BALANCING ACT

### OPEN SOURCE SOFTWARE: WILL IT PROMOTE OR HINDER SOFTWARE DEVELOPMENT?

*Open source software* is software for which the actual program code (or *source code*) is made available free of charge to the general public. The growing number of open source products—such as the *Linux operating system* and *Apache Web server*, two of the most famous examples—are reviewed and improved by a huge number of independent programmers who update the software at no charge for fun, notoriety, or as a programming exercise. Proponents of open source software believe that if a large group of programmers who are not concerned with financial gain work on the program, it will produce a more useful and error-free product much faster than through the traditional commercial software development process. Programs based on open source code are usually available for free, or for a nominal fee (compared to similar software) for documentation and support.

Though open source software has been around for the last five years or so, it wasn't until recently that it became accepted by mainstream companies. Linux is commonly used for business servers and mainframes today, and Apache runs over 50% of the world's Web servers. The main reason companies are switching over to open source software is cost. For example, Amazon.com saved $17 million in one quarter after switching to Linux-based systems. With large commercial software companies—particularly Microsoft—denouncing open source software, many companies are reluctant to talk about their open source software use for fear of reprisals. But most experts predict that open source use will continue to grow. One estimate sees it displacing 20 percent of traditional software licensing revenue by 2004.

If open source use continues to grow as expected, it will definitely impact software as we know it today. Will existing software companies streamline their development process to cut costs? Or will they feel they need to put out products that are better and more reliable than open source competitors? Or will they simply go out of the software business?

### YOUR TURN

Give some thought to the potential impact in the next year or two if the open source software trend continues, and then answer the following questions.

1. Do you think open source software will have a positive or negative impact on the quality of software available for use? Why or why not?
2. Do you feel that commercial software manufacturers would be justified in raising their prices to make up for revenue lost to open source competitors? Do you think that strategy would be effective?
3. How does software piracy affect the cost and availability of commercial software? If commercial software manufacturers increase their copy-protection schemes, do you think it would help or hurt them?
4. What should the government's role be in the software market?
5. Do you think products based on open source code should be able to be sold for commercial gain after they have been modified? Why or why not?

# KEY TERMS

**Instructions:** Match each key term on the left with the definition on the right that best describes it.

a. **byte**

b. **central processing unit (CPU)**

c. **data**

d. **file**

e. **floppy disk**

f. **folder**

g. **hard drive**

h. **information**

i. **ink-jet printer**

j. **input device**

k. **keyboard**

l. **laser printer**

m. **monitor**

n. **motherboard**

o. **mouse**

p. **output device**

q. **random access memory (RAM)**

r. **storage device**

s. **storage medium**

t. **system unit**

**1.** ______ A common pointing device that you slide along a flat surface to move a pointer around the screen and make selections.

**2.** ______ A display device for a PC.

**3.** ______ A group of 8 bits, normally used to represent one character to a computer.

**4.** ______ A group of chips attached to the motherboard that provides a temporary holding place for the computer to store data and program instructions while it is needed.

**5.** ______ A logical named place on a storage medium into which files can be stored to keep the medium organized.

**6.** ______ A low-capacity, removable magnetic disk storage medium made of flexible plastic permanently sealed inside a hard plastic cover.

**7.** ______ A type of hardware that accepts output from the computer and presents it in a form the user can understand.

**8.** ______ A type of hardware that supplies input to a computer.

**9.** ______ A storage system consisting of one or more metal magnetic disks permanently sealed with an access mechanism inside its drive.

**10.** ______ An input device containing numerous keys that the user can press to input letters, numbers, and symbols into a computer.

**11.** ______ A printer that forms images by spraying tiny drops of ink onto a page.

**12.** ______ A printer that prints documents using a laser beam and toner powder; the standard for business documents.

**13.** ______ Data that have been processed into a meaningful form.

**14.** ______ Raw, unorganized facts.

**15.** ______ Something stored on a storage medium, such as a program, document, or graphical image.

**16.** ______ The main box of a computer that houses the CPU, motherboard, memory, and other devices.

**17.** ______ The main circuit board for a computer, located inside the system unit, to which all computer-system components are connected.

**18.** ______ The primary piece of processing hardware, attached directly to the motherboard, that consists of circuitry and other components.

**19.** ______ The name for the part of a storage system where the data is actually stored, such as a floppy disk or CD.

**20.** ______ The name for the part of a storage system, such as a floppy drive or CD drive, that reads data from or stores data on a storage medium.

## SELF-QUIZ

Answers for the self-quiz appear at the end of the book.

### True/False

**Instructions:** Circle **T** if the statement is true or **F** if the statement is false.

**T F 1.** A keyboard is a type of pointing device.

**T F 2.** RAM is the type of memory that is used for temporary storage and is erased when the power to the PC is turned off.

**T F 3.** An ink-jet printer would normally produce a better image than a laser printer.

**T F 4.** A DVD-ROM drive can be used to record data onto DVD discs.

**T F 5.** To start a program in the Windows environment, the Start menu can be used.

### Completion

**Instructions:** Supply the missing words to complete the following statements.

**6.** ______________ are raw facts to a computer; those facts processed into a meaningful form is ______________.

**7.** 250 MB of data is equal to about ______________ bytes.

**8.** A handheld PC would most likely use a(n) ______________ as its primary input device.

**9.** A(n) ______________ can be used to convert flat printed documents into digital form.

**10.** The chip-based device located on the motherboard that does most of the processing for a computer is called the ______________.

**11.** The small areas or dots on a monitor that are used to display images are called ______________.

**12.** A printer is an example of a(n) ______________ device.

**13.** A(n) ______________ located inside the system unit is used to store most of the programs and data used with a PC.

**14.** A piece of hardware used to connect to the Internet is called a(n) ______________.

**15.** Copying and deleting files are examples of ______________.

# PROJECTS

**YOUR OPINION**

## 1. E-Medicine

The chapter Closer Look box took a look at how handheld PCs are being used by physicians for a number of important tasks, such as scheduling appointments, updating patient records, ordering tests, prescribing medication, and so forth. Though this trend is fairly recent, computers have been involved in medical treatment for quite some time. They control the machines used to dispense medicine and monitor patients in intensive care units, they help analyze x-rays and other diagnostic exams, they guide robotic arms and other devices used during surgery, and so forth. Some aspects of computerized care are beneficial. But one can't help wonder if we may depend too much on computers and lose the human touch in patient treatment. And what about the potential for errors due to human input error, a computer virus, natural disaster, or sabotage?

For this project, consider the issues raised above and write a short essay expressing your opinion about the use of computers and computerized devices in medical treatment. Would you feel more comfortable trusting your diagnosis and treatment to a human medical professional or to a computer? Why or why not? What checks and balances (if any) do you believe need to be in place to ensure the safety of patients? List any additional pros and cons of automated medical diagnosis and treatment that you can think of that were not covered here. Submit your opinion on this issue to your instructor in the form of a short paper, not more than two pages in length.

**INDEPENDENT RESEARCH**

## 2. Ports for the Future

As mentioned in the chapter, external hardware connects to the computer via ports located on the exterior of the system unit. Some ports are built directly into the motherboard, and others are created by expansion cards already located inside the PC when it is purchased. The user can add additional expansion cards to create additional ports, as needed, provided there are empty expansion slots inside the PC. Conventional ports include *parallel, serial, joystick, PS/2 (keyboard/mouse), monitor,* and *game ports.* Newer ports include *USB, USB 2,* and *Firewire (IEEE 1394).* Some of the older ports—particularly parallel and serial—are beginning to be referred to as *legacy* ports. They are being omitted from some new computers today, and many people predict that they will eventually be replaced by newer types of ports.

For this project, investigate the ports just listed and provide a description of each port, including its normal use. When performing your research, form an opinion about whether or not any of the older ports could be completely replaced by the newer ones. Determine if there are any types of adapters that can be used to connect a piece of hardware designed for an older type of port to a USB or other type of newer port. Finally, locate two computer advertisements either online, in the newspaper, or in a computer journal, and list all the ports included on each PC, plus how many empty expansion slots are left on each PC. Do these advertisements change your opinion about legacy ports? If so, explain. Summarize your findings in a two- to three-page paper.

**HANDS-ON**

## 3. Will it Fit?

Many new PCs today come with very large—17- or 19-inch—monitors. Though they make output much easier to see, sometimes it may be difficult to get the monitor to fit on your desk.

For this project, find two 17-inch and two 19-inch CRT monitors made by different manufacturers and determine their physical size. (You may use newspaper ads, manufacturer Web sites, or systems for sale at your local stores.) Next, select the desk or table at home that you would use for the PC and measure it. Draw a sketch to scale of the top surface of the desk (bird's-eye view), and then add each monitor to your sketch (drawn to scale) to illustrate how well each one would fit. Are there any significant size differences between the manufacturers you selected? Would you need to eliminate any of these models due to lack of space?

Next, locate two 17-inch and two 19-inch flat-panel monitors and determine their physical size. How much difference is there between these models and the CRT models you tried to fit earlier? Compare prices between the CRT and flat-panel monitors you selected. Do you think the price difference justifies the smaller footprint? Prepare a summary of your findings to turn in to your instructor along with your sketch.

**4. File Practice**

As discussed in the chapter How To box, all operating systems have at least one program you can use to manage your files, such as the Windows Explorer program.

For this project, obtain a floppy disk for the computer you will be using for this course and insert it into the PC. Open the PC's file management program (with Windows, use the Start menu or desktop icon to open My Computer or Windows Explorer). Once the program is open, click or double-click the icon for the floppy drive to display the contents of your floppy disk. Are there any files on the disk? By looking at the status bar at the bottom of the file management program's window, or by right-clicking the A drive icon and selecting *Properties,* determine how much room is available on the disk.

Next, open any word processing program (Word, WordPad, Notepad, etc.). Create a new document consisting of your name at the top of the page. By using the appropriate toolbar button or File menu option, save the document onto your floppy disk (change the save location to the floppy disk drive and use your last name as the filename). Return to your file management program and view the contents of your floppy disk again. Is your new document stored there? If so, how big is it and how much room is left on your disk now? If it is not there, return to your word processor and use the Save As option to save the file again, making sure you are storing it on your floppy disk.

Prepare a short summary of your work to turn in to your instructor, listing the software programs used, the name of the file you saved on your disk, the size of the file, and the amount of space left on your disk once the file was stored on it. Return to your file management program and delete the file you stored on your floppy disk.

GROUP PRESENTATION

**5. Today's CPUs**

As mentioned in the chapter, most processor chips used in PC-compatible desktop computers today are made by Intel or Advanced Micro Devices (AMD).

For this project, form a group to research the CPUs currently available from these two companies. Which chips and clock speeds are available at the present time? Are any new chips expected to come out soon? Do any of the chips have any significant advantages over the others? Your group should check recent ads or search online to determine which CPUs are the most common today and how much Level 1 and Level 2 cache memory are typically available with each chip. Do any have a Level 3 cache? Share your findings with the class in the form of a short presentation. The presentation should not exceed 10 minutes and should make use of one or more presentation aids such as the chalkboard, handouts, overhead transparencies, or a computer-based slide presentation (your instructor may provide additional requirements). Your group may also be asked to submit a summary of the presentation to your instructor.

### 6. Instant Photos

There are a wide variety of digital cameras today—from inexpensive consumer models, to serious replacements for consumer film cameras, to professional-quality cameras.

For this project, form a group to research digital cameras. Determine what the term *megapixel* means and how it relates to digital cameras. Your group should select and compare one inexpensive consumer camera, one medium-priced consumer camera, and one professional-quality camera and review their specifications. Include the types of storage available for use with the cameras you selected, as well as the options for transferring digital photos from the camera to a PC or printer. Share your findings with the class in the form of a short presentation. The presentation should not exceed 10 minutes and should make use of one or more presentation aids such as the chalkboard, handouts, overhead transparencies, or a computer-based slide presentation (your instructor may provide additional requirements). Your group may also be asked to submit a summary of the presentation to your instructor.

### 7. Toxic PCs

**VIDEO VIEWPOINT**

PC hardware contains a variety of toxic and hazardous materials. As more and more computers are replaced by newer models, the problem of how to dispose of obsolete—and potentially dangerous—computer equipment, known as *e-waste*, grows. The accompanying video clip takes a look at the issue of e-waste and features resolutions by the Calvert Group, a self-proclaimed leader in the area of socially responsible investing.

**ONLINE VIDEO**

To view the Toxic PCs video clip, go to www.course.com/morley2003/ch2

After watching the video, think about the impact of e-waste on the environment. Many discarded computers are exported to Asia, which has become a dumping ground for e-waste. Whose responsibility is it to correct this problem? Is the U.S. at fault for allowing the exportation of our e-waste? According to a press release by the Calvert Group, one computer may contain up to 700 different chemical compounds—such as arsenic, lead, mercury, and cadmium—many of which are hazardous. If the materials making up a PC are hazardous, should manufacturers be allowed to continue to use those materials or should they be forced to find alternatives? What if a restriction on these compounds severely limited the types of computer equipment that could be manufactured? Or are landfills full of discarded equipment just the price we pay for being a technological society? What efforts should be made to recycle discarded PCs? Who should bear the cost of the recycling—the manufacturers, the consumers, the government?

**Express your viewpoint:** What impact does e-waste have on society and who is responsible for reducing the amount of e-waste being generated?

Use the video clip and the questions previously asked as the foundation for your response. Your instructor will direct you to be prepared to discuss your position (either in class, via an online class discussion group, or in a class chat room), or to write a short paper stating and supporting your viewpoint on the issue. You may also be asked to do research and provide resources to support your point of view on this issue.

# A QUICK TOUR OF CYBERSPACE

## OUTLINE



## OBJECTIVES

**After completing this chapter, you will be able to:**

- Understand the difference between the Internet and the World Wide Web.
- Explain how Internet addresses are used to identify computers, Web pages, and people on the Internet.
- List several activities that can be performed using the Internet.
- Describe possible options for accessing the Internet.
- Explain how a browser, URLs, and hyperlinks are used to display Web pages.
- Understand how to send and receive electronic mail.
- Discuss some societal implications of the Internet, such as security, privacy, and differences in the way we communicate online.

# CHAPTER 3

## OVERVIEW

As you already know, a computer network is two or more computers connected together so that the users can share resources—such as hardware, software, and data—as well as communicate electronically with each other. Networks that connect to other networks form an *internet*; the largest internet in the world—connecting millions of computers—is called the *Internet*.

Though the Internet has existed in one form or another since 1969, in its early stages it was used solely by government and educational researchers. For the last decade or so, the Internet has become increasingly more accessible to the general public, but it has only been in the last few years that technology has evolved enough to support the Internet activities we've grown accustomed to today—such as downloading music and video files, watching animated presentations, and playing multimedia games with other online players.

This chapter begins with an overview of what the Internet and World Wide Web are, what they can be used for, and how they can be accessed. You'll learn about various options for connecting to the Internet, as well as the basic Web browsing and e-mail skills you will need to do research for class projects and to access the Web-based resources that accompany this book. The chapter closes with a look at some important societal issues regarding cyberspace.

# WHAT ARE THE INTERNET AND WORLD WIDE WEB?

Though the terms *Internet* and *World Wide Web* are often used interchangeably, they do not refer to the same thing. In actuality, the Web is just one part of the Internet.

## The Internet

The **Internet** evolved from an experimental network called *ARPANET*, which was created in 1969 by the U.S. Department of Defense's Advanced Research Projects Agency, or *ARPA*. One objective of the ARPANET project was to create a computer network that would allow researchers located in different places to communicate with each other. Another objective was to build a computer network capable of sending data over a variety of paths to ensure that network communications could continue even if part of the network was destroyed, such as in a nuclear attack or by a natural disaster. Over the years, *protocols* (standards) were developed for transferring data over the network and for ensuring that the data were transferred intact. Eventually, other networks were connected to ARPANET, and the resulting internet evolved into the present-day Internet.

A remarkable characteristic of the Internet is that it is not owned by any person or organization, and no single person or organization is in charge. Each network connected to the Internet is managed individually by that network's *network administrator*, but there is no network administrator for the Internet as a whole. The closest thing to an Internet governing body is a variety of organizations, such as the *Internet Society* and the *World Wide Web Consortium (W3C).* These organizations are involved with such issues as establishing the protocols used on the Internet, making recommendations for changes, and encouraging cooperation between and coordinating communication among the networks connected to the Internet. Another interesting factor is that, because of the protocols used, all computers on the Internet can communicate with each other, access the same resources, and exchange information, regardless of the type of computer or operating system being used.

The Internet infrastructure today can be used for a variety of purposes, such as exchanging *e-mail* and *instant messages*, participating in discussion groups and chat sessions, and transferring files. One of the most widely used Internet resources is the *World Wide Web.*

## The World Wide Web

While the term "Internet" refers to the physical structure of the network we've been discussing, the **World Wide Web** is one resource available through the Internet. The World Wide Web (also frequently called the *Web)* is a collection of documents—called **Web pages**—which are available through the Internet. The Web page files are located on computers (called *Web servers*) that are continually connected to the Internet so they can be accessed at any time by anyone with a computer and an Internet connection.

Web pages are displayed with a software program called a **Web browser.** Web pages today can contain text, graphics, animation, sound, video, and three-dimensional *virtual reality (VR)* objects, and are connected by **hyperlinks**—graphics or text that, when clicked with the mouse, display other Web pages. When a hyperlink is clicked, the appropriate Web page is displayed, regardless of whether the new page is located on the same server as the original page, or on a server in an entirely different state or country. Hyperlinks can also be used to enable Web visitors to download files, such as images, music, or software programs.

## Internet Addresses

**Internet addresses** are used to identify resources accessible through the Internet, such as computers, Web pages, and people. Each Internet address is unique and is assigned to one and only one person or thing. The most common types of Internet addresses are *IP addresses* and *domain names* (to identify computers); *URLs* (to identify Web pages); and *e-mail addresses* (to identify people).

### IP Addresses and Domain Names

**IP addresses** and their corresponding **domain names** are used to identify computers—most commonly Web servers—available through the Internet. IP (short for *Internet protocol*) addresses are numeric, such as *206.68.137.41*, and are commonly used by computers to refer to other computers. To make it easier for people, computers that host information available through the Internet (such as Web pages) also have a unique text-based domain name (such as *microsoft.com*) that corresponds to that computer's IP address. IP addresses and domain names are unique; that is, there can't be two computers on the Internet using the exact same IP address or exact same domain name. To ensure this, specific IP addresses are allocated to each network (to be assigned to network PCs) and there is a central worldwide registration system for domain name registration.

As shown in Figure 3-1, domain names typically identify who owns that computer, followed by a period and then either the type of organization (such as school, commercial business, government, or individual person) or the computer's location. The rightmost part of the domain name (beginning with the period and describing the type or location of the organization) is called the *top-level domain (TLD)*. The original TLDs used in the U.S. include *.com* (for commercial businesses), *.edu* (for educational institutions), *.gov* (for government organizations), *.org* (for noncommercial organizations), *.net* (for network providers and ISPs), and *.mil* (for military organizations). TLDs can also represent a country, such as *.us* for United States or *.jp* for Japan. Because of the high demand for domain names, new top-level domains are periodically proposed and approved by *ICANN* (*Internet Corporation for Assigned Names and Numbers*), the nonprofit corporation that is charged with such responsibilities as IP address allocation and domain name management. For example, three of the newest TLDs are *.biz* (for businesses), *.info* (for all uses), and *.name* (for individuals).

**FIGURE 3-1**

Examples of domain names

| Domain Name | Organization | Type/Location of Organization |
|---|---|---|
| microsoft.com | Microsoft Corporation | Commercial business |
| stanford.edu | Stanford University | Educational institution |
| fbi.gov | Federal Bureau of Investigation | Government organization |
| navy.mil | United States Navy | Military organization |
| royal.gov.uk | The British Monarchy | Government organization<br>United Kingdom |

Though many domain names consist solely of two parts, additional parts can be used to identify an organization more specifically, as in the last example in Figure 3-1. If so, all of the pieces of the domain name are separated by periods.

### Uniform Resource Locators(URLs)

Similar to the way an IP address or domain name uniquely identifies a computer on the Internet, a **uniform resource locator**, or **URL**, uniquely identifies a Web page. URLs are comprised of a combination of the *computer name* (the name assigned to that computer by the system administrator) and the domain name of the computer on which the Web page is stored, plus the Web page's filename and the names of any folders in which that file is stored. For example, the Web page shown in Figure 3-2 is called *index.html*, and is stored in a folder called *arthur* on a Web server called *www* in the *pbskids.org* domain.

FIGURE 3-2

A Web page URL

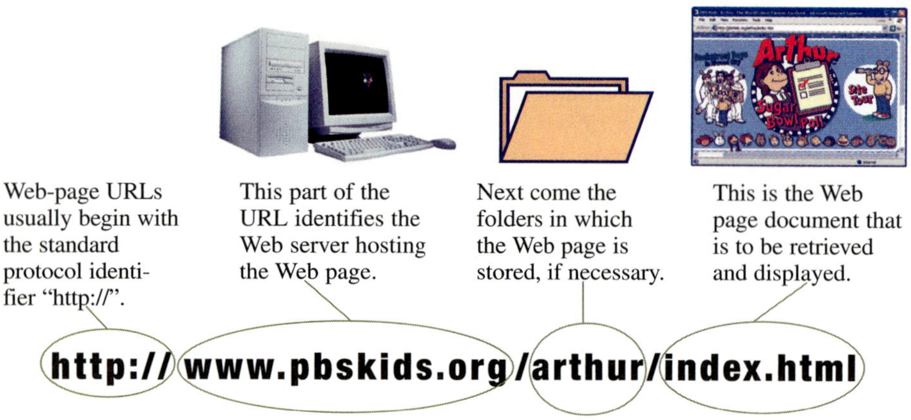


Some characteristics of the URL shown in Figure 3-2 are common to most URLs. The letters *http* stand for *hypertext transfer protocol*—the protocol typically used to display Web pages. Though Web pages are the most common Internet resource accessed with a Web browser, if a different type of Internet resource is being requested, a different protocol indicator is used. For example, the protocol *ftp://* can be used to issue requests to download files using *ftp* or *file transfer protocol.* The *www* at the beginning of the domain name is a very common computer name for a Web server. The file extension *.html* stands for *hypertext markup language*—the language usually used to create Web pages—and is the most common file extension for Web pages. Other file extensions, such as *.htm* (another abbreviation for hypertext markup language) and *.asp* (for *active server pages*, which are commonly used with Web pages that are dynamically created based on user input), are possible.

To request to see a particular Web page, you can type its URL into the specified area (usually called the *Address bar* or *Location bar* and located towards the top of your Web browser window). Some, but not all, Web browsers and Web sites allow you to leave off the *http://* and *www* parts of the URL. It is important to type a URL correctly (using the appropriate spelling, capitalization, and punctuation) or the Web browser will not be able to locate the desired Web page.

### E-Mail Addresses

To contact people using the Internet, you most often use their **e-mail addresses**. An e-mail address usually consists of a **user name** (an identifying name), followed by the @ symbol, followed by the domain name for the computer that will be handling that person's e-mail (such as a *mail server* belonging to a local ISP, America Online, Hotmail, their company, or their school). For example,

```
jsmith@course.com
maria_s@course.com
sam.peterson@course.com
```

are the e-mail addresses of three hypothetical employees at Course Technology, the publisher of this textbook, respectively assigned to jsmith (John Smith), maria_s (Maria Sanchez), and sam.peterson (Sam Peterson). User names are typically a combination of the person's first and last names and sometimes include periods or underscores, but can never include blank spaces. To ensure a unique e-mail address for everyone in the world, user names must be unique within each domain name. So, even though there could be a *jsmith* at Course Technology using the e-mail address *jsmith@course.com* and a *jsmith* at Stanford University using the e-mail address *jsmith@stanford.edu*, their e-mail addresses are unique. It is up to each organization to ensure that one, and only one, exact same user name is assigned under its domain.

### Pronouncing Internet Addresses

Because Internet addresses are frequently given verbally, it is important to know how to pronounce them. A few guidelines are listed next, and Figure 3-3 shows some examples of Internet addresses and their proper pronunciation.

- If a portion of the address forms a recognizable word or name, it is spoken; otherwise it is spelled out.
- The @ sign is pronounced *at.*
- The period (.) is pronounced *dot.*
- The forward slash (/) is pronounced *slash.*

**FIGURE 3-3**

Pronunciation tips for Internet addresses

| Type of Address | Sample Address | Pronunciation |
|---|---|---|
| Domain name | berkeley.edu | berkeley dot e d u |
| URL | microsoft.com/windows/ie/default.asp | microsoft dot com slash windows slash i e slash default dot a s p |
| E-mail address | president@whitehouse.gov | president at whitehouse dot gov |

## WHAT CAN THE INTERNET BE USED FOR?

The Internet is home to an enormous amount of information and activities. It provides access to the World Wide Web and its seemingly limitless information on virtually any subject. It is the medium through which electronic mail and other types of electronic communication can occur. It also provides avenues for e-commerce and distance learning, and is a source for entertainment.

### Information Publishing/Information Retrieval

When people think of the Internet, they likely think of the Web and the vast amount of information that can be found there. To publish information, a person or an organization with access to a Web server—such as through a company computer, a Web-hosting service, or an ISP—can publish Web pages, though sometimes this requires a fee. Once a Web page is published to a Web server, it is available to anyone with access to the Web. Some examples of the type of information available through the Internet are listed in Figure 3-4.

To retrieve information on the Internet from a Web site for which you know the URL (such as www.microsoft.com to get information on Microsoft products or www.switchboard.com to look up someone's telephone number), you can go directly to that site using its URL. If you know what type of information you want to find but don't know which URL to use, a **search site** can be used.

**FIGURE 3-4**

Examples of information available on the Internet

| Type of Information | Examples |
|---|---|
| **Product and company** | Product information (specifications, pricing, instruction manuals, etc.) available through manufacturer and retailer Web sites<br>Corporate information (financial statements, prospectuses, corporate officers, history, stock information, etc.) of interest to employees, current and prospective shareholders, and financial analysts |
| **Education and employment** | Course catalogs, application forms, fee information, and other information of interest to prospective and current students of a college or university<br>Information geared to educate individuals on a particular topic, such as a social cause, environmental concern, or political view<br>Resumes, job listings, and other job-hunting resources and information |
| **Travel** | Travel information, including airline and train schedules, weather, sightseeing, and lodging information |
| **News and history** | Current and past news and magazine articles<br>Biographical information about famous or historical figures, as well as other historical facts |
| **Reference** | Public records, such as birth, death, marriage, and home purchase information<br>Package tracking information (such as for business documents, personal packages, or online shopping deliveries)<br>Maps, ZIP code directories, encyclopedias, dictionaries, and other types of reference information<br>Current stock market quotes, bond rates, currency exchange rates, and other timely financial information |
| **Arts and entertainment** | Photographs or artwork that the creator wishes to share with others<br>Information about popular television shows and their actors and actresses<br>Social information, such as bridal registries and class reunion information |

Search sites are Web pages designed to provide users with links to Web pages that meet their specified conditions. Search sites can use a *search engine* (a program that locates Web pages that match supplied keywords), a *directory* (a collection of categories into which Web pages are classified), or both. After performing a search, hyperlinks to Web pages matching your keywords or selected categories are displayed (these pages are called *hits)*; clicking the hyperlink for a hit displays that page. The How To box at the end of this chapter covers searching in more detail, as well as how to evaluate and properly credit Web sources.

**ONLINE RESOURCES**

For links to a variety of search, reference, and portal sites, go to www.course.com/morley2003/ch3

*Reference sites*—such as those that provide access to encyclopedias, dictionaries, ZIP code directories, telephone directories, or maps—are also useful for specific types of information retrieval. To find an appropriate reference site, type the information you are seeking (*ZIP code lookup*, *topographical map*, etc.) as the key term in a search site. Most **portal** pages (Web pages that want to be your main entrance to the rest of the Web) include search and reference tools, as well as other useful free services to attract repeat visitors. Popular portals include Yahoo!, AltaVista, MSN, AOL, and Bolt.

## E-Mail and Other Types of Online Communications

**Electronic mail** (more commonly called **e-mail**) is the process of sending electronic messages from one computer to another over a network—usually the Internet. If you are connected to the Internet, you can send an e-mail message to anyone who has an Internet e-mail address. As illustrated in Figure 3-5, e-mail messages travel from the sender's PC to his or her ISP, and then through the Internet to the recipient's ISP. When the recipient logs on to the Internet and requests his or her e-mail, it is sent to his or her PC. Because e-mail is stored for an individual until he or she requests it, the sender and the receiver do not have to be online at the same time to exchange e-mail. In addition to text, e-mail messages can include photos and other graphics, as well as attached files.

In order to send or receive e-mail, you use an *e-mail program* that is set up with your name, e-mail address, incoming mail server, and outgoing mail server information. Once your e-mail program has been successfully set up, you don't

**FIGURE 3-5**

**E-mail messages are sent from one computer user to another over the Internet or other network.**

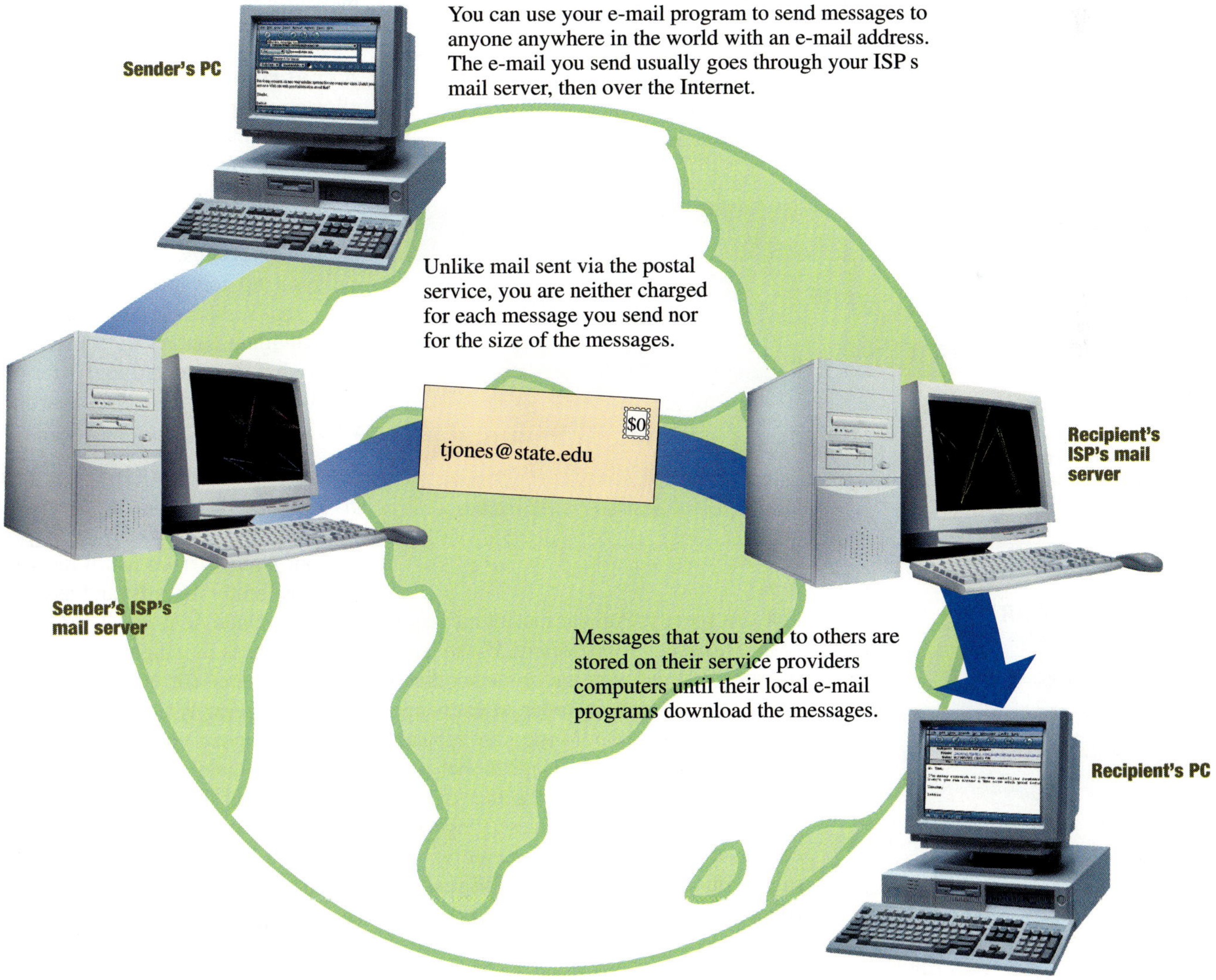

need to specify this information again, unless you want to check mail from a different e-mail account, you change ISPs, or you want to check your e-mail on a different PC.

In addition to e-mail, other types of online communications exist. A few of these applications are illustrated in Figure 3-6.

**Discussion groups** (also called *message boards*, *newsgroups*, or *online forums)* facilitate written discussions between people on specific subjects, such as computers, movies, gardening, music, hobbies, and political views. When a participant posts a message, it is displayed for anyone accessing the message board to read and respond to. Messages are organized by topics (called *threads).* Participants can post new messages in response to an existing message and stay within that thread, or they can post messages that start brand new threads. Some discussion groups can be accessed with just a Web browser; others require a *newsreader* (a special program for handing newsgroup messages that is often incorporated into e-mail programs).

**FIGURE 3-6**

**Examples of additional ways to communicate over the Internet**

**› Discussion groups**

Allow individuals to carry on written discussions with a variety of people on a specific topic. Since messages remain on the site once they are posted, users don't need to be online at the same time to participate.

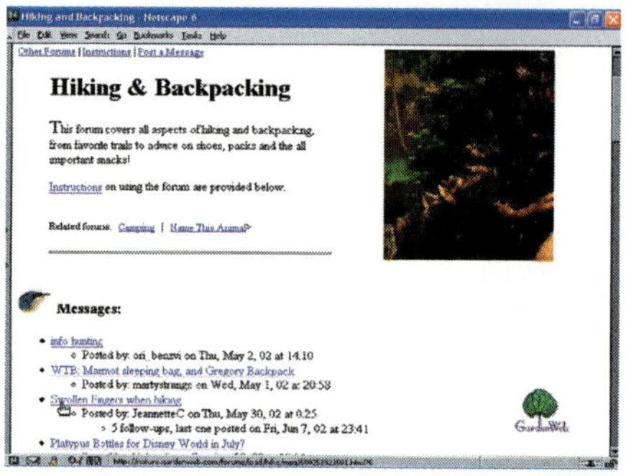


**‹ Instant messaging**

Enables real-time written conversations with friends and other "buddies" who are online at the same time.

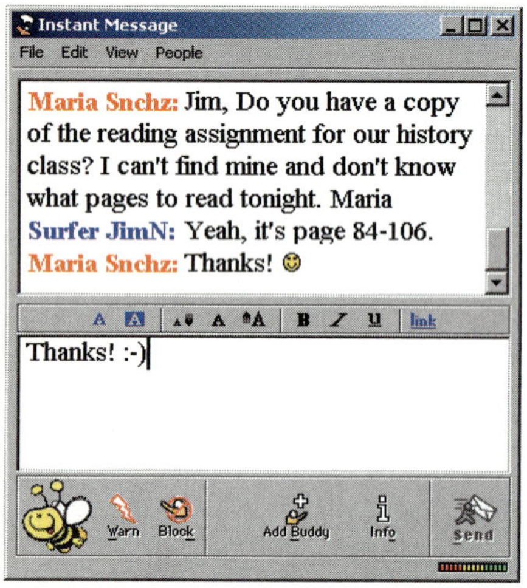


**› Videoconferencing**

Allows multiple individuals to talk with and see each other during a meeting. Some setups allow the use of a shared whiteboard that all participants can write on.

**ONLINE TUTORIAL**

For an online look at how to post discussion group messages and send instant messages, go to www.course.com/morley2003/ch3

A **chat room** is an Internet service that allows multiple users to exchange *real-time* typed messages. Unlike e-mail and discussion groups, chat participants are online at the same time and carry on typed conversations in real time. Like discussion groups, chat rooms are typically set up for specific topics. While most chat sessions are open to anyone, an individual can set up a private chat room that is reserved only for users (typically family, friends, or coworkers) who know the proper password.

**Instant messaging (IM)** is a form of private chat that is set up to exchange real-time messages easily with people on your *buddy list*—a list of individuals (such as family, friends, and associates) that you specify. Popular instant messaging services include *AOL Instant Messaging*, *MSN Messenger*, and *Yahoo! Messenger*. Because there is no single IM standard at the present time, you and your buddies must use the same (or compatible) instant messaging systems in order to exchange instant messages. Whenever one of your buddies is online (the IM program typically indicates which of your buddies are available), you can send a message to that person and it immediately appears on his or her computer. Typically both the messages that you type and that you receive are displayed within the instant messaging window. You can carry on several separate IM conversations at a time in separate windows, and each buddy will see only the messages you send to him or her. Originally a popular communication method between friends, IM has also become a valuable business tool.

**Videoconferencing** (also called *teleconferencing* or *Web conferencing)* refers to the use of computers, video cameras, microphones, and other communications technologies to conduct face-to-face meetings among people in different locations over the Internet. Small videoconferences can take place using the participants' PCs; large group conferences may require a more sophisticated setup, such as a dedicated teleconferencing room set up with video cameras, large monitors, microphones, and other hardware. New uses of one-way Internet videoconferencing include PC cameras located in childcare centers to allow parents to watch live video of their children throughout the day, and surveillance PC cameras set up in homes and offices to check for burglars and other problems when the location is unoccupied.

**Internet telephony** is the process of placing telephone calls over the Internet, usually either from your PC to the recipient's PC or from your PC to the recipient's telephone, depending on the setup. Though some free Internet telephony is available, usually there is a charge for it; however, the fee is typically less than for traditional long-distance phone service.

## Online Shopping and E-Commerce

**E-commerce** refers to performing any type of financial transaction online, such as paying a phone bill, ordering products or services, or buying and selling stock. E-commerce activities can take place between a business and a consumer (called *business-to-consumer* or *B2C* transactions), between two businesses (*business-to-business* or *B2B* transactions), between consumers (*consumer-to-consumer* or *C2C* transactions), or between business and government (*business-to-government* or *B2G* transactions). Some of the most common e-commerce activities involving consumers are illustrated in Figure 3-7.

Since *online fraud*, *credit card fraud*, and *identity theft* (where someone gains enough personal information to order products or otherwise pose as another person) are rising problems, it is important to be cautious when participating in e-commerce activities. To protect yourself, use a credit card whenever possible so that any fraudulent activities can be disputed, but be sure only to enter your credit card number and other sensitive information on a *secure Web page* (look for a locked padlock or a complete—nonbroken—key at the bottom of your Web browser screen, a URL that begins with *https* instead of *http*, or some other indication that a secure server is being used).

### Online Shopping

**Online shopping** is a fast-growing use of the Internet. Products can be purchased directly from large companies—like L.L. Bean, Dell Computer, Wal-Mart, Amazon.com, and Macy's—via their Web sites, as well as from a huge number of small retailers. Typically, a shopper locates the items they'd like to purchase by searching the site or browsing through an online catalog, and then adds them to an online *shopping cart.* When the shopper is finished shopping, checkout procedures are followed—such as supplying the appropriate billing and shipping information—to complete the sale. Most online purchases are paid for using a credit card, though other alternatives—such as using a payment account or smart card, or sending in a check or money order—are sometimes available. After the payment is processed, the item is either shipped to the customer (if it is a physical product) or the customer is given instructions on how to download it (if it is a software program, e-book, music, or some other product in electronic form).

**FIGURE 3-7**

Some e-commerce activities

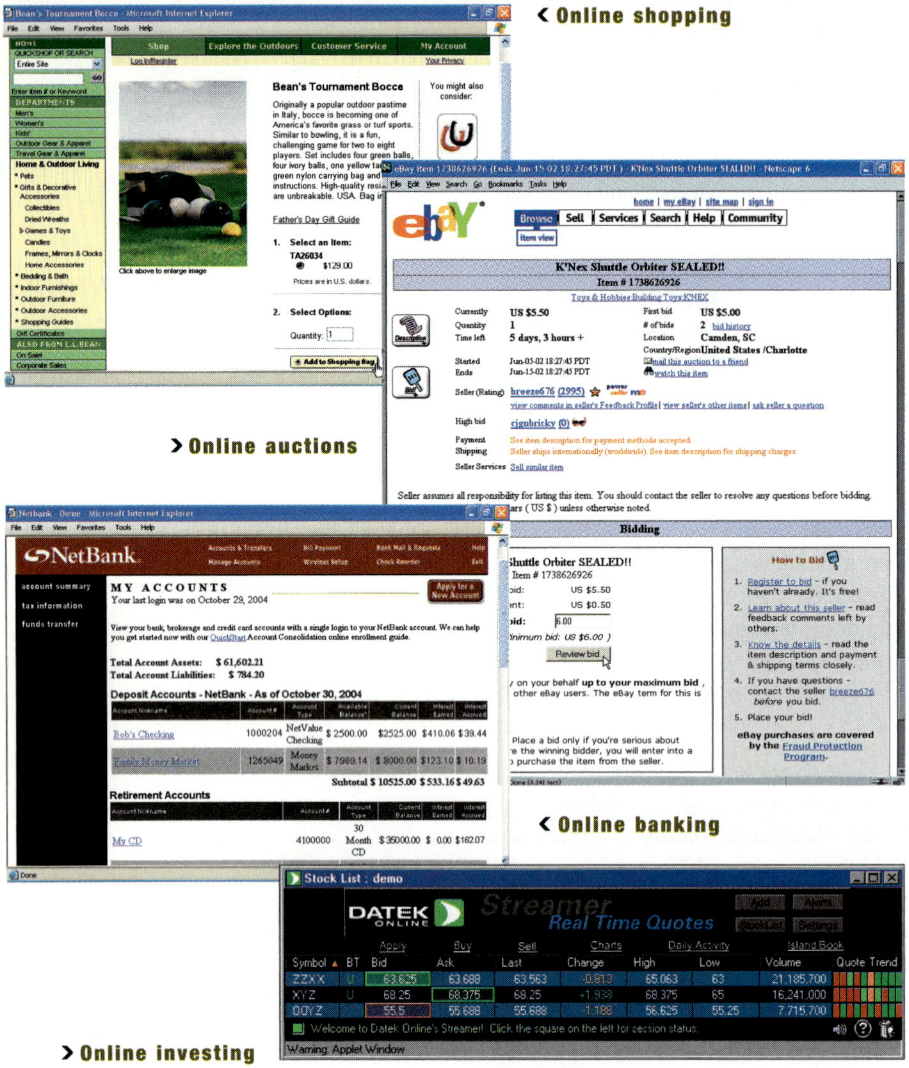


## Online Auctions

**Online auctions** are the most common way to buy items online from other individuals. Once you find an item you'd like to purchase on an auction site (such as eBay or Yahoo! Auctions), you enter a bid and wait. If someone outbids you, you can enter a higher bid. Most auction sites also allow you to enter a maximum bid amount and the auction site will automatically bid for you (using the minimum bid increment for that item) whenever you are outbid, until it reaches your maximum bid. At the time the auction closes, the person with the highest bid is declared the successful bidder and arranges payment and delivery for the item directly with the seller.

## Online Banking

A relatively new online financial application is **online banking.** Though it used to be available separately for a fee, now many conventional banks, such as Bank of America and Wells Fargo, offer free online banking services to supplement in-bank transactions. There are also Web-only banks, such as NetBank and First Internet Bank. Online banking offers many options, including reviewing account activity, sending electronic payments, transferring funds between accounts, and checking your credit card balances.

## Online Investing

Buying and selling stocks, bonds, and other types of securities is referred to as **online investing**. Though it is common to see stock quote capabilities on many search and news sites, trading stocks and other securities usually requires an *online broker.* The biggest advantage for using an online broker is the low transaction fee—often just $10 to $15 per trade, generally much less expensive than comparable offline services. Most online brokers allow you to set up an *online portfolio* that displays the status of the stocks you specify. On many sites, stock price data is delayed 20 minutes, but some brokers offer real-time quotes. Unless the quote or page is automatically refreshed for you on a regular basis, such as with a *Java applet*, it is important to realize that you need to reload the Web page (using your browser's *Refresh* or *Reload* toolbar button) whenever you want to see updated quotes from the Web server.

When conducting any e-commerce activity, be sure to use a secure Web server. The chapter Closer Look box takes a look at another Internet activity that requires a high level of security: Online voting.

## A CLOSER LOOK AT... ONLINE VOTING

### No More Hanging Chads?

Many people view the 2000 U.S. presidential election as a complete breakdown of the voting process. The outcome of the election was delayed for over a month by voting discrepancies, forced recounts, and court battles over the ballots used in Florida (see Figure 3-8). Most of the disputed ballots were punch card ballots—ballot cards in which holes are punched (with a supplied punch device) to identify the voter's choice of candidate or support of a ballot issue. Punch card ballots are read by a special machine that detects the light showing through the punched card.

The Florida controversy centered primarily on the ballots that were not completely punched through, which resulted in a hanging "chad"—the small piece of paper that is supposed to be separated from the ballot when the hole is punched. Depending on whether or not the chad was blocking the punched opening when the ballot was read by the machine, the vote may or may not have been tallied correctly.

The 2000 election problems shifted attention to alternative voting systems. *Optical voting systems*, which have been used in some precincts for years, are considered to be much more accurate and consistent. These systems use optical mark technology where an empty rectangle, circle, oval, or an incomplete arrow is filled in by the voter to indicate his or her choice. The tabulating device reads the votes using "dark mark logic," whereby the computer selects the darkest mark within a given set area as the correct choice or vote.

More recent voting devices are *direct recording electronic (DRE) devices*. A DRE system enables the voter to enter his or her choices directly into a computer or electronic storage device typically using a touch-screen or push-button interface. A keyboard can be used in conjunction with the device to allow write-in votes, if needed. The voter's choices are stored in the voting machine and sent to the main election computer system at periodic intervals.

To either eventually replace or supplement punch card and electronic voting systems, the next likely step will be *online voting* via the Internet. In actuality, Internet voting already exists, though not on a wide-spread basis. In March 2000, Arizona's Democratic Party held the first binding U.S. election in which voters could cast their ballots online. For security purposes, all registered Democrats were mailed a PIN identification number and that number, plus an assortment of personal questions, were used to verify the identity of voters casting their ballots from remote (non-polling place) locations. The response was startling—nearly half of the ballots cast in that election were cast online. England had its first test of online voting at selected locations in 2002, and just under 25% of the voters chose to cast their ballots online. British Commons Leader Robin Cook has said he wants the UK to become the first country in the world to use the Internet for voting, perhaps as soon as the next general election.

Online voting has several advantages, the most obvious of which is convenience. With more than 40% of all U.S. households having Internet access, online voting could increase voter turnout significantly. For elderly individuals and people with limited mobility, it would be a tremendous convenience. Another consideration are the citizens in rural areas who now need to travel great distances to reach a polling place. Kelsey Begaye, President of the Navajo Nation, states that typically only about 40 percent of the people in his Navajo chapter can make it to the polls to cast their votes. For the 2000 Arizona Democratic primary, Begaye and other Navajo Democrats voted from an online polling station set up inside the Navajo Nation, and he believes that "Internet voting will open up underrepresented minority sectors of the population to active participation in the voting process." Many believe that online voting will also entice younger citizens to participate in the elections process, due to the convenience factor and their high level of computer and Internet use.

Potential disadvantages for online voting typically center around security and privacy concerns. How will the system prevent someone from voting as someone else? What will prevent an individual's vote from being stored in a database to be used against him or her at a later time? Could individuals sell their votes to the highest bidder? Possible solutions for voter authentication include using voter PIN numbers (as in the Arizona primary), as well as digital signatures, smart cards, and fingerprint readers as those technologies become more commonly used with home PCs.

**FIGURE 3-8**

**The 2000 U.S. presidential election problems have focused attention on alternate voting methods, including online voting.**

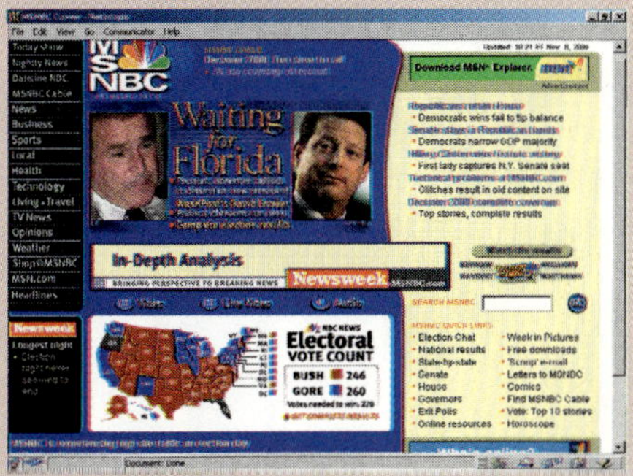

**FIGURE 3-9**

**Examples of Web-based entertainment activities**

**1.** Click to download the file or click one of the other options just to listen to the song.

**2.** Once the file is downloaded to your hard drive, double-click on it to play the song in your default music player program.

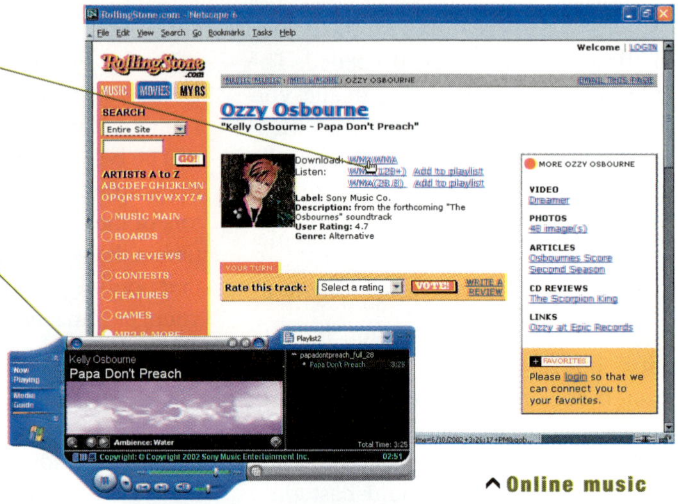

**^ Online music**

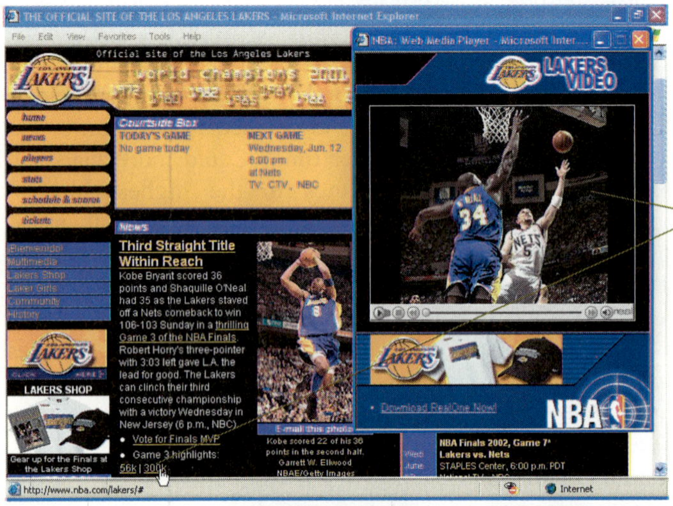

Click to play the video clip in the appropriate player program.

**< Online video**

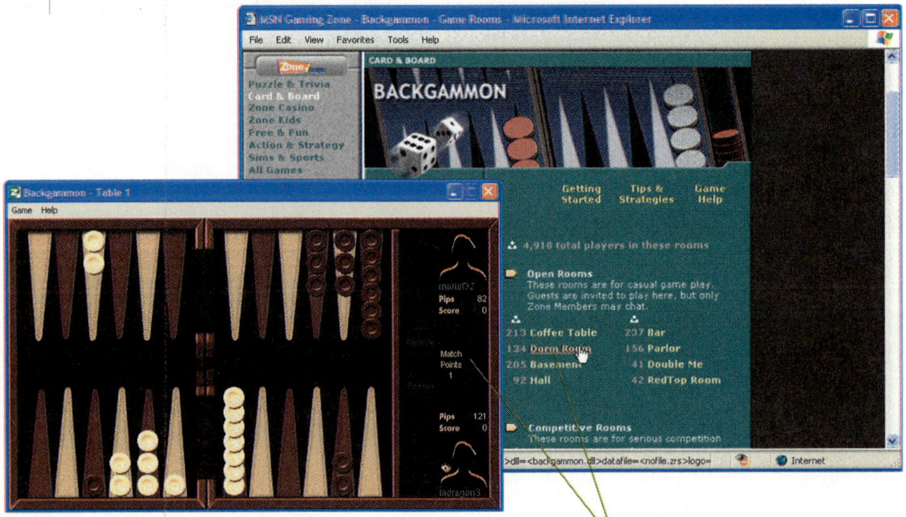

**^ Online gaming**

Click to select a room and opponent, and then the game begins.

## Entertainment

There are an ever-growing number of ways to use the Web for entertainment purposes, such as listening to music, watching videos, and playing games. As shown in Figure 3-9, some of these require special programs (either stand-alone programs or *browser plug-ins)* to play multimedia content.

### Online Music

**Online music** is perhaps one of the hottest Web-based entertainment activities today. Some possibilities include listening to online radio broadcasts, selecting songs to listen to on demand, and downloading songs to be played later on your PC or portable digital music player (such as an *MP3 player).* Online music is often compressed using *MP3 file compression* to reduce its file size from about 10 MB per minute to less than 1 MB per minute, without a noticeable reduction in quality. To avoid copyright violations, all downloaded music should be specified as free downloads (sometimes found on sites featuring new artists, for example) or the site should charge an appropriate fee (for royalties owed to the artist or record label) for the download. Once downloaded, music files can be copied to a CD to create a custom music CD.

Since the introduction of the *Napster* file-sharing service in 1999, controversy flourished over the rights to distribute music via the Internet. Napster and similar sites that allowed users to download MP3 files from other members' computers (called *peer-to-peer file exchange*) were sued by the recording industry. Many of these lawsuits were eventually settled, and most sites facilitating free MP3 downloads stopped their operations. Many people feel the Napster controversy will help to revolutionize the way music and other entertainment is distributed and believe that peer-to-peer services will reemerge stronger in the near future, but more likely as subscription-based services. In May 2002, Napster announced a plan to reorganize with the help of a German media company, but those plans fell through in September 2002 and the company announced they were headed for liquidation.

**ONLINE RESOURCES**

For links to information about the controversy surrounding Napster and other peer-to-peer file sharing sites, go to www.course.com/morley2003/ch3

### Online TV and Videos

Growing more slowly than online music, but still expected to be a significant entertainment option in the future, are television, movies, and video clips delivered through the Internet. Some options at the present time are news clips, movie trailers, music videos, taped interviews, and similar short, prerecorded videos. These clips are usually found on Web sites dedicated to providing multimedia Web content; links to video clips are also widely found on news and entertainment sites. A few live online TV broadcasts exist, but they are fairly rare at the present time.

Online video applications are expected to become much more common in the future as high-speed Internet use continues to grow and the convergence of television, computer, and Internet capabilities continues. Two examples with great potential for the future are *interactive TV* and *video-on-demand.*

*Interactive TV (iTV)* allows the user to perform interactive activities during a television broadcast. Today, many interactive TV shows require the use of some type of *set-top box*, such as the ones used for cable or satellite television services.

*Video-on-demand* allows users to order movies and television shows, which are then typically sent to the user's *digital video recorder (DVR)*—sometimes also called a *personal video recorder* or *PVR*. DVRs (such as *TiVo* or *ReplayTV)* are similar to VCRs, but recordings are stored on a hard disk instead of on videotape. Because a hard disk is a *direct-access* medium (where data at any location on the disk can be immediately retrieved, like a CD or DVD) instead of a *sequential-access* medium (where data is stored and retrieved in a linear fashion, like a videotape), recorded shows can be more easily located. DVRs can also pause the playing of a live TV show while continuing to record the remainder of the show in the background. With video-on-demand, a portion of the movie usually first downloads and then the movie can be played while the rest of the movie is downloading. This type of delivery—called *streaming media*—is also commonly used with both audio and video distributed over the Internet to reduce the time needed to begin to view or hear the selection. Today, video-on-demand is available primarily to cable and satellite TV subscribers in specific areas in a limited number of countries, but many predict the ability for virtually anyone to order video-on-demand through an Internet connection will be available in the fairly near future.

Though some worry about the possibility of movie piracy once movies have been downloaded, the small storage space available in DVRs today, relative to the huge amount of storage space required to store a movie, results in users not being able to keep downloaded movies on their DVRs for long periods of time. Of course, if DVRs and copy-protection schemes eventually allow downloaded movies to be transferred to a DVD disc, legal and ethical concerns similar to the ones raised when VCRs began to be able to copy videotapes may emerge.

An additional privacy concern is the increased availability of pirated copies of movies on the Internet. For example, *Star Wars Episode II: Attack of the Clones* was secretly recorded at a private prerelease screening and copies were made available over the Internet six days before the movie's world-wide release in 2002. A related controversy involves the ability of some of the newer digital video recorders allowing users to transmit recorded shows over the Internet to friends with compatible devices. Whether or not this capability is eventually ruled illegal due to copyright restrictions remains to be seen.

### Online Gaming

**Online gaming** refers to games played over the Internet. Many sites—especially children's Web sites—include games for people to play while visiting the site. There are also sites whose sole purpose is hosting games that can be played online. Some of the games, such as Solitaire, are designed to be played alone. Other *multiplayer* games, such as Hearts, Backgammon, and Quake, can be played online against other online gamers. The Backgammon game featured in Figure 3-9 can be played free of charge without special software; other games (such as Quake) require you to have the appropriate program installed on your PC. Some gaming sites may offer additional premium games that are only available to paid subscribers. Online multiplayer games are especially popular in countries, such as Korea, with high levels of high-speed Internet installations.

While some view these games as harmless, there is growing concern about the addictive nature of online gaming, as well as the violent nature of many games available to children. Some groups advocate the use of a rating system, such as the one used with offline video games, to assign an appropriate age group to each online game based on the levels of sex, nudity, violence, and offensive language contained in that game. If widely available in the future, these ratings—used in conjunction with a browser filtering system—could give parents a means of determining which games their children have access to online.

## Web-Based Training and Distance Learning

*Computer-based training (CBT)* refers to instruction delivered using a computer. Non-Internet activities include educational CD and DVD programs. When CBT takes place over the Internet, it is referred to as **Web-based training (WBT).** Web-based training is typically experienced individually and at the user's own pace, and the content is frequently customized for each individual user, based on his or her mastery of the material already completed. With Web-based training, the content and activities (such as exercises, exams, and animations) are not downloaded, but instead are accessed in real-time, just as other Web pages are. Some advantages of Web-based training include the following:

- *Self-paced instruction.* Students can usually work at their own pace, any time of day or night at their convenience.
- *Flexible location.* Students do not need to live close to any particular facility to take part in the educational program. Web-based training can be accessed from home, while traveling—in fact, basically anywhere the student has access to a computer with an Internet connection.
- *Up-to-date material.* Since all instructional material is hosted on a Web server, it can be updated whenever necessary simply by updating the server's content. Once updated, all users will see the newest version of the instructional material the next time they access the Web site.
- *Immediate feedback and customized content.* Web-based training systems can be set up to provide immediate feedback for exercises, practice tests, simulations, and other online activities. The feedback can include automatically displaying supplementary material for any problem areas identified based on the user's responses. It can also require mastery of material before the student is allowed to move on to the next test or assignment, and can often jump students to more advanced topics as appropriate. This flexibility can result in highly customized content, based on a student's progress and abilities.

Web-based training is often a component in **distance learning**, where students take classes or training from a location different than where the delivery of instruction originates. Distance learning (also called *online learning* and *e-learning)* is available through many colleges and universities; it is also used for professional education and training. Distance learning can be used to train employees in just one task or new skill, as well as for an entire college course or degree program.

Typically a majority of the coursework is completed over the Internet via class Web pages, discussion groups, chat rooms, and e-mail, although schools may require some in-person contact for credit courses, such as for orientation and testing. Although instructors usually develop their own course content, it is becoming increasingly common to use an online course environment available from an e-learning provider to organize this content and other online resources, such as the WebCT example shown in Figure 3-10.

While the advantages of Web-based training and distance learning are numerous, potential disadvantages include the following:

- *Technology requirements and problems*. In order to participate in Web-based training or distance learning, users must have access to a computer and the Internet. Slow PCs or Internet connections can be frustrating for students as they try to download materials or participate in online discussions. Technological problems—such as a computer crash or Web server inaccessibility on a test day—can create significant problems for students and instructors.
- *Anonymity*. Because students are in remote locations, it can be difficult to ensure it is the actual student who is participating in online discussions and online exams. Some instructors choose to require face-to-face exams either at the school or an authorized testing center in the student's geographical area; newer authentication technologies, such as smart cards, fingerprint scanners, and digital signatures, may help to overcome this problem in the near future.
- *Lack of face-to-face contact*. Many educators view the interactive exchange of ideas as a very important part of the educational experience. Though interactivity can take place online via chat rooms and discussion groups, the lack of face-to-face contact for students to see, ask questions of, or have discussions with other students and their instructor is cited as a disadvantage by some educators.

**FIGURE 3-10**

**An e-learning environment**

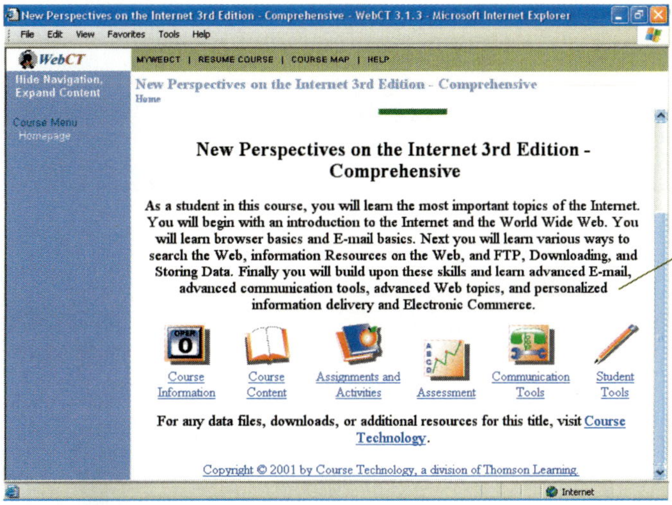


WebCT provides easy access (through a single Web site) to all the tools and information students need to participate in an online course.

## Telecommuting

**Telecommuting** refers to people working at home, connected to their place of business using such means as the Internet, fax machines, personal computers, telephones, and pagers. With such tools, the employee can retrieve company database information and presentation materials, make and receive phone calls, and exchange e-mail messages while away from the main office. Some telecommuting employees work from home on a full-time basis; others spend part of the week at home and part at the office, possibly sharing an office with another telecommuting employee.

Telecommuting enables a company to save on office and parking space and offers employees considerable freedom in choosing when and where they wish to work. As an environmental plus, it also helps cut down on the traffic and pollution derived from traditional work commuting.

Some disadvantages of telecommuting from an employers' standpoint include being less aware of what telecommuting employees do on a regular basis and how many hours per day they are working, and the need to utilize conference calls and other technology to supplement face-to-face meetings. Possible disadvantages from the telecommuters' point of view include less face-to-face interaction with coworkers and people in general, the need to allocate a portion of the home for a home office, and the difficulty of getting away from work. Some telecommuters also report feeling that they have less opportunity for advancement since they are less visible to their employer.

## HOW CAN I ACCESS AND USE THE INTERNET?

In order to use the Internet, your computer needs to be connected to it. Typically, this occurs by connecting your PC to a network (usually belonging to an ISP, your school, or your company) that is continually connected to the Internet. The type of devices used to connect to the Internet can vary from a conventional PC to a smart phone. Some possibilities are shown in Figure 3-11.

It is also becoming more common for public locations to offer Internet access. For example, many Starbucks locations and Internet cafés offer fee-based Internet access, and some taxis and trains offer free Internet service to their riders via a notebook or PDA installed in the cab or train (see Figure 3-12). Free public access is also available at most public libraries.

In addition to PCs being connected to the Internet, smart vending machines and other smart appliances can be online, as discussed in the chapter Trends In box.

**FIGURE 3-11**

Some devices that can be used to access the Internet

^ Desktop PC

^ Internet appliance

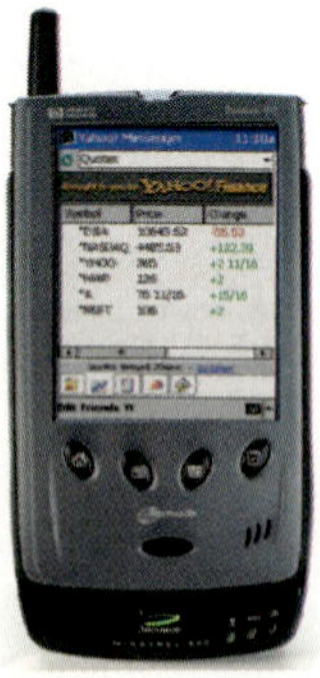

^ Handheld PC

^ Smart phone

## Types of Internet Connections

To connect to the Internet, some type of communications hardware must be used. A PC connecting to the Internet through a local area network would use a *network adapter card*; connecting to an ISP requires a *modem* or similar adapter (see Figure 3-13). Though the term *modem* technically applies only to devices that perform *analog-to-digital* and *digital-to-analog* conversion (such as when transferring digital data over analog telephone lines), it has become common to refer to any device that connects your PC to the Internet as a "modem." The type of modem used depends on the type of Internet connection being used and can be either an internal (in the form of an expansion card inserted into the motherboard inside the system unit of your PC) or an external (a separate device connected to one of your PC's external ports) piece of hardware.

Some Internet connections are *dial-up connections*, which means your PC dials up and connects to your ISP only when needed. Other Internet connections are *direct* or *always-on connections*, which means your computer is always connected to your ISP.

### Dial-Up Connections

**Dial-up connections** usually work over regular telephone lines. To connect to the Internet, your computer dials its modem and connects to a modem attached to a computer belonging to your ISP. While you are connected, your PC can access Internet resources. To end your Internet session, you disconnect from your ISP. Once you are disconnected, another user can connect in your place. One advantage to a dial-up connection is security. Since you are not continually connected to the Internet, it is much less likely that anyone (such as a *hacker*) will gain access to your computer via the Internet, either to access the data located on your PC or, more commonly, to use your computer in some type of illegal or unethical manner.

**FIGURE 3-12**

**Examples of public Internet access**

**< Internet cafés**

This London Internet café offers fee-based public Internet access.

**> Passenger trains**

Yahoo! and Compaq teamed up to offer free Internet access to train passengers in various U.S. locations.

**FIGURE 3-13**

**Common types of modems**

**^ Internal modem**

Located inside your PC; typical for dial-up connections

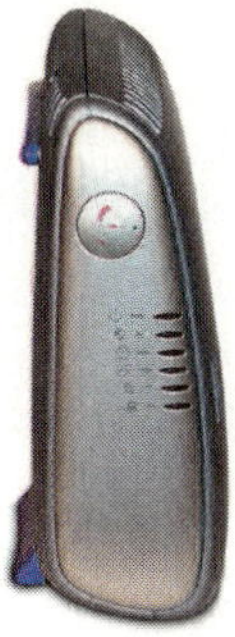

**^ External modem**

Connected to your PC with a cable; common for DSL, satellite, and cable connections

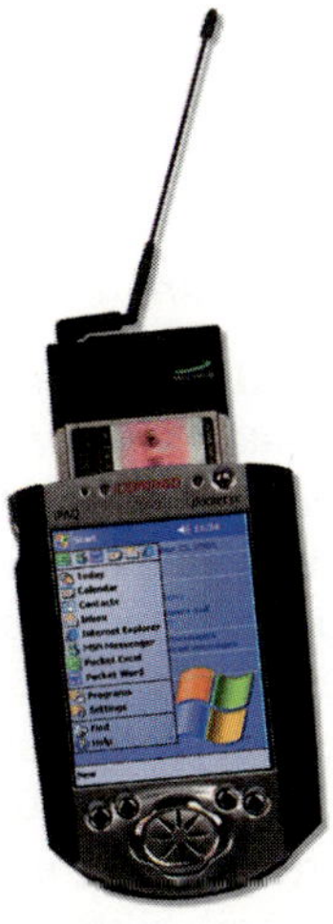

**^ Wireless modem**

Most often used with handheld computers

**^ PC card modem**

Used with notebook PCs; common for dial-up connections

## TRENDS IN... SMART APPLIANCES

You may have seen the television commercial where a young lady presses a button on her cell phone to get a soda from the vending machine. Surprising? Perhaps, but not completely unrealistic since the technology is in place for cashless transactions for small purchases, such as from smart vending machines. It is called *m-commerce*, as in "mobile commerce," and proponents predict it will lead us towards a cashless society. Though debit, credit, and check cards have helped move us in this direction, until recently it was tough to buy a soda or pay for a taxi without cash. With m-commerce, consumers can use their mobile phone (or other wireless device, such as a pager or PDA) to pay for goods and services. To buy a soda from a *smart vending machine*—a vending machine with Internet capability built in—with your mobile phone, for example, you dial the number displayed on the vending machine (see Figure 3-14) and make your selection. The vending machine, which is typically connected to the Internet via a wireless network, adds the charge to your mobile phone bill. If a PDA is used instead, the charge would be deducted from your *digital wallet*—software on your computer that stores an amount of *digital cash* that you can replenish as needed by transferring money from a checking account or credit card.

But m-commerce isn't the only application for *smart appliances* (traditional appliances with some type of computer or communications technology built in). Some smart vending machines use their Internet connections to send details about operating conditions (inventory level, temperatures, malfunction alerts, and so on) to distributors on a regular basis. Some machines even have their own e-mail accounts so that managers can send an e-mail to a malfunctioning machine instructing it how to reconfigure itself. Other examples of smart appliances include laser printers that order new toner cartridges when they are running low and jet engines that notify the airlines of any maintenance that needs to be performed.

Though their use is expected to save consumers time and help businesses cut costs, smart appliances are not without a potential downside. Concerns regarding privacy, security, and the effect of malfunctions will need to be addressed before smart appliances see widespread use.

**FIGURE 3-14**

**A smart vending machine**

One disadvantage of using a dial-up connection is that your telephone will likely be tied up while you are accessing the Internet, unless a second phone line is used. Some Internet call-waiting or call-forwarding services allow you to be notified when you get a telephone call while you are connected to the Internet. They are generally set up to allow the person to leave a short message; some newer systems give you a short window of time to disconnect from the Internet and pick up the telephone call, if desired. Newer dial-up modems help to facilitate some type of call-waiting service, as well. The two most common forms of dial-up Internet service are *standard dial-up* and *ISDN*.

**Standard dial-up** Internet connections use a conventional dial-up modem rated at a maximum data transfer rate of 56 *Kbps (kilobits*—thousands of bits—*per second).* These modems are connected to standard telephone jacks and are commonly used with home PCs and Internet appliances. Portable devices may also use a conventional dial-up modem; if so, they also need to be connected to a standard telephone jack to access the Internet. Some notebook or mobile communications device users may choose to dial up using a cellular modem and cell phone. Standard dial-up Internet service ranges from free to about $25 per month. Advantages of standard dial-up Internet service include inexpensive hardware, ease of setup and use, and wide-spread availability. Disadvantages include slow connection speeds and tying up your phone line while you're online.

**ONLINE RESOURCES**

For links to information about different types of Internet access and ISPs, go to www.course.com/morley2003/ch3

**ISDN** *(integrated services digital network)* also transfers data over ordinary telephone lines, but it is faster than standard dial-up and can use two phone lines to transfer data up to 128 Kbps, or over two times as fast as a typical dial-up connection. If your connection is set up to use one phone line for voice and one for data instead, your phone line won't be tied up during Internet use, but your access speed drops to 64 Kbps. Fairly pricey for the speed at about $70 per month, ISDN requires a special ISDN modem and is used more often in businesses than home connections.

### Direct Connections

Unlike dial-up connections that connect to your ISP only when you need to access the Internet, **direct** *(always-on)* **connections** keep you continually connected to your provider and, therefore, continually connected to the Internet. For example, most office and school PCs are physically connected (using network adapter cards and cables) to a company or school LAN for both network and Internet access. Because direct connections keep your computer connected to the Internet at all times (as long as your PC is turned on), it is important to protect your computer from unauthorized access or hackers. Consequently, all home and office PCs with a direct Internet connection should use a *firewall* program. Firewall programs block access to a PC from outside computers and enable each user to specify which programs on his or her PC are allowed to have access to the Internet.

Travelers and other users on the go can often tap into direct connections provided by airports, coffee houses, and other public locations. Instead of using a physical connection between the LAN and the user's portable PC, however, many public access points use *Wi-Fi* (also known as *Wireless-Fidelity* and *802.11b*), a wireless networking standard that allows users to connect to the Internet once they are within a particular range. Home PC users are increasingly using direct connections, typically via a *DSL*, *cable*, or *satellite* connection.

Direct Internet connections are typically *broadband* connections; that is, connections where more than one signal can be transferred at one time. Broadband Internet connections are much faster than dial-up connections. In theory, they can be up to 100 times as fast as a dial-up connection, but actual speeds at the present time are closer to 25 to 50 times as fast, due to outside factors, such as the speed of and amount of memory in the PC being used, the condition of the transmission media being used, and the amount of traffic currently using the same transmission medium or Web server. Typical download speeds for DSL and cable are about 1.5 Mbps; satellite and *fixed wireless* usually download data between 500 Kbps and 1 Mbps. *Mobile wireless* speeds vary more, typically from slow dial-up to 400 Kbps, depending on the type of service used. Virtually all of these services use slower upload speeds. A discussion of these various types of direct Internet connections follows.

**DSL** *(digital subscriber line)* **Internet access** allows faster data transmission over standard telephone lines than both conventional dial-up and ISDN connections, and uses a technology that doesn't tie up your telephone line. A limitation of DSL is distance: To qualify for DSL, subscribers must be within three miles of a telephone switching station; the speed of the connection degrades as the distance gets closer and closer to the three mile limit. This limitation may eventually be overcome by some type of repeating system to boost the signal over longer distances. Other disadvantages include the fact that DSL is not available in all areas, and each area typically has a small number of DSL providers that can provide service to that area. Typical monthly fees for DSL are around $50.

**Cable Internet access** is the most widely-used type of home broadband connection. Cable connections are very fast and are available to anyone in a location where cable access is available and whose local cable provider supports Internet access. One disadvantage of cable Internet is that all users in an immediate geographical area share the bandwidth of their local cable. Though this may not prove to be a problem all the time, during high-use times of day—such as early evening—the speed of cable Internet service can slow down dramatically as you and your neighbors go online at the same time. Cable is also not widely available in rural areas. Cost is about $45 per month just for Internet access; cable TV is optional, but requires an additional fee.

**Satellite Internet access** is typically a little slower than cable or DSL, but is often the only broadband option for rural areas. In addition to a satellite modem, it requires a *transceiver* satellite dish mounted outside the home or building to receive and transmit data to and from the appropriate satellite. Installation requires an unobstructed view of the southern sky (to have a clear line-of-site between the transceiver and appropriate satellite), and performance may degrade or stop altogether during very heavy rainstorms. Typical cost is about $70 per month.

**Fixed wireless Internet access** is one of the newest options. It is similar to satellite service in that it requires a modem and an outside-mounted transceiver, but it uses radio transmission towers instead of satellites and is typically available only in large metropolitan areas. A clear line-of-sight is required between the transceiver and the provider's radio transmission tower; cost for service is about $50 per month.

**Mobile wireless** (sometimes called *wireless Web)* **Internet access** is most commonly used with handheld PCs, Web-enabled cell phones, and other mobile communications devices to keep them connected to the Internet, even as you carry them from place to place. These devices are typically connected through a wireless network and wireless provider, similar to mobile phone service. The newest mobile communications devices are third-generation devices—referred to as *3G*—which support high-speed digital wireless transmissions. Just becoming available in limited areas in the U.S., 3G is expected to operate at up to 400 Kbps or more, fast enough to access multimedia content with portable PCs or mobile phones, and is viewed as a potentially huge breakthrough in mobile communication applications. Costs for mobile wireless Internet vary widely, with some packages including unlimited Internet, some charging by the number of minutes of Internet use, and some charging by the amount of data transferred.

## Selecting an ISP and Setting Up Your PC

The type of device used (desktop PC or PDA, for example), the type of Internet connection desired (such as conventional dial-up or cable), and your geographical location will likely limit your ISP choices. The pricing and services available through any two ISPs may differ somewhat. For example, some providers simply provide you with an onramp to the Internet; others may include additional content or services, such as instant messaging, music management, Web site hosting, personal online photo galleries, Web site filtering, and a personalized portal page. If multiple providers are available or you are still deciding between two types of Internet connections, the questions listed in Figure 3-15 may be helpful when making your final selection.

The specific steps for setting up your PC to use your new Internet connection depend on the type of connection and the service provider you've chosen to use. Some ISPs provide you with an installation program on CD to install a Web browser, set up your telephone dialing software (for standard dial-up connections only), and walk you through selecting a user name, selecting an access number (if needed), recording your payment data, and any other needed tasks. The installation programs for several common ISPs are also preinstalled on many new PCs. To sign up with one of those providers, just open the appropriate desktop icon or Start menu item with the

**FIGURE 3-15**

Choosing an ISP: Factors to consider

| | |
|---|---|
| **Services** | Can you use the browser of your choice?<br>Does the e-mail support attachments, filtering, multiple mailboxes, and any other features you'd like to have?<br>How many e-mail addresses can you have?<br>What is the size limit on incoming and outgoing e-mail messages?<br>Is there a dial-up number that you can use when you are away from home (for both dial-up and broadband connections)?<br>Are there any special member features or benefits?<br>Is space available for posting a personal Web site or personal photos? |
| **Speed** | How fast are the maximum and usual downstream (ISP to you) speeds?<br>How fast are the maximum and usual upstream (you to ISP) speeds?<br>How much does the service slow down under adverse conditions (high traffic, poor weather, etc.)?<br>If it's a dial-up connection, how often should you expect to get a busy signal? (A customer to modem ratio of about 10:1 or less is optimal.) |
| **Support** | Is 24/7 telephone technical support available?<br>Is any technical support available through a Web site (e-mail support, online knowledge base, etc.)?<br>What is the response time to answer your phone calls or e-mails when you have a problem?<br>Is there ever a charge for technical support? |
| **Cost** | What is the monthly cost for the service?<br>If it's a dial-up connection, is there a local access telephone number to avoid long distance charges?<br>Are there services that can be added or deleted (number of e-mail addresses, Web page hosting, etc.) to increase or decrease the monthly cost?<br>Is there a set-up fee? If so, can it be waived with a 6-month or 12-month agreement?<br>What is the cost of any additional hardware needed (modem, transceiver, etc.)? Can the fee be waived with a long-term service agreement? |

mouse and follow the instructions. Some screens of the installation process with one provider are shown in Figure 3-16; the same general steps would occur with most ISP installation programs, but they might occur in a different order.

Instead of an installation program, smaller local providers may just provide you with instructions on how to set up your Web browser and the phone dialing software (for standard dial-up connections only) located on your PC. If you already have an Internet connection and are looking for a new ISP, the necessary installation programs can typically be downloaded to your PC from ISP Web sites and then run from your PC to begin the setup process.

**ONLINE TUTORIAL**

For an online look at how to download files from the Internet and install them on your PC, go to www.course.com/morley2003/ch3

## Surfing the Web

Once you have finished configuring your PC to use your new ISP, you are ready to start using the Internet. For most individuals, this would mean *surfing the Web*; that is, using a Web browser to visit Web sites and explore what is available on the World Wide Web. In addition to being used to display Web pages, most Web browsers today can be used to perform other Internet tasks, such as downloading files, exchanging e-mail, accessing discussion groups, and participating in chat sessions. The ability to perform a variety of Internet tasks, either as part of the browser program itself or in a separate program that is opened automatically when needed, has made the Web browser a universal tool for exploring and using the Internet.

**FIGURE 3-16**

**Many ISPs have an installation program that walks you through the setup process.**

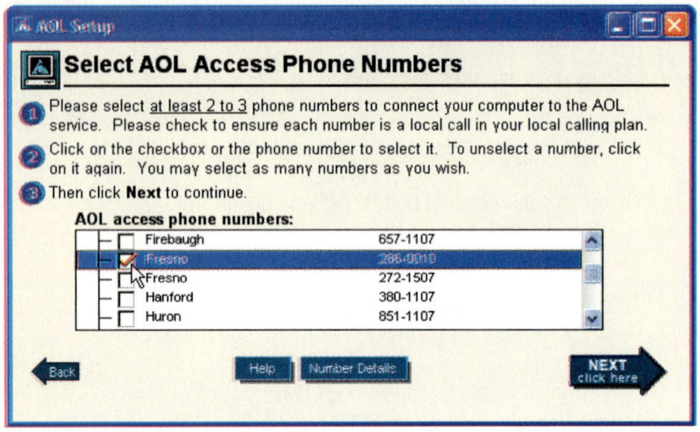


**Step 1: Select an access number**

For dial-up access, you will need to select a local access telephone number for your PC to call when you want to use the Internet.

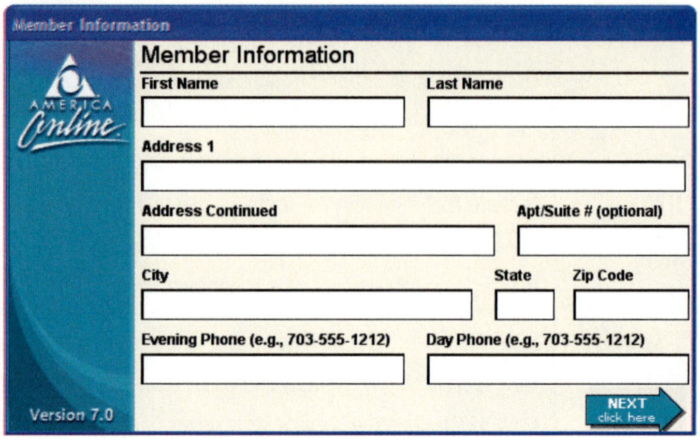


**Step 2: Provide your billing information**

The setup process will include specifying your contact and billing information.

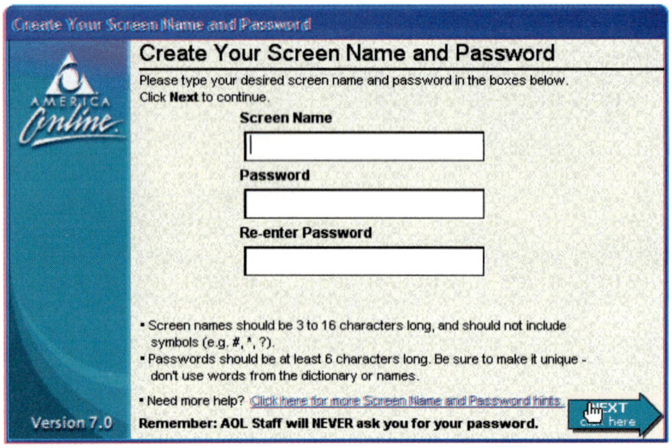


**Step 3: Select a user name and password**

The user name (or screen name) and password you select may be used for logging on to the Internet, as well as for sending and receiving e-mail.

**Step 4: Install and set up browser**

The installation program will install and set up your browser, e-mail program, and dialing program to reflect the choices you made during the setup process.

To start surfing the Web with a direct connection, you need to open your browser using either its desktop icon or Start menu item or a special icon or menu item placed there by your ISP (see Figure 3-17). For dial-up connections, most large ISPs use a desktop icon or Start menu item that opens your browser, dials your telephone, and establishes the Internet connection all in one step; smaller, local dial-up ISPs may require you to open your browser and start your dialing program manually.

Once your Web browser is open and you are connected to the Internet, the Web page currently designated as your browser's starting page or *home page* will be displayed within the browser window. Usually this is the home page for the Web site belonging to your browser, school, or ISP, but you can usually change it to any page—such as a portal page, search site, or any other page you may want to visit regularly—using your browser's Options or Preferences dialog box. From the home page, you can move to any Web page you desire.

Two of the most widely-used Web browsers, *Microsoft Internet Explorer* and *Netscape Navigator*, are illustrated in Figure 3-18. As shown in the figure, Web browsers have navigational tools to help you move forward or backward through the pages viewed in your current session, as well as buttons or menu options to print Web pages when desired. Internet Explorer and Netscape are the browsers that will be used in all of the examples and instructions in this book. If you have a different version of one of these browsers or are using a different browser altogether, the screens and steps shown in this text may look a little different than yours, but should be close enough for you to understand how to perform these actions using your browser.

**FIGURE 3-17**

**Connecting to the Internet**

**1.** Use the desktop icon or Start menu item for your ISP (if one exists) or your browser (if an ISP icon or Start menu item doesn't exist) to open your browser.

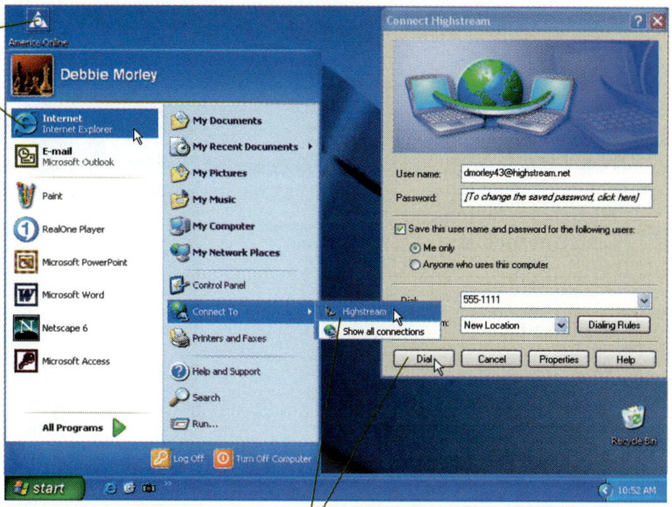


**2.** For dial-up connections only, start your dialing program (if it doesn't start automatically when you start your browser program or if your browser was still open from a previous session), then supply your user name and password, if necessary, and click Dial to connect to the Internet.

## Using URLs and Hyperlinks

To change from your browser's starting Web page to a new Web page for which you know the URL, type that URL in the browser's *Address bar* or *Location bar* and press Enter (see Figure 3-19). You can either edit the existing URL or delete it and type a new one, but be sure to match the spelling, capitalization, and punctuation exactly. If you don't know the appropriate URL to type, you can type the URL for a search site to display that page, and then search for an appropriate page, as illustrated in the How To box at the end of this chapter.

If there is a hyperlink displayed for the page you would like to go to, you can click the hyperlink to display the page associated with that link. Remember, hyperlinks can be either text- or image-based, and, though text-based hyperlinks are often underlined, they may instead be displayed in a different color (as in Figure 3-19) or underlined only when pointed to. If you are not sure if text or a graphic on a page is a hyperlink, rest the mouse pointer on it for a moment. If the item you are pointing to is a hyperlink, the pointer typically changes to a pointing hand (see Figure 3-20).

## FIGURE 3-18

**Most Web browsers have a similar appearance and use similar buttons and commands.**

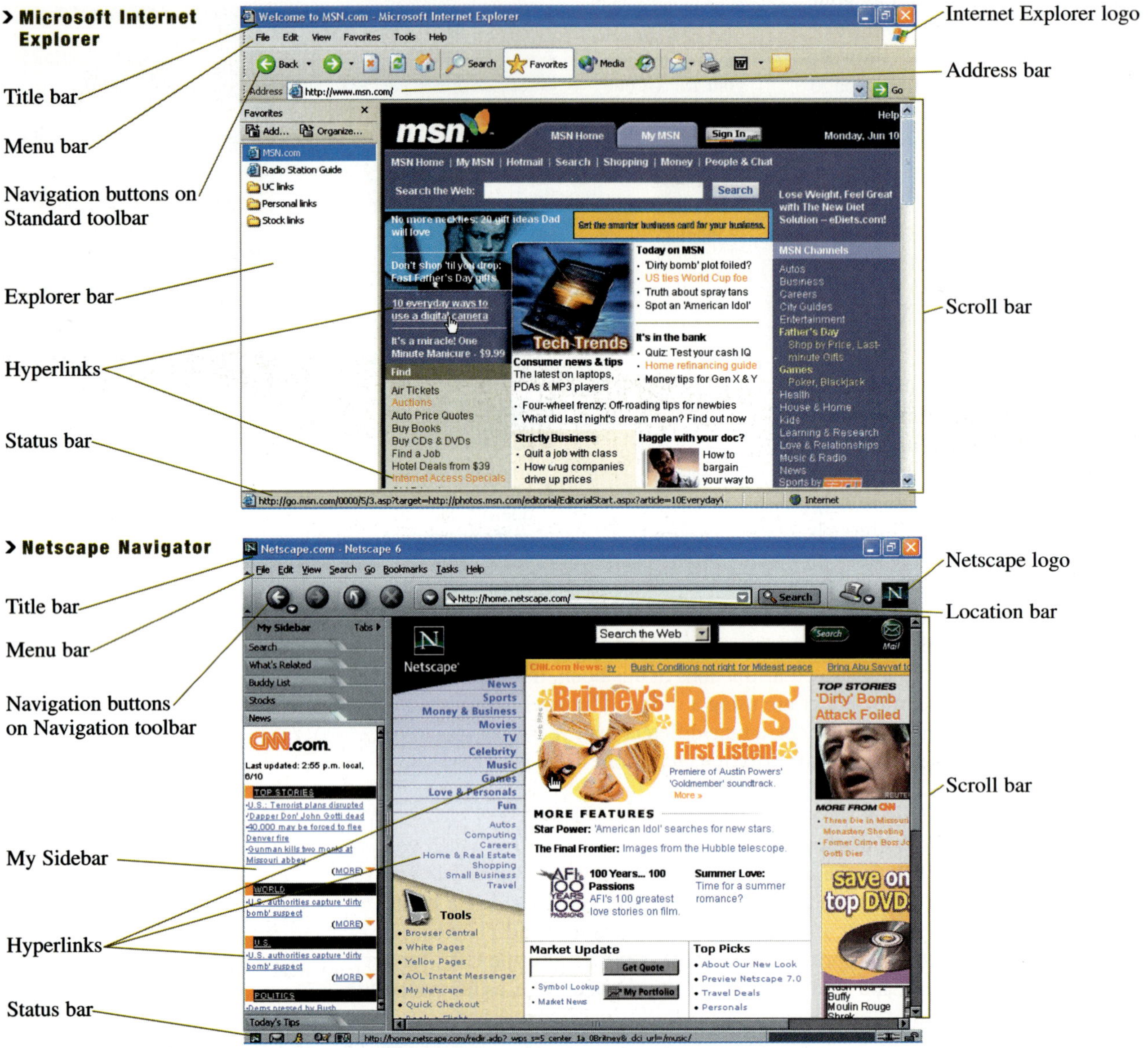


| Internet Explorer | Netscape | Description |
|---|---|---|
| | | *Back* is used to move back to a page that has already been displayed during the current Internet session. |
| | | *Forward* is used to move forward again after using the Back button to move to a previous page. |
| | | *Print* allows you to print the page that is curently displayed. |
| | | *Stop* stops the transfer of a page while it is being loaded (useful when a page is taking a long time to display). |
| | | *Reload* or *Refresh* redisplays the current page (useful if an error prevented the page from loading properly or you want to reload a page that changes frequently, such as one containing stock quotes). |

**FIGURE 3-19**

**How to move around the Web**

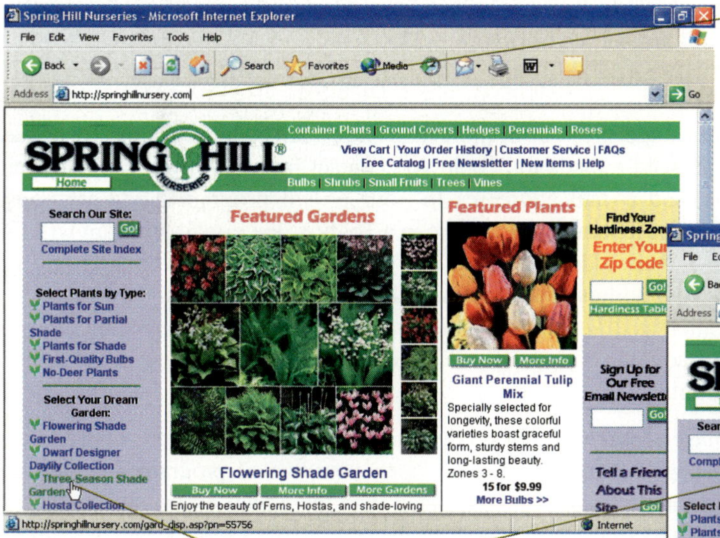


**Type a URL**

Type a URL in the Address/Location bar and press Enter to display the corresponding Web page.

**Use a bookmark**

Click a name on the Bookmarks or Favorites list to redisplay that page in future sessions.

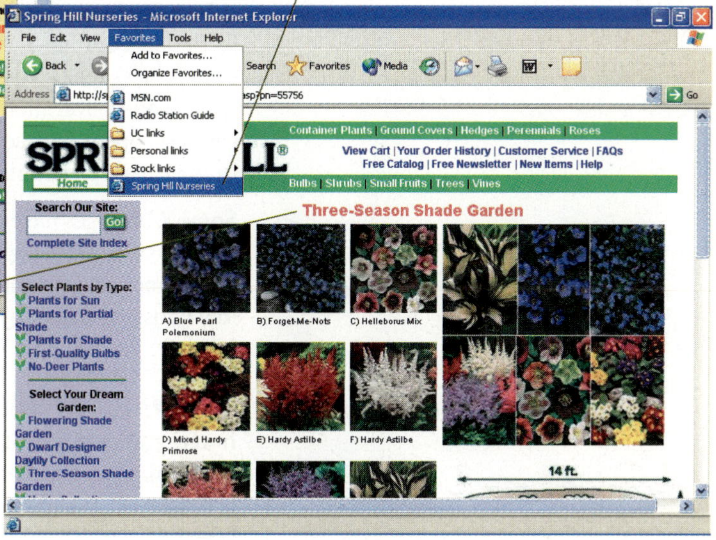


**Click a hyperlink**

Click a hyperlink to display the corresponding page.

## Using Bookmarks and the History List

Virtually all browsers have a **bookmark** or **favorites** feature that will save the Web page addresses you specify so you can return to them easily. It is common to create bookmarks for any page you want to visit on a regular basis. To create a bookmark for a page you are currently viewing, select the appropriate *Add* option from your browser's Bookmark or Favorites menu. Once a page is bookmarked, selecting that bookmark from the Bookmark or Favorites list will redisplay that page. Because bookmark lists can get large and unwieldy, typically browsers have an option on their Bookmarks or Favorites menu that allows you to delete outdated bookmarks or move bookmarks into folders to keep them organized. Some browsers, such as Internet Explorer, can also display the bookmark or favorites list in a separate pane on the screen so they are always available (click the *Favorites* toolbar button to turn this feature on or off in Internet Explorer).

In addition to a bookmark or favorites list, browsers usually maintain a *History list*, which is a record of all Web pages visited in the last week or two (how long a page stays in the History list depends on your browser settings). If you want to revisit a page you've been to recently that isn't bookmarked, click the *History* button (if one is available on your browser) or select the *History* option from the menu (sometimes located under *Tools* on the Tasks menu) to display the History list, then select the desired page.

**FIGURE 3-20**

**The mouse pointer typically changes to a pointing hand when it is moved over a hyperlink.**

**› Hyperlink**

**› Hyperlink**

**› Not a hyperlink**

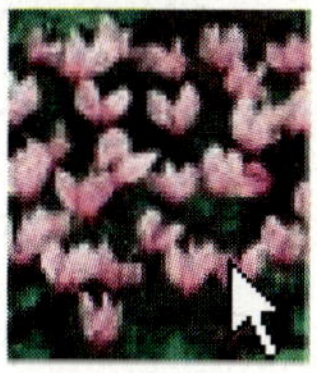

**ONLINE TUTORIAL**

For an online look at how to set up an e-mail program to send and receive e-mail, go to www.course.com/morley2003/ch3

## Sending and Receiving E-Mail

E-mail messages are sent and read using an *e-mail program*, such as *Microsoft Outlook*, *Microsoft Outlook Express*, or *Netscape Mail.* Common steps for sending and receiving e-mail are shown in Figure 3-21.

### Sending E-mail

To send an e-mail message, type one or more than one e-mail addresses in the To: boxes. To make it easier to send e-mails to people you contact frequently, you can add their names, nicknames, and e-mail addresses to your e-mail program's *address book.* When you begin to type a name or nickname in a To: box, the e-mail program will fill in the appropriate e-mail address automatically. To add someone who sent you an e-mail message to your address book, you usually can right-click on the message and choose an option such as *Add Sender to Address Book* from the displayed menu; you can also open your address book to edit it by using a toolbar button or menu option in your mail program.

Some Web pages have *e-mail hyperlinks*—hyperlinks that are linked to an e-mail address instead of a Web page—that automatically open your e-mail program and start an e-mail message directly to the person associated with the e-mail hyperlink. When you run across an e-mail hyperlink (such as sales@abc.com, customer.service@123.com, or johnb@xyz.edu) on a Web page, click that hyperlink to start an e-mail to that person.

### Receiving E-mail

In order to read new e-mail messages, they must be retrieved from your ISP. All new e-mail messages are typically placed in your *Inbox* folder. Once an e-mail message is displayed, it can be printed, replied to, forwarded to someone else, filed into a different folder, or deleted using your e-mail program's toolbar buttons. E-mail messages that you send are usually placed into a folder with a name such as *Sent* or *Sent Items*, and deleted messages are generally moved to a *Trash* or *Deleted Items* folder. Depending on your ISP and how your e-mail program is set up on your PC, your messages may be kept solely on your ISP's mail server, on both your PC and the mail server, or just on your PC. It is important to realize that e-mail messages stored on your ISP's mail server may be deleted periodically. The messages in your Trash or Deleted Items folders remain there until you permanently delete them by selecting *Empty Trash* from Netscape Mail's File menu or *Empty 'Deleted Items' Folder* from Outlook Express' Edit menu. Deleting unneeded messages frees up space on your hard drive.

## FIGURE 3-21

Sending and receiving e-mail

### Sending e-mail using Netscape Mail

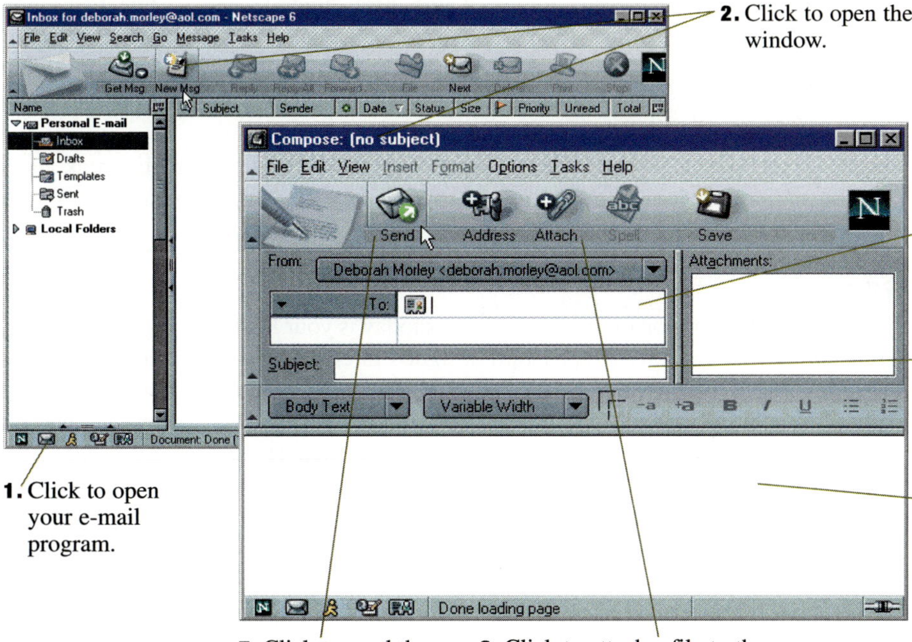


1. Click to open your e-mail program.
2. Click to open the message composition window.
3. Type the recipient's e-mail address here.
4. Type an appropriate subject line here.
5. Type the message here.
6. Click to attach a file to the message, if needed.
7. Click to send the message.

### Receiving e-mail using Outlook Express

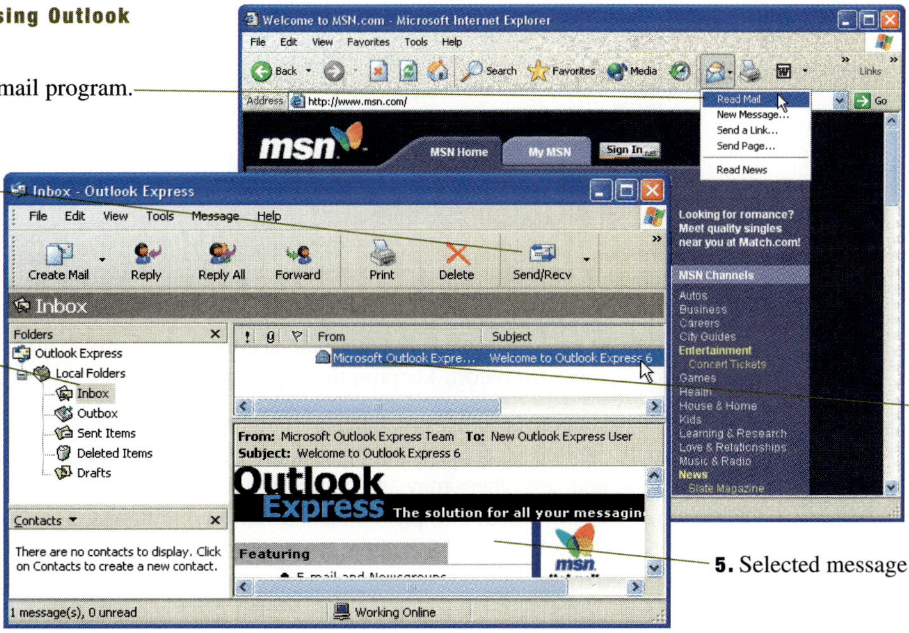


1. Click to open your e-mail program.
2. Click to check for any new mail since the e-mail program was opened.
3. Select the desired mail folder (the Inbox folder is selected here).
4. Click a message to display it.
5. Selected message is displayed here.

# SOCIETAL IMPLICATIONS OF CYBERSPACE

Many people today cannot imagine life without the Internet. The vast amount of useful information and entertainment available through the World Wide Web and other Internet resources has made going online a normal everyday activity for many of us. For countless individuals, exchanging e-mail is as common a means of communication as the telephone. And many of us won't think about making a major purchase (DVD player, computer, refrigerator, etc.) without first researching it online. In fact, it is surprising how fast the Internet and its resources have become an integral part of our society. But despite all its benefits, cyberspace has some risks. How many of us really think about how our online activities might adversely affect us? Some of the most important societal implications of cyberspace surround our security and privacy.

## Security

One of the most common online security risks today is your PC becoming infected with a *computer virus*—a software program designed to change the way a computer operates, without the permission or knowledge of the user. Computer viruses often cause damage to your PC, such as erasing data or bogging down your computer so it doesn't function well. Viruses can be attached to a program (such as one downloaded over the Internet), as well as to an e-mail message. To help protect your computer from viruses, never open attachments from someone you don't know or that have an executable file *extension* (the last three letters in the filename preceded by a period), such as .exe, .com, .vbs, .shs, or .pif, without first checking with the sender to make sure the attachment is legitimate. It is also a good idea to install an *antivirus* program on your PC and set it up to scan all e-mail messages, attachments, and files before they are downloaded to make sure they are virus-free, as well as to scan your entire PC periodically for viruses. If a virus is found, the antivirus program will try to remove it from your system.

Other increasingly common security concerns include identity theft and data loss (due to user error, hardware failure, computer virus, or some other problem).

## Privacy

Some individuals view the potential risk to personal privacy as one of the most important issues regarding our networked society. As more and more data about our everyday activities gets collected and stored in databases, our privacy is at risk because the potential for privacy violations increases. Today, data is collected about practically anything we buy online or offline, though offline purchases may not be associated with our identity unless we use a credit card or make the purchase at a store using a membership or loyalty card. At issue is not that data is collected—with virtually all organizations using computers for record-keeping that's just going to happen—but how the data is used.

Some businesses may use data about our purchases solely for inventory purposes; others may use it to send us marketing material for products related to what we've bought in the past; and still others may sell our data to a mass marketing company, which in turn may use our information to profile us and our buying habits. Many Web sites post a *privacy policy* (see Figure 3-22), which states what they intend to do with any personal data submitted to the site. Some companies, however, have changed their privacy policy without specifically notifying past customers that their data may be used in a manner different from what the privacy policy stated at the time the customers' data was submitted.

## Differences in Online Communication

As you spend more and more time communicating online, you will probably notice some differences between online communication methods (e-mail, chat, and discussion groups, for example) and traditional communications methods (such as phone calls and written letters). In general, online communication tends to be much less formal. This may be because people usually compose e-mail messages fairly quickly and just send them off, often not taking the time to reread and consider their message content or check their spelling or grammar. There is no doubt that e-mail has helped speed up both personal and business communications and has made them more efficient (no more telephone tag, for instance). However, we all need to be careful not to get so casual in our communications—particularly business communications—that our communications become too personal with people we don't know or appear unprofessional.

To help in that regard, a special etiquette—referred to as **netiquette**—has evolved to guide online behavior. A good rule of thumb is always to be polite and considerate of others, and to refrain from offensive remarks. This holds true whether you are asking a question via a company's e-mail address, posting a discussion group message, or chatting with a friend. When the communication involves business, you should also be very careful with your grammar and spelling to avoid embarrassing yourself. Some specific guidelines are listed in Figure 3-23.

**FIGURE 3-22**

**A Web site privacy policy**

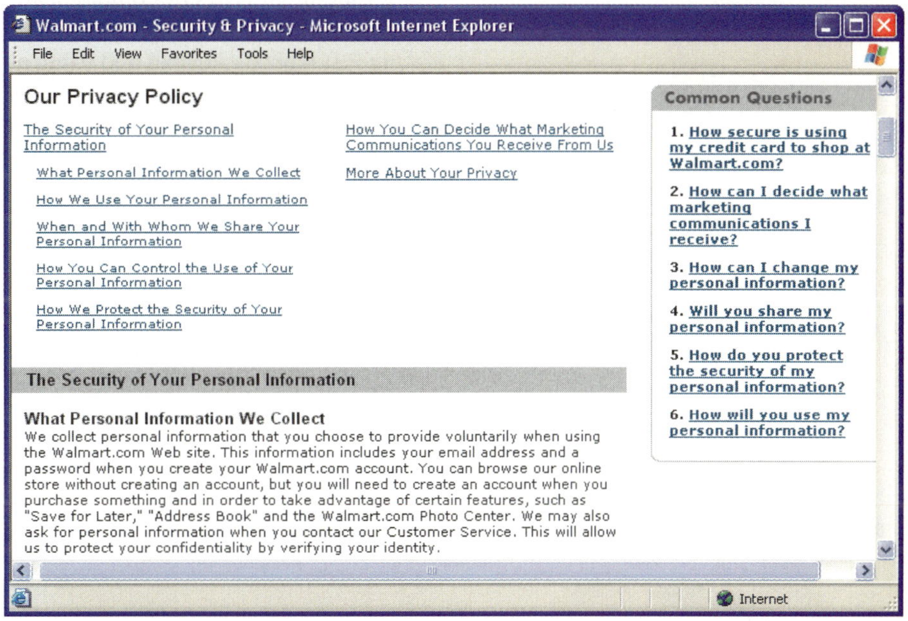


**FIGURE 3-23**

**Netiquette guidelines and common sense can guide you when communicating online**

| | |
|---|---|
| **Use good subject lines** | Use short, descriptive titles for e-mail messages and newsgroup posts. For example, "Question regarding MP3 downloads" is much better than a vague choice, such as "Question." |
| **Don't shout** | SHOUTING REFERS TO TYPING YOUR ENTIRE E-MAIL MESSAGE USING CAPITAL LETTERS. Use capital letters only for emphasizing a few words. |
| **Watch what you say** | Things that you say or write online can be interpreted as being sexist, racist, ethnocentric, xenophobic, or in just general bad taste. Also check spelling and grammar—nobody likes wading through poorly written materials. |
| **Use emoticons and abbreviations** | Use *emoticons* to add emotion to your messages, and use abbreviations and acronyms to save time and make your messages shorter (see Figure 3-24 for some examples). |
| **Avoid e-mail overload** | Don't send *spam mail*—unsolicated bulk e-mails—the Internet equivalent of junk mail. Same goes for e-mail chain letters and e-mailing every joke you run across to everyone in your address book. |
| **Read the FAQs** | *FAQs* are *frequently asked questions* with the corresponding answers. Reading an FAQ list will help you to avoid common mistakes in protocol that could disrupt a newsgroup or waste a company contact's time answering a question already covered in the FAQs. |
| **Lurk, before you leap** | *Lurking* refers to observing a newsgroup's activities for a period of time to get the particular spin of the group, before actively participating. |
| **Avoid flame mail** | Avoid *flame mail*—caustic or inflammatory remarks directed toward specific individuals. That includes taking part in *flame wars*, in which several people participate in sending inappropriate messages. |

Another trend in online communications is the use of abbreviations and *emoticons*. Abbreviations or *acronyms*, such as BTW for "by the way," are commonly used to save time in all types of communications today. A new use for them is in text messaging and e-mail with wireless phones (see Figure 3-24), because text entry is slow using just a phone keypad and using abbreviations helps speed up the entry process. Emoticons—also sometimes called *smileys*—allow people to add emotions to written online communications. Without using these symbols, it is sometimes difficult to tell if a comment is serious or if the person is joking or being facetious, since you can't see the individual's face. Emoticons are illustrations of faces showing smiles, frowns, and other expressions that are created with keyboard symbols, such as the popular :-) smile emoticon (tilt your head to the left to view it). With some programs, emoticons are changed into actual faces, such as ☺. Some common acronyms and emoticons are shown in Figure 3-24. While most people would agree that these symbols are fine to use with personal and casual communications, they are not usually viewed as appropriate for business communications.

**FIGURE 3-24**

Acronyms and emoticons

| ACRONYMS | | EMOTICONS | |
|---|---|---|---|
| **Acronym** | **Stands For** | **Symbol** | **Meaning** |
| ROTFL | "Rolling on the floor laughing" | :-) | Smile |
| LOL | "Laughing out loud" | :-( | Frown |
| BTW | "By the way" | ;-) | Wink |
| IMHO | "In my humble opinion | :-D | Laugh |
| TTFN | "Ta ta for now" | :-P | Sticking out tongue |
| BTDT | "Been there, done that" | :-> | Sarcastic |
| BRB | "Be right back" | >:-< | Angry |
| SAT | "Sorry about that" | <:-) | Dumb |
| GG | "Gotta go" | :-S | Kind of like it |
| YGTBK | "You've got to be kidding" | :-O | Surprise |
| CW2CU | "Can't wait to see you" | (@@) | You're kidding! |
| JAS | "Just a second" | ((H)) | Big hug |

## The Anonymity Factor

By its very nature, online communication lends itself to *anonymity*. Since recipients don't hear senders' voices or even see their handwriting, it is difficult to know for sure who the sender is. Particularly in newsgroups and chat rooms, where individuals traditionally use made-up user names instead of real names, there is an anonymous feel to being online.

Being anonymous gives many individuals a sense of freedom, which makes them feel free to say or do anything online. This sense of true freedom of speech can be beneficial. For example, a reserved individual who might never complain about a poor product or service in person may feel comfortable lodging a complaint by e-mail. In political newsgroups or chat discussions, many people feel they can be completely honest about what they think and can introduce new ideas and points of view without inhibition. Anonymous e-mail is also a safe way for an employee to blow the whistle on a questionable business practice, or to tip off police to a crime or potential terrorist attack.

But, like all good things, online anonymity can be abused. Using the Internet as their shield, some people use rude comments, ridicule, profanity, and even slander to attack people, places, and things they don't like or agree with. Others may use multiple online identities (such as assuming two or more different user names in a discussion group) to give the appearance of increased support for their point of view. Still others, feeling that their identities are protected, may use multiple identities to try to manipulate stock prices (such as by posting multiple negative messages or false information about a company to drive the price down), get buyers to trust an auction seller (by posting fake untrue positive feedback comments about themselves), and other illegal or unethical acts.

Over the last few years, there have been a growing number of lawsuits demanding that ISPs reveal the true identities of people posting controversial or potentially libelous discussion group messages online. Typically ISPs will comply with subpoenas for such information, but free speech advocates fear the use of such lawsuits to silence anonymous critics or punish whistle-blowing employees.

It is possible to hide your true identity while browsing or sending e-mail by removing personal information from your browser and e-mail program, or by using a cloaking service, such as the Anonymizer service available for about $30 per year. Most individuals who use anonymous Web surfing and e-mail do not intend to communicate with terrorists, defraud people, issue online ransom notes, or perform other types of illegal actions. Instead, they usually just want to protect their identity from advertising agencies and other individuals who may want to track their online shopping habits or send them unsolicited e-mail (called *spam*). But, in fact, even when personal information is removed, ISPs and the government may still be able to trace communications back to a particular computer when a crime has occurred, so it's difficult—perhaps impossible—to be completely anonymous online.

## Information Integrity

As stated time and time again, the World Wide Web contains a huge amount of information on a wide variety of topics. While some of the information is factual, other information may be misleading, biased, or just plain wrong. As more and more people turn to the Web for information, it is crucial that they be able to determine if the information they are obtaining is accurate. There have been numerous cases of information intended as a joke being restated on a Web site as fact, or statements being quoted out of context which changed the meaning from the original intent. Consequently, it is smart to evaluate carefully the source of information you read online, and verify important data from multiple sources if possible.

One of the most direct ways of evaluating online content is by considering the source. If you obtain information from news sources that you trust (such as CNN, MSNBC, Fox News, The New York Times, or the Wall Street Journal), you should feel confident that the accuracy of their online information is close to their offline counterparts. For information about a particular product or technology, the originating company is a good source for correct information. For government information, government Web sites are typically better sources for objective information than Web sites belonging to individuals or political organizations that may have a bias.

### Searching the Web

To search for Web pages about a particular topic, you need to perform an Internet search. Though recent browsers include some built-in search capabilities (accessed by typing keywords in the Address/Location bar or by clicking a Search toolbar button), it is more common to use a search site. To begin an Internet search using a search site, type the URL for the desired search site—such as Google, Ask Jeeves, Yahoo!, or AltaVista—in your browser's Address bar or Location bar (see Figure 3-25). At a search site, you may have one or both of the following search options:

- *Keyword Search.* Type keywords in the designated box and press Enter to have a search engine find and display a list of Web pages that either contain that keyword or that have been specified as being appropriate for that keyword. Usually more than one keyword can be typed—most search sites list the pages containing all of the words that you typed higher in the displayed list of matching Web pages.
- *Category Search.* Select an appropriate category from the list displayed on the search site's home page. After clicking a category hyperlink, you will be presented with a list of subcategories for the main category that you selected—keep selecting categories until you see a list of appropriate Web pages.

### Evaluating Search Results

Once a hyperlink to an appropriate Web page appears, clicking it will display the page. Some search strategies and tips for evaluating search results are shown in Figure 3-26.

### Citing Internet Sources

According to the online version of the Merriam-Webster dictionary, the term *plagiarize* means "to steal and pass off the ideas or words of another as one's own" or to "use another's production without crediting the source." Plagiarism from printed material has always been a concern, and it is a growing concern regarding information available on the Internet. The digital format of online information makes it easy to copy and paste from a Web page to another document. However, just because it is easy to do, does not mean it is legal or ethical. In fact, plagiarism is illegal. To ensure Web page content is not plagiarized, Web pages—as well as any other Internet resources—need to be credited appropriately. The guidelines for citing Web page content are similar to that of written material. Figure 3-26 includes some examples from the American Psychological Association Web site (http://www.apa.org).

**FIGURE 3-25**

Search sites may allow you to enter keywords, select categories, or both.

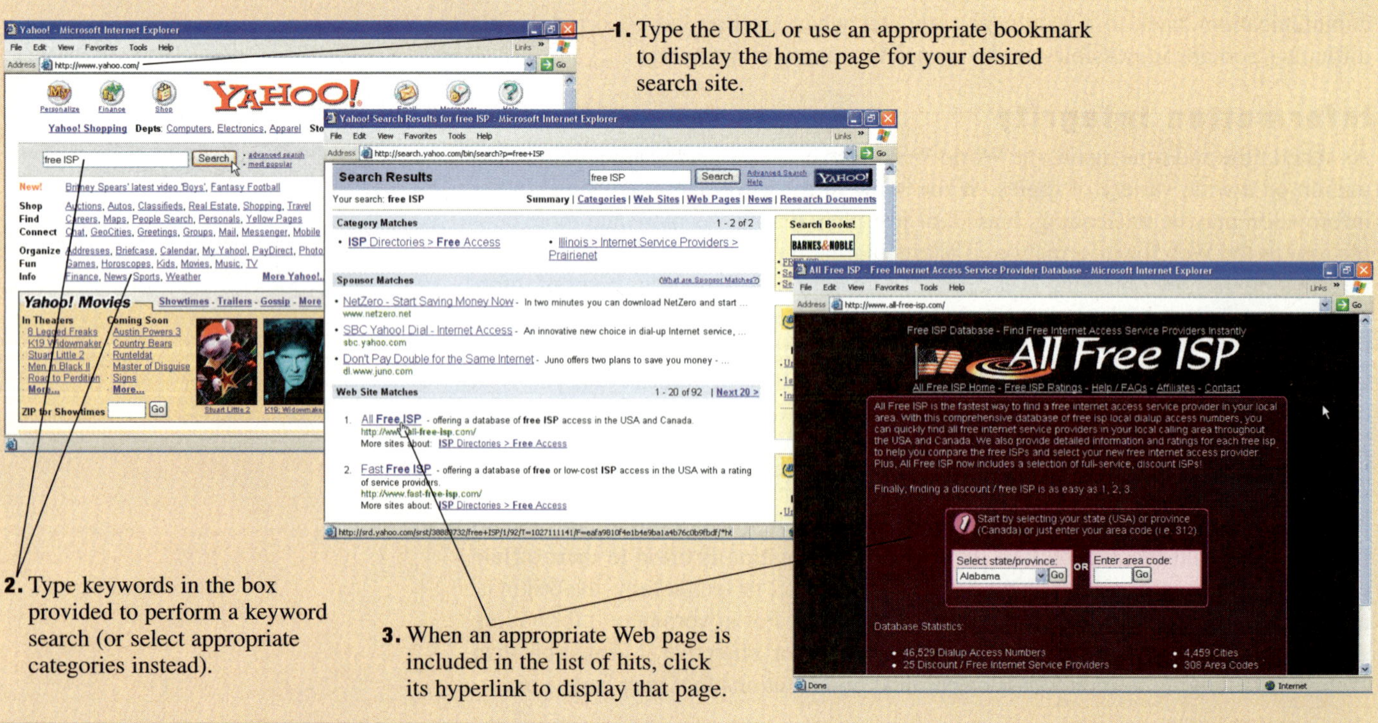

**FIGURE 3-26**

Search strategies, tips for evaluating search results, and Web citation examples

| | |
|---|---|
| **Search Strategies** | |
| **Be efficient** | If an appropriate Web page isn't listed among the first page or two of search results, redo your search to make your search criteria more specific and effective. |
| **Use phrase searching** | Type multiple keywords whenever possible. Check the tips for the search site to see what operators (such as + or –) and other advanced criteria you can use. |
| **Use synonyms and variant word forms** | Use words with similar meanings, alternate forms of a word, and common misspellings, if your initial search results aren't effective. For example, for *hotel*, you could also try *lodging*, *motel*, *B&B*, *lodge*, etc. |
| **Use multiple search sites** | Different sites can return different results; try a new site if your initial search is unsuccessful. |
| **Evaluating Search Results** | |
| **Check the title, description, and URL** | Skim through the title and description to see if it matches what you are looking for. If so, check the domain name listed in the URL to see if you can determine the source of the Web page (the specific company or organization), as well as the type of organization (individual, government, etc.) it is. |
| **Evaluate the source** | After you determine the source of the Web page (from looking at the URL or by clicking on the link), evaluate whether or not it is a good source for the stated information. Information from the company or organization in question is generally more reliable than information found on an individual's Web site; government and educational institutions are typically reliable sources, as well. |
| **Check the timeliness of the information** | Web page content may be updated regularly or posted once and then forgotten. For news articles, always check for a publication date (sometimes it's included in the URL); look for a "last updated" date on other pages containing information that must be current. |
| **Verify the information** | For reports, projects, Web pages, publications, or other documents where accuracy is important, try to locate the same information from two different Web sources to verify the information before you use it. |
| **Web Citation Examples** | |
| **Web site** | The PBS Kids Web site has a variety of fun, educational, interactive activities for children of all ages (http://www.pbs.org/kids). |
| **Web page, no author or date listed** | *GVU's 8th WWW user survey*. (n.d.). Retrieved August 8, 2000, from http://www.cc.gatech.edu/gvu/usersurveys/survey1997-10/ |
| **Exact reprint of a print article, viewed only on a Web page** | VandenBos, G., Knapp, S., & Doe, J. (2001). Role of reference elements in the selection of resources by psychology undergraduates [Electronic version]. *Journal of Bibliographic Research*, *5*, 117-123. |
| **Reprint of a print article, viewed only on a Web page, but the electronic article may be slightly different than the print version** | VandenBos, G., Knapp, S., & Doe, J. (2001). Role of reference elements in the selection of resources by psychology undergraduates. *Journal of Bibliographic Research*, *5*, 117-123. Retrieved October 13, 2001, from http://jbr.org/articles.html |
| **Internet-only article** | Fredrickson, B. L. (2000, March 7). Cultivating positive emotions to optimize health and well-being. *Prevention & Treatment*, *3*, Article 0001a. Retrieved November 20, 2000, from http://journals.apa.org/prevention/volume3/pre0030001a.html |
| **E-mail** | L.A. Chafez (personal communication, March 28, 2001). |

# SUMMARY

**CHAPTER OBJECTIVE 1**

Understand the difference between the Internet and the World Wide Web.

## What Are the Internet and World Wide Web?

The **Internet** evolved from an experimental government network called *ARPANET.* The present-day Internet is the largest *computer network* in the world. The Internet can be used for a variety of purposes; one of the most widely used Internet resources is the **World Wide Web**—an enormous collection of **Web pages** located on *Web servers*. Web pages are viewed with a **Web browser**, and are connected with graphical or text-based **hyperlinks**.

**CHAPTER OBJECTIVE 2**

Explain how Internet addresses are used to identify computers, Web pages, and people on the Internet.

**Internet addresses** identify something on the Internet, such as a computer, Web page, or person. Numerical **IP addresses** and text-based **domain names** identify computers, most often Web servers. The end of a domain name—called the *top-level domain* or *TLD*—identifies the location of the computer or the type of organization the computer belongs to.

Web pages are identified by their **uniform resource locator** or **URL**. Most Web pages begin with the protocol *http://*; the *ftp://* protocol is sometimes used when downloading files. People are identified by their **e-mail addresses**, which are comprised of a **user name**, followed by the @ sign, followed by the domain name of the computer hosting the person's e-mail. Since user names must be unique within a domain, e-mail addresses are completely unique.

It is important to be able to pronounce Internet addresses correctly, since they are frequently given verbally.

**CHAPTER OBJECTIVE 3**

List several activities that can be performed using the Internet.

## What Can the Internet Be Used For?

The Internet contains an enormous amount of information and activities. Information publishing and information retrieval are obvious online activities. A **search site** can be used to locate Web sites containing the information you are seeking; *reference sites* contain handy tools, such as to display maps, look up phone numbers, and map locations. **Portal** pages, such as Yahoo!, AltaVista, MSN, AOL, and Bolt, include search and reference tools and other useful free services to attract repeat visitors.

**Electronic mail (e-mail)** is one of the most frequently used online activities. One of the benefits of e-mail is that the other person does not have to be online at the time the message is sent in order to receive it. Other mediums of online communication include **discussion groups**, **chat rooms**, **instant messaging (IM)**, **videoconferencing**, and **Internet telephony**.

**Online shopping**, **online auctions**, **online banking**, and **online investing** are all common **e-commerce** activities. When performing any type of financial transaction over the Internet, it is very important to use only *secure Web pages*. Online entertainment applications include downloading *MP3* files and other types of **online music**; *interactive TV (iTV)*, *video-on-demand* and other forms of online TV and videos; and **online gaming**. **Web-based training (WBT)** and **distance learning** are online educational options, and **telecommuting** involves using the Internet and other technology to work from home.

**CHAPTER OBJECTIVE 4**

Describe possible options for accessing the Internet.

## How Can I Access and Use the Internet?

To access the Internet, typically your PC connects to a computer belonging to your ISP that is continuously connected to the Internet. Once that connection is established, you have an onramp to the Internet. In addition to a PC, you can connect to the Internet using an Internet appliance or mobile communications device. Public Internet access is also available, such as through an Internet café, library, or other public location. A *modem* or similar communications device is needed to communicate with the other computer. With a **dial-up connection** (such as **standard dial-up** or **ISDN** connection), your PC connects to your ISP over telephone lines when you use the Internet.

With a **direct connection** (such as through a school or company LAN, or though a **DSL Internet access**, **cable Internet access**, **satellite Internet access**, or **fixed wireless Internet access** connection), your PC is continually connected to the Internet. Some **mobile wireless** connections used with handheld PCs, cell phones, and other mobile communications devices are frequently always-on connections, as well. Direct connections are typically *broadband* connections, which are faster than dial-up connections. People using direct connections should protect their systems with *firewalls.*

The procedure for setting up your Internet connection varies, depending on the type of device and ISP used, but in general you'll use an installation program that installs a browser; walks you through specifying your billing information, selecting a user name, and selecting an access telephone number (for dial-up connections only); and sets up your browser.

**CHAPTER OBJECTIVE 5**

Explain how a browser, URLs, and hyperlinks are used to display Web pages.

To start surfing the Web with a direct connection, you need just to open your browser using either its desktop icon or Start menu item or a special icon or menu item placed there by your ISP. With a dial-up connection, you will need to start your dialing program if it doesn't start automatically. Most browsers—such as *Microsoft Internet Explorer* and *Netscape Navigator*—have similar toolbar buttons and commands to allow you to move forward or backward through the pages viewed in your current Internet session, as well as to print Web pages, save Web pages, and other necessary tasks.

To display a new Web page, you can type its URL in the browser's *Address* or *Location bar* or its corresponding hyperlink can be clicked. Favorite Web pages can be **bookmarked** or added to a **favorites** list to access them again more quickly.

**CHAPTER OBJECTIVE 6**

Understand how to send and receive electronic mail.

E-mail messages are sent and received using an e-mail program. Once e-mail messages are received, they can be printed, forwarded to another user, filed into an appropriate folder, or deleted. When messages are sent, they can include attached files in virtually any file format (although the recipient of the file must have a program that can read the file attachment) and they can be sent to multiple users. To create a new e-mail message, open your e-mail program, click the appropriate toolbar button or menu option to open the message composition window, and supply the recipient, subject line, and message in the appropriate areas; your e-mail program's *address book* feature can be used to enter e-mail addresses easily for people you communicate with on a regular basis. To check for new e-mail, open your e-mail program and use the appropriate toolbar button or menu item.

## Societal Implications of Cyberspace

**CHAPTER OBJECTIVE 7**

Discuss some societal implications of the Internet, such as security, privacy, and differences in the way we communicate online.

Societal implications of cyberspace include privacy and security concerns, the differences in online and offline communications, the anonymity factor, and the amount of unreliable information that can be found on the Internet. Special etiquette rules for online behavior are referred to as **netiquette**, and symbols that can be used to express emotion in written online communication are called *smileys* or *emoticons. Acronyms* or abbreviations can also be used to speed up the creation of written online communications.

## BALANCING ACT

### REAL SELF VS. VIRTUAL SELF

The term *virtual* is popular among computer people to describe a situation or activity that is merely conceptual, instead of having a physical reality. For example, a *virtual tour* of a museum allows you to move through photos or 3D images of the museum to see its exhibits; a *virtual mall* is a collection of shopping Web sites that are organized graphically using a mall/store structure; and a *virtual community* is a group of people who meet—often through a *virtual town* Web page—and chat, e-mail one another, and otherwise participate in community activities. To increase the appearance of reality, some virtual towns, chat rooms, and multi-player games sites today allow users to represent themselves with *avatars*—graphical people, objects, or characters that can often be moved and manipulated by users to travel through the virtual community or game, or to express emotions.

The very nature of online communication fosters anonymity. When participating in chat sessions and exchanging e-mail, an individual's physical characteristics (age, gender, race, appearance, etc.) are not visible. Instead, individuals can project any image of themselves that they wish to present, either by what they say or by the avatar they choose to represent themselves. In other words, when they are online, individuals are free to create a *virtual self* that may not necessarily be representative of who they really are. Sometimes this is harmless. Sometimes this is even beneficial, such as for individuals with physical disabilities who can be judged online solely by their ideas, not their appearance. Other times, such as when child molesters masquerade as young people to lure youngsters into real, face-to-face, meetings, it can be downright dangerous and criminal.

### YOUR TURN

Consider the statements made above about how a virtual self can differ from an individual's real self and answer the following questions.

1. Under what circumstances might a person consider giving false or misleading information (age, gender, appearance, education, areas of expertise, and so forth) online? Do you feel that it would be ethical under any of these circumstances? Why or why not?
2. Should chat room and virtual community participants be required to submit their real identities to the person or organization hosting the chat room or community before being allowed to participate? Why or why not?
3. Should the person or organization hosting a chat room or virtual community be responsible for monitoring communications for illegal or unethical behavior? Why or why not?
4. What role should the government take in online communications? Should the government be allowed to monitor online communications and have access to a participant's real identity? If so, under what circumstances?
5. In 1996, the first real virtual wedding was held in an Internet virtual world with the bride, groom, and guests represented by avatars. What is your opinion about "virtualizing" these types of important social events?

## KEY TERMS

**Instructions:** Match each key term on the left with the definition on the right that best describes it.

a. **bookmark**
b. **dial-up connection**
c. **distance learning**
d. **domain name**
e. **DSL Internet access**
f. **e-commerce**
g. **electronic mail (e-mail)**
h. **e-mail address**
i. **hyperlink**
j. **instant messaging (IM)**
k. **Internet**
l. **IP address**
m. **portal**
n. **search site**
o. **uniform resource locator (URL)**
p. **user name**
q. **videoconferencing**
r. **Web browser**
s. **Web page**
t. **World Wide Web**

1. ______ A document, typically containing hyperlinks to other documents, located on a Web server and available through the World Wide Web.
2. ______ A form of private chat set up to allow users easily to exchange real-time typed messages with the individuals they specify.
3. ______ A learning environment where the student is physically located away from the instructor and other students; commonly instruction and communications take place via the Internet.
4. ______ A name that uniquely identifies a person on a particular network; it is combined with a domain name to form an e-mail address.
5. ______ A numeric address that uniquely identifies a computer on the Internet.
6. ______ A program used to view Web pages.
7. ______ A text-based address that uniquely identifies a computer on the Internet.
8. ______ A type of direct broadband Internet service that transfers data over standard telephone lines and doesn't tie up your telephone line.
9. ______ A type of Internet connection where your PC or other device must connect to your service provider's computer before each Internet session in order to use the Internet.
10. ______ A Web site that allows users to search for Web pages that match specified keywords or selected categories.
11. ______ An address consisting of a user name and domain name that uniquely identifies a person on the Internet.
12. ______ An address, usually beginning with *http://*, which uniquely identifies a Web page on the Internet.
13. ______ A Web page that offers a variety of Internet services in hopes of being users' main entrance to the rest of the Web.
14. ______ Electronic messages sent from one user to another over the Internet or another network.
15. ______ Text or an image located on a Web page or other document that is linked to another Web page.
16. ______ The act of doing financial transactions over a network, typically the Internet.
17. ______ The entire collection of Web pages available through the Internet.
18. ______ The largest and most widely used computer network in the world, linking millions of computers all over the world.
19. ______ The saved name and address of a Web page, stored by your browser for future use.
20. ______ Using a computer, video camera, microphone, or other technology to conduct face-to-face meetings among people in different locations.

## SELF-QUIZ

Answers for the self-quiz appear at the end of the book.

### True/False

**Instructions:** Circle **T** if the statement is true or **F** if the statement is false.

**T F 1.** IP addresses are used to identify people on the Internet.

**T F 2.** With instant messaging, both the sender and the recipient must be online at the same time.

**T F 3.** With a direct connection, your computer needs to dial your modem to connect to the Internet.

**T F 4.** It isn't possible to tell if a word or image is a hyperlink until you click it.

**T F 5.** When performing a keyword Internet search, more than one keyword can usually be typed in the search box.

### Completion

**Instructions:** Supply the missing words to complete the following statements.

6. The physical network of the largest network in the world is called the ______________.
7. Web pages are stored on Web ______________.
8. For the e-mail address *jsmith@course.com*, *jsmith* is the ______________ name and *course.com* is the ______________ name.
9. The e-mail address pronounced *bill gee at microsoft dot com* is written as ______________.
10. With a(n) ______________, people bid on products and the highest bidder is allowed to purchase the item.
11. ______________ is a type of direct broadband Internet connection that transmits data over standard telephone lines.
12. Working from home and communicating with the office and others using computers and other technology is called ______________.
13. To save URLs to be able to return to Web pages quickly on a regular basis, ______________ are used.
14. Unsolicited bulk e-mail is called ______________.
15. One of the most common online security risks today is the ______________, a software program designed to change the way a computer operates, without the permission or knowledge of the user, which often causes damage to the PC.

# PROJECTS

YOUR OPINION

**1. E-Voting**

The chapter Closer Look box takes a look at online voting as an alternative to the punch cards and optical mark ballots presently used in most areas in the United States. Consider the concerns raised in the Closer Look box. (For example: How will the system prevent someone voting as another individual? What will prevent a person's vote from being stored in a database so it can be used against him or her at a later time? Could individuals sell their votes to the highest bidder?) Use these questions to help you form an opinion about online voting.

For this project, write a short essay expressing your opinion about online voting in general, and if you believe it will become widely used in the near future. Would you be comfortable casting your vote online? What types of authentication methods would you want in place to verify your identify before being allowed to submit an online ballot? At some point, do you think online voting will become the norm? If so, how would you suggest handling individuals who have no Internet access available to them on Election Day? Submit your opinion on this issue to your instructor in the form of a short paper, not more than two pages in length.

INDEPENDENT RESEARCH

**2. Your ISP**

As discussed in the chapter, ISPs are used to connect to the Internet. You may have a limited number of options for an ISP, depending on where you live and how much you're willing to spend on Internet service.

For this project, research what options you have to connect to the Internet from where you live. Your telephone company should be able to tell you if DSL or ISDN is available to you and what the cost is. If you have access to cable, check with your local cable provider for information on cable Internet. If DSL, ISDN, and cable are not available to you, check into satellite service (such as from StarBand or DIRECWAY). For conventional dial-up, either call a local service provider or go to the Web sites for America Online, Earthlink, Juno, or other large ISPs and determine which ones have a local telephone access number for your area.

After you have completed your research, summarize your findings in a two- to three-page paper. Be sure to include the cost and estimated speed for each service, any limitations on e-mail (such as number of e-mail addresses, mailbox size, or size of attachments), and whether or not each service ties up your telephone line. Be sure to include your opinion as to which service you would choose to use and why.

HANDS-ON

**3. Web Scavenger Hunt**

As illustrated in the chapter How To box, search sites (such as Yahoo!, Google, and AltaVista) can be used to find Web pages containing specific information.

For this project, go to a search site and search for Web pages that you could use to obtain the following information. Once you find each of the items specified below, print the page containing the information using your browser's Print button. After you have found all five items, staple your printouts together and turn them in to your instructor. (Note: Some of the printouts will vary from student to student.)

a. A toll-free telephone number for Dell Computer.

b. The current stock price of IBM Corporation (NYSE symbol IBM).

c. A map of where your house, apartment, or dorm is located.

d. The ZIP code for 200 N. Elm Street, Hinsdale, IL.

e. A recipe for Spicy Chicken Wings, Buffalo Chicken Wings, or something similar.

**4. Safe Online Shopping**

There are a wide variety of online stores where everyday items (such as books, clothes, CDs, and DVDs) can be purchased.

For this project, select a specific product that you might want to buy and find at least three places where you could buy it online. You can go to the Web sites for retail stores (such as Wal-Mart, Target, Bloomingdale's, Macy's, Old Navy, or Circuit City) and try to find the product using the site's search feature or categories. Alternately, you could search for the product using a comparison shopping service (such as MySimon or Pricegrabber), or just a regular search site, to locate online stores that carry your chosen item.

Once you find the item you are looking for, make a note of the price and add the item to your shopping cart. Begin the checkout procedure to try to determine any sales tax and shipping charges (but DON'T actually purchase the item—stop at the point the site requires you to enter a credit card number or other payment information). Does the shopping cart use a secure Web server (look for a locked padlock or a nonbroken key on your browser's status bar or *https:* in the URL showing in the Address or Location bar at the top of your browser's window)? If not, is there a security or privacy statement on the site that states that it uses a secure server later in the checkout process? Also, look for a return policy to see if you can return the product if you are dissatisfied with it. When you have finished researching a site, delete the item from your shopping cart.

After you have found your specified item at three different stores, prepare a one-page summary of the information you gathered. Be sure to include which of the three stores (if any) you would want to buy the item from and why.

GROUP PRESENTATION

**5. Browser Plug-Ins**

A *browser plug-in* is a program that adds the ability to view additional Internet content with your browser, such as to view documents created in certain formats or multimedia elements of a Web page. Common plug-in programs are Adobe Acrobat Reader, Macromedia Flash Player, RealNetworks RealOne Player, Apple QuickTime Player, and Costmo Software Cosmo Player.

For this project, form a group to research the five plug-ins listed above. For each plug-in, determine what types of files or applications the plug-in is used for, at least one location where you can download the plug-in, the cost (if any), what operating systems and browsers the plug-in will work with, and if there are any alternative plug-ins that can be used to view the types of documents or applications associated with the plug-in you are researching.

Share your findings with the class in the form of a short presentation. The presentation should not exceed 10 minutes and should make use of one or more presentation aids such as the chalkboard, handouts, overhead transparencies, or a computer-based slide presentation (your instructor may provide additional requirements). Your group may also be asked to submit a summary of the presentation to your instructor.

### 6. Your Domain

As mentioned in the chapter, domain names are used to identify computers—most commonly Web servers—available through the Internet, and a central registration system is used to ensure that domain names are unique.

For this project, form a group to look into how a domain name is registered. First, select a domain name you would like to use for your group (you can assume you are a business, club, or any other type of organization). Next, visit at least two registrar Web sites (such as NetworkSolutions.com or Register.com) to determine what information you would need to provide to register your domain name and how much it would cost. Also, investigate the top-level domains .com, .net, .org, .info, .name, .biz, and .us to determine who they are designed for. Which top-level domains are available for your group's domain name? Determine any requirements—such as length and allowable characters—for domain names using those top-level domains. Using a lookup feature available on a registration site, see if your group's desired domain name is available. If not, keep trying variations of that name until you find an appropriate available domain name. Finally, find out what *cybersquatting* is and how that may affect your selection of a domain name.

Share your findings with the class in the form of a short presentation. The presentation should not exceed 10 minutes and should make use of one or more presentation aids such as the chalkboard, handouts, overhead transparencies, or a computer-based slide presentation (your instructor may provide additional requirements). Your group may also be asked to submit a summary of the presentation to your instructor.

### 7. Telesurgery

**VIDEO VIEWPOINT**

The Internet, telecommunications technology, and robotics have advanced enough in recent years to allow for *telesurgery*—operating on patients via a PC. The accompanying video clip features Dr. Louis Kavoussi of Johns Hopkins Bayview Medical Center, who performs surgery on patients all over the world from his home office instead of in a hospital operating room. He uses his PC to control robotic surgical tools and cameras, as well as to give surgeons written and verbal instructions.

After watching the video, think about the impact of telesurgery on our society. If, as Dr. Kavoussi believes, telesurgery eventually becomes the norm, what advantages and disadvantages might there be? There are obvious benefits to using telesurgery in remote military and space exploration applications, but will the average citizen go along with having surgery via telecommunications technology? What types of precautions will need to be taken to overcome concerns about software and hardware malfunctions? Is having the best surgeon perform the operation via telesurgery always better than an average surgeon performing the operation via traditional methods? How might an increase in telesurgery impact the medical profession and future physicians? Would you be willing to have telesurgery?

**ONLINE VIDEO**

To view the Telesurgery video clip, go to www.course.com/morley2003/ch3

**Express your viewpoint:** What impact does telesurgery have on personal health and safety, as well as the medical profession in general?

Use the video clip and the questions previously asked as the foundation for your response. Your instructor will direct you to be prepared to discuss your position (either in class, via an online class discussion group, or in a class chat room), or to write a short paper stating and supporting your viewpoint on the issue. You may also be asked to do research and provide resources to support your point of view on this issue.

# COMPUTERS AND SECURITY

## OUTLINE

**Overview**

**Security Concerns**

- Hardware Theft, Damage, and System Failure
- Unauthorized Access and Use
- Computer Sabotage
- Online Theft, Fraud, and Other Dot Cons
- Software Piracy and Digital Counterfeiting
- Personal Safety Issues

**Security Safeguards**

- Protection against Hardware Theft, Damage, and Failure
- Protection against Unauthorized Access and Use
- Protection against Interception of Data and Communications
- Protection against Computer Viruses and Other Types of Sabotage
- Protection against Online Theft, Fraud, and Other Dot Cons
- Protection against Software Piracy and Digital Counterfeiting
- Protection against Cyberstalking and Other Personal Safety Concerns
- Protection against Security Breaches by Employees

**Computer Crime Legislation**

## OBJECTIVES

**After completing this chapter, you will be able to:**

- Discuss security concerns related to computer and Internet use, such as hardware theft, damage, and system failure; unauthorized access and use; and computer sabotage.
- Name several types of dot cons and explain what constitutes software piracy and digital counterfeiting.
- Describe personal safety risks involved with Internet use.
- Understand ways to safeguard a PC against theft, damage, or unauthorized access and use.
- Give suggestions for securely transferring data over the Internet, as well as for protecting against computer sabotage.
- Suggest precautions users can take against online fraud and identity theft.
- Describe ways software piracy and digital counterfeiting may be prevented.
- List ways individuals can protect their personal safety while online, and ways businesses can protect themselves against security breaches by employees.
- Give examples of computer crime legislation.

# CHAPTER 4

## OVERVIEW

The increased use of computers and the Internet helps users finish many tasks quickly and efficiently and adds convenience to many people's lives. However, there is a downside, as well. As more and more personal and business data is stored on computers, the risks and consequences of unauthorized computer access, theft, fraud, and other types of computer crime increase; so do the chances of data loss due to crime, employee misconduct, system malfunction, and disasters. There are even some online activities that can put your personal safety at risk, if you are not careful.

This chapter looks first at a variety of security concerns stemming from the use of computers in our society, including such topics as hardware theft and damage, system failure, unauthorized access and use, computer viruses and other types of sabotage, software piracy, digital counterfeiting, and personal safety issues. Safeguards for each of these concerns are covered next, with an explanation of possible precautions that can be taken to guard against each of these security risks. The chapter closes with a look at computer crime legislation.

# SECURITY CONCERNS

There are a variety of security concerns related to computers and the Internet, most of which can be categorized as **computer crimes**. Computer crime—sometimes referred to as *cybercrime*—includes any illegal act involving a computer. Many computer crimes involve breaking through the security of a computer or network; others include theft of hardware, financial assets, or information. Still other computer crimes involve manipulating data, such as grades, for personal advantage. Increasingly, computer crimes involve acts of sabotage, such as releasing a computer virus or shutting down a Web server. Regardless of its form, computer crime is an important security concern today.

## Hardware Theft, Damage, and System Failure

One of the most obvious types of computer crime is theft of the computer, or other hardware, itself. Other hardware security issues include hardware damage (both intentional and accidental) and *system failure.*

### Hardware Theft

**Hardware theft** occurs when hardware is stolen, such as from a school, business, home, or individual. While stealing desktop PCs, printers, and other larger items during break-ins has been common for some time, stealing notebooks and other types of portable PCs is on the rise. According to the 2002 Computer Crime & Security survey performed jointly by the Computer Security Institute and the FBI, notebook PC theft ranked number two among respondents for financial loss due to attack or misuse. One explanation is that more and more people are traveling with portable PCs, so thieves are increasingly targeting airports, hotels, and cars. Although security experts stress that the vast majority of hardware theft is done for the value of the hardware itself, key executives of certain companies and employees of some government agencies may be targeted for computer theft for the information contained on their PCs.

### Hardware Damage

PCs consist of sensitive electronic devices and delicate components that can be damaged easily. Power fluctuations, heat, dust, and static can all damage computer hardware. Dropping a notebook computer, monitor, printer, or other piece of hardware will often break it; spilling a drink or otherwise getting a keyboard or other hardware component wet will also likely cause some damage. In addition to accidental damage, burglars, vandals, disgruntled employees, and other individuals sometimes intentionally damage the computers they have access to.

### System Failure and Other Types of Disasters

Although many of us would prefer not to think about it, **system failure**—the complete malfunction of a computer system—and other types of computer-related disasters do happen. From accidentally deleting a file to having your computer just stop working, computer problems can cost you a great deal of time, money, and headaches. When the system contains your personal documents and data, it is a problem. When it contains the only copy of your company records or controls a vital system—such as a nuclear power plant—it can be a disaster.

System failure can occur because of a hardware problem. It can also occur because of a natural disaster (such as a tornado, fire, flood, or hurricane), which can wreak havoc on computer hardware and data. Unfortunately, sabotage and terrorist attacks can also be the cause of system failure, hardware damage, and data loss. The terrorist attack on the New York City World Trade Center Twin Towers on September 11, 2001 illustrated this all too clearly. When the Twin Towers collapsed, nearly 3,000 people were killed and hundreds of private and government offices—over 13 million square feet of office space—were completely destroyed; another 7 million square feet of office space was damaged (see Figure 4-1). In addition to the terrible human loss, the offices located in the WTC lost their computer systems—including all the equipment, records, and data stored at that location. The ramifications of the data loss and system failures were felt around the world by all the businesses and people connected directly or indirectly to these organizations.

**FIGURE 4-1**

**The attacks on New York's World Trade Center killed nearly 3,000 people and destroyed hundreds of business offices, including critical telephone switches and cables located at this Verizon building adjacent to Ground Zero.**

## Unauthorized Access and Use

**Unauthorized access** occurs whenever an individual gains access to a computer, network, file, or other resource without permission. **Unauthorized use** involves using a computer resource for unapproved activities. Unauthorized access and unauthorized use are criminal offenses in the United States and many other countries and can be committed by strangers, employees, students, or other individuals. For instance, a student looking at faculty payroll files would likely be unauthorized access, and an employee checking personal e-mail at work might fall under unauthorized use, depending on the policy of the company. Whether or not these types of unauthorized access and unauthorized use are illegal depends on the circumstances, as well as the specific company involved. To explain acceptable computer use to their employees, students, or other users, many organizations and educational institutions publish guidelines. These rules are frequently called *codes of conduct* (see Figure 4-2).

### Hacking

**Hacking** refers to the act of breaking into a remote computer system; the person doing the hacking is called a *hacker*. By its definition, hacking involves unauthorized access. Two exceptions to this statement are *professional hacking* that takes place at the request of an organization to test the security of its system, and hacking into computers set up (usually by hacker organizations) specifically to enable hackers to practice their skills legally. Unless it is authorized, hacking in the United States and many other countries is a crime and is being prosecuted vigorously. For example, Kevin Mitnick—one of the world's most famous hackers—was arrested in 1995, was jailed until he pled guilty to wire fraud and computer fraud in 1999, and then spent an additional year in prison. As a condition of his supervised release in 2000, he was not permitted to use a computer or any type of wireless device for three years. The recent *USA Patriot Act* expands the government's authority to prosecute hacking activities and increases the penalties for unauthorized hacks.

**FIGURE 4-2**

**A sample code of conduct**

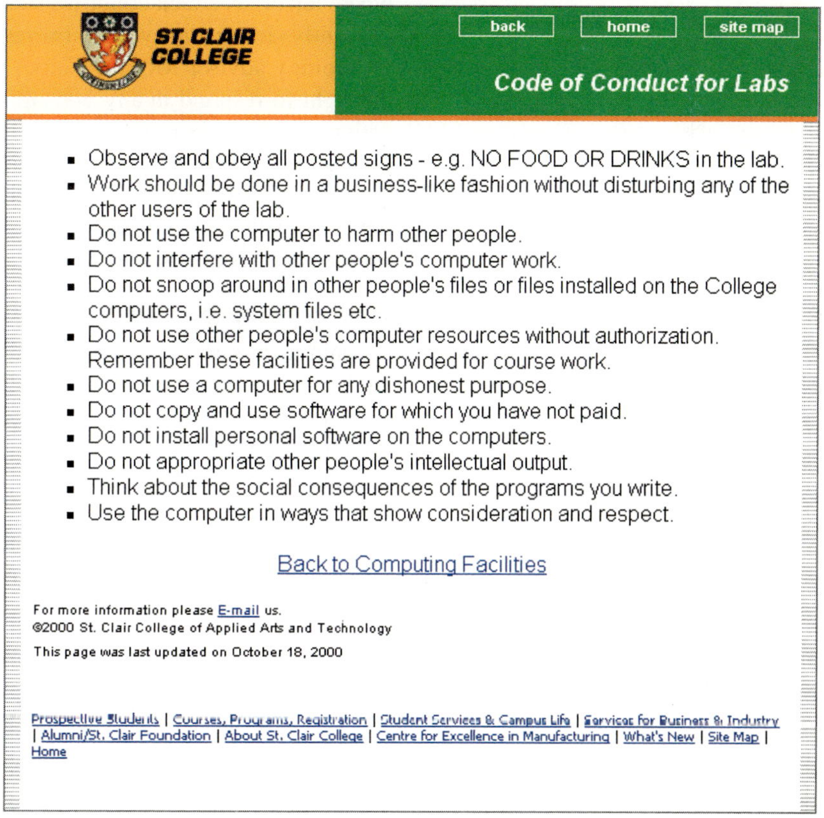

In addition to unauthorized access, hacking may also involve unauthorized use, depending on what actions the hacker takes once he or she has gained access to the system. Usually the motivation for hacking is to steal information or sabotage a computer system, which would constitute unauthorized use. Sometimes hackers break into a system just to prove their computer expertise, to expand their knowledge, or to bring attention to a social cause. Both types of hacking are illegal, and the general public tends to use the term *hacker* to refer to any type of computer break-in regardless of what activities take place after the security breach. But many hackers differentiate between these two types of hacking and prefer the term *cracker* when referring to individuals who break into systems for destructive purposes or material gain.

A recent example of what some hackers consider hacking (not cracking) is the collection of attacks in 2002 from two hackers calling themselves the *Deceptive Duo*. These two individuals broke into secured databases and published selected information from those databases onto government Web sites to prove that the databases had been accessed. Some of the systems breached included a Midwest Express Airlines database containing flight schedules and passenger manifests, a NASA Ames Research Center employee database, a Union Bank database, and a U.S. Defense Department Defense Logistics Agency (DLA) database containing names and ID numbers of DLA employees. In their explanation regarding the motivation for the attacks, the Deceptive Duo claimed that they hacked into the secure systems to bring attention to the systems' vulnerabilities. At the time of this writing, the case was under investigation by the FBI and the duo had been identified, but had not yet been formally charged.

As illustrated by this example, hacking can be a serious problem for both businesses and the government. In fact, hacking is considered to be a very serious threat to our nation's security. With the increased number of computers and systems online and the abilities of hackers today, some experts believe the risk of *cyberterrorism*—where terrorists attack countries such as the U.S. via the Internet—has increased significantly in recent years. In response to this possible threat, White House technology adviser Richard Clarke announced in early 2002 that the U.S. "reserves the right to respond in any way appropriate" to Internet warfare, including military action against cyberterrorists. Current concerns are attacks against the computers controlling such vital systems as the nation's power grids, banks, and water filtration facilities. Clarke has announced that the U.S. will spend billions of dollars in the next few years to prepare against cyber attacks; a "National Strategy to Secure Cyberspace" is also in the works and expected to be released by early 2003.

### Interception of Communications and Transmissions

To gain access to data stored on a particular computer, some criminals attempt to hack directly into that computer. It is also possible, however, to gain unauthorized access to data, files, e-mail messages, and other content as they are being sent over the Internet. Once intercepted, the content can be read, altered, or otherwise used for non-intended purposes. Though it is unlikely that anyone would be interested in intercepting your personal e-mail to friends and relatives, proprietary corporate information and sensitive personal information (such as credit card, bank account, or brokerage account information) is at risk if it is sent over the Internet unsecured.

Wireless networking standards, such as 802.11b (Wi-Fi), as well as the huge increase in the use of wireless mobile communications devices, have opened up new opportunities for data interception. Because information from a PC using a wireless network is transmitted over the airwaves, interception is easier than with wired connections. *Wi-Fi nodes*—the hardware that receives the wireless transmissions and relays it to the network—also provide a natural entry point for hackers trying to break into a system. Wi-Fi nodes are commonly found in parks, airports, coffee houses, and other public locations, in addition to being located inside companies and homes. It is possible to access a public Wi-Fi node if you are located within 300 feet of the node; unless it is protected in some manner, this applies to private Wi-Fi nodes, as well. For instance, a movie pirate recently used his neighbor's Wi-Fi home network to gain access to the neighbor's broadband Internet service, which he then used to send a pirated movie over the Internet. Although some security features are currently built into Wi-Fi networks, new improvements to wireless networking standards are expected to provide increased security, Until then, wireless users should realize that data transmitted via wireless networking is less secure and more open to interception than is data transmitted over physical media.

## Computer Sabotage

Unfortunately, *sabotage*—an act of malicious destruction—is a common type of computer crime today. There are several forms computer sabotage can take, including releasing a computer virus, launching a *denial of service attack*, or changing data or programs located on a computer. Acts of sabotage can take place by employees of a company, as well as by outsiders, and are estimated to cost individuals and organizations billions of dollars per year. Just one incident can be extraordinarily expensive, averaging just over $2 million according to a 2001 study by the Computer Security Institute and the FBI. The most expensive computer virus to date—the LoveLetter virus released in 2000—was estimated to cost almost $9 billion, primarily in labor cost for virus removal and for lost productivity.

### Computer Viruses and Other Types of Malware

**Malware** is the generic term used to refer to any type of malicious software. Malware programs are intentionally written to do destructive acts, although some researchers believe that many young malware creators don't really realize the potential consequences of their actions and the huge amount of destruction and expense that can result from releasing this type of software into cyberspace. The most widely-known type of malware is the **computer virus**—a small software program that is installed without the permission or knowledge of the computer user, is designed to alter the way a computer operates, and can replicate itself to infect any new media it is given access to. Computer viruses are embedded into program or data files and are spread whenever the infected file is downloaded from the Internet or another network, is transferred to a new computer via an infected removable disk, or is e-mailed to another computer (see Figure 4-3). Once a copy of the infected file reaches a new computer, it typically embeds itself into program, data, or system files on the new PC, infecting that computer. Once a computer is infected and the virus is stored on the computer, it remains there until it is discovered and removed.

Most computer viruses are programmed to harm the computers they are transmitted to—such as by damaging programs or deleting files located on those PCs, or by completely erasing the entire hard drive. This damage can take place immediately after infection or it can begin when a particular condition is met. A virus that activates when it detects a certain condition, such as when a particular keystroke is pressed or an employee's name is deleted from an employee file, is called a *logic bomb.* A logic bomb whose trigger is a particular date or time is called a *time bomb.* In addition to destructive computer viruses, there are so-called "benign" viruses that aren't designed to do any permanent damage, but instead make their presence known by displaying a text or video message, or by playing a musical or audio message. Even though benign viruses may not cause any lasting harm (although some do unintentional damage because of programming errors), they are annoying, can require enormous amounts of time to get rid of, and can disrupt communications for the organizations involved.

**FIGURE 4-3**

**How a computer virus or other type of malicious software might spread**

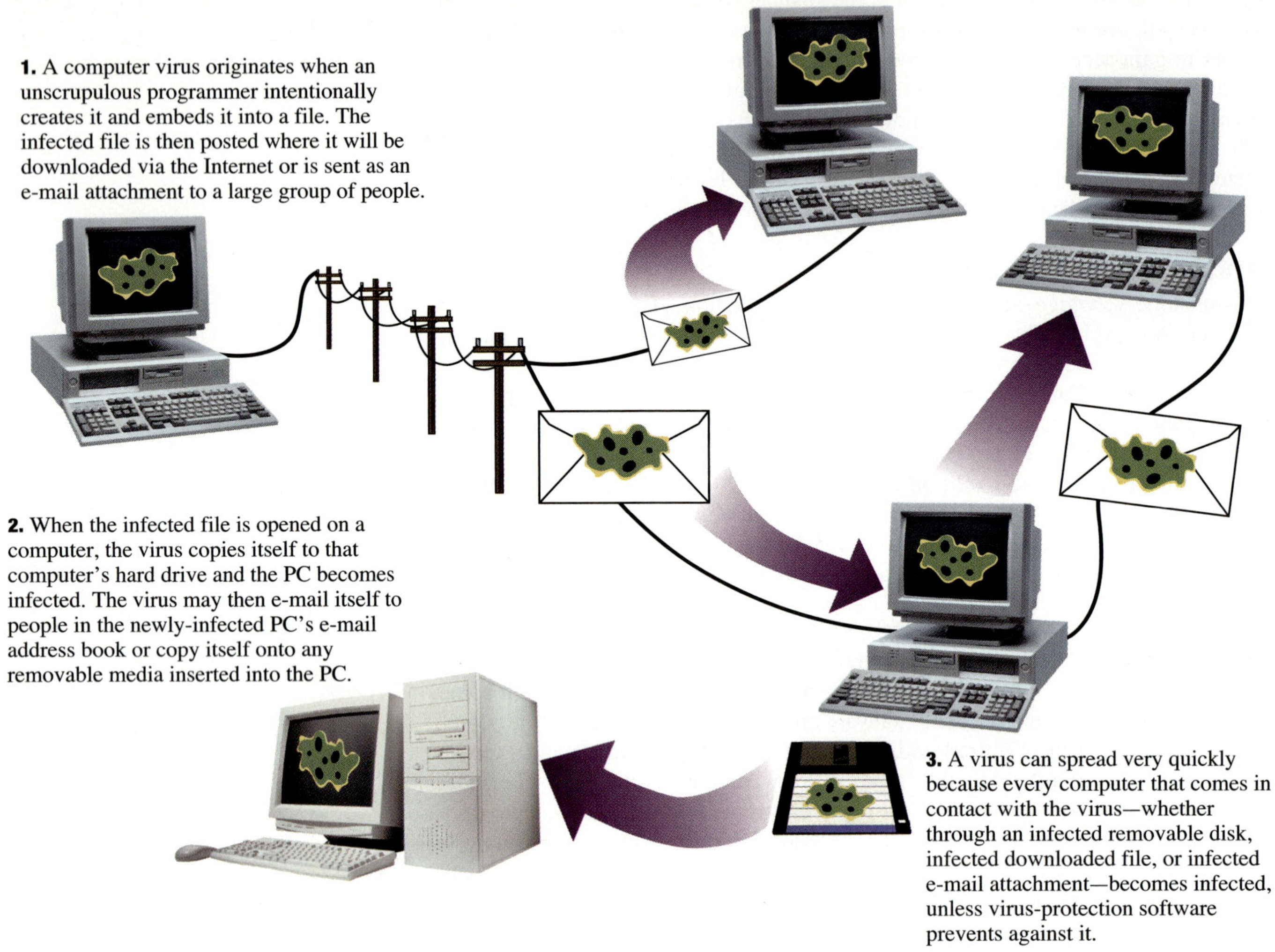


Writing a computer virus or even posting the code for a computer virus on the Internet isn't illegal, but it is considered to be highly unethical and irresponsible behavior. Distributing a computer virus, on the other hand, is illegal. David Smith, creator of the 1999 Melissa virus, is thought to be the first individual in the U.S. to receive jail time for unleashing a computer virus. This virus, released on Friday, March 26, 1999, infected over 100,000 computers by the end of the weekend and caused an estimated $80 million of damage. Smith was sentenced in May 2002 to 20 months in federal prison.

Although there are other types of malware in addition to computer viruses, it is common practice for all types of malware to be generically referred to as "viruses," even though they may not technically be true computer viruses. Two other common forms of malware are *computer worms* and *Trojan horses*.

A **computer worm** is a malicious program designed to cause damage, similar to a computer virus. Unlike a computer virus, however, a computer worm doesn't embed itself into other computer files to replicate itself; instead, it is usually embedded initially inside a host document and spreads by creating copies of itself (by creating copies of the host document) and sending those copies to other computers via a network, usually as e-mail attachments. After an infected attachment file is opened by an individual, the worm inflicts its damage, and then automatically sends copies of itself to other computers, typically using the addresses in the e-mail address book located on the newly infected PC. When those e-mail messages and their attachments are opened (and they frequently are because they usually look like they came from the person whose address book was used), those new computers become infected and the cycle continues.

Because of its distribution method, a worm can spread very rapidly. And, unfortunately, new worms are getting smarter. For example, the Klez worm released in late 2001 has the ability to generate a number of different subject lines and file attachment names. Klez is also particularly persistent. Unlike many viruses that peak and then become controlled in a short period of time, Klez was still going strong at the time of this writing—more than nine months after its introduction—due in part to its design and to the newer Klez variants released during that time period. Today worms require that an attachment be opened before the worm can replicate itself, although it is expected that newer worms may be able to execute when the user just opens the e-mail message.

A **Trojan horse** is a malicious program that masquerades as something else—usually an application program. When the seemingly legitimate program (such as what appears to be a game or utility program, for example) is run, the destructive program executes instead. Unlike viruses and worms, Trojan horses can't replicate themselves and are usually spread by being downloaded from the Internet. A Trojan horse may also be sent as an e-mail attachment, either from the Trojan horse author or forwarded on by individuals not realizing the program is a Trojan horse.

### Denial of Service Attacks

A **denial of service (DoS) attack** is an act of sabotage that attempts to flood a network or Web server with so many requests for action that it shuts down or simply cannot handle legitimate requests any longer, causing legitimate users to be denied service. For example, a hacker might set up one or more computers to continually *ping* a server (contact it with a request to send a responding ping back) with a false return address or to continually request nonexistent information. If enough useless traffic is generated, the server has no resources left to deal with legitimate requests (see Figure 4-4).

**FIGURE 4-4**

**How a denial of service (DoS) attack might work**

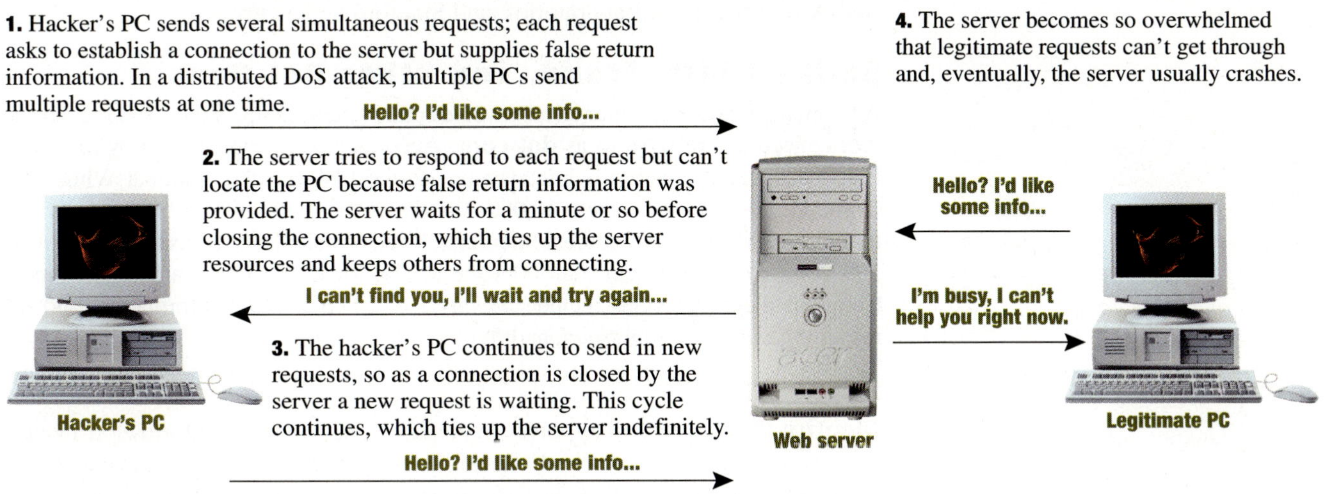

During the past few years, many leading Web sites (such as those belonging to Microsoft, Yahoo!, eBay, CNET, Amazon.com, E*Trade, CNN, ABC News, and ESPN) have been the victims of DoS attacks. Most of these attacks utilized multiple computers (referred to as a *distributed denial of service* or *DDoS attack*). To perform DDoS attacks, hackers have begun more frequently to access and use unprotected PCs with direct Internet connections (such as those located in schools, businesses, or homes). These computers—referred to as *zombies*—participate in the attacks without the owners' knowledge. Because home PCs tend to be less protected than school and business PCs, hackers are increasingly targeting them for use as zombie PCs. It is against the law to launch a denial of service attack in the U.S., and it can be very costly in terms of business lost—such as when an e-commerce site is shut down—as well as the time and expense required to bring the site back online.

Related to a DoS attack is *malicious spamming*, where so many bogus e-mail messages are sent to a mail server that the mail server shuts down. Like a DoS attack, malicious spamming is targeted at a specific company, such as in the case of a former Southern California man who was convicted recently of maliciously bombarding the computer system of his ex-employer with thousands of e-mail messages; he faces up to five years in federal prison.

### Data or Program Alteration

Another type of computer sabotage occurs when a hacker breaches a computer system in order to delete or change data, modify programs, or otherwise alter the data and programs located there. For example, students have been caught changing grades in their schools' database, such as the Florida high school student who recently admitted charging students $5 each to change their grades. Other examples include disgruntled or former employees who alter programs so they work incorrectly; delete important projects, customer records, or other critical data; or randomly change data in the company's database. The usual motivation for these types of acts is revenge—such as for being passed over for a promotion or for recently being terminated. Like hacking, data and program alteration is illegal.

Another example of data alteration that has become more common over the past few years is defacing or otherwise changing Web sites—sometimes classified as a type of *cybervandalism*. This has become a widely used method for hackers who want to draw attention to themselves or a specific cause (see Figure 4-5). Sites modified by hackers in the last few years include those belonging to the Library of Congress, FBI, New York Times, CNN, Secretary of Defense, Sandia National Laboratories, NASA Jet Propulsion Laboratories, and Stanford University.

## Online Theft, Fraud, and Other Dot Cons

A booming area of computer crime involves online theft, fraud, scams, and related activities collectively referred to as **dot cons**. According to a report issued by the Internet Fraud Complaint Center—a joint venture of the FBI and the National White Collar Crime Center—approximately 10,000 Americans reported losing a total of nearly $18 million in 2001 due to fraudulent Internet activities. While the victims ranged from 10 to 100 years old, those older than 60 were at risk for losing larger amounts of money. Common illegal activities include *identity theft*; theft of data, information, and other resources; *online auction fraud*; and *Internet offer scams.*

### Identity Theft

**Identity theft** occurs when someone obtains enough personal information about you (such as your name, date of birth, Social Security number, address, phone number, or credit card numbers) so that they can masquerade as you for a variety of activities. Typically, identity theft begins with obtaining a person's name and Social Security number (see Figure 4-6), such as from a credit application, rental application, or similar form. Once the thief finds that individual's home address (either from the same form or by using a telephone book), he or she usually has enough information to order a copy of the individual's birth certificate over the phone, to obtain a "replacement" driver's license, and to open credit or bank accounts in the victim's name. Assuming the thief requests a change of address for these new accounts after they are opened, it may take quite some time—often until a company or collections agency contacts the victim about overdue bills—for the victim to become aware that his or her identity has been stolen. Although identity theft often takes place via the Internet today, information can also be gathered from trash dumpsters, mailboxes, and other locations. In 1998, the federal government passed the *Identity Theft and Assumption Deterrence Act of 1998*, which made identity theft a federal crime.

**FIGURE 4-5**

**Examples of Web site defacements**

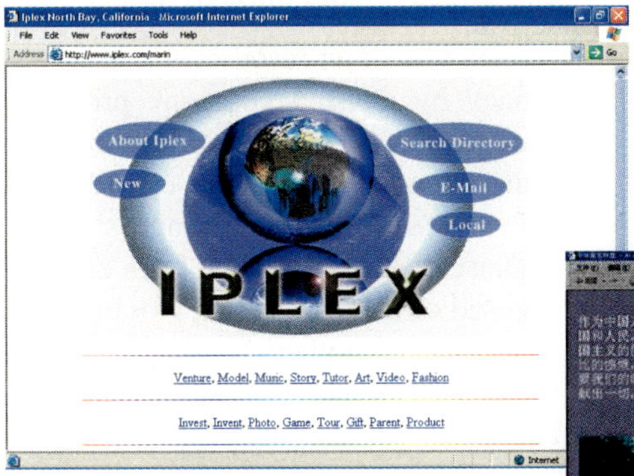


**^ Normal appearance of the Iplex Web site**

**Defacements by political groups**

A number of Chinese hackers hacked U.S. Web sites (like this one) immediately following the mid-air collision between a U.S. spy plane and a Chinese fighter jet that occurred in 2001.

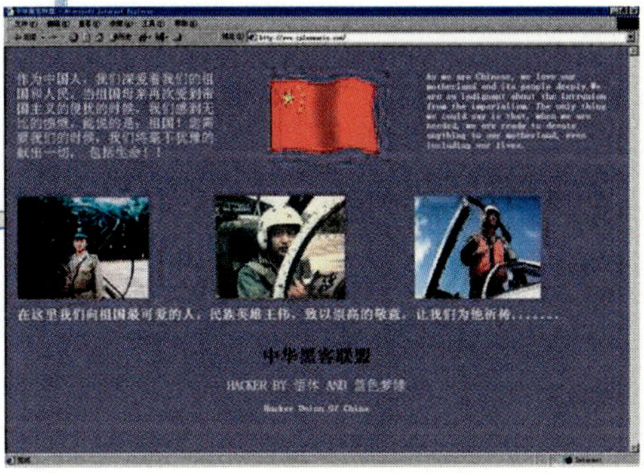

**> Iplex Web site after being altered by a hacker**

**^ Normal appearance of the Stanford Cardiology Web site**

**Defacements by individuals**

The individual who hacked this Web site appears to have done so for no underlying political motivation.

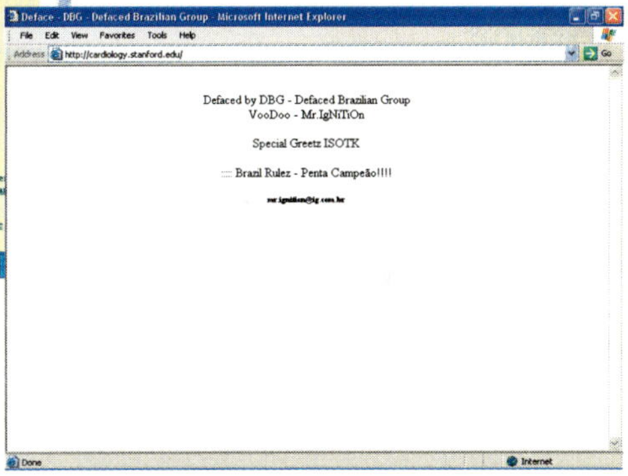


**> Stanford Cardiology Web site after being altered by a hacker**

Unfortunately, identify theft is on the rise—some estimates place it as high as half a million cases in the U.S. each year. Identity theft can be extremely distressing for victims, can take years to straighten out, and can be very expensive. According to the Identity Theft Resource Center, identity theft victims spend an average of 175 hours trying to clear their names. Some victims, like Michelle Brown, believe that they will always be dealing with their "alter reality" to some extent. For a year and a half, an identity thief used Brown's identity to obtain over $50,000 in goods and services, to rent properties—even to engage in drug trafficking. Although the culprit was apprehended eventually, she continued to use Brown's identity; the real Michelle Brown was even detained by U.S. customs agents when returning from a trip to Mexico because of the criminal record of the identity thief. Brown states that she has not traveled out of the country since, fearing an arrest or other serious problem resulting from the theft of her identity, and estimates she has spent over 500 hours trying to correct all the problems related to the identity theft.

### Theft of Data, Information, and Other Resources

*Data* or *information theft*—the theft of data or information usually located on a computer—can take place by stealing an actual PC; it can also take place over the Internet after a hacker gains unauthorized access to a computer system. Common types of data and information stolen include proprietary corporate information and personal customer data, such as credit card numbers and Social Security numbers, that can be used to perform *credit card fraud*, identity theft—even extortion. For example, a Russian hacker stole 300,000 credit card numbers from an online music site in 2000 and

**FIGURE 4-6**

**Identity theft often begins with determining an individual's Social Security number.**

posted many of them on the Internet for anyone to see after the retailer refused to pay a $100,000 ransom for their safe return. Stolen credit card numbers are often exchanged or sold through hacker chat rooms.

Money is another resource that can be stolen via a computer. Insiders sometimes steal money by altering company programs to transfer small amounts of money—for example, a few cents' worth of bank account interest—from a very large number of transactions to an account controlled by the thief. This type of crime is sometimes called *salami shaving.* Salami-shaving victims generally are unaware of the crime because the amount taken from each individual is very small. Some stores have been accused of salami shaving by not diligently updating their pricing database to reflect sale prices. Another example of monetary theft using computers involves hackers transferring money illegally from online bank accounts, traditional bank accounts, or accounts at *online payment services* such as *PayPal* or *eBay Payments.*

### Online Auction Fraud

**Online auction fraud** (sometimes called *Internet auction fraud*)—where you pay for merchandise but it is never delivered or it is delivered but it is not as represented—is an increasing risk for online auction bidders. According to the Internet Fraud Complaint Center, online auction fraud accounted for nearly 64% of all reported Internet fraud in 2001 with the average loss for a typical complaint amounting to $395. Items up for bid at fraudulent auctions are most commonly small collectable stuffed animals (such as Beanie Babies), video consoles and games, computers, cameras, camcorders, and jewelry.

Like other types of fraud, online auction fraud is illegal, but these criminals are often difficult to stop, as well as to identify and prosecute. As is the case in many types of Internet cons, prosecution is more difficult because usually multiple jurisdictions are involved. In addition, many online auction fraud victims pay by personal check or money order and know very little about the seller's identity. Although most online auction sites have policies that suspend sellers with a certain number of complaints lodged against them, it is very easy for those sellers to come back using a new e-mail address and identity. One recent successful federal prosecution for online auction fraud was of a former Los Angeles Ram football player. He was sentenced to 2½ years in federal prison for collecting over $60,000 in eBay auctions during the years 1998 through 2000, but never delivering the merchandise.

### Internet Offer Scams

**Internet offer scams** cover a wide range of scams offered through Web sites or unsolicited e-mail messages. The anonymity of the Internet makes it very easy for con artists to appear to be almost anyone they want to be, including a charitable organization or a reputable-looking business. Common types of scams include work-at-home cons, pyramid and multilevel marketing schemes, bogus credit card offers, and fraudulent business opportunities and franchises. These offers typically try to sell potential victims nonexistent services or worthless information, or they try to convince potential victims to voluntarily supply their credit card details and other personal information, which are then used for fraudulent purposes.

One recent case involved con artists sending e-mails to individuals posing as their ISP, stating that their account information needed updating or their credit card had expired. The e-mails requested that the customers e-mail back the requested information as soon as possible to keep their accounts active. After sending back that data (such as a credit card number and current expiration date), the victims eventually found out that the supplied data was used for fraudulent charges. Other Internet scams include e-mails soliciting donations for charitable organizations that turn out to be nonexistent and pornographic sites that require a valid credit card, supposedly to prove you're 18 or older, but which is then used for credit card fraud.

Some of these cons can be very expensive. For example, an on-going Nigerian letter fraud scheme, which requests use of the potential victim's bank account to supposedly facilitate a wire transfer of a substantial amount of money and some up-front cash to pay for nonexistent fees, resulted in an average reported loss of $5,575 to its many victims in 2001.

## Software Piracy and Digital Counterfeiting

Instead of stealing an existing computer program, object, or other valuable that belongs to someone else, *software piracy* and *digital counterfeiting* involve creating duplicates of these items, and then selling them or using them as authentic items.

### Software Piracy

**Software piracy**, the unauthorized copying of a computer program, is illegal in the United States and many other—but not all—countries. Because of the ease with which computers can create exact copies of a software program, piracy is a widespread problem. In a recent report, the *Business Software Alliance (BSA)*—an organization formed by a number of the world's leading software developers that has anti-piracy programs in 65 countries worldwide—estimates that approximately 40% of all business application software globally (and about 25% of all business application software in the U.S.) is installed illegally. It estimates that the monetary loss due to software piracy worldwide during 2001 was nearly $11 billion.

Software piracy can take place in many forms, including individuals making an illegal copy of a program to give to a friend, businesses installing software on more computers than allowed for in the program's *end-user license agreement* (see Figure 4-7), loading unlicensed copies of software on PCs sold to consumers, and large-scale operations in which the software and its packaging are illegally duplicated and then sold as supposedly legitimate products. Pirated software is also commonly distributed via the Internet. One recent investigation indicates that more than 60% of software programs sold through Internet auction sites are pirated copies and more than 90% are sold in violation of the publisher's license agreement. Microsoft Corporation estimates that it alone has discovered and requested the removal of more than 117,000 online auctions and Internet sites offering illegal copies of Microsoft software worldwide during a recent two-year period.

**FIGURE 4-7**

**An end-user license agreement usually specifies how many PCs the software can be installed on, if it can be resold, etc.**

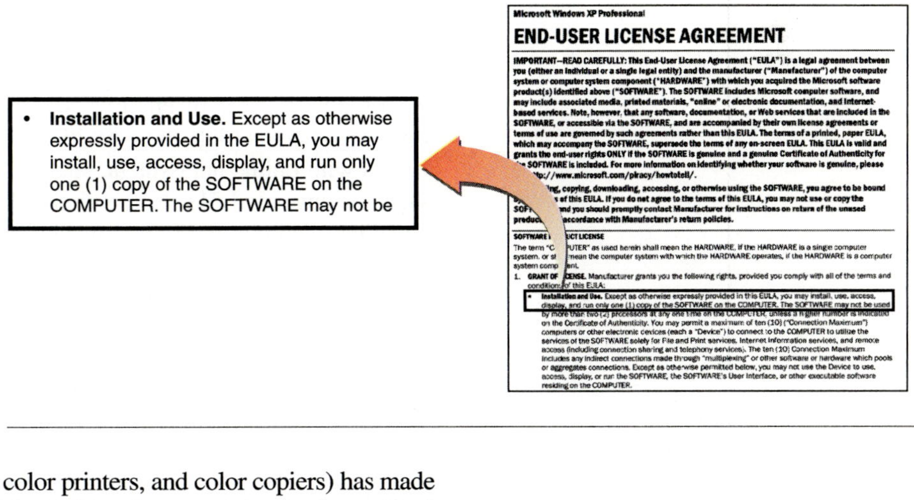


### Digital Counterfeiting

The increasing availability of high-quality full-color imaging products (such as scanners, color printers, and color copiers) has made **digital counterfeiting**—creating counterfeit copies of currency and other printed resources using computers and other types of digital equipment—more prevalent. According to the U.S. Secret Service, many of today's counterfeiters have moved from the traditional method of offset printing to digital counterfeiting. They estimate that 47% of the counterfeit money made in 2000 was digitally produced—up from 0.005% in 1995.

With digital counterfeiting, the bill (or other item to be counterfeited) is either scanned into a computer and then printed, or it is color-copied. In addition to counterfeiting currency, some criminals may choose to create fake business checks or printed collectibles, such as baseball cards, celebrity autographs, even T-shirts. For instance, it has been estimated that in the first three months following NASCAR racer Dale Earnhardt's death in 2001, over $20 million of counterfeit Earnhardt products and collectibles were sold. Other common counterfeiting activities include creating fake identification papers, such as corporate IDs, driver's licenses, passports, and visas (see Figure 4-8).

**FIGURE 4-8**

**Many of today's counterfeit documents are created with computers and other types of digital equipment.**

Counterfeiting is illegal in the U.S. and is taken very seriously. For example, for creating or knowingly circulating counterfeit currency, offenders can face up to 20 years in prison for each offense. Although the majority of counterfeit currency is produced by serious criminals—such as organized crime, gangs, and terrorist organizations—the Secret Service has seen a dramatic increase in counterfeiting among high school and college students. This is attributed primarily to the ease of creating counterfeit bills—though not necessarily high-quality counterfeit bills—with digital technology. Because the paper used with real U.S. currency is very expensive and cannot legally be made by paper mills and because bills contain a number of other characteristics that are difficult to reproduce accurately, the majority of the counterfeit money made by amateurs is easily detectable.

## Personal Safety Issues

Cybercrime can be expensive (as in the case of theft and online fraud) and a huge inconvenience (as in the case of identity theft); it can also be physically dangerous. Although most of us may not ordinarily view using the Internet as a potentially dangerous activity, cases of physical harm due to Internet activity do happen. For example, children and teenagers have become the victims of pedophiles who arranged face-to-face meetings by using information gathered via e-mail, discussion groups, or chat rooms. Adults have fallen for unscrupulous or dangerous individuals who misrepresented themselves online; they have also been victims of *cyberstalking*. In addition, the availability of personal information online has made it more difficult for individuals to hide from people who may want to do them harm, such as abused women trying to hide from their abusive husbands.

### Cyberstalking

**Cyberstalking** can be defined as repeated threats or harassing behavior conducted via e-mail or another Internet communications method. Cyberstalkers often find their victims—typically women—in chat rooms and begin to harass them; there have also been reported cases of employers being stalked online by ex-employees who were fired or otherwise left their position under adverse conditions. Cyberstalking often begins with online harassment, such as sending harassing or threatening e-mail messages or unwanted files to the victim, posting inappropriate messages in chat rooms about the victim or as the victim, signing the victim up for offensive or pornographic e-mail newsletters, or publicizing the victim's home address and telephone number. Although there is no one exact definition of cyberstalking, the generally accepted standard covers any harassing online activity in which a reasonable person would experience fear, or some sense of dread or threat. There are as yet no specific federal laws against cyberstalking, but most states have made it illegal and some federal laws do apply if the online actions include computer fraud, crime, or a threat to personal injury.

It has been estimated that approximately 200,000 people stalk someone online each year. Most cyberstalkers are not caught, however, due in part to the anonymity of the Internet, which assists cyberstalkers in concealing their true identities. Cyberstalking can lead to offline stalking and possibly physical harm—in at least one case, it led to the death of the victim.

### Online Pornography

There is a variety of controversial and potentially objectionable material on the Internet. One of concern to many parents is the huge amount of pornography available online. Although there have been attempts to ban this type of material from the Internet—for example, the *Communications Decency Act* signed into law in 1996 made it a criminal offense to distribute patently indecent or offensive material online—they have not been successful (the Communications Decency Act was ruled unconstitutional in 1997 by the U.S. Supreme Court). However, like its printed counterpart, online pornography involving minors is illegal. Because of the strong link they believe exists between child pornography and child molestation, many experts are very concerned about the amount of child pornography that can be found and distributed via the Internet. They also believe that the Internet makes it easier for pedophiles and other predators to act out, such as by striking up "friendships" with children in chat rooms and convincing them to meet them in real life. And this can have devastating consequences, such as for a 13-year-old girl from Danbury, Connecticut who was strangled to death in 2002—a 25-year-old man she met in an online chat room allegedly confessed to the crime and was awaiting sentencing at the time of this writing.

One legal gray area that exists at the moment is *virtual child pornography*, where computer-generated photos are used to make it appear that children are involved in pornographic acts (either innocent photos of children altered to be placed in different surroundings or on different bodies, or photos of adults manipulated to make them look like children). The *Child Pornography Prevention Act of 1996* made virtual pornography illegal, but was overturned in 2002 by the U.S. Supreme Court on the basis that it was written too broadly. Although several child protection laws pertaining to areas such as online predators and virtual pornography are in the works, no legislation had been signed into law at the time of this writing.

# SECURITY SAFEGUARDS

The first part of this chapter took a look at the various forms computer crime and other potential security problems related to computer use can take. This next part focuses on how computer users can protect themselves against theft, security breaches, sabotage, and other computer security concerns.

## Protection against Hardware Theft, Damage, and Failure

To protect against hardware theft, damage, and failure, there are a number of precautions that can be taken. Locks can be used to prevent theft, proper care of hardware can prevent some types of damage, and *backups* and disaster preparedness can help recover from a major system failure.

### Door and Computer Equipment Locks

Simple theft deterrences, such as locked doors and equipment, can go a long way in preventing computer theft. For instance, until it became commonplace to secure PCs to desks or tables, many educational institutions found their equipment walking out the door at an astounding rate. Today, cable locks (see Figure 4-9) are typically used to secure desktop PCs and other semi-permanent equipment in most schools and in many other organizations. Cable locks can also be used to secure a portable PC to a table or other object whenever that is feasible. While on the go, the best anti theft measure is common sense; for example, portable PCs should never be left unattended in public locations, such as restaurants and airports.

FIGURE 4-9

Securing PCs with cable locks

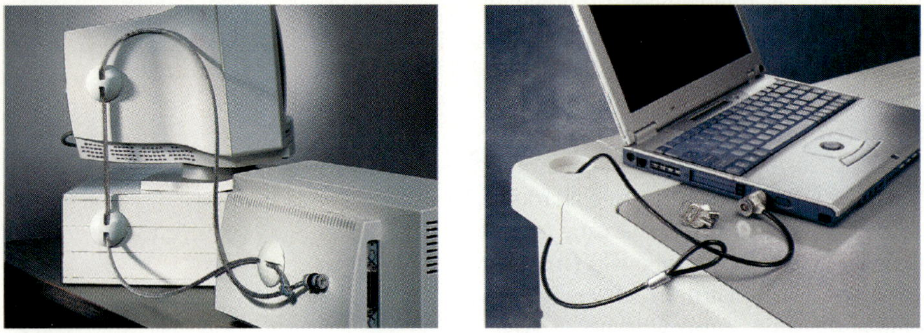

^ Desktop PC

^ Notebook PC

Doors to facilities and storage cabinets should also be locked whenever possible to deter theft. In addition to computers, extraneous components of a computer system—such as removable hard drives, high-capacity disks, toner cartridges, and other expensive supplies and components—should be secured. To safeguard against theft by employees, only a limited number of employees should have access to the keys used to secure computers and storage cabinets.

### Proper Hardware Care

Proper care of hardware can help to avoid serious damage to a computer system, including the data that is stored on it. Safeguards include protecting against power surges, damaged storage media, dust, heat, and static.

A **surge suppressor** connects all of the powered components in your computer system (system unit, monitor, powered speakers, printer, etc.) to a standard electrical outlet. It is similar to a regular power strip, but it has protection against electrical fluctuations built in to prevent them from harming your system. A typical consumer surge suppressor is shown in Figure 4-10; there are also industrial models, some of which can even protect against the huge surges caused by a direct lightning hit on a power line.

FIGURE 4-10

A surge suppressor

For users who cannot afford to have the power to their systems go out without warning, *uninterruptible power supply (UPS)* units are available. A UPS is a device containing a built-in battery that switches on automatically when the power goes off in order to prevent the computer from shutting down. UPSs designed for use by individuals usually provide power for a few minutes before the batteries need to be recharged; this should be enough time for the user to save all open documents and shut down the computer system properly. Most industrial-level UPSs can run for a significantly longer amount of time; some are continuous systems, in which the computer always runs off of battery power (even when the electricity is on) to provide a more stable source of power (usually the battery is continuously being recharged when the power is on). Many UPS devices have surge suppression built in—if not, a separate surge suppressor should be used.

Floppy disks, hard disks, CDs, and DVDs are all extremely sensitive storage media that work well over time with appropriate care. Floppy disks should be kept out of extremely hot or cold temperatures—they can melt in the sun or freeze in extremely cold conditions just like any other plastic object. CDs and DVDs should be kept in their protective jewel cases and handled carefully to prevent fingerprints and scratches on the data sides of the disc (usually the bottom, unprinted side on a one-sided disc). Hard drives, which are located inside the system unit, need to be protected against jostling or other excess motion that can result in a *head crash*, where a hard drive's read/write head actually touches the surface of a hard disk. To protect against head crashes, which can cause a great deal of damage, system units should be kept in a location they won't be tripped over or bumped into when the computer is turned on.

Dust, heat, and static can also be dangerous to a PC. Don't place your PC equipment in direct sunlight or in a dusty area. Small handheld vacuums made for electrical equipment can be used periodically to remove the dust from the keyboard and from inside the system unit. Also, be sure the system unit has plenty of ventilation, especially around the fan outlet. To prevent static electricity from damaging the inside of your PC when installing a new expansion board or other internal device, turn off the surge suppressor and unplug the power cord from the PC before removing the cover from the system unit, and then discharge static electricity from your fingertips by touching the outside of the power supply module inside the system unit before touching any other components. An antistatic wristband can be used as an extra precaution while working inside a PC; antistatic mats are available to place under desk chairs for an additional safeguard when using a PC where static electricity is a problem.

### Backups and Disaster Preparedness

Virtually every computer veteran will warn you that, sooner or later, you will lose some critical files. Maybe a storm will knock down power lines, causing your electricity to go out and shutting off your PC—erasing the document that you haven't saved yet. Perhaps your PC will stop working in the middle of finishing that term paper that's due tomorrow. Or, more likely, you'll accidentally delete or overwrite an important file or the file just won't open properly anymore. And don't forget major disasters—a fire or flood can completely destroy your PC and everything that is stored on it.

Creating a **backup** means making a duplicate copy of important files so that when a problem occurs, you can restore those files using the backup copy. Theoretically, you can back up any file on your computer system, but generally users are most concerned about backing up data files. Depending on their size, backup data can be placed on a floppy disk, recordable or rewritable CD disc, second hard drive, or virtually any other storage medium. Good backup procedures can help protect against data loss.

**ONLINE TUTORIAL**

For an online look at how to back up your PC, go to www.course.com/morley2003/ch4

It is essential for all businesses to have backup procedures in place to back up either all data files or all data files that have changed since the last backup. Backups should occur on a frequent, regular basis—such as every night—and a rotating collection of backup media should be used so it is possible to go back to a previous day's backup, if needed. Individuals, however, tend to back up in a less formal manner. Personal backups can be as simple as copying an important document to a floppy disk or e-mailing that document to a second PC you have access to, or as comprehensive as backing up the entire contents of your PC. You can perform backups by manually copying files using your file management program, but there are programs that make the backup process easier (see Figure 4-11). These programs can typically back up the files you specify on demand or be set up to back up specified files on a regular basis (such as every Friday night). Many backup programs can also create a backup of your entire PC once all programs have been installed and the system is configured correctly. You can use this backup to restore your system to that configuration quickly if something goes wrong with your PC at a later time, which saves you the time and bother of having to reinstall your operating system and all your programs and settings manually. Once your entire system has been backed up, you can just back up data from that point on, unless you make enough major changes to your system to warrant a new full system backup. To protect against fires and other physical disasters, backup media should be stored in a different physical location than your PC or inside a fire-resistant safe.

**FIGURE 4-11**

**Backing up a hard drive**

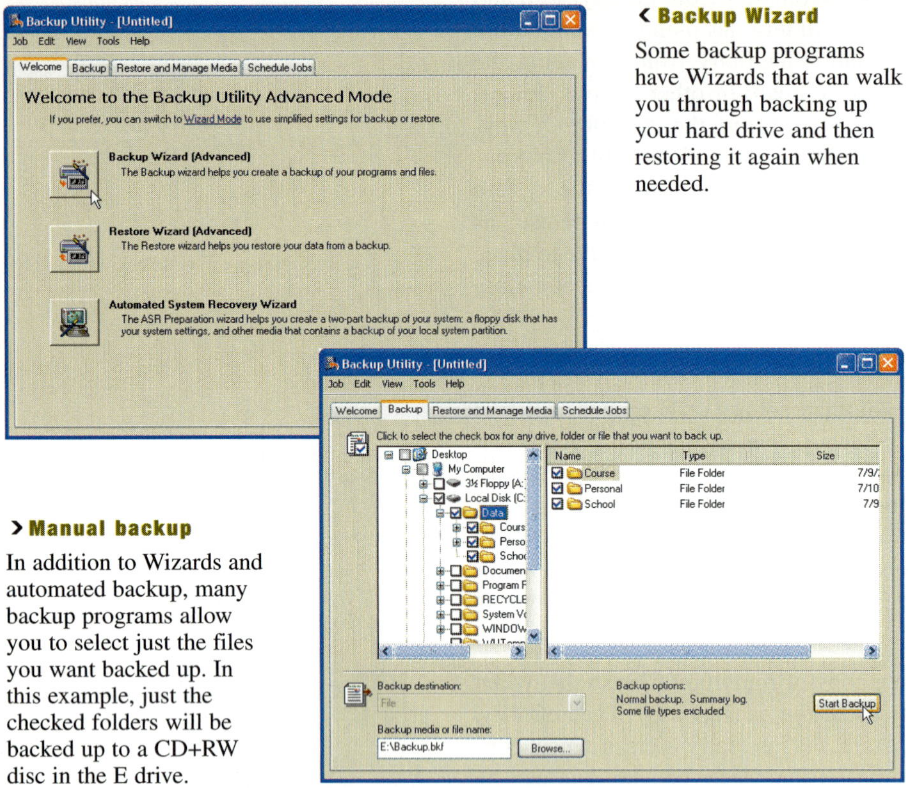


**< Backup Wizard**

Some backup programs have Wizards that can walk you through backing up your hard drive and then restoring it again when needed.

**> Manual backup**

In addition to Wizards and automated backup, many backup programs allow you to select just the files you want backed up. In this example, just the checked folders will be backed up to a CD+RW disc in the E drive.

For a quick backup before editing a document, you can use the *Save As* option of the program's File menu to make a duplicate copy of the file onto your hard drive. Although this backup won't be any help in case of fire or system failure, it can be used to restore the original file if you make a major mistake while editing the document or for some other reason would prefer to start again with the original document. When editing a document, it is a good idea to save it to your hard drive every few minutes, in case of a power failure or a problem with the program you are using that causes that program to close. Most Windows programs allow you to use the quick Ctrl+S keyboard shortcut to save a document under its current name. Performed using the left hand, users can save documents in just a split second with that key combination. Many application programs also have an *auto backup* option that can save the current version of an open document at regular intervals, so that the last saved version can be retrieved following a power failure or if the program shuts down unexpectedly. While the auto backup feature is helpful, experts say you shouldn't rely on this feature but instead, you should save your documents deliberately on a regular basis as you are modifying them.

To supplement backup procedures, organizations should have a **disaster-recovery plan**—a plan that spells out what an organization will do to prepare for and recover from a disruptive event. Disaster-recovery plans should include such information as who will be in charge immediately after the disaster has occurred, what alternate facilities and equipment can be used, when data should have been backed up last and where the backup medium is located, the priority of getting each operation back online, disaster insurance coverage information, and so forth. Copies of a disaster-recovery plan should be located off site, such as at an appropriate employee's home and at the office of an associated organization located in a different city.

Disaster-recovery plans are sometimes made for specific anticipated potential problems—such as the preparations many businesses and individuals made in anticipation of possible computer difficulties stemming from the *Y2K (Year 2000)* event. Other plans are generic for use with any type of major disaster. The importance of a good disaster-recovery plan was made obvious following the collapse of the World Trade Center towers in 2001. Minutes following the first airplane hitting the towers, corporate executives, disaster-recovery firms, and backup storage companies began arranging for employees and backup data to be moved to prearranged temporary offices. As a result, many businesses—such as bond-trader Cantor Fitzgerald who lost 700 employees and all the equipment and data located in its WTC offices—were operational within two days of the attacks, despite the complete destruction of their facilities.

To accomplish this, like many large organizations Cantor's disaster-recovery plan included a *hot site*—a designated alternative facility that can be used to house a business' operations any time the primary facility becomes unusable. Hot sites are equipped with the computers, cabling, desks, and other equipment necessary to keep the business' operations going. Like many businesses located in the WTC, Cantor's backup data was housed by a data recovery company called Recall Corporation. Recall employees spent the day of the attack gathering backup tapes belonging to clients located in and near the attacks, using bar-code scanners to locate the needed 30,000 tapes out of the 2 million in their secure storage facility. Cantor received their tapes the day after the attack and was able to begin trading the next morning. Although Cantor—like the other organizations located in the WTC—suffered enormous human loss, good disaster-recovery planning enabled Cantor to restore the records containing client accounts and portfolios completely, helping to avoid other potential fallout from this disaster.

## Protection against Unauthorized Access and Use

A number of security risks can be reduced or eliminated by carefully controlling access to an organization's facilities and computer system. To prevent unauthorized access of these resources, an *identification* procedure can be used to verify that the person trying to access the facility or system is listed as an authorized user. An *authentication* system can be used to determine whether or not the person attempting access is actually who he or she claims to be. Some of the strongest access control systems include both identification and authentication procedures. *Firewalls* and other types of access prevention software can also protect against hackers and other unwanted intruders.

**ONLINE TUTORIAL**

For an online look at how various types of identification and authentication systems work, go to www.course.com/morley2003/ch4

### Possessed Knowledge Systems

A **possessed knowledge** system is an identification system that requires the individual requesting access to provide information only the authorized user is supposed to know. *Passwords*, user names, and *PIN numbers* fall into this category.

**Passwords**, the most commonly used type of possessed knowledge, are secret words or character combinations associated with an individual. They can be used to restrict access to a facility or, more commonly, to a network or other computing resource. For example, one password might be required for anyone requesting access to a corporate or school computer system, and then a different password may be required to access any drives, folders, or documents on that network containing sensitive or confidential information.

When using passwords, it is important to select good ones and to change them frequently. One of the biggest disadvantages of password-only systems is that passwords can be forgotten; they can also be guessed or deciphered by a hacker's PC easily if good password selection strategies are not applied. For example, it was discovered that the Deceptive Duo hackers were able to access the databases from which they retrieved information because the system administrator passwords for those databases had never been changed from the programs' default passwords. As illustrated by this example, any individual possessing an authorized password will be granted access to the system because the system recognizes the password, regardless of whether or not the person using the password is the authorized user. Some strategies for selecting good passwords are listed in Figure 4-12.

Two other types of possessed knowledge—user names and *PIN (personal identification) numbers*—are typically not used by themselves, but are instead combined with a password or other type of access control method, such as a *possessed object* or *biometric* characteristic, to add another level of security.

**FIGURE 4-12**

Strategies for creating good passwords

| PASSWORD STRATEGIES |
|---|
| ▪ Make the password at least 8 characters, if allowed by the application. A four- or five-character password can be cracked by a computer program in less than a minute. A 10-character password, in contrast, has about 3,700 trillion possible character permutations and could take a regular computer decades to crack. |
| ▪ Choose an unusual sequence of characters to create a password that will not be in a dictionary—for instance, mix in numbers and special characters with abbreviations or unusual words you will remember. The password should be one that you can remember, yet one that doesn't conform to a pattern a computer can readily figure out. |
| ▪ Keep a written copy of the password in a place where no one but you can find it. Many people place passwords on Post-it notes that are affixed to their monitors or taped to their desks—a practice that's almost as bad as having no password at all. |
| ▪ Don't use your name, your kids' or pets' names, your address, your birthdate, or other public information as your password. |
| ▪ For Web site accounts that remember your settings or profile, such as online news, auction, shopping, or bookstore sites, use a different password than for your highly sensitive activities such as online banking or stock trading; passwords used on non-sensitive Web sites are usually more easily obtained by criminals than those on high-security sites. |
| ▪ Change your passwords frequently. |

**FIGURE 4-13**

Possessed objects, such as the magnetic card being used here, prevent against unauthorized access.

## Possessed Object Systems

**Possessed objects** are physical objects that are used for identification purposes. Common possessed objects used to access a facility or computer system are smart cards, encoded badges, and magnetic cards that are similar to credit cards (see Figure 4-13). One disadvantage of using possessed objects to restrict access to facilities or systems is that the object can be lost or, similar to passwords, used by an unauthorized individual. These disadvantages can be overcome by using a password or biometric characteristic in conjunction with the possessed object.

For a look at the growing use of smart cards on college campuses to identify students, grant access to facilities, and more, see the Trends In box.

## Biometric Systems

**Biometrics** is the study of identifying individuals based on measurable biological characteristics. **Biometric devices** are used to identify users by a particular unique physiological characteristic (such as their fingerprint, hand, face, or iris), or personal trait (such as their voice or signature). Since the means of access (usually a part of the body) cannot be lost or forgotten and because it cannot be used by anyone other than the authorized individual, biometric access systems can perform both identification and authentication. For a look at how biometric devices are being used to identify terrorists and other criminals in public locations, see the Closer Look box.

To grant access using biometric data, devices (such as *fingerprint readers*, *hand geometry readers*, *face readers*, and *iris scanners*) are typically used in conjunction with software and a database to match a person's identity with his or her biometric characteristic previously stored in the database. In general, biometric systems are very accurate since even identical twins (who have the same DNA structure) have different fingerprints and irises. According to IrisScan, a leading iris-recognition company, the odds of two different irises being declared a match is 1 in $10^{78}$. Systems based on physiological characteristics (traits that rarely change, such as a person's face, iris, hand geometry, or fingerprint) tend to be more accurate than those based on a personal trait (which may change, such as an individual's voice being affected by a cold or a written signature being affected by a broken wrist).

## TRENDS IN... SMART CARDS ON CAMPUS

At Pennsylvania State University, the traditional school ID card has become much more than just an ID card. With its magnetic stripe now augmented with smart card technology (see Figure 4-14), the *Penn State id+ card* can be used for banking, long distance phone services, public transportation, and library services; in designated laundry, vending, and copy machines; and at a variety of retail stores and restaurants located both on and off campus. To facilitate purchases, the Penn State smart card chip can hold a digital cash value. When the cash value stored in the card is used up, the card can be reloaded at a card value center using cash or a credit card. The card can also be used to identify students for exams and meal service, and to provide access to secure areas, such as labs and residence halls.

Smart card ID systems like this are not unique to Penn State. In fact, the Smart Card Alliance estimates that close to one million smart cards are being used on college campuses today. The convenience of smart ID cards is a good fit with college students, who need to carry their ID around anyway. Now using their smart ID cards, students can buy lunch or a soda, or make copies, without having to worry about how much cash they have on hand.

The storage capability of the chip on the typical smart card—up to 500 times more than traditional magnetic stripe cards and growing all the time—opens up many opportunities for new applications for smart college ID cards. Possibilities include using the card to access school records, check test scores, register for classes, store medical information, make travel arrangements, encrypt and sign digital files, and even shop online. Using any computer with Internet access and a smart card reader, students could use their smart cards to access their school information from anywhere in the world, as well as sign in for distance learning exams and other online activities.

The biggest drawback of college smart cards is they can be lost. In addition to losing their means of identification (a big problem, since all students and faculty need to use their cards on a daily basis), losing a preloaded card is the same as losing cash, since schools don't refund the cash value remaining on a lost card. However, colleges report that card loss is generally fairly low, mainly because students tend to keep good track of them.

**FIGURE 4-14**

**The Penn State University id+ smart card can be used for a wide variety of on and off campus activities.**

**Smart card circuitry**

Biometric identification systems offer a great deal of convenience, because they require little effort on the part of the user. Consequently, biometric systems are increasingly being used to replace possessed objects and passwords for granting access to secure facilities (such as corporate headquarters, university residence halls, and prisons), logging onto computer systems and secure Web sites, punching employees in and out of work, and confirming consumers' identities at ATM machines and check-cashing services. Some examples of the most commonly used types of biometric systems are shown in Figure 4-15; their primary advantages and disadvantages are listed in Figure 4-16.

**FIGURE 4-15**

Types of biometric devices

**^ Fingerprint reader**

Typically used to protect access to office PCs, to log on or replace Web site passwords on home PCs, to pay for products or services, and to access resources (Welfare benefits, transportation tickets and passes, etc.).

**^ Hand geometry reader**

Typically used to control access to facilities (government offices, prisons, military facilities, etc.) and to punch in and out of work.

**^ Face reader**

Typically used to control access to highly secure areas, as well as to locate terrorists and criminals in public locations.

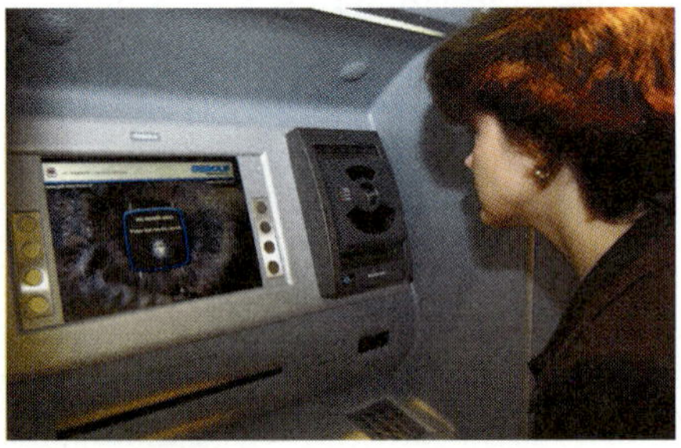

**^ Iris scanner**

Typically used to control access to highly secure areas, such as nuclear facilities and prisons; beginning to be used to authenticate users of ATMs and other banking facilities.

### Firewalls and Other Crime-Prevention Software

A **firewall** is a security system that acts as a protective boundary between a computer or network and the outside world. *Personal firewalls* are typically software-based systems that are geared towards protecting home PCs from hackers attempting to access those computers through their Internet connections. Hackers who gain access to these PCs can access the information on them (such as passwords stored on the hard drive), as well as use those computers in denial of service attacks and other illegal activities. Consequently, all PCs with direct Internet connections (such as DSL, cable, fixed wireless, or satellite) should use a firewall (PCs using dial-up Internet access are relatively safe from intrusion). Firewalls designed to protect business networks may be software-based, hardware-based, or a combination of the two. They can typically be used both to prevent network access from hackers and other outsiders, and to control employee Internet access.

**FIGURE 4-16**

Advantages and disadvantages of various biometric technology

| Biometric Characteristic | Advantages | Disadvantages |
|---|---|---|
| **Fingerprint** | Easy to use; inexpensive | Sometimes harder to read on older individuals; usually requires contact with scanner; negative social image |
| **Hand** | Easy to use | Usually requires contact with scanner; fairly expensive |
| **Face** | Requires no direct contact with user; can be used without the person's cooperation | Lighting, disguised appearance, and other factors may affect results |
| **Iris** | Requires no direct contact with user; easy to use | Mirrored sunglasses and light conditions may affect results; expensive |

## A CLOSER LOOK AT... BIOMETRICS AND CRIME PREVENTION

A variety of biometric techniques exist to identify individuals. While most of the time these techniques are used to locate an individual in a database of authorized users or to confirm that a person matches a supplied name or ID card, they can also be used to locate terrorists and other criminals in public locations.

Because it requires no contact with the reading device and can be performed from a distance, face recognition is a logical choice for these types of systems, which are increasingly being used by the government and law enforcement agencies. To locate known criminals and terrorists, cameras installed in public locations—such as airports, parks, and sporting events—take photos and try to match those photos with the individuals in crime photo databases. These systems can be effective at reducing crime; for instance, since a face recognition system using 300 cameras in outdoor locations was installed in Newham, England, crime in that area of the city has dropped 40 percent (see Figure 4-17).

One of the first public incidents of this technique was during the Super Bowl XXXV in Tampa Bay, Florida in 2001. Dubbed the "Snooper Bowl" by critics, law enforcement agents used cameras to snap photos of the 100,000 or so fans as they stepped through the turnstiles. The photos were then compared to known criminals, terrorists, and con artists located in databases of the Tampa Police Department, the FBI, and other state and local law enforcement agencies. Although the surveillance system only picked out 19 people (all petty criminals) from the database, the system pushed face recognition—and its corresponding privacy issues—into the public spotlight.

Other recent face recognition crime-prevention applications include guarding access to the vault holding the Olympic medals at the 2002 Winter Olympic games and looking for known terrorists in the New York harbor loading area for the ferry to Ellis Island and the Statue of Liberty.

Following the 9/11 terrorist attacks, attention turned to the potential use of face recognition technology at airports and border crossings both to prevent known terrorists from entering the country and to assist in apprehending them. These systems compare live video frames of individuals proceeding through security checkpoints to photos of known terrorists and other serious criminals located in Department of Justice and FBI databases. A positive match, which can usually occur in less than one second, sets off an alarm or otherwise notifies the proper authorities that a match has been made.

Law enforcement agencies contend that face recognition systems are no different than the many video surveillance systems in place today in a wide variety of public locations. They view it as just one more tool to be used to protect the public, similar to scanning luggage at the airport. Privacy advocates fear being under perpetual police surveillance and the eventual expansion of these security surveillance systems, such as using them to look for "deadbeat Dads" or other applications not vital for national security. How accepting the public will be about being in a digital lineup at the grocery store and while pumping gas remains to be seen, but a recent study by Saflink Corporation found that over 80% of Americans supported the use of biometric devices to enhance airline security and approximately 60% were accepting of their use at public events.

**FIGURE 4-17**

**Control room for Newham, England face recognition system**

Firewalls work by closing down all external *communication port addresses*—the electronic connections that allow a PC to communicate with other computers—to unauthorized computers and programs for both incoming and outgoing activities. While business firewalls are set up by the network administrator and those settings cannot typically be changed by end users, personal firewalls will usually notify the user when an application program on the PC wants Internet access or a computer on a home network tries to access a firewall-protected PC. At that point, the user may either grant or deny access. As shown in Figure 4-18, some personal firewall programs also let you view all of the access attempts that were blocked automatically by the firewall. In addition to protecting your PC from outside access, many firewall programs also protect

**FIGURE 4-18**

**A personal firewall program**

against inside attacks from Trojan horses and other malicious programs that may have slipped through your virus protection. If not blocked, these programs can open ports and send data from your PC to a hacker at the hacker's request.

In addition to firewalls, organizations may use other crime-prevention software, such as programs that record all attempts (both successful and unsuccessful) to access network resources by both outsiders and employees. This data is then analyzed to try to identify any potential problems, such as attempted network access by a hacker, attempted access by employees to resources that should not be available to them, or a possible DoS attack.

## Protection against Interception of Data and Communications

More and more confidential information is being transmitted over the Internet. As a result, it is extremely important to prevent sensitive information submitted on Web site forms or via e-mail from being intercepted and read by anyone other than the intended recipient. It is also becoming increasingly important to ensure that Web sites and individuals with whom you communicate via the Internet are who they actually claim to be, and that any information transmitted to or from them cannot be modified in transit. There are a variety of tools that can be used to secure information sent electronically, as well as to authenticate business partners, e-commerce sites, and other entities with whom sensitive transactions may take place.

### Secure Web Servers

To protect against interception of sensitive information sent via a Web page form (such as online shopping, banking, stock trading, or other financial transactions), only *secure Web pages* should be used. A secure Web page is located on a **secure Web server**, which is protected against unauthorized access and *encrypts* (scrambles) data going to and coming from the server. To indicate that a secure Web page is being viewed, most Web browsers display a locked padlock or a solid (unbroken) key on the status bar at the bottom of the browser window; many URLs will also begin with *https:* instead of *http:* when a secure server is being used (see Figure 4-19).

### E-Mail and File Encryption

Although it may not seem likely that the e-mail messages you send and receive might be intercepted and read by someone else, it is a possibility if they are not secured. To secure e-mail messages and other documents sent over the Internet, **encryption** techniques are used. An encrypted document is essentially scrambled and as such is unreadable until it is *decrypted*—or unscrambled—correctly. Both files and e-mail messages can be encrypted before they are sent over the Internet; individual files can also be encrypted before they are stored on a hard drive so they will be unreadable if opened by an unauthorized person. In addition, encryption can be used to protect the content of instant messages.

FIGURE 4-19

Sensitive information should only be submitted via secure Web pages.

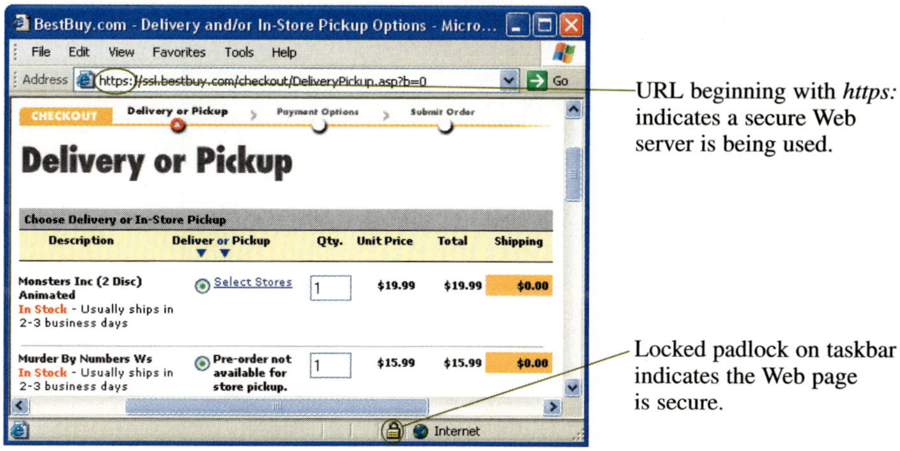


One of the most common types of encryption used today is **public key encryption**, which utilizes two encryption *keys*—very long numbers that are mathematically related—to encrypt and decrypt documents. Specifically, public key encryption uses a pair of keys that have been assigned to a particular individual; the *public key* is available for anyone to use, but the *private key* is used only by the individual to whom it was assigned (passwords are often required when using a private key to protect against unauthorized use). Documents or messages encrypted with a public key can only be decrypted with the matching private key, and documents encrypted with a private key can only be decrypted with the matching public key. To send someone an encrypted message, typically the sender uses the recipient's public key (which was obtained from the recipient) to encrypt the file and then when the message is received, the recipient uses his or her private key to decrypt the file (see Figure 4-20).

Encryption can be performed by third-party encryption programs, such as *Pretty Good Privacy (PGP)* or FileLock. Public/private key pairs are either generated by the encryption program being used or are obtained through a *Certificate Authority (CA),* such as VeriSign or Thawte. Keys obtained from a Certificate Authority need to be installed in your browser, e-mail program, and any third-party encryption program before they can be used, although often this is done automatically for you if your keys are downloaded from the Internet. Obtaining a business public/private key pair usually requires a fee, but free keys are available for personal use through some Certificate Authorities. Some encryption programs (such as PGP) are also available without charge for personal use.

To send an encrypted message to someone using public key encryption, you need to have access to his or her public key. If that person has previously sent you an encrypted document, his or her public key will likely have been stored by your e-mail program in your address book or by your encryption program in a special *key ring* feature used by that program. In either case, that public key would be available whenever you wanted to send that person an encrypted document. If you don't already have the appropriate public key for the individual to whom you wish to send an encrypted message, you will either need to request it from that person, look up the individual in a public key directory available through some Certificate Authorities, or send the document unencrypted.

To avoid the need to obtain the recipient's public key before sending that person an encrypted e-mail, *Web-based encryption* can be used. With this type of service, documents are uploaded via a secure Web server and encrypted, and the recipient is usually sent an e-mail notice that they have a secure e-mail waiting for them. Using a link in that e-mail notice, the recipient can then securely download and decrypt the document. Alternatively, some secure Web-based e-mail services require both the sender and recipient to have accounts through the service, and any new e-mail messages are decrypted and displayed whenever the recipient checks his or her e-mail through that service. Typically Web-based encryption service is available on a subscription basis, such as with a set monthly fee and/or a fee for the volume of e-mail sent each month. Using third-party and Web-based encryption is illustrated in the Chapter 5 How To box.

**FIGURE 4-20**

**Using public key encryption to secure an e-mail message**

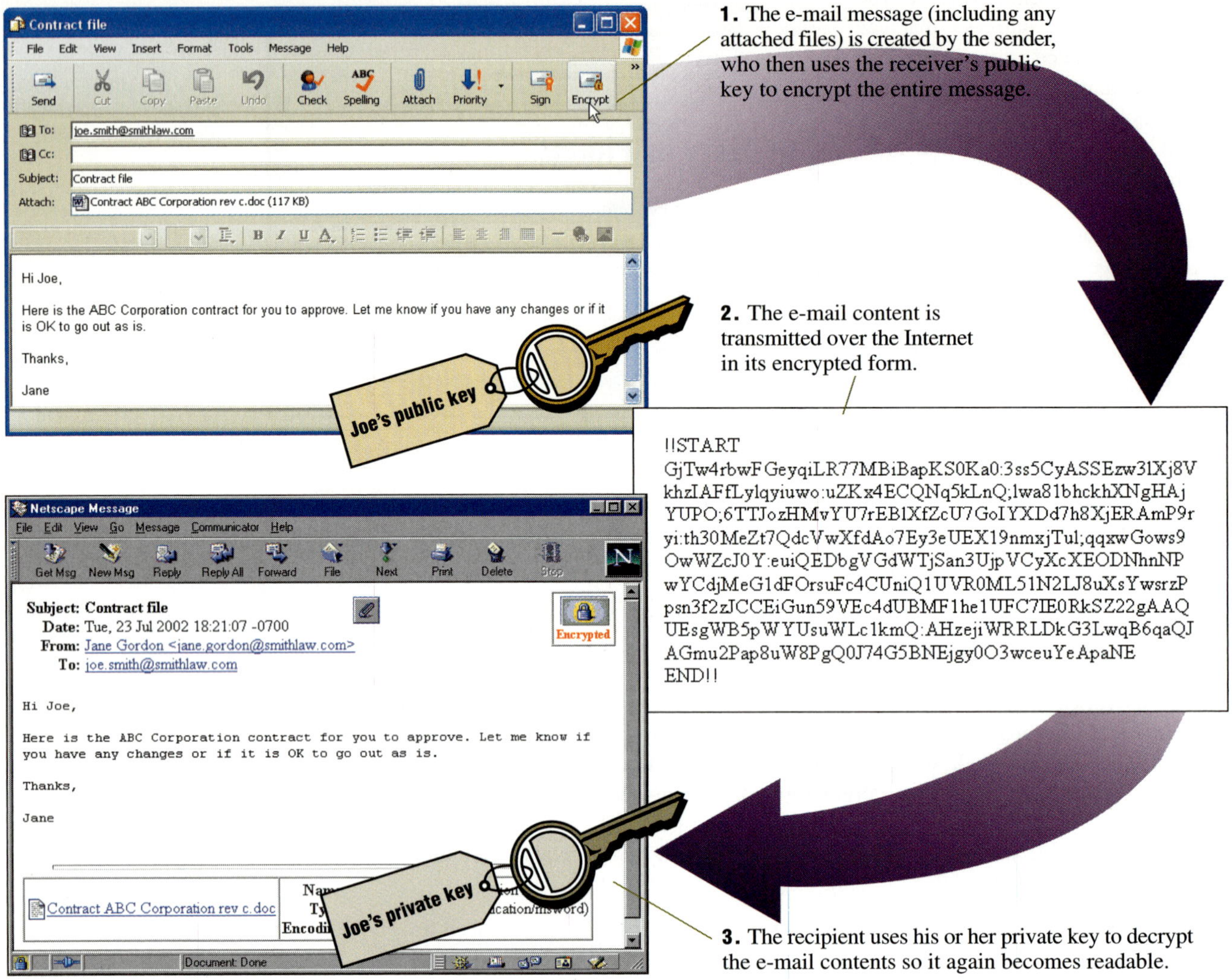


There are various strengths of encryption available; the stronger the encryption, the more difficult it is to crack. Earlier 40-bit encryption (which can only use keys that are 40 bits or 5 characters long) is considered to be weak encryption. Stronger encryption is available today, such as strong 128-bit encryption (which uses 16-character keys) and military-strength 2,048-bit encryption (which uses 256-character keys), although not without some objections from law enforcement agencies and the government, who state that terrorists routinely use encryption methods to communicate and appropriate agencies need access to those communications to protect our national security. Current commercial encryption programs are so strong that it can take government agencies days or even weeks to crack them and typically requires the use of a supercomputer. As might be expected, the encryption issue moved into the forefront after the 9/11 attacks. To avoid the situation where documents from criminals cannot be decrypted by these agencies in a timely manner, the government has long proposed a *key escrow system*, where independent third-party escrow companies would hold copies of all private keys to be used for law enforcement and national security purposes when authorized by a court order. Civil liberties groups, on the other hand, have vowed to fight a key escrow or similar system, calling it an invasion of personal privacy. At the present time, this issue is still being debated and no solution has been reached.

## Digital Signatures

While encryption is used to ensure that a document cannot be intercepted or altered during transmission, the purpose of a **digital signature**—sometimes called an *e-signature*—is to verify the identity of the sender of the document. Digital signatures typically use public key encryption, but the actual signature (a unique digital code that is created with the individual's private key and which is based on the user's identity and the content of the document being signed) is different with each signed document. Some encryption programs include the capability to digitally sign documents; third-party digital signature programs are also available. When a document with a digital signature is received, the recipient's computer uses the sender's public key and the digital signature code to verify that the document was signed with the matching private key and that the document contents were not modified since it was signed (see Figure 4-21). Some digital signature programs can display a scanned image of the sender's actual signature along with an indicator to show that the document was digitally signed; more commonly, the digital signature indicator appears as a statement at the bottom of the e-mail or a button that can be clicked to see the identity of the verified sender.

Digital signatures are used more often by businesses than individuals and are expected to become extremely important as contracts and other legal documents begin to be exchanged more frequently over the Internet. *The Federal Electronic Signatures in Global and National Commerce Act*, signed into law in 2000 with a digital signature, makes electronic signatures as legally binding as handwritten signatures for e-commerce transactions. Designed to facilitate consumer transactions, this law enables people and businesses to buy insurance, get a mortgage, open a brokerage account, or finalize other transactions that require signed authorization, without waiting for physical documents to be mailed back and forth.

**FIGURE 4-21**

**Using digital signatures**

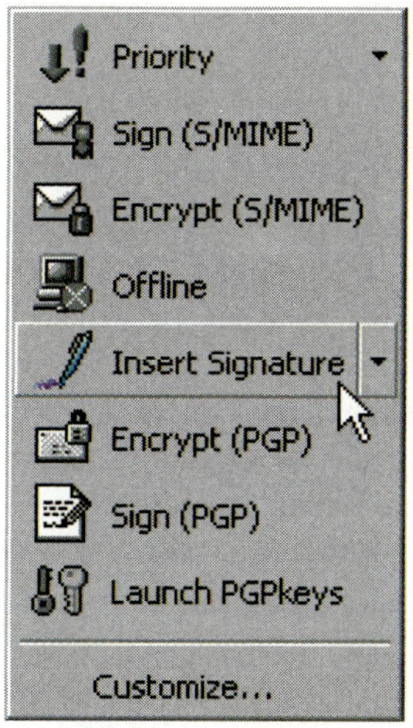


**‹ Signature command**

Many digital signature programs work in conjunction with your regular office suite and e-mail programs, so an option to sign the file or e-mail can be found on a menu.

**⌄ Signing a document**

To add your signature to a document or e-mail message, you may be asked to select the desired signature and then supply the appropriate password.

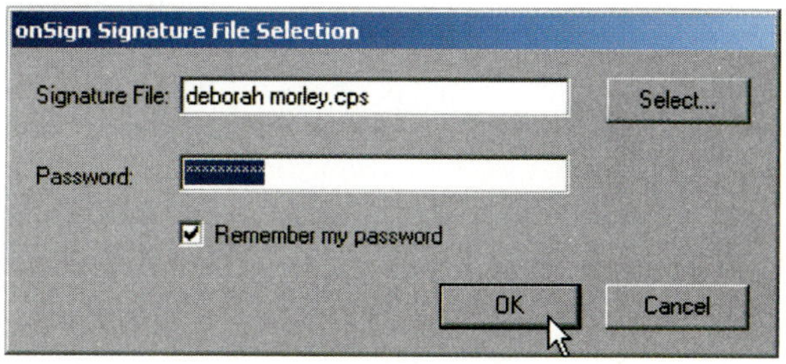


**› Validity indicators**

The file or e-mail message will either display a signature with a notice stating whether or not the signature is valid, or a message or button stating that the file is signed, which can be clicked to verify the signature.

A signature is marked invalid if the content of the file or e-mail was changed since it was signed.

## Digital Certificates

When a business or individual obtains a public/private key pair from a Certificate Authority, it is usually awarded as part of a **digital certificate.** A digital certificate (also called a *digital ID*) typically contains the name of the person, organization, or Web site being certified along with a certificate serial number, an expiration date, and a copy of the certificate holder's public key. The Certificate Authority guarantees that individuals or organizations granted digital certificates are, in fact, who they claim to be, usually only after verifying their identity with a financial institution.

**FIGURE 4-22**

**Viewing digital certificate information**

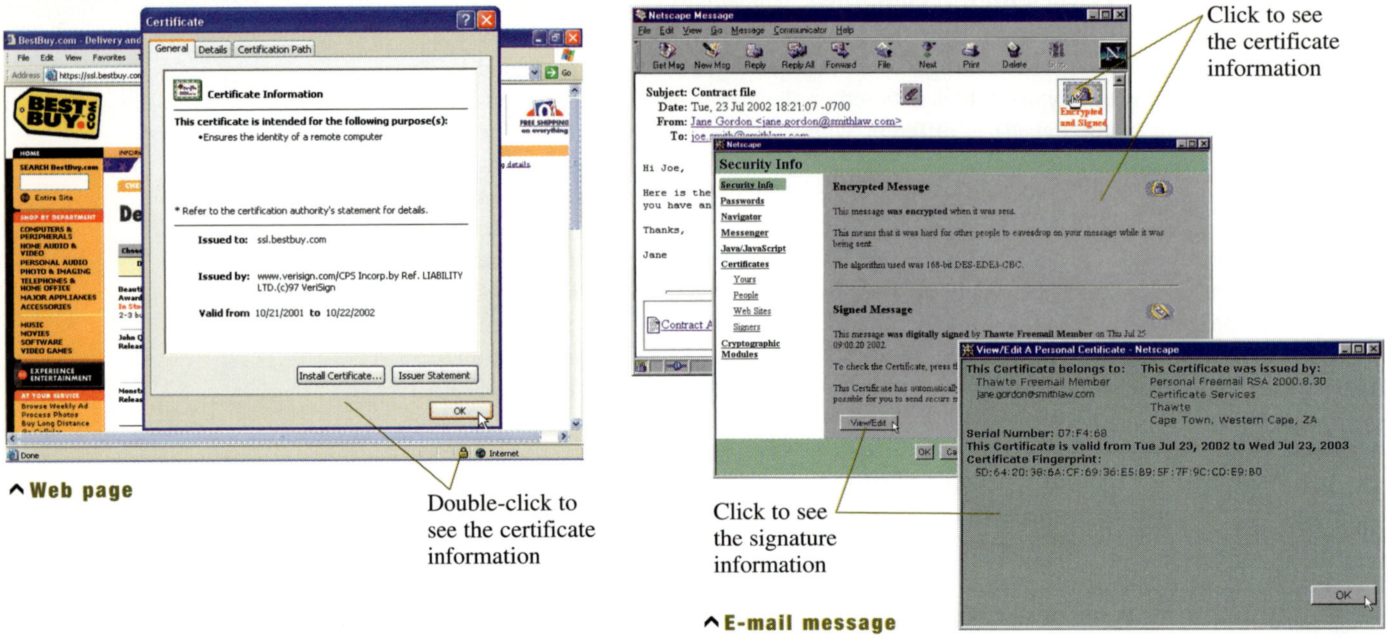


Digital certificates are used with secure Web sites to guarantee that the Web site is secure and actually belongs to the stated organization (so users can know for sure who their credit card number or other sensitive data is really being sent to). Certificates issued to businesses and individuals are typically installed in their browser, e-mail program, and any third-party encryption program so that information is available for use whenever a file or e-mail message needs to be digitally signed or encrypted. To see the certificate information for a secure Web page, click on the security indicator on your browser's taskbar; for a digitally signed or encrypted e-mail message, click the appropriate hyperlink located in the message (see Figure 4-22).

### Virtual Private Networks (VPNs)

While e-mail and file encryption can be used to transfer individual messages and files securely over the Internet, when a business needs a continuous secure channel a **virtual private network (VPN)** can be used. A VPN is a private network created over a public communications system, such as the Internet. VPNs use encryption and other security mechanisms to ensure that only authorized users can access the network and that the data cannot be intercepted. Since it uses a public infrastructure instead of an expensive private physical network, VPNs can provide a secure environment over a large geographical area at a manageable cost.

## Protection against Computer Viruses and Other Types of Sabotage

A good firewall system can go a long way towards protecting against some types of sabotage, such as data and program alteration and Trojan horses. Although denial of service attacks are virtually impossible to prevent completely, good firewall and network security protections can lessen the chance of being a target, as well as prevent an individual PC from being enlisted as a zombie PC in a DoS attack.

To protect against computer viruses and other types of malware, **antivirus software** should be installed on all PCs—both in homes and in offices—and it should be set up to run continuously whenever your computer is on. Antivirus software can protect against getting a virus in the first place, as well as detect and remove any viruses or worms that may find their way onto your PC (see Figure 4-23). If a known virus is found, the program can remove it and try to repair its damage. Most antivirus programs can be set up to scan files and e-mail messages automatically before they are downloaded or opened—this is an excellent precaution. If a virus is found in a file or e-mail message not yet opened, the program will inform you so you can either cancel the download or delete the file before it is opened.

Because new viruses are introduced all the time, virtually all antivirus programs have regular updates available through the software company's Web site. Many programs come with one year of free updates; additional years can be purchased after that.

**ONLINE RESOURCES**

For links to information about computer viruses and virus detection, go to www.course.com/morley2003/ch4

**FIGURE 4-23**

**Antivirus software**

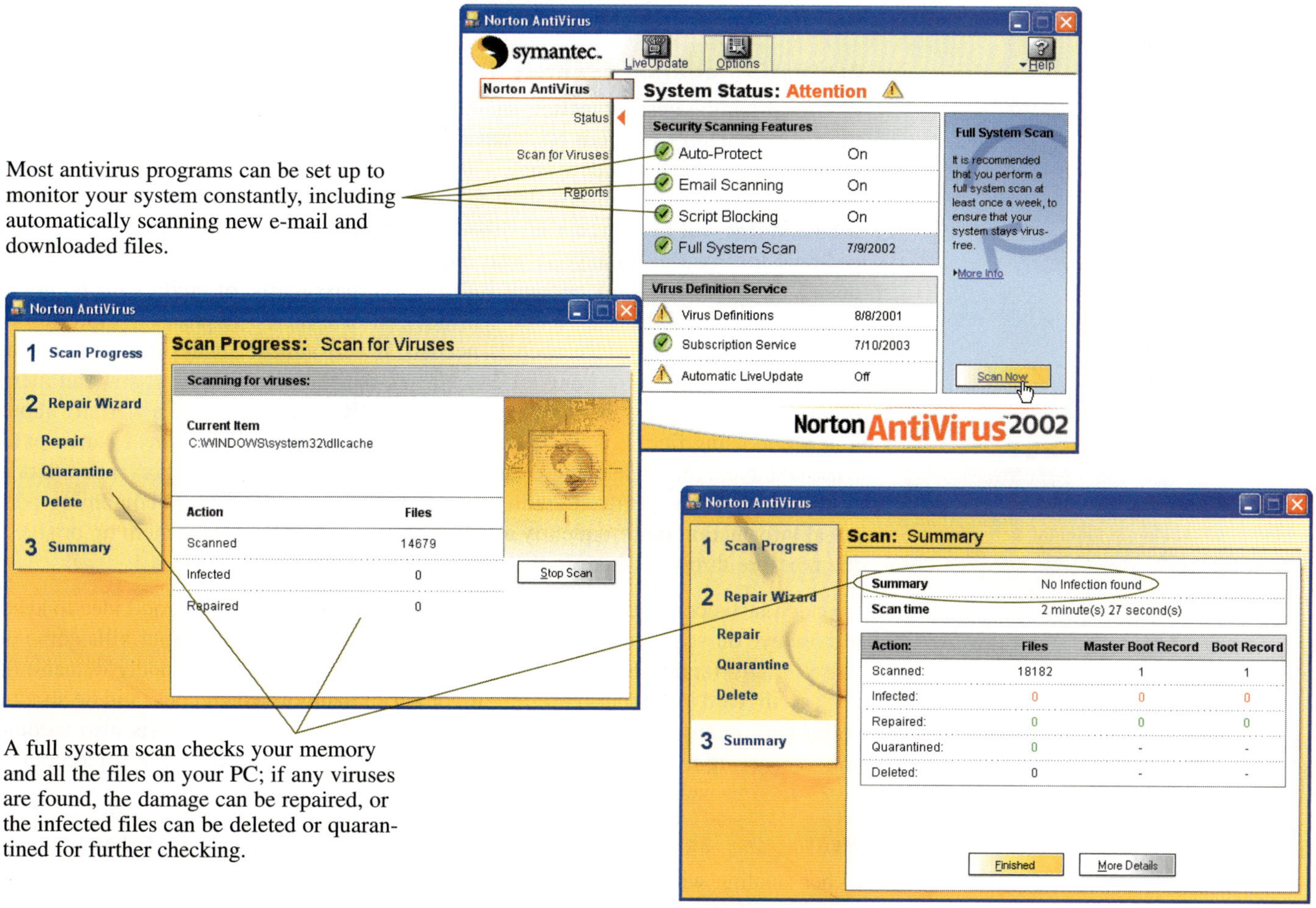


Most antivirus programs can be set up to monitor your system constantly, including automatically scanning new e-mail and downloaded files.

A full system scan checks your memory and all the files on your PC; if any viruses are found, the damage can be repaired, or the infected files can be deleted or quarantined for further checking.

In addition to using up-to-date antivirus software, additional virus-prevention techniques include the following:

- Limit sharing disks and other removable storage media with others.
- Only download programs from reputable Web sites.
- Only open e-mail attachments from people that you know and that don't have an executable file extension (such as .exe, .com, or .vbs). (If you think an executable file might be a legitimate attachment, double-check with the sender before opening it.)
- Regularly download and install the latest security patches available for your e-mail program to correct known security holes.

## Protection against Online Theft, Fraud, and Other Dot Cons

Businesses and consumers can both help to prevent some types of online theft—businesses by using good security measures to protect the data stored on their computers, and consumers by only sending sensitive information to secure servers. Various other techniques can help protect against identity theft, online auction fraud, and other types of dot cons.

### Protecting against Identity Theft

In a nutshell, the best protection against identity theft is to protect your identifying information. Don't give out personal information—especially your Social Security number or mother's maiden name—unless it is absolutely necessary and, before revealing any personal information to a new organization, find out how it will be used and if it will be shared with other organizations. Also, never give out sensitive personal information to anyone who requests it over the phone or by e-mail. Most businesses that need bank account information, passwords, or credit card numbers already have that information and will not call or e-mail a request for more information. If additional information is needed, it will almost always be requested in writing, but be sure to respond only to written requests for your bank and call them to question any request that seems peculiar. The IRS recently issued a warning about a new con using fictitious bank correspondence and phony IRS forms to attempt to trick taxpayers into disclosing their personal and banking data. To prevent someone from using the preapproved credit card offers and other documents containing personal information that frequently arrive in the mail, be sure to tear them up or shred them before throwing them in the trash.

**ONLINE RESOURCES**

For links to information about how to prevent identity theft and online auction fraud, as well as how to deal with it if it occurs, go to www.course.com/morley2003/ch4

To catch instances of credit card fraud or identity theft early, it is a good idea to keep a close eye on your credit card bills and credit history. Make sure your bills come in every month (some thieves will change your mailing address to delay detection), read credit card statements carefully to look for unauthorized charges, and be sure to follow up on any calls you get from creditors. Some security experts also recommend ordering a full credit history on yourself once a year to check for accounts listed in your name that you didn't open and any other problems.

### Protecting against Online Auction Fraud and Other Dot Cons

When dealing with other individuals online in auctions and other person-to-person activities, it makes sense to be cautious. Before bidding on an auction item, check out the seller's feedback rating to see comments written by other auction sellers and buyers (see Figure 4-24). Whenever possible, pay for auctions and other online purchases using a credit card so you can dispute the item, if needed. Auctions where the sellers accept payment using a payment service (such as PayPal or e-Bay Payments) can typically be paid for using a credit card. If you have any questions about an

## FIGURE 4-24

Smart online auction buying

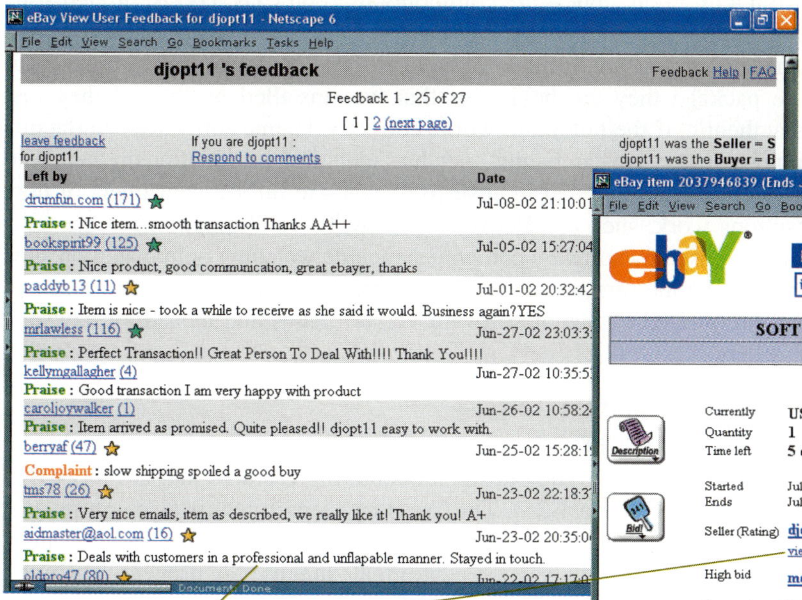


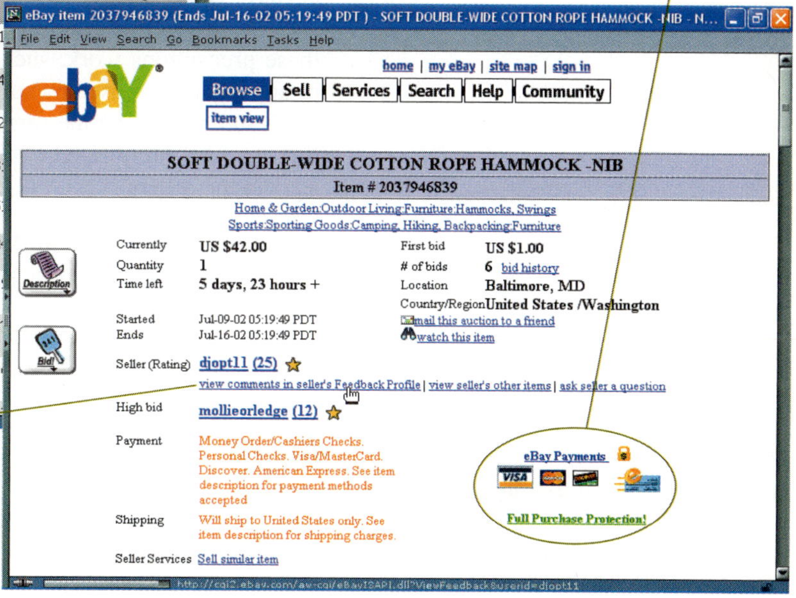


**Credit card payments**

Look for auctions that allow credit card payments so you can dispute the charge if the item doesn't arrive or isn't as specified.

**Seller feedback**

Before bidding on an item, check the seller's feedback to look for any problems with previous auctions.

auction—such as whether a DVD is a Region 1 disc manufactured for use in North America or an Asian import, or whether a painting or collectible comes with a certificate of authenticity—be sure to e-mail the seller before bidding on the item.

To avoid Internet offer scams, be very wary of investment or income opportunities that arrive unsolicited via e-mail. Similarly, be cautious of deals that seem to offer something for nothing. As the old adage goes, if it seems too good to be true, it probably is. If you do decide to try a "no obligation" free trial of a service, be sure to cancel within the prescribed period if you don't want the service to continue, and watch your credit card and telephone bills for any erroneous or fraudulent charges.

## Protection against Software Piracy and Digital Counterfeiting

Software piracy and digital counterfeiting affect more than just big businesses and the government. Because software pirates cost software developers a great deal of money, higher prices and less money available for research and development hurt law-abiding consumers. In addition, it has been estimated that piracy and counterfeiting has cost hundreds of thousands of American jobs, due to a flooded market and the resulting reduced demand for legitimate products.

### Education, Holograms, and Other Anti-Piracy Tools

One noteworthy tool the software industry is using in an attempt to prevent software piracy is education. By educating businesses and consumers about the legal use of software and the negative consequences possible for breaking piracy laws, the industry hopes to significantly reduce intentional use of illegal software. Paired with this, the industry is also continually working on strengthening anti-piracy laws and adapting them to fit new technology, such as broadband Internet and rewritable DVDs.

To make it more difficult for criminals to create pirated copies of software, *holograms*—printed text or images that change when the item containing the hologram is tilted or looked at from a different angle—are commonly used on CDs, DVDs, printed software documentation, and stickers located on new PCs containing preinstalled software. Because holograms are difficult to duplicate, end users can feel confident that the software package they are buying or that was installed on the PC they just received is authentic, if the hologram works correctly. (Some software manufacturers have launched extensive campaigns—such as including information on their Web sites, in product information, and in advertisements—to inform consumers of how these precautions work, such as Microsoft's "How To Tell" program.) Other antipiracy techniques used by software companies include watching online auction sites daily and requesting the removal of suspicious items, mandatory software registration, and buying pirated copies of software via Web sites and then filing lawsuits against the sellers.

### Preventing Digital Counterfeiting

To prevent counterfeiting of U.S. currency, the Treasury Department is in the process of releasing new currency designs containing features that are more difficult to duplicate (see Figure 4-25). The Treasury Department is also continually working on developing new technological means to prevent currency from being copied, as well as to track the devices used in the counterfeiting process. For example, many color copiers print invisible codes on copied documents, making counterfeit money copied on those machines traceable. This type of technology is also thought to be incorporated into many scanners. In fact, printer and scanner manufacturer Canon has revealed that they have been incorporating anticounterfeiting technologies into their products since 1992, but the company is prohibited by the government from disclosing any information about those technologies.

Prevention against the counterfeiting of other types of documents—such as collectible souvenirs, checks, and identification cards—include using holograms, watermarks, and other difficult-to-reproduce content; using *digital watermarks* (subtle alteration of images, audio files, or other digital content that isn't noticeable when the work is viewed or played, but that can be read using special software to authenticate the item); and educating consumers about how the appearance of fake products differs from authentic products.

**FIGURE 4-25**

**Anticounterfeiting measures used with U.S. currency**

A thread embedded in the paper contains several items that can be seen when held up to the light or placed in front of an ultraviolet light.

The enlarged portrait has more detail and is harder to duplicate.

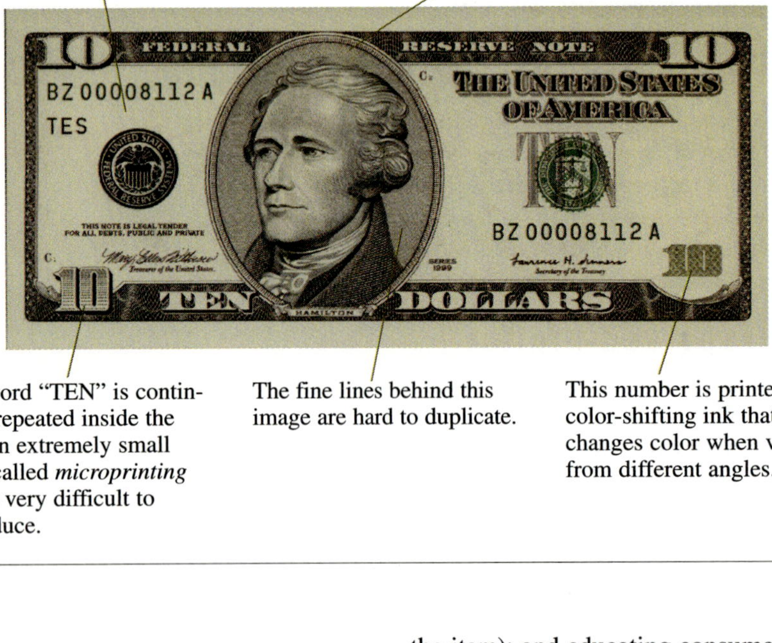


The word "TEN" is continually repeated inside the "10" in extremely small print called *microprinting* that is very difficult to reproduce.

The fine lines behind this image are hard to duplicate.

This number is printed in color-shifting ink that changes color when viewed from different angles.

## Protection against Cyberstalking and Other Personal Safety Concerns

There is no surefire way to protect against cyberstalking and other online dangers completely, but some common sense precautions can reduce the chance of a serious personal safety problem due to online activities.

### Safety Tips for Adults

It is wise to be cautious and discreet in chat rooms, discussion groups, and other online locations where individuals communicate with strangers. To protect yourself against cyberstalking and other types of harassment, use gender-neutral, non-provocative identifying names, such as *jsmith*, instead of *janesmith* or *iamcute*. Don't reveal personal information—such as your real name, address, or telephone number—to people you meet in a chat room. Though they may feel like new friends, they are in actuality strangers and you have no idea who they really are or what they are like in real life.

### Safety Tips for Children

Most experts agree that the best way to protect children from online dangers is to stay in close touch with them as they explore the Internet. To be able to check up on their online activities easily and frequently, it is a good idea for children to use a PC in a family room or other public location, instead of their bedroom. They should also be informed of what activities are allowed, what types of Web sites are off limits, and why. In addition, it should be made clear that they are never to reveal personal information about themselves online without a parent's permission.

## Protection against Security Breaches by Employees

When most of us think of a security breach, we think of a hacker outside the system trying to break in. Although that is the case in most instances, a significant number of business security breaches are committed by insiders. A 2002 joint study by the Computer Security Institute and FBI found that about one-third of the security breaches reported by the companies surveyed came from within. Consequently, it pays employers to be cautious with their employees. Some suggestions are listed next.

### Screen Potential New Hires Carefully

Employers should carefully investigate the background of all potential employees. Some people falsify résumés to get jobs. Others may have criminal records. One embarrassing mistake made by Rutgers University was to hire David Smith, the author of the Melissa virus, as a computer technician when he was out on bail following the arrest for that crime.

### Watch for Disgruntled Employees and Ex-Employees

The type of employee who is most likely to commit a computer crime is one who has recently been terminated or passed over for a promotion, or one who has some reason to want to "get even" with the organization. Limiting access for each employee to only the network resources needed for his or her job can help prevent some types of sabotage by disgruntled current employees. Any attempts by an employee to access off-limit areas should be seriously investigated. In addition, whenever an employee leaves the company for any reason, all access to the system (user name, password, e-mail address, etc.) should be removed immediately.

### Develop Policies and Controls

All companies should develop policies and controls regarding security matters. Employees should be educated about computer crime and the conditions that foster it, informed of the seriousness and consequences of computer crime, and instructed what to do when they suspect a computer crime is taking place or is about to occur. Policies such as shredding sensitive documents that are no longer needed, limiting employee access to only needed parts of the network, immediately removing access for any employee who leaves the company, and separating employee functions as much as possible are all wise precautions. So is creating a procedure to review and approve all content before it is posted on the company Web site.

### Ask Business Partners to Review their Security

In this networked economy, many organizations provide some access to internal resources for business partners. If those companies are lax with their security measures, attacks from business partners' employees are possible. Consequently, in addition to making sure their own security measures are sufficient, it is important for businesses to be sure their business partners maintain adequate security policies and controls.

## COMPUTER CRIME LEGISLATION

Federal law has had mixed results deterring computer crime. The main piece of legislation regarding using a computer in a criminal manner—the *Computer Fraud and Abuse Act*—has been regularly updated to broaden its scope and to clarify its intent (see the list of selected federal computer crime laws in Figure 4-26). The law currently forbids unauthorized access to data stored in federal government computers and federally regulated financial institutions. It also outlaws the deliberate implantation of computer viruses in those computers. Actions taken with intent to harm are classified as felonies, while actions performed merely with reckless disregard are considered to be misdemeanors. Critics say the law doesn't go far enough in that a hacker who is merely curious may not be found guilty of a crime at all. Newer laws, such as the USA Patriot Act, *Digital Millennium Copyright Act*, and Identity Theft and Assumption Act, address more recent security concerns.

One problem with computer crime legislation is jurisdiction. Because the criminal and the victim may be located in different cities, states, or countries, determining which laws apply and whose job it is to enforce them can be difficult. Complicating matters is the fact that hackers and other computer criminals can make it appear that the criminal activity is coming from a different location than it really is. An additional problem is that many existing laws do not transfer well to computer networks. For example, should e-mail, chat, and other online communications methods be treated like telephone conversations or conventional written mail? Although there have long been laws addressing such offenses as sending indecent material through the mail, libel, harassment, inciting hatred, and the like, these laws don't specifically address computer networks and so must be modified.

**FIGURE 4-26**

Some important computer crime laws

| DATE | LAW AND DESCRIPTION |
|---|---|
| 2001 | **USA Patriot Act (USAPA)**<br>Grants federal authorities expanded surveillance and intelligence-gathering powers, such as broadening the ability of federal agents to obtain the real identity of Internet users, intercept e-mail and other types of Internet communications, follow online activity of suspects, expanded wiretapping authority, and more. |
| 1999 | **Digital Millennium Copyright Act (DMCA)**<br>Makes it illegal to circumvent antipiracy measures built into commercial software, as well as outlawing the manufacturing or sale of devices used to illegally copy software or other copy-protected resources. |
| 1998 | **Identity Theft and Assumption Deterrence Act of 1998**<br>Makes it a federal crime to knowingly use someone else's means of identification, such as their name, Social Security number, or credit card, to commit any unlawful activity. |
| 1997 | **No Electronic Theft (NET) Act**<br>Expands computer piracy laws to include distribution of copyrighted materials over the Internet. |
| 1996 | **Anticounterfeiting Consumer Protection Act of 1996**<br>Expands counterfeit law to include computer programs, documentation, packaging, and other audio-visual works, as well as the ability of law enforcement to seize counterfeiting property and equipment. |
| 1996 | **National Information Infrastructure Protection Act**<br>Amended the Computer Fraud and Abuse Act to punish information theft crossing state lines and crack down on network trespassing. |
| 1994 | **Computer Abuse Amendments Act**<br>Extends the Computer Fraud and Abuse Act to include computer viruses and other harmful code. |
| 1991 | **Telephone Consumer Protection Act**<br>Requires telemarketing companies to respect the rights of people who do not want to be called and significantly restricts the use of recorded messages. |
| 1986 | **Computer Fraud and Abuse Act of 1986**<br>Amends the 1984 law to include federally regulated financial institutions. |
| 1984 | **Computer Fraud and Abuse Act of 1984**<br>Makes it a crime to break into computers owned by the federal government. |

In addition, responsibility is an issue. Whose job is it to monitor the massive amounts of data sent over computer networks daily? Is it anyone's responsibility or obligation? Will the right to personal privacy be compromised? Will the public be willing to pay for the potentially exorbitant cost of having networks policed? These and similar issues need to be addressed when crafting new computer crime legislation. At the time of this writing, new computer crime legislation was being considered and expected to be implemented in the near future.

All computer users should take specific actions to protect their PC. In this world of viruses, worms, hackers, and "buggy" (error-prone) software, it pays to be somewhat cautious. Though safeguards were covered in detail throughout this chapter, some specific precautionary steps all computer users should follow are summarized in this box.

**Step 1: Protect your hardware.**

Be sure to plug all components of your computer system (system unit, monitor, printer, scanner, powered subwoofer, etc.) into an industry-approved surge protector. Be careful not to bump or move the computer when it is on. Don't spill food or drink onto the keyboard or any other piece of hardware. Store your disks and CDs properly. If you ever need to work inside the system unit, turn off the PC, unplug it, and ground yourself by touching the power supply before touching any other component inside the system unit.

**Step 2: Install and use an antivirus program.**

Install a good antivirus program and set it up to scan all files and e-mail messages before they are downloaded to your PC, as well as perform a full-system scan periodically, such as every Friday night. To detect the newest viruses and types of malware, your antivirus program must be updated on a regular basis. For example, activating the Norton Antivirus Automatic LiveUpdate (as shown in Figure 4-27) instructs the program to update your virus definitions every four hours. Typically about $10 per year keeps you up-to-date, once your free update subscription expires.

**Step 3: If you have an always-on Internet connection, install a personal firewall.**

As mentioned in the chapter, a firewall protects you from a hacker accessing your PC through the Internet. Although full-featured firewall programs, such as Sygate's Personal Firewall Pro or Zone Labs' ZoneAlarm Pro, can be purchased for business use, home users can download a free version of either of these programs. For additional protection if you have a home network, be sure only to turn on file-sharing for files and folders that really need to be accessed by other users. To turn file-sharing on or off in the Windows environment, right-click on the file or folder and select the *Sharing* or *Sharing and Security* option. As shown in Figure 4-28, shared items have a different appearance than non-shared items.

**Step 4: Back up regularly.**

Once you have your new PC set up with all your programs installed and the menus and other settings the way you like them, do a full backup so the PC can be restored to that configuration in case of a major problem with your computer or hard drive. Be sure also to back up your data files on a regular basis. Depending on how important your documents are, you may want to back up all your data every night, or copy each document onto a floppy disk or rewritable CD after each major modification. To

**FIGURE 4-27**

**Update your antivirus program on a regular basis**

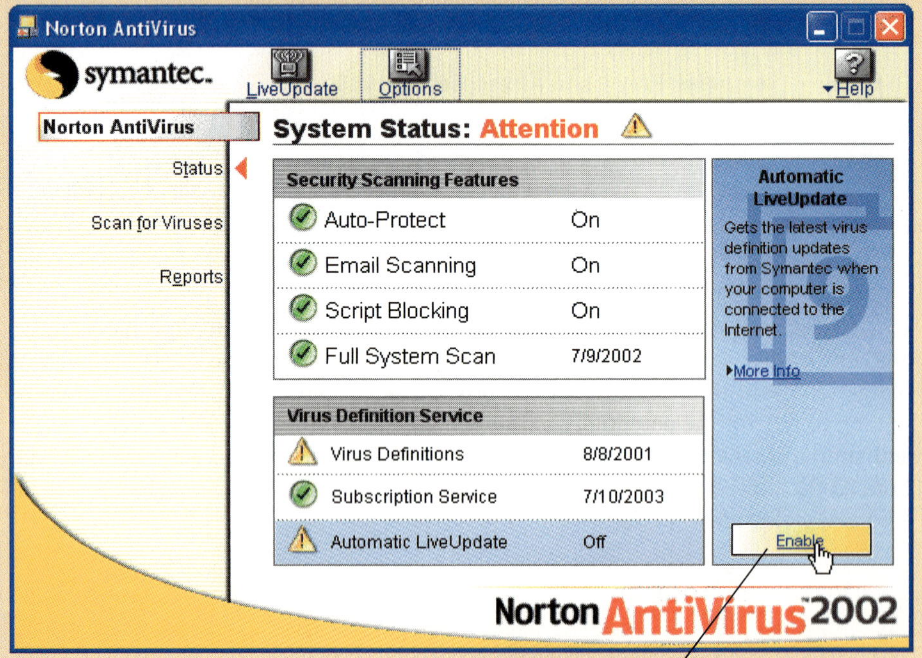


Turning LiveUpdate on in this program instructs the program to check for and download any new virus information regularly (provided the user is connected to the Internet at that time).

facilitate data backup, keep all your data organized in folders (such as all in a main folder called "Data" as in Figure 4-28). For an even higher level of security, install a second hard drive just for data. That way, if your main hard drive ever becomes unstable and needs to be reformatted, your data drive will remain untouched. Backups on removable media should be stored in a different location than your PC or in a fire-resistant safe.

### Step 5: Update your operating system, browser, and e-mail program regularly.

Most companies that produce operating systems, browsers, or e-mail programs regularly post updates and *patches*—small programs that take care of specific problems or *bugs* with their software, such as a security hole—on their Web sites. Some programs include an option within the program to check online for updates; for other programs, you'll need to go to each manufacturer's Web site directly to check for any critical or recommended updates. Because malware frequently takes advantage of security holes in these types of programs, particularly the Microsoft Outlook e-mail program, it is important to keep them up-to-date.

### Step 6: Test your system for vulnerabilities.

There are several free tests available through Web sites to see if any of your PC's ports are accessible to hackers. These tests, such as the one on the Symantec Web site shown in Figure 4-29, should be run once you believe your antivirus software, firewall, and any other protective components you are using are set up correctly, to check for any remaining vulnerabilities.

**FIGURE 4-28**

**Share files and folders only as necessary and store all data in a single location for easier backup**

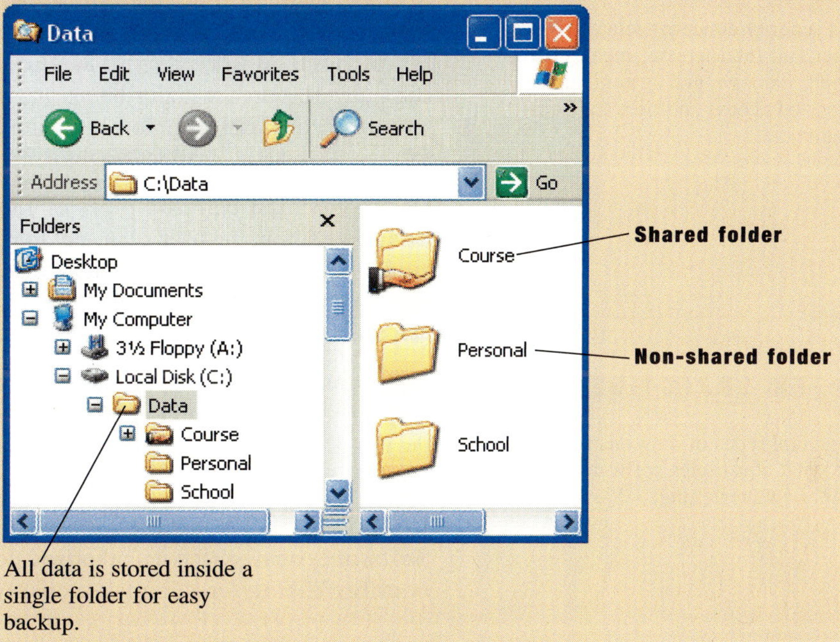


**FIGURE 4-29**

**Free online security checkups can help identify your PC's vulnerabilities**

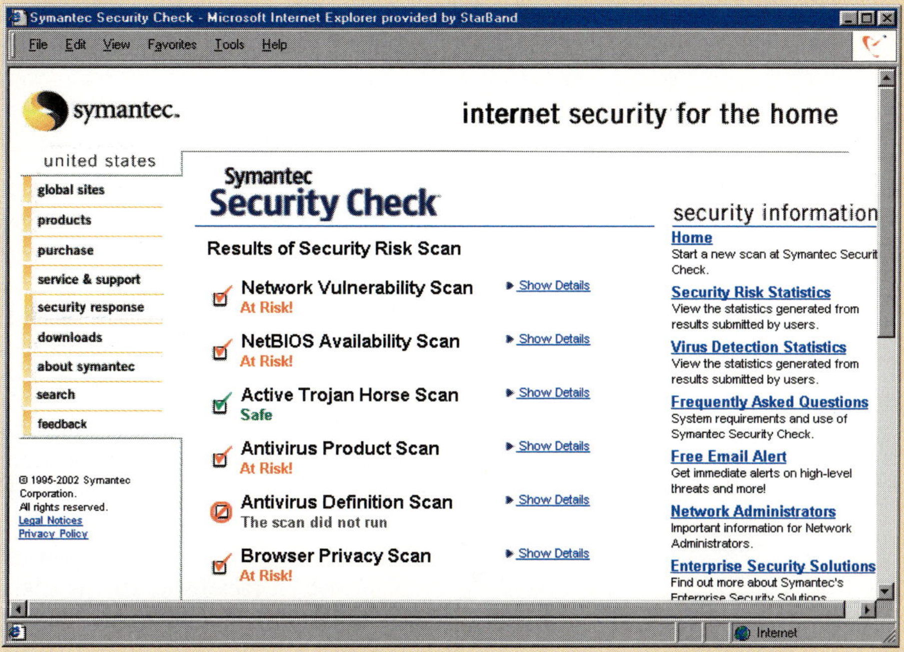

# SUMMARY

## Security Concerns

**CHAPTER OBJECTIVE 1**

Discuss security concerns related to computer and Internet use, such as hardware theft, damage, and system failure; unauthorized access and use; and computer sabotage.

There are a number of important security concerns related to computers and the Internet. Many of these are **computer crimes**. **Hardware theft**, damage, and **system failure** are important concerns for all users to be aware of. **Unauthorized access** (such as **hacking**) occurs when someone gains access to a computer resource without being an authorized user; **unauthorized use** occurs when someone uses a computer resource for unapproved activities. The interception of data, files, and e-mail messages sent over the Internet is another growing concern.

One of the most common types of *sabotage* is the **computer virus** (a program installed without the user's consent that is typically designed to cause damage to the system and replicate itself). Other types of **malware** include **computer worms** and **Trojan horses**. Computer sabotage can take the form of a **denial of service (DoS) attack** or data or program alteration.

**CHAPTER OBJECTIVE 2**

Name several types of dot cons and explain what constitutes software piracy and digital counterfeiting.

**Dot cons** are a growing problem for consumers. **Identity theft**—where an individual's identity is used to make purchases and other unauthorized activities—is on the rise and can result in serious hardship for the individual whose identity is stolen. Theft of data, information, or other resources via the Internet is another possibility, as are **online auction fraud** and **Internet offer scams**.

**Software piracy** (the unauthorized copying of a computer program) and **digital counterfeiting** (creating fake copies of currency and other printed resources) are illegal in the U.S. They cost manufacturers billions of dollars each year, some of which must be passed on to law-abiding consumers.

**CHAPTER OBJECTIVE 3**

Describe personal safety risks involved with Internet use.

There are personal safety risks for both adults and children stemming from Internet use. **Cyberstalking**—online harassment that frightens or threatens the victim—is more common in recent years, even though most states have passed laws against it. The vast amount of pornography available online and the possibilities of encountering pedophiles online can increase personal safety risks for children and other young Internet users.

## Security Safeguards

**CHAPTER OBJECTIVE 4**

Understand ways to safeguard a PC against theft, damage, or unauthorized access and use.

There are a number of safeguards that individuals and businesses can use to prevent the possible problems discussed. To protect against hardware theft, door and equipment locks can be used. To protect against accidental hardware damage, **surge suppressors**, proper storage media care, and precautions against excess dust, heat, and static are important. To be prepared for data loss, **backups** are essential for both individuals and businesses—most businesses should also develop a **disaster-recovery plan** for natural and man-made disasters.

To guard against unauthorized access of facilities, programs, and data, *identification* and *authentication* systems can be used. The most common types of systems include **possessed knowledge** systems, which typically use **passwords**; **possessed object** systems, which typically use smart cards, magnetic cards, or badges; and **biometric** systems, which use **biometric devices** to authenticate a user based on a biometric characteristic. **Firewalls** act as a protective boundary between a computer or network and the outside world to prevent against access by hackers.

Sensitive transactions should be performed only on **secure Web servers**; sensitive files and e-mails should be secured from prying eyes with **encryption** techniques, such as **public key encryption**. Public key encryption can be performed by third-party encryption programs as well as by many e-mail programs, once an individual has obtained a set of encryption *keys*. *Web-based encryption* is also available. The strength of an encryption method is measured by the length of its keys, such as weak 40-bit encryption and the strong 128-bit encryption that is very difficult to crack.

When encryption isn't needed, but the identity of the sender needs to be verified, a **digital signature** can be used. **Digital certificates**, obtained through a *Certification Authority (CA)*, typically include a public key to be used with both encryption and digital signatures. Digital certificates can also be used to verify the identity of secure Web pages. When a business desires a private network that can use the Internet or other public network structure, a **virtual private network (VPN)** can be used.

**CHAPTER OBJECTIVE 5**

Give suggestions for securely transferring data over the Internet, as well as for protecting against computer sabotage.

One of the most important safeguards against computer sabotage is the consistent use of up-to-date **antivirus software** to prevent and remove computer viruses. Other precautions include only downloading software from reputable Web sites and never opening executable e-mail attachments without first checking with the sender.

To protect against identity theft, individuals should guard their personal information carefully. To check for identity theft, bills and credit history should be watched. When interacting with other individuals online or buying from an online auction, it is wise to be conservative. Check auction sellers' feedback records and see if they take credit cards before placing an online bid, and steer clear of offers that seem too good to be true.

**CHAPTER OBJECTIVE 6**

Suggest precautions users can take against online fraud and identity theft.

Various tools, such as consumer education and holograms, can be used to prevent software piracy. Many businesses are also aggressively pursuing pirates in court in an attempt to reduce piracy. The government has various methods in place to prevent digital counterfeiting of currency, such as using difficult-to-reproduce materials and features.

**CHAPTER OBJECTIVE 7**

Describe ways software piracy and digital counterfeiting may be prevented.

To protect their personal safety, adults should be cautious and discreet in online communications. Both adults and children should be wary of revealing any personal information or meeting online acquaintances in person. To protect children, parents should keep a close watch on their children's online activities.

Taking common-sense precautions with employees—such as screening new hires, watching for disgruntled employees, and developing good policies—can help businesses avoid crimes from internal sources.

**CHAPTER OBJECTIVE 8**

List ways individuals can protect their personal safety while online, and ways businesses can protect themselves against security breaches by employees.

## Computer Crime Legislation

There is some amount of computer crime legislation in place, such as the *USA Patriot Act*, the *Identity Theft and Assumption Act*, and the *Computer Fraud and Abuse Act*, but the rapid growth of the Internet and jurisdictional issues have contributed to the lack of legislation for some types of computer crimes.

**CHAPTER OBJECTIVE 9**

Give examples of computer crime legislation.

# BALANCING ACT

## SECURITY VS. PERSONAL FREEDOM

There are some basic types of security we all depend on. We expect the military to protect us from invasions or attacks from other countries, we depend on our local police to keep our towns safe, and we expect our employers to provide a safe workplace. As the level of potential danger in our lives increases, it tends to limit our own personal freedom. For example, many citizens of large cities avoid walking the streets alone at night, even though they have the right to do so, and many Americans avoid traveling to the Middle East, South America, and other locations thought to be dangerous for Americans at the present time. Ironically, security measures established to protect us sometimes tend to limit our personal freedom as well; for example, having to submit to personal and baggage searches before boarding an airplane or showing identification to gain admittance to your workplace. Most citizens are willing to give up some level of personal freedom in order to protect their personal safety, but the difficulty is determining the balance—how much loss of freedom is worth a certain level of additional security?

It's not surprising that the answer to this question varies from person to person. Some individuals are willing to trade some personal freedom and privacy for convenience, such as the frequent travelers who are signing up for expedited airport-screening programs. After a background check and entering personal data and a biometric characteristic into a computer database, these programs allow the travelers to speed past the identity checks required of other passengers. Other individuals, however, may not be so willing to compromise their personal privacy and personal freedom and might view these types of systems as an infringement on personal privacy and a step toward restricted personal freedom for all. Still others may believe that adequate security is possible without any loss of personal freedom.

### YOUR TURN

Consider the statements made above regarding finding the balance between security and personal freedom and answer the following questions.

1. Do you think it's necessary to sacrifice some degree of personal freedom in order to improve national security? Why or why not?
2. Do you think a national ID card (such as a hard-to-forge national driver's license containing a thumbprint or other biometric data) could help prevent terrorist attacks, such as the 9/11 attacks? If so, do you think Americans would support their use?
3. There has been an increased use of video surveillance and facial recognition systems in public locations to try to identify terrorists or known criminals so they can be apprehended. While some privacy advocates strongly object, law enforcement views these systems as a necessary tool. What is your opinion?
4. According to U.S. and foreign officials, Osama bin Laden and his associates are using encryption methods that hide maps, photographs, instructions for terrorist activities, and other data in images posted on Web sites. Whose responsibility is it to try to stop this type of communication? If encryption programs are used to plan a terrorist attack or other criminal activity, should the program author be held accountable? Why or why not? Do you support the use of a key escrow system to make decryption easier for government agencies? Explain.
5. As we get further and further from the 9/11 attacks, do you think public support regarding fingerprint scans at airports, a national ID card, and other methods viewed as terrorist preventions will begin to wane? Why or why not?

## KEY TERMS

**Instructions:** Match each key term on the left with the definition on the right that best describes it.

a. **antivirus software**

b. **backup**

c. **biometric device**

d. **computer crime**

e. **computer virus**

f. **cyberstalking**

g. **denial of service (DoS) attack**

h. **digital counterfeiting**

i. **digital signature**

j. **disaster-recovery plan**

k. **encryption**

l. **firewall**

m. **hacking**

n. **identity theft**

o. **online auction fraud**

p. **password**

q. **software piracy**

r. **surge suppressor**

s. **unauthorized use**

t. **virtual private network (VPN)**

**1.** ______ A combination of secret words or character combinations used to gain access to a computer system or facility.

**2.** ______ A device that identifies and authenticates users based on a unique physiological characteristic (such as their fingerprint, hand, face, or iris) or personal trait (such as their voice or written signature).

**3.** ______ A device that protects a computer system from damage due to electrical fluctuations.

**4.** ______ A duplicate copy of data or other computer contents in case the original version is destroyed.

**5.** ______ A method of scrambling e-mail messages or files to make them unreadable if they are intercepted by an unauthorized user.

**6.** ______ A private network set up through a public communications network, such as the Internet.

**7.** ______ A security system that is designed to protect a computer or computer network from outside attack.

**8.** ______ A software program, installed without the user's knowledge, designed to alter the way a computer operates or to cause harm to the system.

**9.** ______ A unique digital code that can be attached to an e-mail message or document to verify the identity of the sender and guarantee the message or file was unchanged since it was signed.

**10.** ______ A written plan that describes the steps a company will take following the occurrence of a disaster.

**11.** ______ An act of sabotage that attempts to overwhelm a network or Web server with enough disruptive requests for action that the network or Web server becomes unable to fulfill valid user requests.

**12.** ______ Any illegal act involving a computer.

**13.** ______ Repeated threats or harassing behavior via e-mail or another Internet communications method.

**14.** ______ Software used to detect and eliminate computer viruses.

**15.** ______ The unauthorized copying of a computer program.

**16.** ______ The use of computers or other types of digital equipment to make illegal copies of currency, checks, collectibles, and other print-based items.

**17.** ______ Using a computer resource for unapproved activities.

**18.** ______ Using a computer to penetrate the security of a computer system.

**19.** ______ Using someone else's identity to purchase goods or services, obtain new credit cards or bank loans, or otherwise illegally masquerade as that individual.

**20.** ______ When an item purchased through an online auction is never delivered after payment, or the item is not as specified.

# ✓ SELF-QUIZ

Answers for the self-quiz appear at the end of the book.

## True/False

**Instructions:** Circle **T** if the statement is true or **F** if the statement is false.

**T F 1.** Computer viruses can be spread via e-mail.

**T F 2.** As long as a business has purchased one legal copy of a software program, it can always legally install the program on all the computers in its offices.

**T F 3.** It is OK to leave floppy disks and CDs in your car in the summer since they are very durable.

**T F 4.** To help protect against your PC being used in a denial of service (DoS) attack, firewall software can be used.

**T F 5.** A password is an example of a possessed object.

## Completion

**Instructions:** Supply the missing words to complete the following statements.

**6.** A(n) ______________ is a person who attempts to gain unauthorized access to a computer or network, typically through the Internet.

**7.** Color-copying money is an example of ______________.

**8.** To protect yourself against computer viruses, you should never open e-mail ______________ with executable file extensions.

**9.** A(n) ______________ is a destructive program that is hidden inside a seemingly legitimate program.

**10.** A(n) ______________ Web page will have a locked padlock or unbroken key displayed on the browser's status bar.

**11.** With ______________ encryption, two keys are used—one to encrypt the file or e-mail message and one to decrypt it.

**12.** A(n) ______________ contains a built-in battery to keep a PC functional during a power failure, at least long enough to shut it down properly.

**13.** ______________ technology is used to try to identify or authenticate individuals using a live photo and a photo database.

**14.** A(n) ______________ typically includes the name of an individual, organization, or Web site and a copy of their public key and guarantees the entity's identity.

**15.** A(n) ______________ can help a business get operational again following a fire, act of sabotage, or similar disaster.

# PROJECTS

## 1. Smart IDs

**YOUR OPINION**

The chapter Trends In box discusses the growing use of smart cards as campus ID cards. Some credit cards are now being issued as smart cards, and smart cards have been proposed to replace conventional drivers' licenses, medical insurance cards, bank ATM cards, and other important identification cards. The ability of a smart card to hold a larger amount of personal data than a conventional magnetic stripe card is viewed as a benefit by some; the additional information potentially available through a card (such as an individual's medical history or purchasing record) is viewed as a privacy risk to others.

For this project, consider the points raised above and write a short essay expressing your opinion about using smart cards to replace conventional magnetic stripe cards. If it isn't already, would you want your campus ID card to become a smart card? Why or why not? Do you think smart cards will be used any differently by consumers than conventional magnetic stripe cards? List any pros and cons of replacing magnetic stripe cards with smart cards and provide a concluding paragraph stating other possible uses for smart cards that might be beneficial and/or accepted by the general public. Submit your opinion on this issue to your instructor in the form of a short paper, not more than two pages in length.

## 2. Hacktivism

**INDEPENDENT RESEARCH**

*Hacktivism* can be defined as the act of hacking into a computer system for a politically or socially motivated purpose. The individual who performs an act of hacktivism is said to be a *hacktivist*. While some view hacktivists no differently than other hackers, hacktivists contend that they break into systems in order to bring attention to political or social causes. Two recent examples of hacktivism include the Web defacements in 2002 by two individuals calling themselves the "Deceptive Duo" and the Web defacements following the death of a Chinese airman when his jet fighter collided with a U.S. surveillance plane in 2001.

For this project, research the two examples of hacktivism mentioned above, plus any other use of hacktivism you can find that occurred within the last year or two. Were any of the hackers identified or found guilty of a crime? What seemed to be the motivation behind the hacks? Form an opinion about hacktivism in general, such as whether or not it is a valid method of bringing attention to specific causes, and whether or not hacktivists should be treated any differently when caught than other types of hackers. Summarize your findings in a two- to three-page paper.

## 3. Virus Hoaxes

**HANDS-ON**

In addition to the valid reports about new viruses found in the news and on antivirus software Web sites, reports of viruses that turn out to be hoaxes abound on the Internet. In addition to being an annoyance, virus hoaxes waste time and computing resources. They may also eventually lead some users routinely to ignore all virus warning messages, leaving them vulnerable to a genuine, destructive virus.

For this project, visit at least two sites dedicated to identifying virus hoaxes, such as those on Web sites of antivirus companies (for example, Symantec and McAfee software) and sites sponsored by the government (such as the Hoaxbusters site currently found at hoaxbusters.ciac.org). Explore the sites to find information about recent hoaxes, as well as general guidelines for identifying hoaxes, chain letters, and other similar items. At the end of your research, prepare a one-page summary of your findings to turn in to your instructor.

### 4. Digital Certificates

When you want the capability to both digitally sign and encrypt e-mail messages, a digital certificate is typically your best bet. Though some digital certificates require a fee, free personal certificates are available.

For this project, locate a Certificate Authority (CA) that provides free digital certificates for personal use. Determine the minimum amount of information needed to obtain one and, if you have Internet access at home, sign up for a free certificate using your home PC. When the digital certificate is sent to you, install it on your home PC for use with your e-mail program and then send yourself an e-mail that is signed or encrypted. Retrieve the e-mail to make sure it came through in one piece and to see what it looks like on the recipient's end.

Prepare a one-page summary of your research, including what identification data was required to obtain a basic certificate, if a more secure certificate is available after further authentication, and how the signed or encrypted e-mail process worked. Be sure to include an opinion about the ease of use of this system and whether or not you would want to use it to secure or sign sensitive e-mails.

**GROUP PRESENTATION**

### 5. Auction Pirates

Pirated software being sold via online auctions is reaching epidemic proportions. One estimate by the Software and Information Industry Association is that over 90% of all software sold through online auctions is pirated. Pirated movies are prevalent as well, often being available over the Internet before they are released on DVD—sometimes even before they are released worldwide in the theater.

For this project, form a group to participate in the following scenario: While on an online auction site, you run across what looks like a great deal on a DVD movie that was just in the movie theater a few months ago, and you have the highest bid when the auction closes. After receiving and cashing your personal check, the seller ships your DVD. When it arrives, the return address on the package is from Thailand and the text on the cover of the DVD isn't English, so you realize that you have just bought an Asian import DVD. When you contact the seller, he says that he bought the DVD in a store in his country, so it can't be a bootleg copy.

Your group should research the legality of selling DVDs in the U.S. that are produced in other countries. If a DVD is available for retail sale in a foreign country, does that mean it can be bought there by an individual and then brought into the U.S., or imported to the U.S. for resale? Is there any way to check whether or not a DVD bought via an online auction is legitimate? Your group should also discuss the scenario explained above and come up with some ways this problem might have been avoided in the first place, and what (if anything) could be done after the fact, if you weren't happy with your purchase.

Share your findings with the class in the form of a short presentation. The presentation should not exceed 10 minutes and should make use of one or more presentation aids such as the chalkboard, handouts, overhead transparencies, or a computer-based slide presentation (your instructor may provide additional requirements). Your group may also be asked to submit a summary of the presentation to your instructor.

### 6. Biometric Databases

It is becoming increasingly common for biometric devices to be used to grant or deny access to corporate and government facilities. They are also beginning to be used to identify consumers for financial transactions, such as making ATM withdrawals or cashing checks. Because these applications just need to authenticate that the person trying to gain access is really who he or she claims to be, the system can use *one-to-one matching* (where the system knows which person it is to authenticate) instead of *one-to-many matching* (where the system tries to identify a person by matching him or her up with a photo in a database, such as when facial recognition is used to see if a person photographed at an airport is someone in a database containing known criminals or terrorists). With one-to-one matching, the system needs to be provided with the identity of the person to be authenticated, usually by the individual entering in a PIN number or swiping an ID card. Then the system can obtain the appropriate biometric data (via a hand scanner or iris reader, for example) and check whether or not that data matches the data for the specified individual. With one-to-one matching, the biometric data can be stored either in a database on the computer or on an ID card or other type of possessed object supplied by the user.

For this project, form a group to discuss the pros and cons of having biometric data stored in a database, versus it being stored solely on a possessed object. From a convenience standpoint, is one method preferable? What about from a privacy standpoint? In what situation might one system be preferred over the other? If your school or company was going to implement a biometrics system to grant access to facilities, which method would the members of your group prefer? Why? If possible, locate a school or business in your area that uses a biometric access system and find out where the individuals' biometric data is stored. Have there been any objections from the students or employees at this organization?

Share your findings with the class in the form of a short presentation. The presentation should not exceed 10 minutes and should make use of one or more presentation aids such as the chalkboard, handouts, overhead transparencies, or a computer-based slide presentation (your instructor may provide additional requirements). Your group may also be asked to submit a summary of the presentation to your instructor.

### 7. Homeless Hacker

**VIDEO VIEWPOINT**

Hackers who try to gain access to business and government computers are a growing problem. Some hackers do it for monetary gain, others supposedly to bring attention to system vulnerabilities or other, purportedly more noble, purposes. The accompanying video clip features 21-year-old Adrian Lamo, a freelance security consultant who regularly tries to hack into systems without authorization, looking for their security holes.

After watching the video, think about the impact of hackers breaching the security of business and government computers. If hackers like Lamo continue to use real networks and Web servers to practice and improve their hacking skills, what are the implications? Will it expose the data located on those networks to greater danger, or will it result in tightened security and, ultimately, a more secure system? Lamo says that, while he is an intruder, he is guided by a sense of curiosity and he is helping corporations and consumers understand the limits of Internet security. Should these types of hacks be treated any differently than hackers who break into systems to steal data or other resources? Should hackers who don't steal any information still be prosecuted? Or, as Lamo charges, are companies at fault by leaving their networks unprotected? Are there varying degrees of criminal hacking or is a hack just a hack, regardless of the motivation? Lamo has begun publicizing his successful hacks through the media, instead of contacting the company directly. Does that make his motives more questionable?

**ONLINE VIDEO**

To view the Homeless Hacker video clip, go to www.course.com/morley2003/ch4

**Express your viewpoint:** What impact does hacking have on businesses, the government, and individuals and how should it be treated?

Use the video clip and the questions previously asked as the foundation for your response. Your instructor will direct you to be prepared to discuss your position (either in class, via an online class discussion group, or in a class chat room), or to write a short paper stating and supporting your viewpoint on the issue. You may also be asked to do research and provide resources to support your point of view.

# COMPUTERS AND PRIVACY

## OUTLINE

**Overview**

**Privacy Concerns**

- Web Browsing Privacy
- E-mail Privacy
- Databases and Electronic Profiling
- Spam and Other Marketing Activities
- Electronic Surveillance and Monitoring

**Privacy Safeguards**

- Protection of Web Browsing and E-mail Privacy
- Protection of Personal Information
- Protection of Workplace Privacy

**Privacy Legislation**

## OBJECTIVES

**After completing this chapter, you will be able to:**

- Define and discuss various privacy concerns related to Web browsing and e-mail, including cookies, Web bugs, spyware, and e-mail privacy.
- Describe some privacy concerns regarding databases, electronic profiling, spam, adware, telemarketing, and various types of electronic surveillance and monitoring.
- Identify ways individuals can protect their privacy while surfing the Web.
- List steps individuals can take to safeguard their e-mail addresses and other personal information.
- Suggest some ways to filter out or reduce objectionable Web content, spam, and telemarketing activities.
- Understand how individuals can protect their workplace privacy.
- Discuss the status of privacy legislation.

# CHAPTER 5

## OVERVIEW

Almost all of us have some aspects of our lives that we prefer to keep private. These may include an indiscreet incident from the past, sensitive medical or financial facts, or certain tastes or opinions. Yet we can appreciate that sometimes selected people or organizations have a legitimate need for some of this information. A doctor needs accurate medical histories and lifestyle information about his or her patients. Financial information must be disclosed to credit card companies, loan officers, and college scholarship committees. A company or the government may need to probe into the lives of people applying for unusually sensitive jobs or who are under investigation for a crime.

No matter how legitimate the need, however, there is always the danger that information will be misused. Facts may be taken out of context and used to draw distorted conclusions. Private information may end up being distributed without one's consent or knowledge. Erroneous facts may cause individuals to be denied services that they are entitled to or to be accused of actions they didn't take.

This chapter explores these and other important issues relating to privacy and how our computer-oriented society has created new risks for personal privacy violations. The chapter opens with a discussion of various privacy concerns, followed by ways privacy can be safeguarded. The chapter closes with a discussion of privacy legislation.

# PRIVACY CONCERNS

**Privacy** can be defined as "the state of being concealed or free from unauthorized intrusion." The term **information privacy** refers to the rights of individuals and companies to control how information about them is collected and used. The problem of how to protect personal privacy—that is, how to keep personal information private—existed long before computers entered into the picture. For example, sealing wax and unique signet rings were used centuries ago to seal letters, wills, and other personal documents to guard against their contents being revealed to unauthorized eyes.

But today's computers, with their ability to store and manipulate unprecedented quantities of data in a very short amount of time, combined with the fact that databases containing our personal information can be accessed and shared via the Internet, have added a new twist to the issue of personal privacy. While many concerns center around these databases, other important privacy issues include *cookies*, *Web bugs*, *spyware*, e-mail privacy, spam and *telemarketing,* and *electronic surveillance* and monitoring.

## Web Browsing Privacy

One area of concern for many individuals who browse the Web on a regular basis is maintaining the privacy of where they go and what they do at Web sites. You may wonder: Does anyone keep track of which Web sites I visit, what hyperlinks I click on, how long I stay on a Web site, and what things I download and buy? What about the information I provide to a Web site? Can I specify who gets to see it? The answer to each of these questions is "yes" to some extent, but it depends on the specific Web sites visited, the settings on your PC, and what precautions you have taken to protect your privacy.

### Cookies

**ONLINE TUTORIAL**

For an online look at how cookies work, go to www.course.com/morley2003/ch5

Many Web pages today use **cookies**—small text files that are stored on your hard drive by a Web server, typically the one hosting the Web page being viewed—to identify return visitors and their preferences. For example, if you visit Amazon.com and place items in your shopping cart, a cookie is sent from the Amazon.com Web server to your hard drive with information that will help the Amazon.com Web site retrieve your shopping cart when you revisit the site at a later time. The cookie information can also be used to personalize the Amazon.com Web page based on your shopping preferences the next time you visit. The information stored in a cookie file typically includes the name of the cookie, its expiration date, the domain that the cookie belongs to, and either selected personal information that you have entered while visiting the Web site or an ID number assigned by the Web site that allows the Web site's server to retrieve your information from its database.

The database used in conjunction with a Web site is usually located on the Web site's server and may contain two types of information: *personally identifiable information (PII)* and *non-personally identifiable information (Non-PII).* Personally identifiable data is connected with a specific user's identity—such as his or her name, address, and credit card number—that was provided to the site, typically during the process of ordering goods or services. Non-personally identifiable information is anonymous data—such as which products were looked at or which advertisements located on the site were clicked—that is not directly associated with the visitor's name or any other personally identifiable characteristic.

Some individuals view all cookies as a potentially dangerous invasion of privacy, but the use of cookies can provide some benefits to consumers. For example, cookies can enable a Web site to remember preferences for customized Web site content, as well as retrieve a shopping cart containing items selected during a previous session, as illustrated in Figure 5-1. Other Web sites may use cookies to remember log-on information, though increasingly operating systems—such as recent versions of Windows—can also keep track of Web site passwords, for those users who would prefer not to use cookies for that purpose. Some Web sites may also utilize cookies for marketing purposes to keep track of which pages on their Web sites each person has visited, in order to display advertisements or products on return visits that match his or her interests.

Individual cookies are relatively safe from a privacy standpoint. Web sites can only read their own cookie files; they can't read other cookie files on your PC or any other data on your computer, for that matter. A cookie also cannot track activity from one Web site to the next. Cookies are typically stored in a *Cookies* folder on each user's hard drive, and can be looked at, if desired, although sometimes deciphering the information contained in a cookie file is difficult. Figure 5-2 shows the contents of the cookie file generated by shopping at the BestBuy site shown in Figure 5-1. Notice that the cookie file contains information about both the shopping cart contents and the signed-in user.

One of the factors that fueled objections to cookie use involved the practice of advertising companies, such as *DoubleClick,* trying to track an individual's Web activity by using multiple cookies. Because DoubleClick places banner ads on literally thousands of different Web sites, that company was in the unique position of being able

**FIGURE 5-1**

**Examples of Web site cookie use**

**‹ Personalized content**

Many Web sites use cookies to keep track of display preferences, such as for the customized news, weather, stock quote, and TV listing information shown here for a Yahoo! user.

The user's identity and shopping cart contents are remembered when the site is revisited.

**› Shopping cart content**

Online stores frequently use cookies to remember the contents of your shopping cart (even if you close your browser between sessions) so you can continue shopping at a later time without starting over.

**FIGURE 5-2**

**Viewing a cookie file**

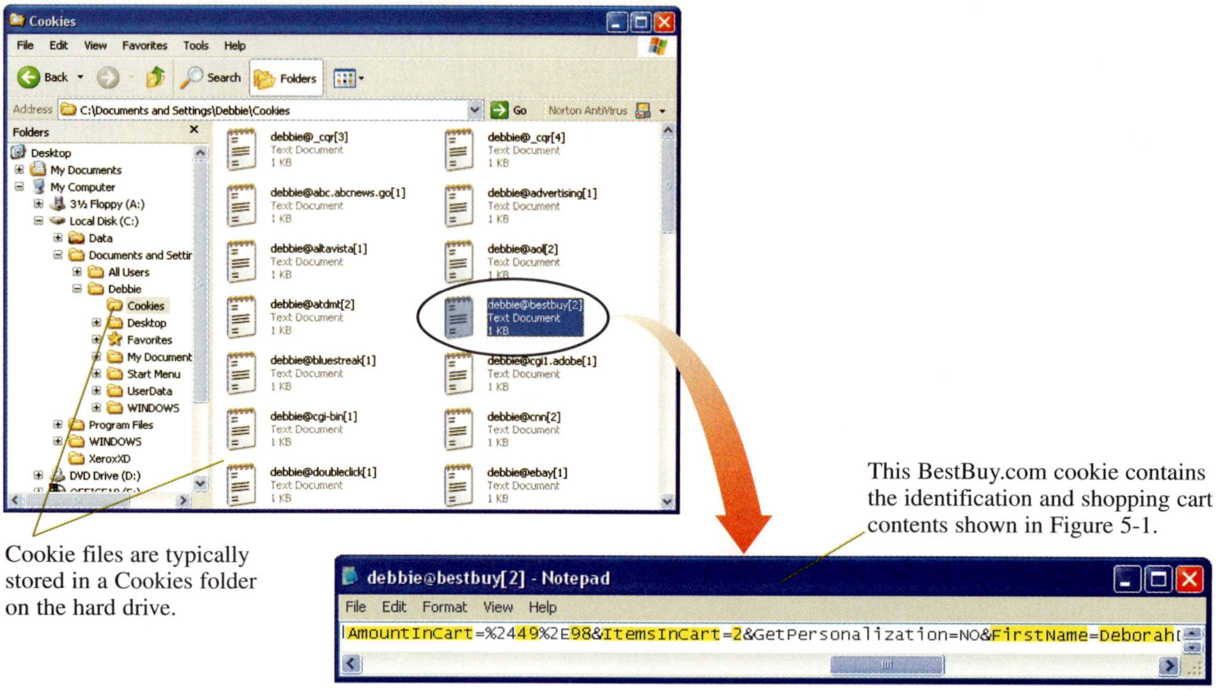


to place many cookies on a single user's hard drive—one for each site the user visited that contained a DoubleClick ad. DoubleClick then used all of the DoubleClick cookies located on that user's hard drive to get an idea of his or her overall Web activity. Although the data collected wasn't associated with the person's actual identity, privacy advocates and other individuals were concerned by the fact that the information was collected and analyzed, and then used to determine the most appropriate advertisements to be displayed for each user. This issue came even more to the forefront in late 1999 when DoubleClick bought a catalog marketing company and announced plans to combine the previously anonymous consumers' online activity data with the newly-acquired marketing company's information in order to track users' Web activity under their actual identity. The announcement of DoubleClick's intent to sell the resulting information really caused an uproar. A flood of privacy lawsuits were filed, such as the one by the privacy watchdog group *EPIC* (*Electronic Privacy Information Center*), which eventually led DoubleClick to agree, in 2002, to obtain permission from consumers before combining any personally identifiable data with Web surfing history.

As a result of the DoubleClick fiasco, there has been some demand for Congress or the Federal Trade Commission (FTC) to legislate how Web surfing data can be used. It is legal and generally accepted that cookies can be placed on a user's hard drive without direct permission by companies known to the user (such as the site the user is visiting). Some people, however, believe that *third-party cookies* (cookies placed by companies other than the one related to the Web site the user is currently visiting, such as advertising firms who have placed ads on that page) should not be able to be installed without direct permission from the user. Currently the advertising industry is pushing for voluntary adherence to usage standards, in lieu of legislation. It has formed the *Network Advertising Initiative* or *NAI* and worked with the FTC and the U.S. Department of Commerce to develop a self-regulatory process governing NAI members, which includes DoubleClick and several other large Internet advertising companies. These standards detail under what conditions non-personally identifiable information can be merged with personally-identifiable information, as well as require that consumers be given the choice to opt out from data collection entirely.

### Web Bugs

A **Web bug** is a very small (often 1 pixel by 1 pixel) image on a Web page that transmits data about a Web page visitor back to the Web page's server. Usually Web bug images are invisible because they are so tiny and typically match the color of the Web page's background. Web bugs can be used to retrieve information stored in cookies, if the Web bug and cookie are both from the same Web site or advertising company. Consequently, Web bugs can be used by third-party advertising companies to compile data about individuals—similar to the multiple-cookie scenario. Web bugs are used extensively by DoubleClick and other Internet advertising companies.

In addition to being used in conjunction with cookies, Web bugs can also relay the IP address of the computer being used to view the Web page. This might be done, for example, in order to cause a different banner ad to be displayed on PCs using an IP address belonging to a commercial ISP, such as Earthlink, (assumed to be home users) versus someone browsing on a PC using a corporate IP address. Web bugs are also used to gather usage statistics about a Web site, such as the number of visitors to the site, the most visited pages on the site, and the time of and the Web browser used for each visit. Perhaps the biggest objection to Web bugs is that they are not visible to users, which means users typically are not aware of this potential invasion of their privacy.

### Spyware

**Spyware** is the term used for any software that is installed without the user's knowledge that secretly gathers information about the user and transmits it through his or her Internet connection to advertisers. Similar to cookies and Web bugs, the information gathered by the spyware software is typically not associated with a person's identity; it is usually used to provide advertisers with information to be used for marketing purposes, such as to help them select advertisements to display on each PC. Like Web bugs, people aren't normally aware when spyware is being used. Instead of being embedded into a Web page like a Web bug, however, spyware programs are usually installed—unknowingly to the users—at the same time another program is installed on the user's computer.

The inclusion of the spyware program is sometimes mentioned in the hosting program's licensing agreement, but most spyware is installed without the user's knowledge. Part of the reason is that studies show most users don't read licensing agreements before clicking *OK* or checking an "I agree" box to install a software program. This is at least partially blamed on the complexity and difficult wording found in some agreements (one analysis of an agreement for a software program containing spyware found its sentences to be over three times as complex as a standard tax form, and the agreement was judged to be written at a $16^{th}$ grade reading level). Once a spyware program is installed on a PC, it typically does not show up on any list of installed programs, making it difficult for users both to realize that the spyware program has been installed and to uninstall it.

Some examples of spyware that became known to the public recently include an ad that automatically downloaded and installed a toolbar from SearchExplorer.com if a user's mouse moved over the ad while it was displayed (the toolbar was used for tracking Web activity for advertising purposes). According to the advertising company that placed the ads, over one million people downloaded the software over a four-week period in 2002 (the ad has subsequently been changed on virtually all Web sites to eliminate the mouse-over download feature). In another example, millions of people who downloaded and installed the popular *Kazaa* file-sharing software program also installed several third-party programs, including one program intended to be used for a new peer-to-peer network. The new peer-to-peer service—called *Altnet*—went online in mid-2002 and works within the Kazaa service to disseminate music and other content available from different companies. It also has the capability of using the individual PCs' processing power for distributed computing, such as performing complicated research-oriented computing tasks for clients. As a result of the backlash from customers outraged that their personal computers' resources could be used for free by other individuals, Kazaa has since made most of its third-party software programs optional, though at least one—an ad server program—must remain installed in order to use the Kazaa service.

Privacy advocates object to spyware because it collects and transmits data about individuals to others, as well as uses up the users' system resources and Internet bandwidth, all without the user's consent. As an additional annoyance, many spyware programs are not removed if the original hosting program is uninstalled.

**FIGURE 5-3**

**Unless e-mail messages are encrypted, they cannot be assumed to be private.**

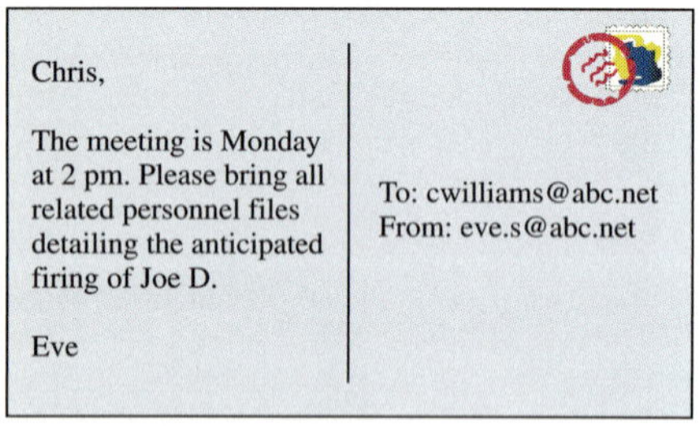


**^ Regular (nonencrypted e-mail) = postcard**

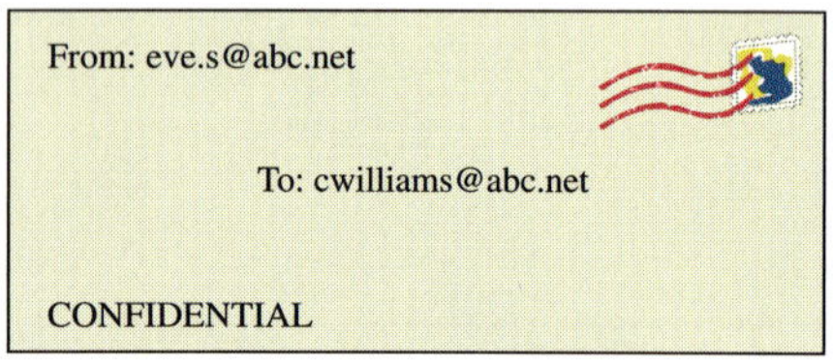


**^ Encrypted e-mail = sealed letter**

## E-mail Privacy

Many people mistakenly believe that the e-mail they send and receive is private and won't ever be read by anyone other than the intended recipient. Since it is transmitted over public media, however, nonencrypted e-mail can be intercepted and read by someone else. Although it is unlikely this will happen to your personal e-mail, only encrypted e-mail can be transmitted privately. It is also important to realize that your employer and your ISP have access to the e-mail you send through those organizations and will often *archive* (keep copies of) it. There have been many cases where e-mail sent by criminal suspects, such as computer hackers and stalkers, has been retrieved by law enforcement from the suspects' ISPs and used to prosecute them. Consequently, it is wise to view nonencrypted e-mail as more like a postcard than a letter, from a privacy standpoint (see Figure 5-3).

## Databases and Electronic Profiling

Information about individuals can be located in several different types of databases. For example, most educational institutions maintain databases containing student information, most organizations have an employee database for employee information, and most physicians and health insurance providers maintain separate databases containing individuals' medical information. From a privacy standpoint, these databases, provided they are adequately protected from hackers and other unauthorized individuals, are not of significant concern to consumers because the information can rarely be shared without the individuals' permission. On the other hand, *marketing* and *government databases* are associated with a higher risk of privacy violations.

**Marketing databases** contain data about people, such as where they live, what they are inclined to do, and what they buy. This information is used for marketing purposes, such as to send advertisements that fit each individual's interests (via regular mail or e-mail) or to try to sign people up over the phone for some type of service. Virtually anytime you provide information about yourself online or offline—for example, when you subscribe to a magazine, fill out a sweepstakes entry, or buy a product or service with a credit card—there's a good chance that information will find its way into a marketing database.

Information about individuals is also available in **government databases**. Some information, such as Social Security earnings and income tax returns, is confidential and should only be seen by authorized individuals. Other information—such as birth records, marriage certificates, and property purchases—are available to the public, including the marketing companies that specialize in creating marketing databases.

In the past, the various types of data about any one individual were stored in several separate locations, such as at different government agencies, individual stores, and the person's bank and credit card companies. Because it would be extremely time-consuming to locate all the information about one person from all these different places, there was a fairly high level of information privacy. Today, however, most of an individual's data is stored on computers that can communicate with each other via the Internet, which means accessing personal information about someone is much easier than it used to be. For example, a variety of information about individuals is available for free through the Internet (see Figure 5-4); there are also paid services that perform online database searches. Although sometimes this capability is an advantage—such as checking the background of potential employees to see if they have a criminal record or looking up a misplaced phone number—it does raise privacy concerns.

Collecting a variety of in-depth information about an individual is known as **electronic profiling**. Marketing companies create electronic profiles on individuals from data acquired from a variety of sources—for instance, product and service purchases that are personally identifiable and public information, such as land values, vehicle registrations, births, marriages, and deaths. Electronic profiles are frequently very specific and can include information about an individual's name, current and previous addresses, telephone number, marital status, number and age of children, spending habits, and product preferences. The information contained in electronic profiles is then sold to companies upon request to be used for marketing purposes (see Figure 5-5). For example, one company might request a list of all individuals in a particular state whose street addresses are considered to be in an affluent area and who buy baby products. Another company might request a list of all SUV owners in a particular city that haven't bought a car in five years.

**FIGURE 5-4**

**A variety of databases can be searched online for free.**

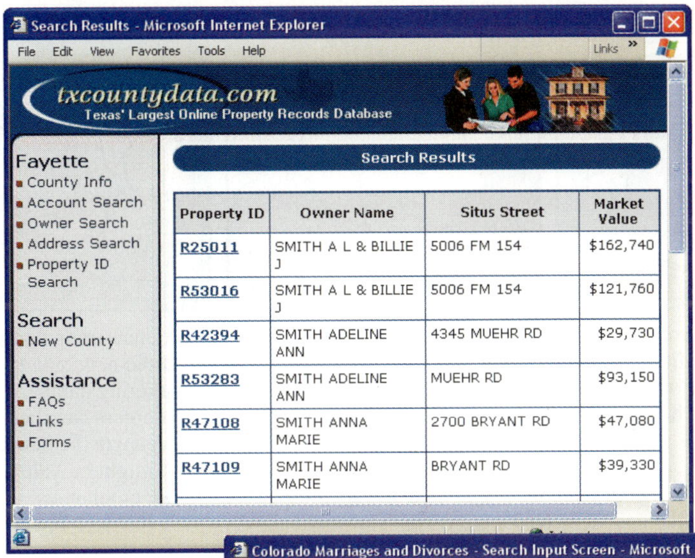


**Property value search**

Some states permit searches for property located in that state, such as the Texas database shown here that allows searches by address or owner name and displays the owner's name, address, and property value.

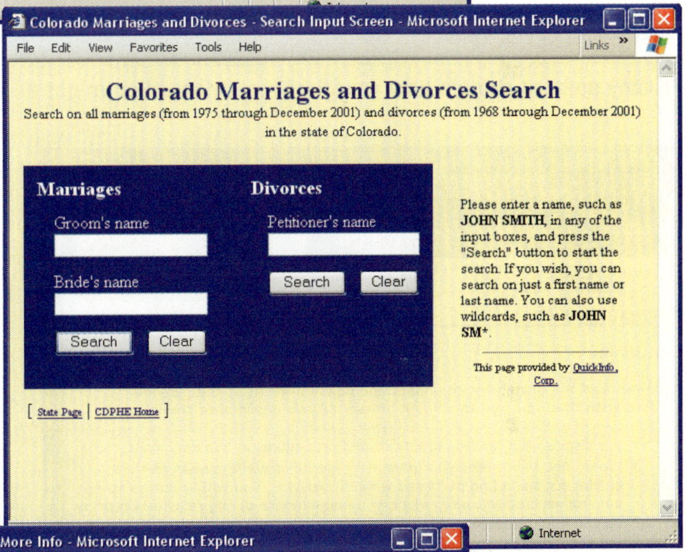


**Marriage or divorce search**

Some states allow anyone to search for recent marriages or divorces that occurred in that state (such as Colorado, as shown here) by the name of the bride, groom, or divorce petitioner.

**Address and phone number search**

Any information listed in a U.S. telephone book can be found using this site. You can search either by name or telephone number to view the available information.

## FIGURE 5-5

**How electronic profiling might work**

When you make an electronic transaction, information about who you are and what you buy is recorded.

The identities of people and what they buy are sold to marketing companies.

The marketing companies add the new data to their marketing databases; their computers can then reorganize the data in ways that might be valuable to other companies.

The marketing companies create lists of individuals matching the specific needs of companies; the companies buy the lists for their own marketing purposes.

## FIGURE 5-6

**Privacy policies explain how your personal information might be used.**

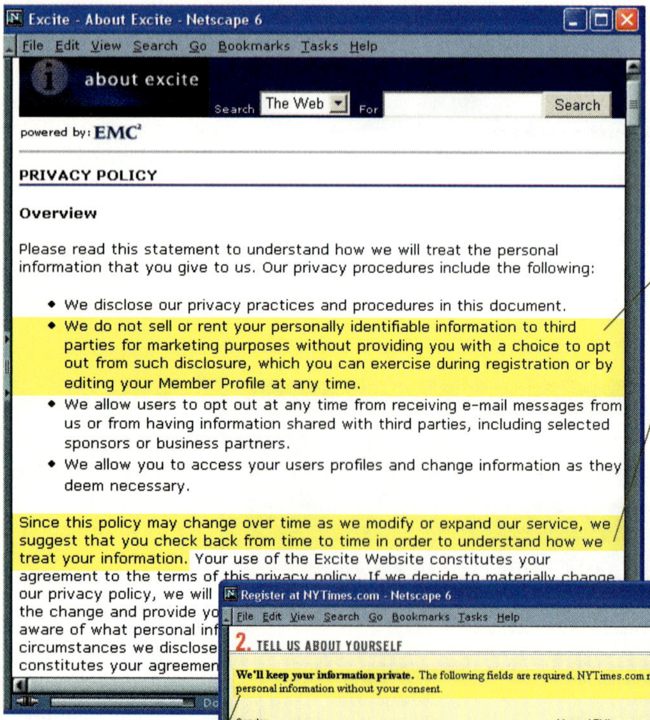


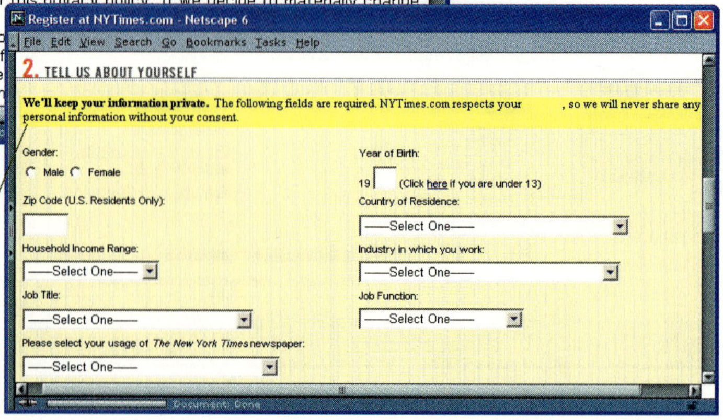


The privacy policy displayed on this Web site indicates that your personally-identifiable information may be disclosed to third parties unless you specifically opt out. It also reserves the right to change the policy at a later time, so suggests you check back periodically.

According to this privacy statement, information provided during registration will not be shared with others without your consent.

Many Web sites have a **privacy policy** (see Figure 5-6) that discloses how the personal information you provide while visiting that Web site or while completing a product registration will be used. As long as their actions do not violate their privacy policy, it is legal for businesses to sell the personal data that they collect. One problem with privacy policies is that they are sometimes difficult to decipher; in addition, many businesses periodically change their privacy policy without warning, requiring consumers to reread privacy policies frequently or risk their personal information being used in a manner that they didn't agree to when the information was initially provided. For example, BestBuy changed its online privacy policy in mid-2002 to allow the company to combine customer information from its Web site with data collected in its stores and to reserve the right to share information collected from surveys or reviews on its Web site with third parties. Other companies recently adapting their privacy policies include eBay, Amazon.com, and Yahoo. Some companies notify customers by e-mail when their privacy policies change, but more commonly they expect customers to check the current policy periodically and notify the business if any new actions are objectionable.

## Spam and Other Marketing Activities

**Spam** refers to unsolicited e-mail sent to a large group of individuals at one time. The electronic equivalent of junk mail (see Figure 5-7), spam most often originates from commercial sources, such as Web sites selling a product or service; a great deal of spam involves pornographic or other potentially offensive materials. Spam can also be generated by individuals forwarding on e-mail messages they receive (such as jokes, recipes, or new possible virus alerts or health concerns) to everyone in their address book. In addition to spam, most individuals receive marketing e-mails either from a company to whom they supplied their e-mail addresses or from another company with whom their e-mail addresses were shared. While these latter types of marketing e-mail messages don't technically fit the definition of spam since they were permission-based, many individuals consider them to be spam.

Large ISPs such as America Online often have millions of pieces of spam clogging their networks each day, and the problem is getting worse all the time. Spam is currently estimated to account for over 25% of all messages received—more than even job-related or personal e-mail, according to Ferris Research. Because spam is much less expensive than other marketing activities (one marketing resource offers 15 million e-mail addresses for about $100) and seems to be working (one spammer reports that the typical response rate is 4 to 5%), the amount of spam and other types of marketing e-mail sent to individuals is expected to continue to increase at a rapid pace. Although legislation is currently being drafted at both federal and state levels to curb spam abuse, it is complicated since spam is regarded as commercial speech and is therefore protected by the First Amendment.

One of the most common ways of getting on a spam mailing list is as a result of signing up for a free online service, such as a sweepstakes, newsletter, or discussion group. Once you use your e-mail address to register a product, place an order, or respond to an online or e-mail offer, chances are you are opening yourself up to receiving spam as well. At best, large volumes of spam are an annoyance to recipients and can slow down a mail server's delivery of important messages. At worst, they can disable a mail network completely. Many view spam as an invasion of privacy because it arrives on computers without permission and costs them time and other resources (such as bandwidth, mailbox space, and hard drive space). With spam beginning to arrive on smart phones, pagers, and other wireless devices—which usually charge on a per-message basis—spam may soon become a very expensive annoyance for individuals and businesses that use wireless devices.

Other unsolicited marketing activities that can be viewed as privacy violations because of their intrusion factor include *pop-up* and *pop-under ads*, *telemarketing*, and *adware*. Pop-up and pop-under ads are Web-based advertisements that show up in a separate browser window when you are surfing the Web, typically generated by viewing a particular Web page. As their names suggest, pop-up ads appear on top of all other browser windows; pop-under ads appear beneath all other browser windows and so may not be noticed until a later time. **Telemarketing**—a marketing activity that many individuals encounter almost every day—consists of unsolicited offers that come via the telephone. Unlike pop-up and pop-under ads, which are typically displayed in response to a Web page just displayed, most telemarketing is targeted to individuals based on the data contained in a marketing database, compiled from both a user's offline and online activities.

**Adware**—free or low cost software that is supported by onscreen advertising—is another very common online marketing tool today. Many free programs that can be downloaded from the Internet, such as the free version of the NetZero e-mail program and the Gator e-Wallet, include some type of onscreen advertising. Some programs

**FIGURE 5-7**

Examples of spam

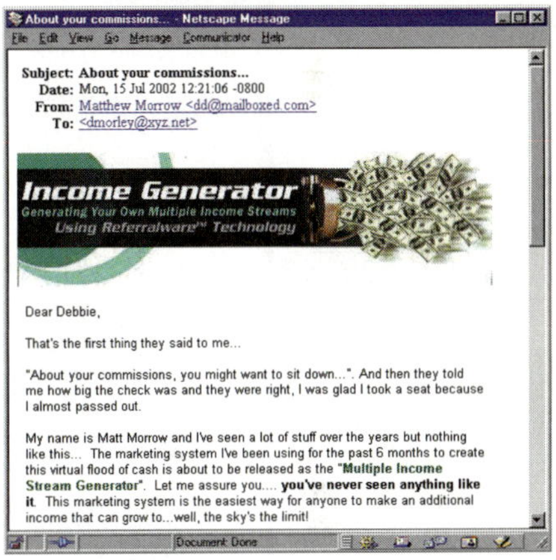

that incorporate adware into their free version also have a paid (without advertising) version available as well (see Figure 5-8). Although some adware may display banners ads on the PC it's installed on, similar to some spyware programs, adware differs from spyware in that it doesn't secretly gather data about the individual and then use his or her Internet connection to relay that information to someone else. One advantage of adware from a marketing standpoint is that it enables advertisers to reach consumers when they are at work—a period of time that traditionally has been off-limits.

**FIGURE 5-8**

**Some programs are available in both free (with adware) and paid (without adware) versions.**

The paid version doesn't display ads.

The free version includes adware.

## Electronic Surveillance and Monitoring

There are many ways electronic tools can be used to watch individuals, listen in on their conversations, or monitor their activity. Some of these tools—such as devices used by individuals to eavesdrop on wireless and cordless telephone conversations—aren't legal. Other products and technologies, such as the GPS devices that are built into some cars so they can be located if they are stolen or the monitoring ankle or wrist bracelets used for offenders sentenced to house arrest, are used solely for law enforcement purposes. Still others, such as *computer monitoring software* and *video surveillance* equipment, can sometimes be used legally by individuals and businesses, in addition to being used by law enforcement agencies.

### Computer Monitoring Software

While cookies, Web bugs, and spyware can keep track of some Web activity, **computer monitoring software** is available specifically for the purpose of recording keystrokes or otherwise continually monitoring someone's computer activity. These programs are typically marketed towards parents (to check on their children's online activities), spouses (to determine if a spouse is having an affair, viewing pornography, or participating in activities that are unacceptable to the other spouse), or employers (to ensure employees are using company computers and time only for work-related activities). Computer monitoring programs can be set up to keep a log of all computer keystrokes, but more commonly are set up to record activity pre-designated as questionable (such as visiting certain Web sites) or to take screen shots at specified intervals (see Figure 5-9).

Although it is legal to use computer monitoring software on your own computer or the computers of your employees, installing it on PCs without the owners' knowledge to monitor their computer activity is usually an illegal activity. For example, in 2001 a Michigan man installed monitoring software on the computer of his estranged wife, who was living in a separate residence at the time. The software recorded all of her computer activity, including all e-mail messages sent and received and all Web pages visited, and sent that information to the man's e-mail account. After mentioning information that he should not have known to a friend of his wife, the matter was investigated and the man was charged with four felony counts (installing an eavesdropping device, eavesdropping, using a computer to commit a crime, and having unauthorized computer access). Faced with up to 5 years in prison and fines of up to $19,000, the man pled guilty to two of the charges and was sentenced to 2 years probation plus court costs and fees.

**FIGURE 5-9**

**An example of a computer monitoring program**

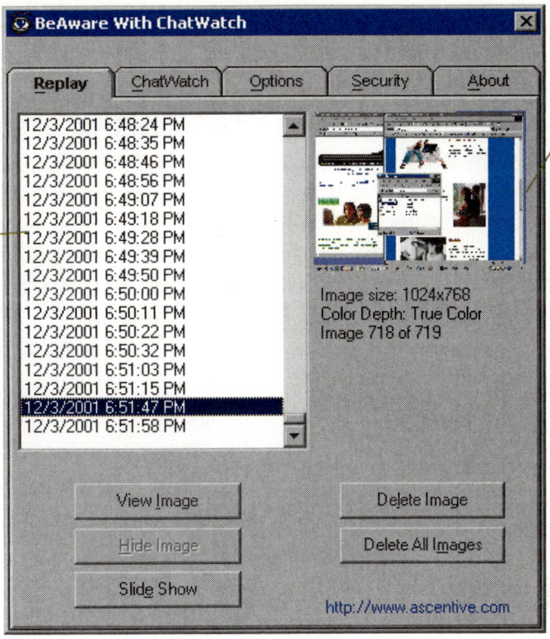


This program is set up to take captures of the screen about every 10 seconds.

Captured images can be previewed here or viewed using the options at the bottom of the screen.

In addition to consumer monitoring products, there are also monitoring programs available only for use by law enforcement and other government agencies. Similar to wiretapping, electronic monitoring of computer activity requires a court order or similar authorization to be lawful. The Closer Look box describes how one monitoring program—the FBI's **Carnivore** project—can be used to intercept e-mail and other Web activities from individuals suspected of criminal activity. This program has been highly controversial since its inception, mainly due to questions about the possibility of it being used improperly.

One limitation of the Carnivore program from a law enforcement standpoint involves encrypted documents. If a file or e-mail is encrypted, although it can still be intercepted using the Carnivore program, it must be decrypted in order to be understood. The decryption process can take a long time, since the government agency doesn't have access to the needed encryption key. To overcome this limitation, monitoring software that records all keystrokes can be used to record e-mail messages and documents before they are encrypted, as well as to record encryption passwords. For example, the FBI used a keystroke monitoring system in 1999 in the investigation of the son of a reputed former Philadelphia mob boss. Although he was suspected of heading a New Jersey loan-sharking operation with ties to organized crime, encryption software prevented the FBI from being able to read his intercepted electronic communications. After obtaining a court order to enter the suspect's house and install the system on his computer, the FBI was able to obtain enough information to indict him.

Virtually all computer monitoring programs need to be physically installed on the PC that is to be monitored—a big disadvantage for law enforcement agencies who wish to monitor the activities taking place on a suspect's PC. To overcome this limitation, the FBI is reportedly developing a keystroke logging program known as *Magic Lantern.* Like other keystroke logging programs, Magic Lantern software records all keystrokes performed on the computer on which it is installed, but is designed to be installed on a suspect's PC using a computer virus sent over the Internet to the suspect, instead of having to be physically installed in person.

## A CLOSER LOOK AT... THE FBI'S CARNIVORE PROGRAM

### Legitimate Law Enforcement or Invasion of Privacy?

Carnivore, the FBI's e-mail and Web activity monitoring system that has recently been renamed a less-threatening-sounding *DCS1000*, has had many privacy advocates up in arms since its existence was first confirmed. Originally, the idea behind the system was to monitor the e-mail traffic sent from a criminal suspect; it has subsequently been expanded to monitor other types of Web activity performed by a criminal suspect, such as Web pages viewed and files downloaded.

Carnivore is a *packet sniffing program*—a program that can monitor all of the information passing over a network; in this case, the Internet. As data passes over the Internet, the program looks at, or "sniffs," each packet to see if it is a packet the program is looking for. To use Carnivore to monitor a suspect's activities, the FBI and the suspect's ISP work together to identify an access point that contains all Internet traffic involving the suspect, with as little other Internet traffic as possible—that access point is the location where the Carnivore system is installed. All packets passing through the access point are bypassed through the Carnivore system, which identifies and makes copies of all packets coming from the criminal suspect's PC. The copies are run through a filter and only the packets meeting the specifications of the court order are stored; all other packets are discarded (see Figure 5-10).

Although the FBI stresses that the Carnivore system is to be used only when permitted by a court order or other authority as allowed by law (similar to a telephone wiretap) and only the communications sent by the suspect are looked at by agents, privacy advocates remain concerned. They argue that Carnivore differs from a wiretap in that it has access to all messages passing through the ISP, not just those going to or coming from the criminal suspect's PC, so there is grave potential for abuse. The FBI counters that using Carnivore in any way other than as specified in the court order is illegal. Carnivore is currently used to gather evidence against criminal suspects in several specific areas, such as child pornography, espionage, fraud, and terrorism—in fact, it was used extensively in the hours following the 9/11 attacks to try to identify the responsible parties and to obtain information about any additional attacks yet to come.

Communications networks are routinely used in the commission of serious criminal activities, so law enforcement agencies say the ability to conduct lawful electronic surveillance of the communications of suspected criminals is essential for preventing serious criminal behavior. The FBI must work continuously to break any new encryption procedures that criminals may use to disguise their electronic communications, in addition to developing other computer surveillance methods, such as the Magic Lantern keystroke logging program, that work around the encryption problem.

Since the 9/11 terrorist attacks, public support for electronic surveillance methods for national security purposes has increased. A Harris poll taken in late September 2001 indicated that 63% of Americans favored law enforcement monitoring of online communications taking place in chat rooms, and 54% favored expanded government monitoring of cell phones and e-mail to intercept communications from terrorists and other criminals.

**FIGURE 5-10**

**The FBI's Carnivore program uses a packet sniffer to filter out Internet traffic coming from a criminal suspect.**

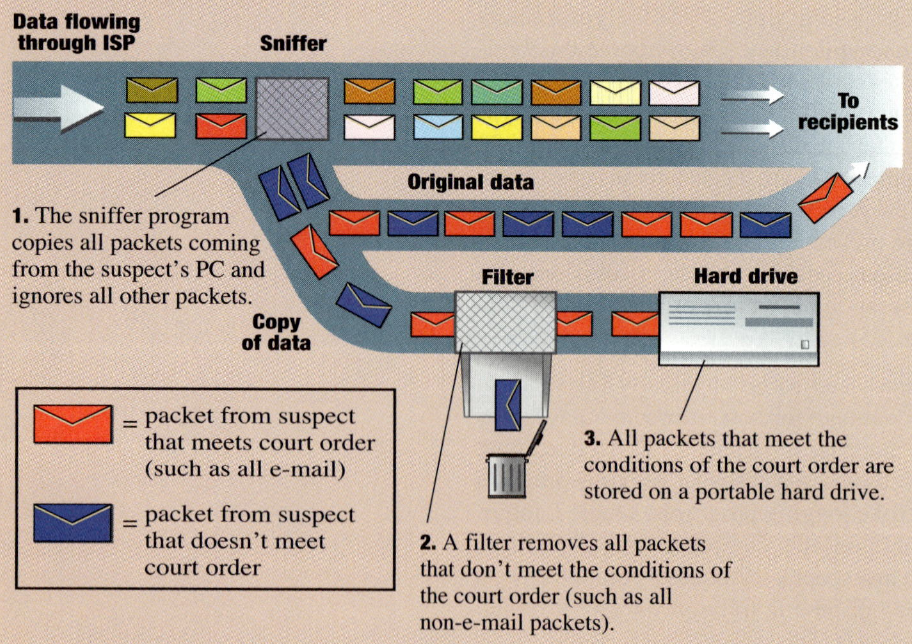

## Employee Monitoring

**Employee monitoring** refers to companies recording or observing the actions that their employees take while on the job. With today's technology, employee monitoring is very easy to perform and much of it can be done through the use of computers. Although many employees feel that being watched at work is an invasion of their personal privacy, it is legal and it is on the rise. According to a recent study by the American Management Association (AMA), the majority (about 75%) of all U.S. companies use some type of electronic surveillance with their employees, typically reviewing e-mail messages, monitoring telephone calls, checking downloaded files, and reviewing Web usage.

**ONLINE TUTORIAL**

For an online look at various types of employee monitoring, go to www.course.com/morley2003/ch5

Tools employers can use to monitor employees include monitoring software, cameras, and *proximity cards.* A proximity card is similar to the magnetic stripe ID cards that have been used for years to grant access to facilities or computer systems, but has smart card capabilities built in (see Figure 5-11) to give it additional functionality. For monitoring purposes, proximity cards can identify the location of each employee wearing one on a continual basis—an application that some privacy advocates feel crosses the line between valid monitoring of activity and an invasion of privacy. Other less controversial uses for proximity cards include regular access capabilities (like conventional access cards), automatically locking an employee's PC when they get a certain distance away from it (to eliminate the problem of nosy co-workers), and automatically unlocking the PC when the employee returns (to eliminate the need for passwords).

**FIGURE 5-11**

**Proximity cards with smart card capabilities can be used for facility access, PC access, and employee monitoring.**

Although some employees may view workplace monitoring as an invasion of their personal privacy, employers have several valid reasons for monitoring employee activities, such as security concerns, productivity measurement, legal compliance, and legal liability. For example, management has a responsibility to the company (and to its stockholders for publicly held corporations) to make sure employees do the job that they are getting paid to do. If any employees are spending too much time away from their desks chatting with other employees, answering their personal e-mail, or placing online bids at eBay, the company has the right to know and the responsibility to stop that misuse of company time. In addition, the company needs to protect itself against lost business (due to employee incompetence or poor client skills, for example) and lawsuits (such as from employees if offensive e-mail messages are circulated among the office or inappropriate Web sites are displayed on someone's PC).

Even though employee monitoring can be expensive, many companies view the cost as insignificant compared to the risk of a multimillion dollar lawsuit. For instance, one study showed that 11% of U.S. firms have battled sexual harassment and/or racial discrimination claims stemming from employee e-mail and Internet use, and Chevron was recently ordered to pay female employees $2.2 million to settle a sexual harassment lawsuit stemming from inappropriate e-mail sent by male employees.

Case law strongly supports employee monitoring, since the equipment and network the employee uses belong to the employer; even e-mail messages sent or received at work have been ruled to be the employer's property. There have been several cases where employees have learned this fact the hard way, such as the case in December 1999 when 23 New York Times employees were fired for sending inappropriate e-mail messages to one another over the company's network. A very worrisome trend for employers is the high occurrence of e-mail or Web activity involving pornography or other potentially offensive content that leaves the employer liable for lawsuits. The AMA study found that 46% of the companies surveyed initiated disciplinary action against employees for sending sexually suggestive or explicit material via office e-mail, and 36% had disciplined employees for downloading, uploading, or viewing pornography.

To reduce cost and objections from employees, some businesses have found employee training and education to be an effective and cost-efficient alternative to continuous monitoring. Regardless of the techniques used, it is wise for businesses to inform employees about their monitoring practices, although they are not required by law to do so at the current time. Legislation has been introduced to set minimum standards for employee notification, but no legislation has yet been signed into law.

### Video Surveillance

The idea of video surveillance is nothing new. Closed-circuit cameras have been monitoring activities in such places as retail stores, banks, and office buildings for years. What is new, however, is the increased use of video cameras in public locations for law enforcement purposes.

Often used in conjunction with face recognition technology, video cameras are now being used in such locations as sporting arenas, airports, and public parks, in hopes of identifying known terrorists and other criminals and preventing crimes. Although one of the first public trials of this technology at the 2001 Super Bowl in Atlanta resulted in a huge public outcry, since 9/11 public opinion has become more tolerant of video surveillance. In a September 2001 Harris poll, an astounding 86% of the Americans polled approved of the use of face recognition technology to scan for suspected terrorists at various public locations and events. This poll shows a clear shift in some Americans' priorities from personal privacy to personal safety. It remains to be seen whether or not public opinion will revert back to being more critical of public video surveillance as we move further away from the events of 9/11.

Not surprisingly, the focus of video camera installations since 9/11 has been in Washington D.C. and New York. In many cases, the cameras are hidden from view or disguised, such as being installed inside a lamp fixture, as shown in Figure 5-12. More obvious video surveillance setups have also been installed at potential targets during high-profile times, such as the ones used in July 2002 to monitor the Fourth of July celebration at the National Mall in Washington D.C. and to screen ferry passengers bound for the Statue of Liberty (refer again to Figure 5-12).

**FIGURE 5-12**

**Examples of video surveillance performed by the government and law enforcement agencies**

Camera is inside the light fixture

**‹ Subtle surveillance**

For most ongoing surveillance locations, cameras are non-obtrusively placed to blend into their surroundings.

**› Obvious surveillance**

Some surveillance setups are intentionally obvious, such as at airports and other public places, in hopes of deterring criminal acts by their presence.

### Presence Technology

**Presence technology** refers to the ability of one computing device (such as a desktop PC, PDA, or smart phone) on a network (such as the Internet) to locate and identify another device on the same network and determine its status. In theory, it can be used to tell when someone on the network is using his or her computer or mobile phone, as well as where that device is physically located at any given time. For example, when an employee at a company using presence technology (sometimes called *presence management* when used in a business context) has a question that needs answering, he or she can check the directory displayed on his or her PC or mobile phone to see which team members are available for a quick telephone call or instant message, regardless of where those team members are physically located (see Figure 5-13). Presence technology is also expected to be used on regular Web pages, so visitors—usually potential or current customers—can see which salespeople, service representatives, or other contacts are currently available. Another expected application is including dynamic presence buttons in e-mail messages—the presence button would display one message (such as "I'm online") if the sender is online at the time the e-mail message is read, and a different message (such as "I'm offline") if the sender is not signed in at that time.

Although future presence technology applications are expected to go way beyond instant messaging (IM), at the moment IM is the most widely available presence application. Today's instant messaging doesn't tell you where a PC or mobile communications device user is currently located and only works with people on your pre-designated buddy list, but the instant messaging window does indicate to individuals when people on their buddy lists sign on and off. According to industry estimates, more than 50 million people in the United States use instant messaging, and many of those people say that one of their favorite aspects of the technology is the ability to know whether or not a buddy is online.

Though presence technology is currently in the early stages, it has been in the works since 1996 in the form of an FCC **enhanced 911 (e911)** mandate for mobile phones. The e911 mandate was prompted by the tremendous increase in 911 calls made from mobile phones (now estimated to be one wireless call to 911 in the U.S. every four seconds) paired with the fact that 911 operators are unable to locate the position of mobile callers, unlike callers using a land-based telephone. The e911 mandate regulations specify that new cell phones must have built-in GPS capabilities to enable emergency services personnel to pinpoint the location of people calling 911 using a mobile phone. Phase I requires only the location of the nearest cell tower; phase II, which began in October 2001 and is scheduled to be fully implemented by the end of 2005, requires more precise location information. Though designed to assist in emergency services, phone vendors and advertising agencies are expected to develop other uses for these location services. Possibilities include seeing ads targeted to where you happen to be physically located at the moment (such as close to a particular restaurant at lunchtime), as well as being able to tell if a family member or friend is available for a telephone call before dialing the number.

One group currently working on developing presence technology applications and specifications is the *Wireless Village.* Founded by Ericsson, Motorola, and Nokia, the Wireless Village—also called the *Mobile Instant Messaging and Presence Services (Mobile IMPS) Initiative*—was formed in April 2001 to define and promote a set of universal specifications for instant messaging and presence services used in conjunction with wireless devices. Under the current specifications, consumers will be able to determine the information about themselves—such as their availability, location, call status, and connection status—that they want to be available to others. For example, individuals could specify status information such as "In meeting," "Outside," "Busy," or "Available" to be transmitted to the individuals in their buddy list located on their mobile phone or other mobile communications device.

Though some aspects of presence technology are intriguing (such as being able to tell that a loved one's flight arrived safely when you notice his or her cell phone is turned on again or knowing if a friend or colleague is finished with a meeting), privacy advocates are pushing for legislation and standards to ensure that presence technology providers protect users' security and privacy. At the time of this writing, a bill had been introduced in the House of Representatives that requires informed customer consent for the use of wireless presence information, but the bill was still in committee.

**FIGURE 5-13**

**An example of presence technology in use**

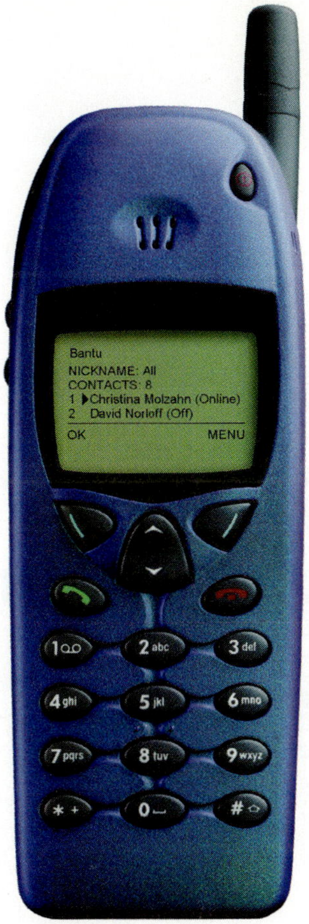

# PRIVACY SAFEGUARDS

Although there isn't any way to ensure that your personal information is 100% protected in today's information society, there are precautions you can take to help protect your Web browsing and e-mail privacy, prevent electronic profiling, reduce spam and other marketing activities, know if you are being electronically monitored, and otherwise safeguard your privacy. Some precautions can be implemented by making adjustments to your computer settings, others involve using third-party software, and still others are based on using common sense or other offline procedures.

## Protection of Web Browsing and E-mail Privacy

One way to protect your privacy while browsing the Web is to control the use of cookies, spyware, and Web bugs. Another way is to reduce the amount of personal information you allow your Web browser to give out. Both of these privacy safeguards can be carried out to some degree by changing settings in your Web browser; for users who want a higher level of control and protection, third-party software or services can be used. E-mail messages and other communications sent via the Internet can be made private through the use of encryption.

**FIGURE 5-14**

**Browser cookie management**

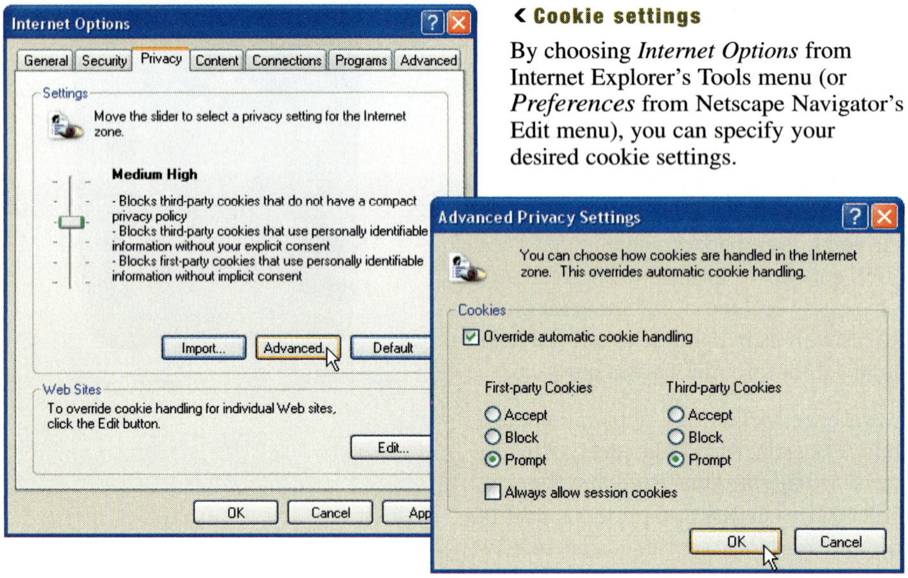


**‹ Cookie settings**

By choosing *Internet Options* from Internet Explorer's Tools menu (or *Preferences* from Netscape Navigator's Edit menu), you can specify your desired cookie settings.

**⌄ Cookie prompts**

After turning on a "Prompt" or "Warn me" cookie feature, you will be prompted to accept or reject cookies as they are encountered. You can usually view more information about the cookie before allowing or blocking it, as well as apply that decision to all future cookies sent from that site.

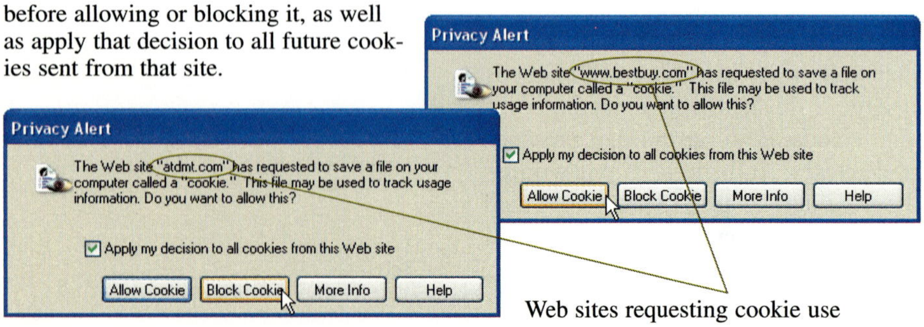


Web sites requesting cookie use

### Cookie, Spyware, and Web Bug Control

As shown in Figure 5-14, Web browsers offer some level of cookie control, from allowing all cookies to turning off cookies entirely (which may make some features—such as a shopping cart—on some Web sites inoperable). The *Medium* and *Medium High* privacy settings in Internet Explorer are widely used choices since they allow the use of regular cookies, but block most cookies using personally identifiable information without permission, and prevent any software (such as spyware) from being installed automatically without consent. Both Internet Explorer and Netscape Navigator users who want more individual control over cookies can choose to accept or decline cookies as they are encountered. Although this option interrupts your Web surfing frequently, it is interesting to see the cookies generated from each individual Web site. For example, the two cookie prompts shown in the bottom of Figure 5-14 were both generated while visiting the BestBuy.com Web site after turning on this feature. Although the first cookie request came from the BestBuy.com Web site directly, the second was a third-party cookie from Atlas DMT, an online marketing company. Another alternative for controlling cookies is periodically deleting the cookie files stored on your hard drive, either by using an option available through your Web browser or by finding the Cookie folder located on your hard drive and deleting its contents using your file management program.

**ONLINE RESOURCES**

For links to information about controlling cookies and detecting Web bugs and spyware, go to www.course.com/morley2003/ch5

For an even greater control over cookies, third-party **cookie management software** (such as the Cookie Crusher and the free-for-home-use WebWasher programs) can be used; some firewall programs also include cookie-blocking capabilities. Cookie programs can prevent the use of cookies by Web bugs, although it is not possible at the present time to suppress Web bugs themselves. To see if a Web page contains a Web bug, some programs—such as Bugnosis—can be used. These programs typically check all suspicious graphics located on a Web page as it is first opened, make any Web bugs hidden on the page visible so you can see them, and provide information about each Web bug found. Firewall programs can protect against spyware programs transmitting information over your Internet connection, since firewalls typically control outgoing computer traffic as well as incoming. To prevent spyware from being installed on your computer in the first place, it is a good idea to see if the program you would like to download is on a list of known spyware programs (such as by using the Spychecker Web site shown in Figure 5-15) before downloading the program. Spyware programs (as well as other items, such as adware and cookies, that may involve privacy risks) already installed on your PC can be detected by special programs designed for that purpose, such as LavaSoft's Ad-aware Plus (also shown in Figure 5-15). These programs typically both identify and allow you to remove any risky components found.

**FIGURE 5-15**

**Ways to detect and avoid spyware**

**‹ Spyware prevention**

Web sites such as this can be used to check whether or not a specific program is known spyware.

Computer resources to be scanned

Spyware and other potential nuisances found (like this DoubleClick cookie); checking an item and continuing will delete it.

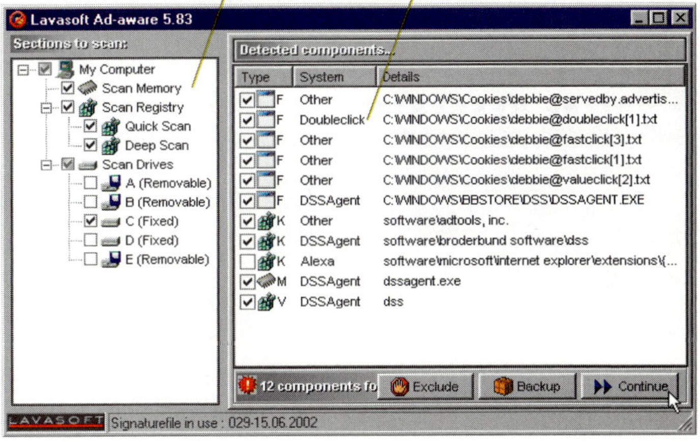


**› Spyware detection and removal**

Spyware programs are often difficult to identify and remove; spyware removal programs can identify any spyware on your PC and remove it if you instruct it to do so.

## Anonymous Web Browsing

Although you can hide your identify somewhat by removing your name and e-mail address from your browser information (see Figure 5-16), for a truly anonymous online experience a third-party service or software program is needed. Third-party products and services, such as the Anonymizer service shown in Figure 5-16, hide individuals' personal information, as well as their computer's IP address and other identifying indicators. Some of these types of programs or services also include other useful features, such as cookie management, hiding the browser's history and

**FIGURE 5-16**

**Anonymous Web browsing**

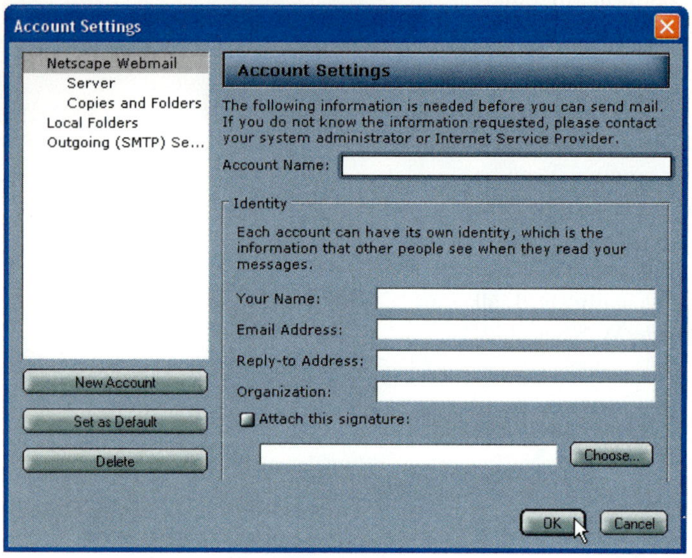


**‹ Removing personal information from a browser**

If you don't use the e-mail component of a browser, remove your name and e-mail address from the e-mail settings so that information isn't available while your browser is being used (select *Mail/News Account Settings* from the Edit menu to get to this screen in Netscape Navigator).

This button turns the Anonymizer service off or on.

**› Using a third-party anonymity service**

For more complete online anonymity, third-party Internet privacy services or programs can be used, such as this one that routes all Web page information through its secure server before displaying the page.

bookmark information, and suppressing annoying pop-up ads. Internet privacy software is often sold on a subscription basis; it typically can be updated on a regular basis throughout the subscription period and costs about $30 to $50 per year.

### E-mail Privacy Protection

As discussed in detail in Chapter 4, to protect sensitive files and e-mail messages, encryption programs—which ensure that messages and file content are unreadable if they are intercepted by someone other than the intended recipient—can be used. Encryption options are available as part of some e-mail programs, with a third-party encryption program, or through a Web-based service. The chapter How To box explains how to use encryption to protect the privacy of e-mail messages and files sent over the Internet.

## Protection of Personal Information

There are a number of precautions that can be taken to protect the privacy of personal information. Safeguarding your e-mail address and other personal information is a good start. You can also *opt out* of some marketing activities and use filters to limit exposure to spam and objectionable Web content.

### Safeguard Your E-mail Address

Protecting your e-mail address is one of the best ways to avoid spam. One way to accomplish this is to use one e-mail address for family, friends, colleagues, and other trusted sources. For online shopping, signing up for free offers, discussion groups, product registration, and other activities that typically lead to junk e-mail, use an alternative *disposable* or **throw-away e-mail address**—such as a second address from your ISP or a free e-mail address from Yahoo! or Hotmail. Although you will want to check your alternate e-mail address periodically, such as to check for online shopping receipts or shipping notifications, this method can prevent a great deal of spam from getting to your regular e-mail account. Another advantage of using a throw-away e-mail address for only non-critical applications is that you can quit using it and get a new one if spam begins to get overwhelming or too annoying.

To comply with truth-in-advertising laws, an *unsubscribe* e-mail address included in an unsolicited e-mail must be a working address. If you receive a marketing e-mail from a reputable source, you may be able to unsubscribe by clicking on the supplied link or

**ONLINE RESOURCES**

For links to information about obtaining e-mail addresses, go to www.course.com/morley2003/ch5

otherwise following the unsubscribe instructions. Since spam from less-legitimate sources often has unsubscribe links that don't work or are present only to verify that your e-mail address is genuine—a very valuable piece of information for future use—some privacy experts recommend never replying back to or trying to unsubscribe from any spam.

### Be Cautious of Revealing Personal Information

In addition to protecting your real e-mail address, protecting your personal information is a critical step to safeguarding your privacy. Consequently, it makes sense to be cautious about revealing your private information to anyone. Privacy tips for safeguarding personal information include the following:

- Read a Web site's privacy policy (if one exists) before providing any personal information. Look for a phrase saying that the company will not share your information with other companies under any circumstances. If the Web site reserves the right to share your information if the company is sold or unless you specifically notify them otherwise, it is best to assume that any information you provide will eventually be shared with others. Web sites displaying certification from a privacy organization, such as the *TRUSTe trustmark* shown in Figure 5-17, either follow the privacy guidelines of that organization or have a policy that has been reviewed by that organization.
- Just because a Web site or registration form asks for personal information from you doesn't mean you have to give it. Supply only the required information (these are often marked with an asterisk or colored differently than non-required fields—if not, you can try leaving fields blank and seeing if the form will still be accepted), and if you are asked for too much personal information, look for an alternate Web site for that product or service. Either way, don't provide an e-mail address (or else use a throw-away address) if you don't want to receive offers or other e-mail from that company (see Figure 5-18).
- Don't supply personal information online to people you meet in chat rooms. Although they may seem like close friends, due to the nature of online communications, it is important to realize that you don't know for sure who they are or what they are like in real life.
- Avoid putting too many personal details about yourself on your Web site. If you'd like to post photographs or other personal items for faraway friends and family members to see, consider using a password protected service (such as PictureTrail or Yahoo! Photos).
- Beware of Web sites offering prizes or the chance to earn free merchandise in exchange for your personal information. Chances are good that the information will be sold to direct marketers, which will likely result in additional spam. If you choose to sign up for services from these Web sites, use your throw-away e-mail address.

**FIGURE 5-17**

**Web sites displaying the TRUSTe trustmark must follow TRUSTe guidelines for setting and adhering to privacy policies.**

reviewed by TRUST e site privacy statement

**FIGURE 5-18**

**Completing only the required information on forms found both on- and offline can help protect your privacy.**

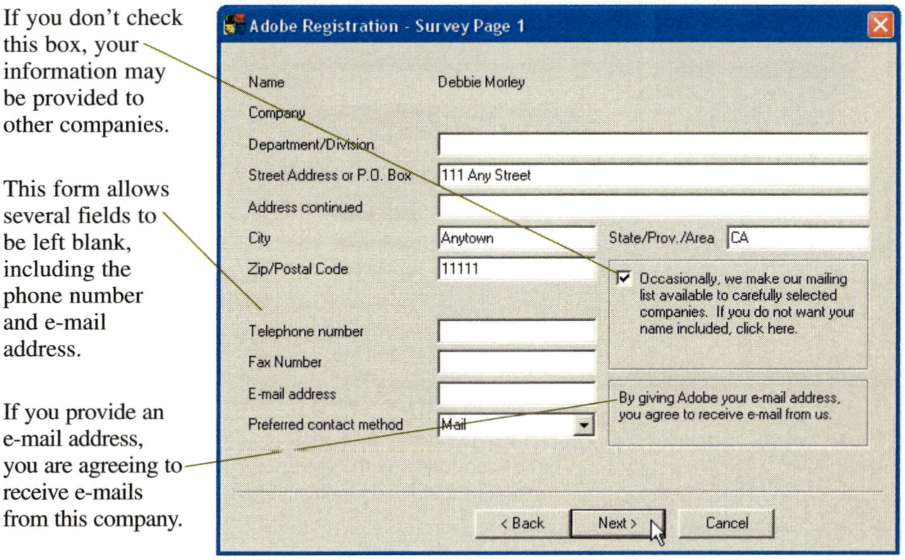

- If you are using a public computer (such as at a school, library, or Internet café), be sure to change back any personal e-mail settings you changed in the e-mail program during the current session, as well as clear the browser's *cache* (copies of frequently visited Web pages that are stored on your hard drive to speed up browsing), cookies, and any other temporary Internet files that might reveal the Web sites you visited during your session.

The chapter Trends In box takes a look at one way companies are working on storing consumers' personal information so it is available to the consumers online on a continual basis, alleviating the need to supply this information again and again on online forms.

### Dealing with Spam and Other Marketing Activities

Keeping your personal information—particularly e-mail address, mailing address, and telephone number—as private as possible can help to reduce spam and some other direct marketing activities, such as direct mail and telemarketing. One common way to deal with spam that makes it to your PC is to use *e-mail filters*—set up either through your ISP or e-mail program. Fee-based filtering services are also commonly used—particularly by businesses.

E-mail filters typically are used to route messages automatically into particular folders based on stated criteria (see Figure 5-19). For example, you could specify that keywords frequently used in spam subject lines, such as *free*, *porn*, *opportunity*, *last chance*, etc., be routed into a folder named Possible Spam, and you could specify that all e-mail messages from your boss be routed into an Urgent folder. Although you would need to check the Possible Spam e-mails periodically to locate any e-mail messages mistakenly filed there before you permanently delete those messages, filtering can help you find the important messages more easily in your e-mail Inbox.

**FIGURE 5-19**

**Creating an e-mail filter**

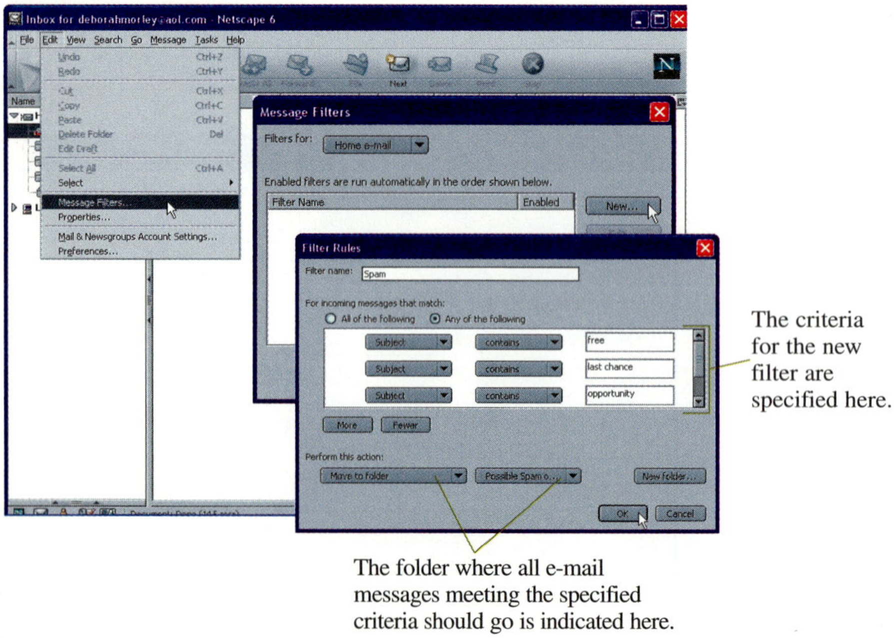


Instead of—or in addition to—filtering spam, you can try to reduce your amount of spam and other direct marketing activities by **opting out**. Opting out refers to following a predesignated procedure to remove yourself from marketing lists or otherwise preventing your personal information from being obtained or shared with others. You might want to opt out for a variety of reasons, such as the following:

- To prevent your bank, insurance company, investment company, and any other financial institution from sharing your personal data with third parties;
- To stop direct marketing companies from sending you junk mail or having telemarketers call you on the telephone;
- To prevent online marketing companies from displaying targeted advertisements in your browser.

# TRENDS IN... DIGITAL IDENTIFICATION

## Online National IDs?

National ID systems for the United States, England, and various other countries have long been proposed. In fact, in August 2002 Japan began issuing 11-digit ID numbers to citizens as part of its new national ID system. The potential benefits of a national ID system include better control of borders and reduced credit card fraud, identity theft, and other serious problems resulting from misuses of the current ID systems—assuming that the new ID cards would contain biometric data to make the cards extremely difficult to forge or otherwise misuse. Disadvantages, according to privacy experts, include the increased centralization of personal data and the resulting reduction in personal privacy.

While the debate continues about a physical national ID card, Microsoft and other companies are developing similar digital IDs for online purposes. Beginning with their *Passport* system introduced in 1999, Microsoft has been working to get public acceptance of a single digital ID. The purpose of the single digital ID is to store in one place a variety of personal information that is frequently needed online, such as log-on names and passwords, shipping and billing addresses, credit card numbers, and more. With the number of user names and passwords any one individual needs to remember today, plus the inconvenience of supplying the same information over and over again on Web page forms, the idea has appeal to many. Originally designed to store only user names and passwords, Microsoft's current .NET version of its Passport system—called *.NET Passport*—is capable of remembering much more data, including the desired e-mail address, name, state, country, ZIP code, language, time zone, gender, birth date, and occupation to be associated with a particular individual for online transactions. The optional .NET Passport Express Purchase Service is a free *digital wallet* service available to consumers that can store shipping, billing, and payment information for faster online purchasing at Web sites supporting .NET Passport.

Microsoft reports that it has issued about 200 million Passport products worldwide, though the Gartner Group estimates the number of actual users to be closer to 14 million. This discrepancy may be due in part to the fact that all users signing up for free Microsoft Hotmail accounts are automatically given a .NET Passport account (see Figure 5-20), but they may never use it. Despite its obvious head start, Microsoft has some new competition in the digital ID arena. Formed in late 2001 by Sun Microsystems and 33 other large companies including American Express, Hewlett-Packard, America Online, MasterCard, Nokia, United Airlines, and RSA Security, the *Liberty Alliance* project is developing a nonproprietary alternative to Microsoft .NET Passport. Where Microsoft originally planned to be the sole custodian of data submitted to its Passport system (although they changed their mind due to customer and developer resistance), Liberty is developing open standards and specifications for *federated network identity*, where an individual's personal information is administered by the user and distributed to appropriate parties as needed, instead of using a central authority. The initial Liberty specifications are complete, and Liberty-enabled products and services are expected to be available by the end of 2002. With the huge number of powerful companies behind it, Liberty is expected to give Microsoft .NET Passport strong competition.

Convenience is the main benefit of a single digital ID because it enables ID holders to visit any Web site and be given personalized attention, and it ensures that the ID holder never has to fill out another form to order products or services. However, precautions must be taken by the developers of digital ID systems to protect users' identities and personal information. For example, what is to prevent someone from creating a Web site with a false Passport sign-on logo to fool customers into entering their log-on names and passwords? And could hackers gain access to the databases containing the personal information? Both Microsoft and Liberty emphasize that security and encryption procedures would ensure the protection of stored consumer data, but all privacy concerns have not been alleviated as of yet. Some experts predict that a single standard will evolve for digital ID systems so that they will work together and personal data will eventually be held by a highly secure independent custody firm, instead of each individual digital ID company, to reduce some objections from privacy advocates in the future.

**FIGURE 5-20**

**Signing up for a Hotmail account automatically creates a .NET Passport account**

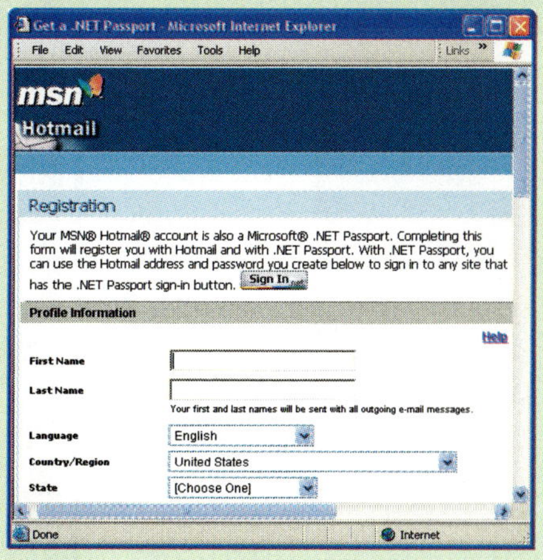

To opt out from a particular company or direct marketing association, you can contact them directly—many organizations include opt out instructions in their privacy policies. For registered online accounts, opt out options are sometimes included in your personal settings and can be activated by modifying your personal settings at that site. Opt out instructions for financial institutions and credit card companies are often included in the disclosure statements that are periodically mailed to customers.

**ONLINE RESOURCES**

For links to information about opting out, go to www.course.com/morley2003/ch5

To assist consumers with the opting out process, there are a number of Web sites, such as the Center for Democracy and Technology and PrivacyRightsNow!, that provide tools to help consumers opt out. For example, these sites help visitors create opt out letters that can be sent to the appropriate companies (see Figure 5-21). For online marketing activities, organizations such as the Network Advertising Initiative have options on their Web sites to help consumers opt out of online targeted ads. Typically, this process replaces the advertiser's marketing cookie with a general *opt-out cookie*. The opt-out cookie prevents another marketing cookie belonging to that particular advertiser from being placed on that user's hard drive as long as the opt-out cookie is present (usually until the user deletes the opt-out cookie file).

At the present time, opting out procedures are confusing and time consuming, and don't always work well. Consequently, some privacy groups are pushing to change to an *opt in* process, where companies would need to obtain an individual's consent before collecting or sharing any personal data. Until there is a change in legislation, however, the general practice in the business community will remain that they can use your information as allowed for by their privacy policy unless you specifically opt out.

**FIGURE 5-21**

**Opting out**

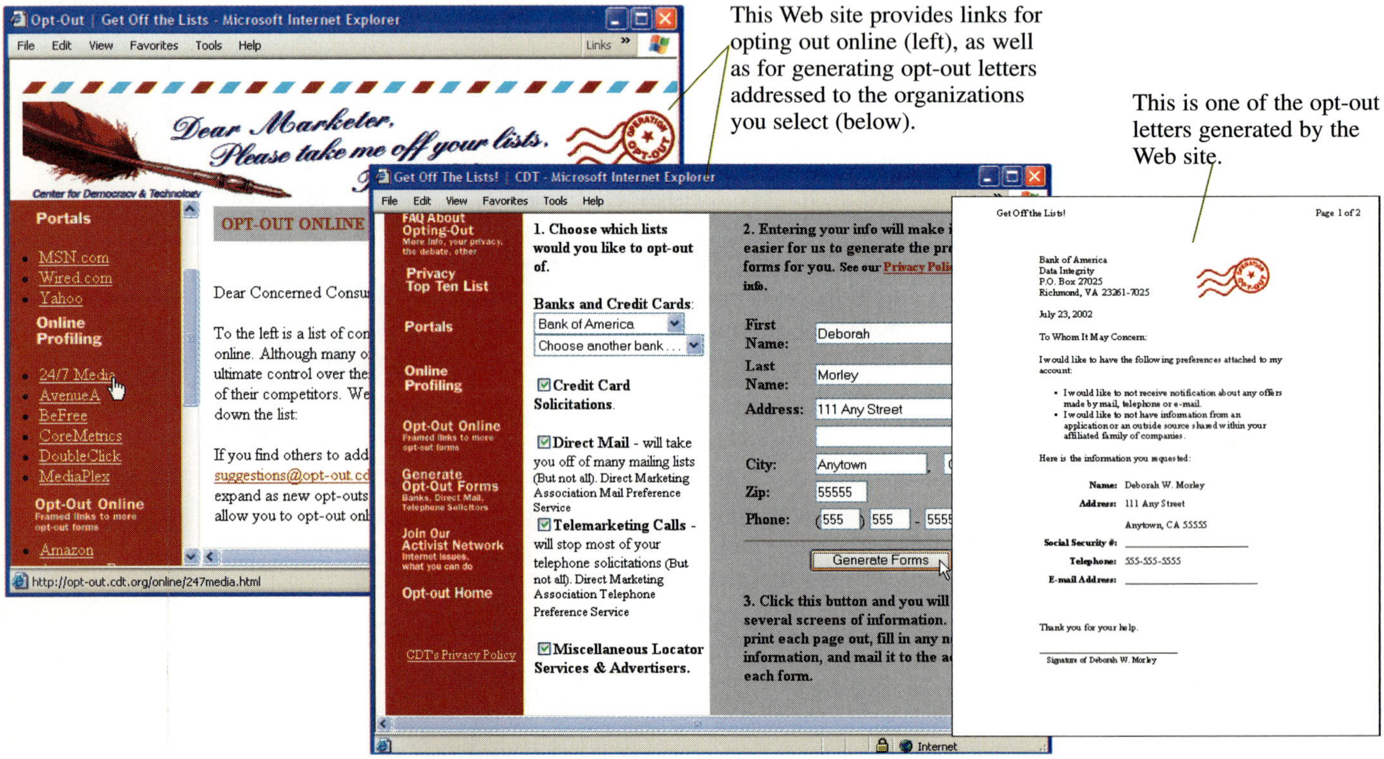

### Filtering Out Objectionable Content

Another type of filtering that can be used for privacy purposes is **Internet filtering**, which is used to prevent objectionable material from being displayed on your PC. It can be used by individuals for their home computers (such as by individuals to protect themselves from material they would view as offensive or by parents to protect their children from material they feel is inappropriate). It is also commonly used by employers to try to keep non-work-related material out of the workplace. Available through both browser settings (see Figure 5-22) and standalone programs, Internet filtering typically restricts access to Web pages that contain specified keywords or that exceed a rating for potentially offensive categories, such as language, nudity, or violence (typically these ratings are assigned by the content provider, not an independent rating organization). Some filtering services are offered at the ISP level, as well.

An on-going debate has been whether or not public libraries should use Internet filtering. Pro-filtering advocates want to protect children at public locations (such as libraries and schools) from accessing adult material. Individuals and organizations against Internet filtering at libraries and schools believe the filtering violates patrons' First Amendment rights to free speech. *The Child Internet Protection Act (CIPA)* that went into effect in 2001 required public libraries and schools to use filtering software to block Internet access to certain materials in order to receive public funds, but that law was ruled unconstitutional by a federal court in 2002.

## Protection of Workplace Privacy

While individuals' privacy concerns typically center around protecting their personal privacy, there are additional privacy issues that businesses and organizations need to consider. They have a responsibility to keep private information about their employees, the company, and their customers safe. Strong security measures, such as firewalls and access-prevention methods for both computer data and facilities, can help to protect against unauthorized access by hackers. They should take precautions against both intentional

**FIGURE 5-22**

**Browser settings can be changed to deny access to Web pages with objectionable content**

**‹ Content Advisor**

Internet Explorer's Content Advisor can be used to specify the maximum allowable levels of Web site language, nudity, sex, and violence.

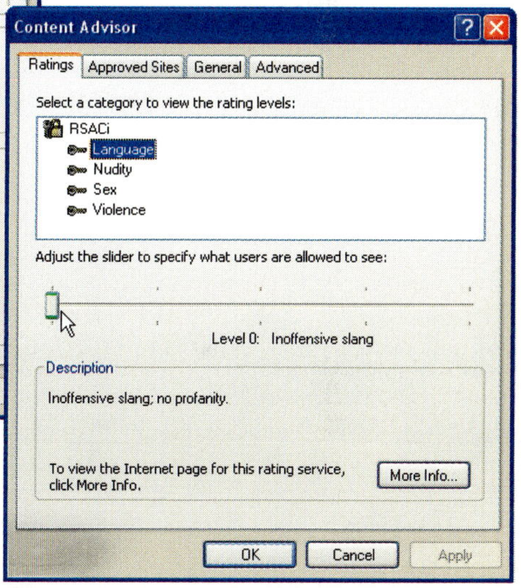


**˅ Supervisor password**

A supervisor password can be used so that unauthorized individuals cannot change the Content Advisor settings.

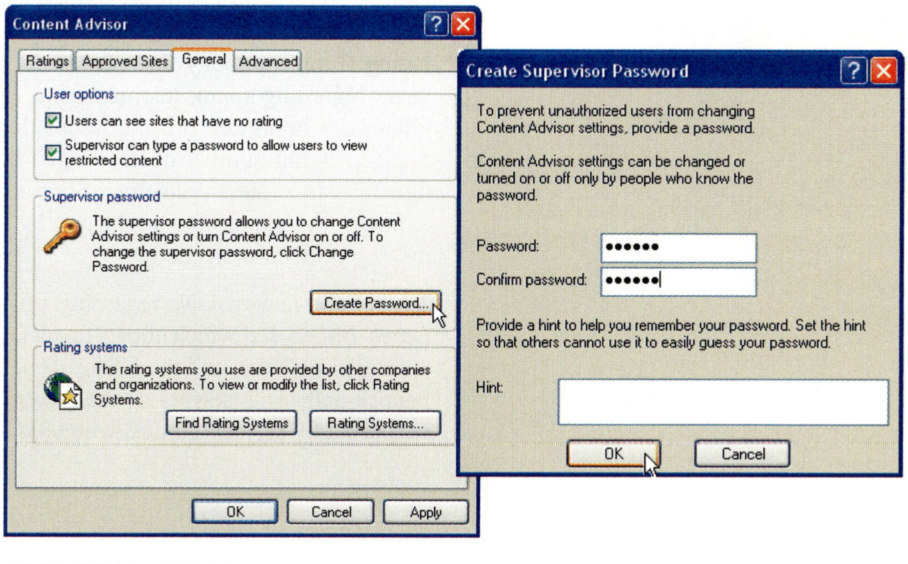

and accidental breaches of privacy by employees. For example, an error during Hillary Clinton's senate campaign in 2000 resulted in the e-mail addresses of everyone being sent a campaign update (including the private e-mail addresses of media stars and campaign insiders) being visible to all recipients instead of being hidden from view. Finally, businesses and organizations also have the responsibility to monitor their employees' activities to ensure workers are productive. In general, businesses must protect the privacy of their customers and employees, while at the same time avoid leaving the company vulnerable to lawsuits and maintain a safe and productive workplace environment.

### Employee Policies

To inform employees of what personal activities (if any) are allowed during company time or on company equipment, as well as what employee activities (such as Web surfing, e-mail, telephone calls, and documents stored on an office PC) may be monitored, all businesses should have a detailed employee policy. This policy—sometimes called a *code of conduct*—should be available to all employees; for example, as part of their employee handbook or posted on the company intranet.

### Separate Business and Personal Activities

Since at-work activities may legally be monitored by your employer, it is wise—from a privacy standpoint—to avoid personal activities at work entirely. Even if personal activities are allowed (such as checking your personal e-mail on your lunch hour), it is safer to perform personal activities at home. Be especially careful with any activity, such as sending a joke via e-mail to a co-worker, that might be interpreted as harassment. For personal phone calls, use your cell phone or a pay phone outside during your lunch hour or rest break.

## PRIVACY LEGISLATION

The high level of concern regarding personal privacy has led state and federal legislators to pass a variety of laws since the 1970s in an attempt to curb privacy abuses (see Figure 5-23). Although Internet privacy is viewed as one of the top policy issues facing Congress today and numerous bills have been proposed in the last several years regarding spam, telemarketing, spyware, identity theft, online profiling, and other very important privacy issues, legislation has been slow in coming. The fact that a growing number of state legislators have concluded that industry self-regulation fails to protect consumers' online privacy may help to speed up the process, although the matter is complicated by having differing opinions about the levels of privacy protection needed.

Two of the newest laws regarding privacy—the *Financial Modernization (Gramm-Leach-Bliley) Act*, which allows financial institutions to share consumer data unless the consumer opts out, and the *USA Patriot Act*, which expands the surveillance and intelligence-gathering powers of the government and law enforcement—are not widely supported by privacy groups, who view them as detriments to personal privacy.

**FIGURE 5-23**

Some important federal privacy laws

| Date | Law and Description |
|---|---|
| 2001 | **USA Patriot Act (USAPA)**<br>Grants federal authorities expanded surveillance and intelligence-gathering powers, such as broadening the ability of federal agents to obtain the real identity of Internet users, intercept e-mail and other types of Internet communications, follow online activity of suspects, expanded wiretapping authority, and more. |
| 1999 | **Financial Modernization (Gramm-Leach-Bliley) Act**<br>Extends the ability of banks, securities firms and insurance companies to share consumers' non-public personal information, but requires them to notify consumers and give them the opportunity to opt-out before disclosing any information. |
| 1998 | **Children's Online Privacy Protection Act**<br>Regulates how Web sites can collect information from minors and communicate with them. Also provides an exception from Internet tax moratoriums for Web sites providing material that is harmful to minors (unless access to such material is restricted to those 18 or over), and for ISPs (unless they offer screening software that allows customers to limit access to Internet material that is deemed harmful to minors). |
| 1998 | **Telephone Anti-Spamming Amendments Act**<br>Applies restrictions to unsolicited, bulk commercial e-mail. |
| 1992 | **Cable Act**<br>Extends the Cable Communications Policy Act to include companies that sell wireless services. |
| 1991 | **Telephone Consumer Protection Act**<br>Requires telemarketing companies to respect the rights of people who do not want to be called and significantly restricts the use of recorded messages. |
| 1988 | **Computer Matching and Privacy Act**<br>Limits the use of government data in determining federal-benefit recipients. |
| 1988 | **Video Privacy Protection Act**<br>Limits disclosure of customer information by video-rental companies. |
| 1986 | **Electronic Communications Privacy Act**<br>Extends traditional privacy protections governing postal delivery and telephone services to include e-mail, cellular phones, and voice mail. |
| 1984 | **Cable Communications Policy Act**<br>Limits disclosure of customer records by cable TV companies. |
| 1978 | **Right to Financial Privacy Act**<br>Provides guidelines that federal agencies must follow when inspecting an individual's bank records. |
| 1974 | **Education Privacy Act**<br>Stipulates that, in both public and private schools that receive any federal funding, indivduals have the right to keep the schools from releasing such information as grades and evaluations of behavior. |
| 1974 | **Privacy Act**<br>Stipulates that the collection of data by federal agencies must have a legitimate purpose. |
| 1970 | **Fair Credit Reporting Act**<br>Prevents private organizations from unfairly denying credit to individuals and provides individuals the right to inspect their credit records for truthfulness. |
| 1970 | **Freedom of Information Act**<br>Gives individuals the right to inspect data concerning them that are stored by the federal goverment. |

# HOW TO... ENCRYPT E-MAIL MESSAGES AND FILES

To keep the content of e-mail messages and files private during transit, encryption methods can be used. There are three primary options for encrypting e-mail messages and files: Using an e-mail program's built-in encryption capabilities, using a third-party encryption program, or using Web-based encrypted e-mail.

### Using an E-mail Program's Built-in Encryption

As discussed in Chapter 4, many e-mail programs can use public key encryption, in which the sender needs to know the recipient's public key. Once someone sends a digitally signed or encrypted e-mail, his or her public key is typically stored in the recipient's e-mail program's address book and is used automatically when an encrypted e-mail message is sent to that person (encryption is typically requested by selecting an option or clicking a toolbar button in the message composition window before sending the e-mail). When the recipient receives the encrypted e-mail, his or her e-mail program will use his or her private key to decrypt the message automatically, or the program will ask the recipient to supply the private key password and then decrypt the message.

### Using a Third-Party Encryption Program

Instead of public key encryption, some third-party encryption programs use *private key* or *symmetric key encryption*, which utilizes a single secret key both to encrypt and to decrypt the file. When a third-party private key encryption program is used to send an encrypted file to someone else, the sender and the recipient must first agree on the encryption password to be used; for obvious security reasons that password should not be sent in an e-mail message with the encrypted file. To decrypt the file, the recipient must supply the appropriate password. Depending on the program used and on how the file was encrypted, the recipient may need to have an encryption program installed on his or her PC that is compatible with the sender's encryption program; some programs are capable of creating *self-decrypting* files that can decrypt themselves without the recipient needing to use any special software—just the appropriate password is required (see Figure 5-24).

**FIGURE 5-24**

**Example of a third-party encryption program using private key encryption**

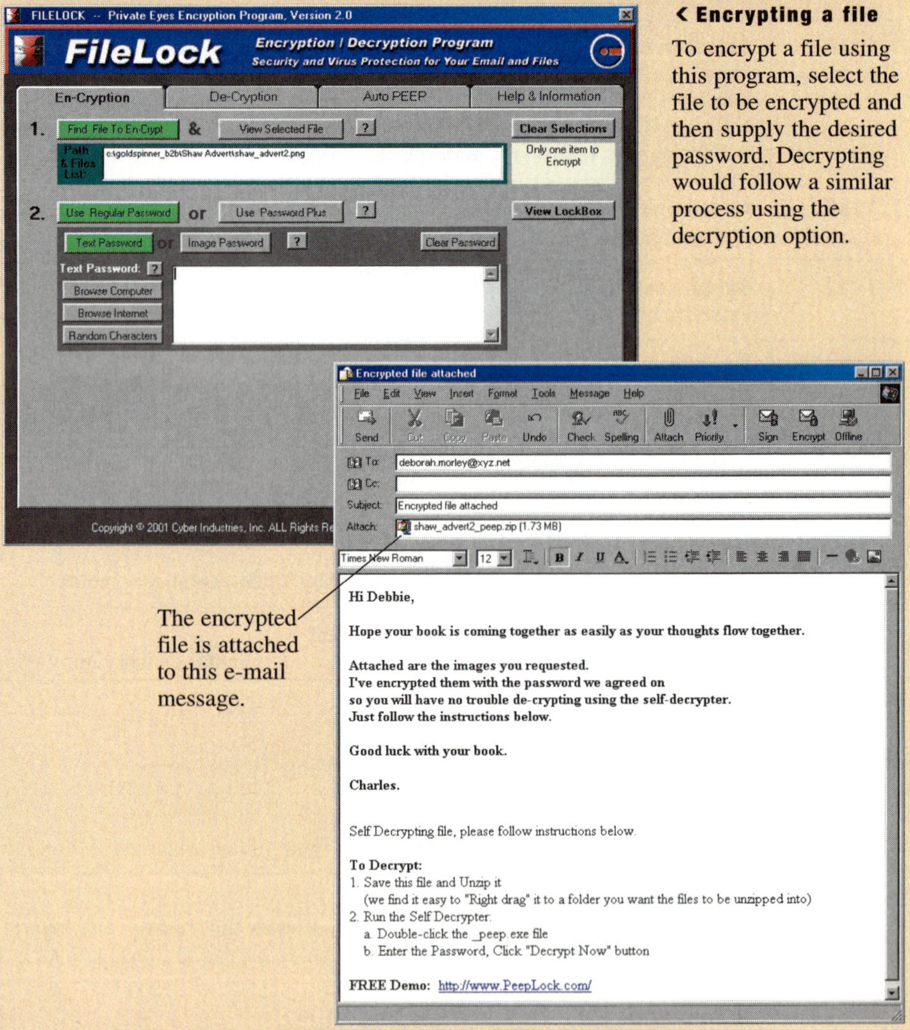


**< Encrypting a file**

To encrypt a file using this program, select the file to be encrypted and then supply the desired password. Decrypting would follow a similar process using the decryption option.

**^ E-mailing an encrypted file**

Encrypted files can be e-mailed to others as attachments. If private key encryption is used, the recipient must know the appropriate password to decrypt the file. In this example, the file is self-decrypting so no additional software is required on the recipient's end to open the encrypted attachment—just the agreed upon password.

## Using Web-Based Encrypted E-mail

Web-based encrypted e-mail usually works similarly to regular Web-based e-mail (where e-mail is composed and viewed on a Web page belonging to the Web-based e-mail service), but it uses a secure Web server to host the Web pages where e-mail messages are both composed and read. With some encrypted Web-based e-mail systems, the e-mail message is sent (via a secure Web page) to the secure server and the recipient is notified via his or her regular e-mail address that an encrypted e-mail message is waiting. Using the link included in the e-mail message, the recipient can view the message on a secure Web page. With this type of system, often only the sender is required to have an account through the encrypted Web-based e-mail service. Other encrypted Web-based e-mail systems—such as the free HushMail service shown in Figure 5-25—require both the sender and recipient to have accounts through that system. Since all e-mail sent through the service is automatically encrypted, users just log on to the HushMail Web page and provide their password when requested to decrypt and view any new encrypted e-mail sent to their HushMail e-mail address.

**FIGURE 5-25**

**Example of encrypted Web-based e-mail**

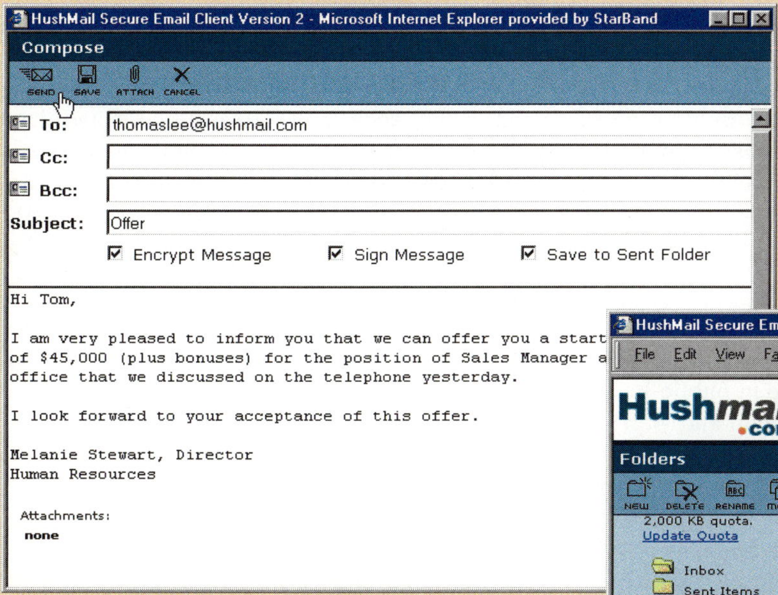


**‹ Sending e-mail**

E-mail messages are composed after the sender logs on to the secure e-mail site (using his or her password) and selects the appropriate option to compose a new e-mail message. Once the Send button is clicked, the message is encrypted and sent to the recipient.

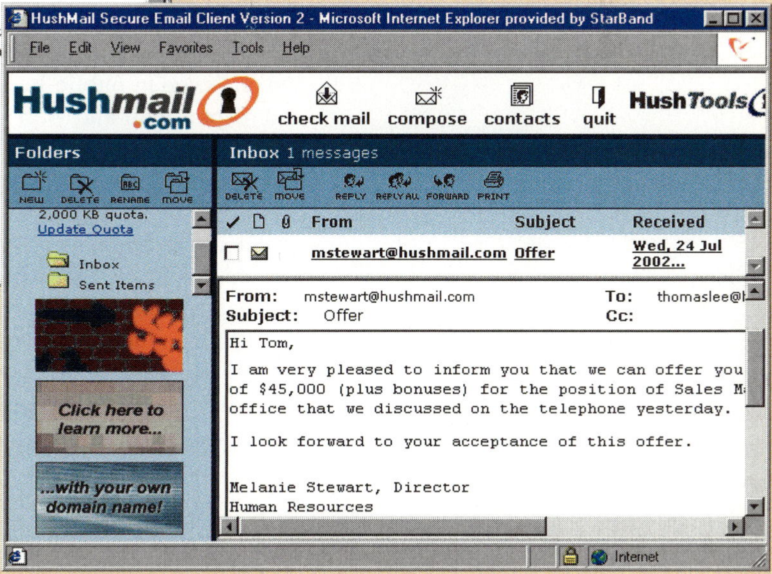


**› Receiving e-mail**

When the recipient logs onto his or her e-mail account (using his or her password) and requests new mail, the e-mail message is decrypted and displayed.

# SUMMARY

**CHAPTER OBJECTIVE 1**

Define and discuss various privacy concerns related to Web browsing and e-mail, including cookies, Web bugs, spyware, and e-mail privacy.

## Privacy Concerns

**Information privacy** refers to the rights of individuals and companies to control how information about them is collected and used. One **privacy** concern for individuals is the use of **cookies**. Some cookies can add helpful features to a Web site; others are used to target advertising. Although individual cookies can't track your Web activity, multiple cookies placed by the same company may be able to. **Web bugs** are small images on a Web page that can transmit data back to a Web page server. Sometimes Web bugs are used in conjunction with cookies. Another source of concern is **spyware**—programs typically installed without a user's knowledge that transmit information over the user's Internet connection to outsiders.

Many people mistakenly believe that the e-mail they send and receive is private. This isn't true, both because it can be intercepted and read if it isn't encrypted and because businesses and ISPs typically archive e-mail that passes through those organizations. This archived e-mail can be retrieved at a later time if appropriate, such as if subpoenaed for a lawsuit or if needed for a law enforcement investigation.

**CHAPTER OBJECTIVE 2**

Describe some privacy concerns regarding databases, electronic profiling, spam, adware, telemarketing, and various types of electronic surveillance and monitoring.

The extensive use of **marketing databases** and **government databases** brings concern to both privacy organizations and individuals. Information in marketing databases is frequently sold to companies and other organizations; information in some government databases is available to the public. Some database information can be retrieved via the Web. **Electronic profiling** is the collection of diverse information about an individual, such as information collected from these databases. An organization's **privacy policy** addresses how any personal information submitted to that company will be used. Other privacy issues concerning individuals include the vast amounts of **spam** (unsolicited bulk e-mail), **adware** (programs that display onscreen advertising), and **telemarketing** that occur today.

**Computer monitoring software** that can record an individual's computer use can be viewed as a privacy violation by some, as can the increased use of *video surveillance* in public locations. The FBI's **Carnivore** project, which is used to intercept e-mail and Web activity from individuals suspected of criminal activity, has met strong objection from privacy advocates. Though allowed by law, some employees view **employee monitoring** (such as monitoring computer use, telephone calls, and an individual's location using *proximity cards* or video surveillance) as an invasion of their privacy. **Presence technology**—the ability of one computer on a network to know the status and location of another computer on that network—was originally developed in response to an **enhanced 911 (e911)** mandate that required 911 operators to be able to identify the location of callers using a mobile phone. Though in the early stages, presence technology is expected eventually to allow users of computers, mobile phones, and other devices used for communication to be able to determine the availability of other individuals before contacting them.

**CHAPTER OBJECTIVE 3**

Identify ways individuals can protect their privacy while surfing the Web.

## Privacy Safeguards

There are a number of precautions individuals can take to protect their personal privacy while online. To control cookies, either browser settings or third-party **cookie management software** can be used; cookies can also be deleted manually from your hard drive. Firewalls can be used to protect against spyware programs gaining outside access, and anti-spyware programs can detect and remove spyware and other potential nuisances. Web bugs themselves cannot be prevented (though cookie control can prevent their use of cookies), but special programs can be used to see if a Web bug is included in a particular Web page.

To browse anonymously, third-party software or a browsing service can be used. Often anonymous browsing services also include other helpful features, such as cookie control and suppressing onscreen ads. Typically these services are available on a subscription basis. A limited amount of privacy can be achieved by removing all personal information from your browser's e-mail program, if that program is not needed for exchanging e-mail.

Protecting your e-mail address is one of the best ways to avoid spam. A **throw-away e-mail address** can be used for any activities that may result in spam; then your personal e-mail address can be used only for those communications that should not result in spam. Before providing any personal information on a Web page, it is a good idea to review the Web site's privacy policy to see if the information will be shared with other organizations. Consider whether or not the Web site is requesting too much personal information, and only provide the required data. Do not provide personal details in chat rooms and personal Web sites. Unless you don't mind spam or are using a throw-away e-mail address, avoid completing online forms to enter sweepstakes, win free merchandise, or take part in other marketing tactics.

**CHAPTER OBJECTIVE 4**

List steps individuals can take to safeguard their e-mail addresses and other personal information.

*E-mail filters* can be used to manage an individual's e-mail, including spam. To try to reduce the amount of spam, junk mail, online ads, and telemarketing calls an individual is already subjected to, he or she can **opt out**. Typically this requires contacting each company directly, though some Web sites provide links to online opt out forms or create form letters that can be printed and mailed to the appropriate companies.

**CHAPTER OBJECTIVE 5**

Suggest some ways to filter out or reduce objectionable Web content, spam, and telemarketing activities.

**Internet filtering** can be used to prevent objectionable material from being displayed on a PC. It is typically used by individuals (to protect their personal privacy against this type of material), parents (to protect what their children are exposed to), and employers (to ensure that only work-related Web pages are accessed).

Businesses have a responsibility to keep private information about their employees, the company, and their customers safe. Firewalls, password-protected files, and encryption can help secure this information. Businesses also have the responsibility to monitor employee activities to ensure that employees are performing the jobs they are being paid to do, not causing lost business, and not leaving the company open to lawsuits. To inform employees of allowable activities, an employee policy or *code of conduct* should be developed and distributed to employees. For the highest level of privacy while at the workplace, employees should perform only work-related activities on the job.

**CHAPTER OBJECTIVE 6**

Understand how individuals can protect their workplace privacy.

## Privacy Legislation

Although Internet privacy is viewed as one of the top policy issues facing Congress today, legislation to protect privacy is slow in coming. Two of the newest laws regarding privacy include the *Financial Modernization (Gramm-Leach-Bliley) Act* and the *USA Patriot Act*.

**CHAPTER OBJECTIVE 7**

Discuss the status of privacy legislation.

# BALANCING ACT

## PERSONAL PRIVACY VS. THE GOVERNMENT'S RIGHT TO KNOW

It has been several years since Sun Microsystems' co-founder and CEO Scott McNealy delivered his famous statement about consumer privacy: "You have zero privacy anyway. Get over it." Since then, as more and more of our personal data has become centralized and shared at an astounding rate, the privacy debate has escalated. What amount of personal privacy should individuals demand today? Have we given up some right to privacy by using the Internet and other tools that have added convenience to our lives? And, more importantly in this time of national insecurity, will giving the government access to more data about us as individuals help to protect us and the country as a whole?

Most people would go along with the statement that the government needs some information about us to do its job. Certain agencies need to know where we live, how much money we make, and if we have a criminal record. But does the government need to know where we shop, what Web sites we visit, and what we say in our personal e-mail messages? Some individuals might believe that the government has the right to know anything about us if it helps to prevent crime and gives us a safer society to live in. Others may believe that trading privacy for an additional sense of security is unacceptable.

Accepting the fact that lots of data about individuals is going to be collected and stored on computers today, some privacy advocates want us to think about protecting data that can cause harm, rather than trying to protect all personal data. For example, most individuals probably wouldn't object to some personal information—such as our listed telephone numbers—being available over the Internet. However, many probably would object to their medical records becoming public knowledge.

### YOUR TURN

Give some thought to the balance between personal privacy and the government's right to know, and then answer the following questions.

1. Do you think the level of personal privacy that most individuals view as essential has shifted in the last few years? Why or why not?
2. Should the government be given access to all information it feels is needed to protect its citizens? To protect the country?
3. There has been increased talk of developing a national ID card since the 9/11 terrorist attacks. How might such a card be beneficial from the government's standpoint? Are their benefits from a citizen's standpoint? How might such a card affect personal privacy?
4. The technology now exists to implant a microchip under an individual's skin so that his or her personal data, such as identity and medical history, can be obtained by emergency room or law enforcement personnel using a special scanner. What is your opinion about this technology? Do you view it as a possible replacement for identification cards? What if consumer applications (such as being able to unlock your house or log on to your computer) or safety applications (such as ensuring only company airline pilots use the controls of an aircraft) were added? Would that change your opinion of this technology? Why or why not?

# KEY TERMS

**Instructions:** Match each key term on the left with the definition on the right that best describes it.

a. **adware**

b. **Carnivore**

c. **computer monitoring software**

d. **cookie**

e. **cookie management software**

f. **electronic profiling**

g. **employee monitoring**

h. **enhanced 911 (e911)**

i. **government database**

j. **information privacy**

k. **Internet filtering**

l. **marketing database**

m. **opt out**

n. **presence technology**

o. **privacy policy**

p. **spam**

q. **spyware**

r. **telemarketing**

s. **throw-away e-mail address**

t. **Web bug**

1. ______ A collection of data about people that is collected and maintained by the government.
2. ______ A collection of data about people that is stored in a large database and used for marketing purposes.
3. ______ A monitoring program used by the FBI to intercept and monitor e-mail and Web activity from suspected criminals.
4. ______ An e-mail address used only for nonessential purposes and activities that may result in spam; the address can be disposed of and replaced if spam becomes a problem.
5. ______ An FCC mandate requiring that all mobile phones contain technology that enables 911 operators to identify the location of callers using mobile telephones.
6. ______ A policy, commonly posted on a company's Web site, that explains how personal information provided to that company will be used.
7. ______ A small file stored on a user's hard drive by a Web server, commonly used to identify personal and marketing preferences for that user.
8. ______ A software program often installed on a user's PC without the user's knowledge that secretly collects information and sends it to an outside party via the user's Internet connection.
9. ______ A very small (often 1 by 1 pixel) image on a Web page that transmits data back about the Web page visitor to a Web server.
10. ______ Using electronic means to collect a variety of in-depth information about an individual, such as their name, address, income, and buying habits.
11. ______ Free or low cost software that is supported by onscreen advertising.
12. ______ Observing or reviewing employees' actions while they are on the job.
13. ______ Software that can be used to control the use of Web page cookies.
14. ______ Software that can be used to record an individual's computer usage, typically either by capturing images of the screen or by recording the actual keystrokes used.
15. ______ Technology that enables one computer to locate and identify another computer on the same network.
16. ______ To request that you be removed from marketing activities or that your information not be shared with other companies.
17. ______ The rights of individuals and companies to control how information about them is collected and used.
18. ______ Unsolicited, bulk e-mail sent over the Internet.
19. ______ Unsolicited marketing activities that take place via the telephone.
20. ______ Using a software program or browser option to restrict access to particular Web pages or types of Web pages.

## ✓ SELF-QUIZ

Answers for the self-quiz appear at the end of the book.

### True/False

**Instructions:** Circle **T** if the statement is true or **F** if the statement is false.

**T F 1.** Some Web bugs use cookies.

**T F 2.** The FBI's Carnivore program is used to monitor telephone communications from individuals suspected of crimes.

**T F 3.** One way of safeguarding your e-mail address is to use a single e-mail address for all Internet activity, including your personal communications, online shopping, and completing online surveys.

**T F 4.** Very few major U.S. companies monitor the online activities of their employees.

**T F 5.** Encryption can be used for privacy purposes in addition to security purposes.

### Completion

**Instructions:** Supply the missing words to complete the following statements.

**6.** Many Web sites today remember personal settings and preferences via the use of ______________ files stored on your hard drive.

**7.** A program that secretly transmits information about a user via the Internet connection is referred to as ______________.

**8.** ______________ uses information from marketing databases and other sources to create a collection of in-depth information on specific individuals.

**9.** The most widely used presence technology application today is ______________.

**10.** ______________ cards can be used to tell employers where their employees are, as well as to unlock and lock each individual's PC automatically as they approach and leave their desks.

**11.** ______________ cookies are placed by an organization other than the one belonging to the Web site you are viewing, such as by an advertising agency.

**12.** An e-mail ______________ can be used to route suspected spam automatically into a separate e-mail folder.

**13.** Web sites such as HushMail use ______________ techniques to protect the privacy of e-mail messages.

**14.** If you ______________ from a company's marketing list, you aren't supposed to receive any more marketing mail or telephone calls from that organization.

**15.** Internet ______________ can be used to restrict children's access to Web pages containing inappropriate content.

# PROJECTS

YOUR OPINION

## 1. Double Duty

The chapter Trends In box discussed the Microsoft .NET Passport system—a digital ID system about which many privacy groups have expressed concern. One objection is the way users are automatically signed up for a .NET Passport when they create a free Hotmail account. Although users are allowed to change their privacy preferences for their .NET Passport after it is created, there apparently is no way of avoiding creating a .NET Passport account when your Hotmail account is created.

For this project, consider the issue of additional programs or services being installed when only one service is requested (such as a .NET Passport with a Hotmail account or a spyware program with a shareware program) and write a short essay expressing your opinion about this issue. Consider the following questions before forming your opinion: Is there any difference between what Microsoft is doing and what spyware publishers do? Is this something that should be regulated by the government or is it legitimate for a company to make additional products mandatory when a consumer wishes to use another one of its other products? What if the consumer is informed that the second program or service is being installed along with the first, or if the program or service is a fee-based product or service versus a free product or service? Submit your opinion on this issue to your instructor in the form of a short paper, not more than two pages in length.

INDEPENDENT RESEARCH

## 2. Fourth Amendment

The Fourth Amendment to the U.S. Constitution is frequently mentioned in the privacy debate. For this project, locate the text of the Fourth Amendment and analyze it. Does it address personal privacy? If you think so, which part of the amendment applies to personal privacy? If you don't think it addresses privacy, why do you think this amendment is quoted so often in pro-privacy arguments? Next, find at least two articles (either in print or online) where the Fourth Amendment is mentioned in relation to personal privacy. In what context is the Fourth Amendment used in the articles? Do you agree with the stated opinions? Why or why not? Do you believe the Fourth Amendment guarantees all Americans privacy? Summarize your findings in a two- to three-page paper.

HANDS-ON

## 3. Employee Monitoring

As mentioned in the chapter, it is not unusual for organizations to monitor their employees' activities, including telephone calls, e-mail, Web activity, and downloaded files.

For this project, select an organization (such as your school, place of business, or another organization in your community) and research employee monitoring at that organization (you will likely need to contact the human resources department of that organization to obtain the needed information). Determine such information as what activities the organization monitors, how frequently monitoring takes place, and how the employees to be monitored are selected. Is there a written employee policy regarding this? If not, are employees notified that monitoring may take place? After gathering information about the monitoring from an employer perspective, contact two employees of that organization and interview them regarding what they know about it. Does their perception of the employee monitoring that takes place at the organization differ from the organization's policy? If monitoring does indeed take place at the organization, were the employees aware of it? Prepare a short summary of your findings to turn in to your instructor. Be sure to include an opinion of whether or not the employee monitoring practices at this organization would influence whether or not you would like to work there.

### 4. Browser Settings

There are a variety of settings in a Web browser that pertain to privacy, such as cookie, cache, history, and e-mail settings. Cookie settings determine how cookies can be used, the browser's cache and history list store information about Web pages recently visited, and e-mail settings contain personal information.

For this project, find a public computer (such as in a computer lab at your school or at your local public library) on which you are permitted to make changes to the browser and e-mail settings (ask permission first if you are not sure). Open the available browser and check the current settings (in Internet Explorer, select *Internet Options* from the Tools menu and look at the General and Privacy tabs; in Netscape Navigator, select *Preferences* from the Edit menu and look under the Navigator and Advanced options). Find the appropriate options to clear the cache (temporary files), history list, and cookie files. Also, open the associated e-mail program and delete any current e-mail settings (in Outlook Express, select *Accounts* from the Tools menu and click the Mail tab; in Netscape Mail 6 or 7, select *Mail/News Account Settings* from the Edit menu; in earlier versions of Netscape, select *Preferences* from the Edit menu and click the Mail & Newsgroup option).

Next, return to the browser and visit at least five different Web sites to build up a history and cookie list. You may want to go to a shopping Web site and add items to your shopping cart (but don't complete the checkout process) or personalize a portal page, such as specifying your ZIP code at MSNBC.com. Find the appropriate menu option or toolbar button to display your history list. Are the Web sites you visited listed there? Display the browser settings again and find the option to view the cookie files. Were any new cookies added during your browser session? If so, are all of them from the Web sites you visited or are any of them third-party advertising cookies? Delete all temporary Internet files (cache, cookie files, and the history list), then close the browser window. Prepare a short summary of your work to turn in to your instructor.

**GROUP PRESENTATION**

### 5. Privacy Policy Flip-Flops

Although a company's privacy policy may look acceptable when you read it before submitting personal information to that company, there is no guarantee that the policy will not be changed later.

For this project, form a group to research privacy policies. Locate three different policies on Web sites and analyze and compare them. Do any of the organizations reserve the right to change their policy at a later time without notice? If so, will they notify consumers? Do any of the policies allow for any sharing of data to third-party organizations? If so, is the data personally identifiable and can customers opt out? Can you find any additional clauses in the policies that might be of concern to users? Also, find the most recent publicized examples of companies changing or violating their privacy policies and determine if there is any new or impending related legislation. As a group, discuss your opinions regarding a company's right to change its privacy policy and the impact such a change may have on customer loyalty.

Share your findings with the class in the form of a short presentation. The presentation should not exceed 10 minutes and should make use of one or more presentation aids such as the chalkboard, handouts, overhead transparencies, or a computer-based slide presentation (your instructor may provide additional requirements). Your group may also be asked to submit a summary of the presentation to your instructor.

### 6. Spam

Many Internet users today are flooded with unsolicited e-mail messages, or "spam." Typically, the more often you share your e-mail address with companies, the more spam you will receive.

For this project, form a group to discuss spam. For those group members with personal e-mail addresses, is spam a problem? Has anyone in the group had the experience of signing up for something at a Web site or clicking a particular Web page ad and shortly thereafter receiving spam related to that action? Do the members in your group typically just delete spam messages or do they try to unsubscribe? For those that unsubscribe, does it seem to work? For an experiment, obtain a free e-mail address for your group (such as from Yahoo! or Hotmail). Set up a browser with that e-mail address and a fictitious name, and visit several different Web sites. Set customized settings at a portal page, and submit the group's e-mail address to at least two Web sites to sign up for a newsletter, enter a sweepstakes, download coupons, or receive some other service. As you surf, click on several different banner ads, as well. Be sure to record the sites you visited and the advertisements you clicked on. Wait one or two days (depending on the time allotted for this project) and then check the group's e-mail. Do you have any spam messages? If so, can you identify why you received each message, based on the online activities your group performed? Does this experiment change your group's opinion in any way about spam?

Share your findings with the class in the form of a short presentation. The presentation should not exceed 10 minutes and should make use of one or more presentation aids such as the chalkboard, handouts, overhead transparencies, or a computer-based slide presentation (your instructor may provide additional requirements). Your group may also be asked to submit a summary of the presentation to your instructor.

### 7. Washington DC Security Camera Network

**VIDEO VIEWPOINT**

Individual live surveillance cameras are being used at an increasing number of public locations. Washington DC is going one step further—it is building what will be the nation's largest network of surveillance cameras. The system is expected to include hundreds of cameras to watch over mass transit stations, public schools, traffic intersections, shopping malls, national monuments, and more. The accompanying video takes a look at the system and some of the objections to it from privacy groups.

After watching the video, think about the impact of live public video surveillance. Is it a valid crime prevention tool or an invasion of privacy? Does the government have the responsibility to use every means possible to protect the country and its citizens? Or do citizens have the right not to be watched in public? What if it was a live police officer stationed at each video camera location instead of a camera? Is that more acceptable from a privacy standpoint? If people don't plan to commit criminal acts in public, should they be concerned that law enforcement personnel may see them?

**ONLINE VIDEO**

To view the Washington DC Security Camera Network video clip, go to www.course.com/morley2003/ch5

**Express your viewpoint:** What impact does public video surveillance have on our society and who should have the final say regarding how (or if) it will be used?

Use the video clip and the questions previously asked as the foundation for your response. Your instructor will direct you to be prepared to discuss your position (either in class, via an online class discussion group, or in a class chat room), or to write a short paper stating and supporting your viewpoint on the issue. You may also be asked to do research and provide resources to support your point of view on this issue.

# ETHICS AND INTELLECTUAL PROPERTY RIGHTS

## OUTLINE



## OBJECTIVES

**After completing this chapter, you will be able to:**

- Understand the concept of intellectual property rights and how they can be protected legally.
- Explain what ethics are and how they relate to computer use.
- List several types of copyrighted materials and describe how they can be used ethically.
- State several ethical issues related to the use of school or business resources and information.
- Explain what computer hoaxes and digital manipulation are and how they relate to computer ethics.
- Identify several ethical issues surrounding business practices and decisions.
- Discuss the current status of legislation related to intellectual property rights and ethics.

# CHAPTER 6

## OVERVIEW

Computers have unarguably changed the way many of us work and live. We typically use them at work to assist with job-related tasks, and at home to shop, pay bills, correspond with others, and overall help facilitate routine tasks. We use them as a means of entertainment and as a tool for homework and for work we bring home from the office. While computers often make daily tasks easier, they also make it easier to perform some types of illegal or unethical acts. For example, computers today can be used to launch computer viruses, create high-quality copies of software programs and music CDs, and copy information from a Web page and present it as your own work. But just because technology enables us to do something, does that make it right? Is legality the only measuring stick, or are there some acts that are legal, but still morally or ethically wrong? Is there only one set of ethics, or can ethics vary from person to person? These questions are the subject of this chapter.

Many legal issues, such as hacking, computer theft, software piracy, and other computer crimes were discussed in Chapter 4. This chapter opens with one additional legal issue with which all computer users should be familiar—intellectual property rights. The different types of intellectual property rights are discussed along with what types of property each one protects. Next comes a discussion of ethics, including what they are and a variety of ethical issues surrounding computer use by individuals and businesses. Topics include the ethical use of copyrighted material, ethical uses of resources and information, unethical use of computer hoaxes and digital manipulation, and ethical business practices and decision-making. The chapter closes with a look at legislation related to ethics and intellectual property rights.

# WHAT ARE INTELLECTUAL PROPERTY RIGHTS?

**ONLINE RESOURCES**

For links to information about intellectual property rights, go to www.course.com/morley2003/ch6

**Intellectual property rights** are the legal rights to which the creators of *intellectual property*—original creative works—are entitled. Intellectual property rights indicate who has the right to use, perform, or display the creative work; how long the creator retains rights to the property; and other related restrictions. Examples of intellectual property include original music compositions; drawings, paintings, computer graphics, sculptures, and other works of art; essays, poetry, books, and other types of written work; architectural drawings; symbols, names, and designs used in conjunction with a business; and inventions. The three main types of intellectual property rights are *copyrights*, *trademarks*, and *patents*.

## Copyrights

A **copyright** is a form of protection available to the creator of an original artistic or literary work, such as a book, movie, software program, musical composition, or painting. Copyright protection in the U.S. gives the copyright holder the exclusive right to publish, reproduce, distribute, perform, or display the work. Immediately after creating a work in some type of material form (such as on paper, film, canvas, videotape, disk, CD, or DVD) the creator automatically owns the copyright of that work. The creator is then entitled to copyright protection of that work and has the right to make a statement such as "Copyright © 2003 by John Smith. All rights reserved." Although not required on works created in the United States after March 1, 1989 to retain their copyright protection, it is wise to display this type of copyright statement on a published work to remind others that the work is protected by copyright law and that any use must comply with copyright restrictions. Only the creator (or his or her employer if the work is created as a *work for hire*; that is, within the scope of employment) of a work can rightfully claim copyright. Copyrights can be registered with the U.S. Copyright Office. Although registration is not required for copyright protection, it does offer several legal advantages if the need to prove ownership of a copyright ever arises, such as during a copyright infringement lawsuit.

Anyone wishing to reproduce copyrighted materials or otherwise use them in a manner not authorized by copyright law must first obtain permission from the copyright holder and pay any required fee. One exception is the legal concept of *fair use*, which permits limited duplication and use of a portion of copyrighted material for such purposes as criticism, commentary, news reporting, teaching, and research. For example, a teacher may legally distribute a copyrighted poem for discussion in a poetry class, and a news photographer may take a photograph of a newly installed sculpture to show on the evening news. Copyrights apply to both published and unpublished work and last until 70 years after the creator's death. Copyrights for works registered by an organization, anonymous works, and other types of works in which the creator's identity is not revealed to the Copyright Office last 95 years from the date of publication or 120 years from creation, whichever is shorter.

To protect their rights, some creators of digital content—such as art, music, photographs, and movies—incorporate a **digital watermark** into their works. A digital watermark is a subtle alteration of digital content that isn't noticeable when the work is viewed or played but that identifies the copyright holder. Usually viewed with special software—and sometimes only by the copyright holder who knows the proper password—digital watermarks typically contain either a unique identification code that identifies the copyright owner or complete copyright information.

It is important to realize that purchasing a copyrighted item—such as a book, painting, or movie—does not change the copyright protection afforded to the creator of that item. Although you have purchased the right to use the item, you cannot legally duplicate it or portray it as your own creation. Some of the most widely publicized copyright infringement issues today center around individuals distributing copyright-protected music and movies via the Internet, as discussed in the Trends In box.

## Trademarks

A **trademark** is a word, phrase, symbol, or design (or a combination of words, phrases, symbols, or designs) that identifies and distinguishes one good or service from another. Trademark rights prevent others from using a confusingly similar mark, but they do not prevent others from making or selling the same goods or services under a clearly different mark. Trademarks that are claimed, but are not registered with the U.S. Patent and Trademark Office, can use the mark ™; registered trademarks can use the symbol ®. Trademarked words and phrases—such as Windows® XP and BLOCKBUSTER®—are common; so are trademarked logos (see Figure 6-1). Domain names that match a company's trademark, such as Amazon.com and Lego.com, are also protected by trademark law.

**FIGURE 6-1**

Examples of trademarked logos

There have been a number of claims of online trademark infringement in the last few years, particularly involving domain names that contain, or are similar to, a trademark. For instance, several celebrities—such as Madonna—have fought to be given the exclusive right to use what they consider to be their rightful domain names (Madonna.com, in this example). Other examples include Microsoft's complaint against another organization using the domain name microsof.com and Radio Shack's objection to a private individual using shack.com for the Web site of his business called DesignShack.

Disputes such as these are typically first brought to the Arbitration and Mediation Center of the *World Intellectual Property Organization (WIPO)*, which has the power to award the disputed domain name to the most appropriate party. If the domain name appears to have been acquired by someone other than the holder of the trademark for the purpose of harming the trademark holder or selling the domain name at an inflated price—an act referred to as *cybersquatting*—the trademark holder generally prevails. If the current domain name holder has a legitimate reason for using that name and doesn't appear to be a cybersquatter, WIPO may allow them to continue to use that domain name. For instance, WIPO ruled that microsof.com was confusingly similar to the trademark already owned by Microsoft and its owner had no legitimate interest in that domain name, so WIPO transferred the disputed domain name to Microsoft Corporation. However, the owner of DesignShack (whose nickname is "Shack") was allowed to keep the shack.com domain name because it was ruled that he had a legitimate interest in that name.

## TRENDS IN... PEER-TO-PEER FILE SHARING

Chances are you've heard of Napster, the first widespread music sharing service which was started in 1999. Napster facilitated the ability of users to share MP3 files, located on their own computers, with other individuals over the Internet. This differs from music download sites, where the files to be downloaded are located on a central server. To use the Napster service, a person had to register with Napster for a free membership and download the Napster file-sharing software program. To make files accessible to other Napster members, each Napster member would designate the drives and folders on his or her PC that contained the MP3 files to be shared. Anytime that person was online, those folders were accessible to all other Napster members. To download a file, a Napster member would use the search feature on the Napster Web site to specify a particular song, and a list of all users currently online with the specified song stored on their hard drives would be displayed. The person requesting the song would select a host user, and then the Napster software would copy the MP3 file from the host user's computer to the requesting user's PC. This type of file sharing is referred to as **peer-to-peer (P2P) file sharing**.

Although Napster was eventually forced to stop its file-sharing service (see Figure 6-2) as a result of copyright infringement lawsuits by the recording industry, peer-to-peer file sharing of music, videos, and more through other P2P file-sharing sites is still going strong. Any P2P services that are used to transfer copyrighted material are facing the same legal issues that Napster did. For instance, is the company responsible if users violate copyright law? Or, just by providing the service, is the company violating copyright law? Is it the company's responsibility to make sure no copyright violations occur?

Because they are not actually distributing copyright-protected material to others since the files are transferred directly from one user's hard drive to another's—not from the P2P service's server—some peer-to-peer services argue that they cannot be held responsible if users violate copyright laws. This was the same argument that Napster used, but it wasn't supported in the courts. The music and motion picture industries are continuing to file lawsuits against other popular file-sharing services—such as Morpheus, Kazaa, and Madster—that they believe are being used to share copyrighted material. For example, at the time of this writing, a federal judge had just granted a preliminary injunction against Madster on the basis that the service appears to facilitate and contribute to copyright infringement on a massive scale. Some believe that prosecution of individual file traders isn't far off.

In addition to copyright concerns, security is an issue that all peer-to-peer users should consider. Because P2P applications typically allow other individuals access to your hard drive, it is important to ensure that only the desired folders and drives can be accessed by others. Though most P2P services allow users to specify the shared resources, a recent study of Kazaa users released by HP Labs indicated that P2P users frequently expose personal data to other users. According to the researchers, the majority of users in the study was unable to tell which files they were sharing, and sometimes incorrectly assumed they were not sharing any personal files when in fact they were sharing all files on their hard drive. As an experiment to determine whether P2P users were taking advantage of this vulnerability, the researchers placed dummy personal files with titles such as Credit Card.xls and Inbox.dbs on a PC set up for the Kazaa service and made those files available to Kazaa members. In a 24-hour period, the credit card file was downloaded by four individuals and the inbox file was downloaded by two individuals. This experiment underscores the fact that all users who choose to participate in P2P activities should make sure that only the files they want shared are accessible to other users.

A new application using peer-to-peer technology is the sharing of movies and television shows. Some of these activities, such as exchanging *bootleg* copies of movies over the Internet, are unarguably illegal. Others, such as sharing television shows recorded onto a *digital personal video recorder* (often referred to as a *DVR* or *PVR*), are more debatable. The release of recent models of SONICblue's ReplayTV DVR, which is capable of storing up to 320 hours of televised shows and sharing those recordings with other ReplayTV users via the Internet, has brought peer-to-peer file sharing back into the spotlight. As a result of lawsuits by Viacom, Disney, NBC, TimeWarner Entertainment, and Columbia Pictures, SONICblue was ordered to design software to monitor ReplayTV users' viewing habits and distribution of material. Although that order was overturned, the lawsuits have yet to be settled. It is expected that the results of these and other current lawsuits will have a significant impact on the future of both peer-to-peer sharing and DVRs.

**FIGURE 6-2**

**The Napster peer-to-peer file sharing service was eventually shut down due to copyright infringement lawsuits.**

The *U.S. Anticybersquatting Act*—also called the *Trademark Cyberpiracy Prevention Act*—passed in 1999 allows for penalties of up to $300,000 for each willful registration of a domain name that infringes on a trademark. Sometimes, whether or not a domain name was registered in bad faith is a difficult judgment call. For example, 2002 California Assembly candidate Dan Dow set up campaign Web sites at DanDow.com, plus three other sites related to the name of his opponent John Dutra: JohnDutra.com, JohnDutra.net, and JohnDutra.org. He was able to do this because the domain names were available—John Dutra's campaign hadn't yet registered them. Dutra views Dow's actions as unethical and in violation of the law. However, Dow disagrees, stating that his JohnDutra Web sites are educational, used to inform the voters about Dutra and his views. At the time of this writing, Dow still had possession of the JohnDutra domain names.

## Patents

Unlike copyrights (which protect artistic and literary works) and trademarks (which protect a company's logo and brand names), a **patent** protects inventions by granting exclusive rights of an invention to its inventor for a period of 20 years. A patented invention is typically a unique product, but can also be a process or procedure that provides a new way of doing something or that offers a new technical solution to a problem. Like trademarks, patents are applied for and are issued by the U.S. Patent and Trademark Office; a recent patent issued to Casio for a new handheld computer design is shown in Figure 6-3.

The number of patent applications—particularly for computer- or Internet-related products—has skyrocketed in recent years. Also growing are the number of patents requested for business methods and models, such as CoolSavings.com's Internet coupon distribution method, Amazon.com's one-click purchase procedure, and Priceline.com's name-your-own-price business model. When a product or business model is patented, no other organization can duplicate it without paying an agreed-on royalty to the patent holder or risking prolonged patent litigation. Patents can be difficult, expensive, and time-consuming to obtain—for example, a single U.S. patent application can cost up to $20,000 in legal fees for U.S. use only—which puts patents out of the price range of many new firms or individual inventors. However, patents can also be very lucrative. For instance, IBM—which is frequently identified by the U.S. Patent and Trademark Office as the top patenting company, such as in 2001 when it was issued over 3,400 patents—earns an estimated $1.7 billion per year from its patents.

**Figure 6-3**

**A patent for a new handheld computer design**

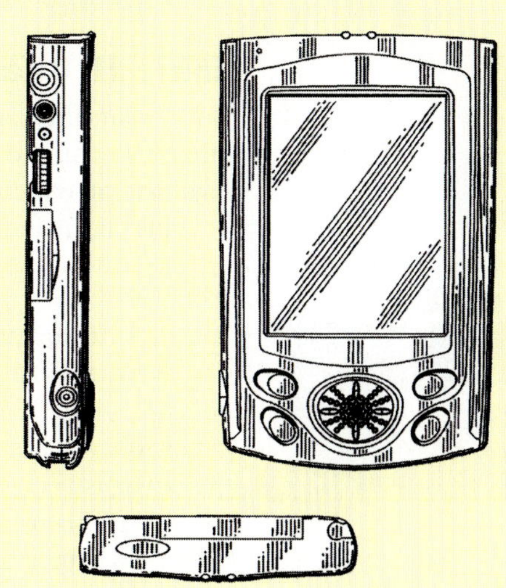

US00D461185S

(12) **United States Design Patent** (10) **Patent No.:** **US D461,185 S**
**Ando** (45) **Date of Patent:** ** **Aug. 6, 2002**

(54) **HANDHELD COMPUTER**

(75) Inventor: **Toshiya Ando,** Higashikurume (JP)

(73) Assignee: **Casio Keisanki Kabushiki Kaisha,** Tokyo (JP)

(**) Term: **14 Years**

(21) Appl. No.: **29/149,284**

(22) Filed: **Oct. 5, 2001**

(51) **LOC (7) Cl.** .......... **14-02**
(52) **U.S. Cl.** .......... **D14/341**
(58) **Field of Search** .......... D14/341–346; D18/1, 2, 7; 235/145 A, 145 R; 341/22, 23; 345/156, 168, 169, 172, 173; 349/12

(56) **References Cited**

U.S. PATENT DOCUMENTS

D397,679 S * 9/1998 Hawkins et al. .......... D14/342
D408,372 S * 4/1999 Ota et al. .......... D14/346
D416,237 S * 11/1999 Miyahara et al. .......... D14/346
D420,987 S * 2/2000 Miyahara et al. .......... D14/346
D442,583 S * 5/2001 Ohta et al. .......... D14/346

* cited by examiner

*Primary Examiner*—Freda Nunn
(74) *Attorney, Agent, or Firm*—Frishauf, Holtz, Goodman & Chick, P.C.

(57) **CLAIM**

The ornamental design for a handheld computer, as shown.

**DESCRIPTION**

FIG. **1** is a left side elevational view of a handheld computer, showing my new design;
FIG. **2** is a front elevational view thereof;
FIG. **3** is a right side elevational view thereof;
FIG. **4** is a rear elevational view thereof;
FIG. **5** is a top plan view thereof; and,
FIG. **6** is a bottom plan view thereof.

**1 Claim, 1 Drawing Sheet**

# WHAT ARE ETHICS?

The term **ethics** refers to standards of moral conduct. For example, telling the truth is a matter of ethics. An unethical act isn't always illegal, although it might be, but illegal acts would be viewed as unethical by most people. For example, purposely lying to a friend is unethical but usually not illegal, while perjuring oneself in a courtroom as a witness is both illegal and unethical. Whether or not criminal behavior is involved, ethics play an integral role in our lives since they guide our behavior.

Much more ambiguous than the law, ethical beliefs can vary widely. What is viewed as ethical behavior by one individual may be viewed as unethical by another. Ethical beliefs may vary depending on such characteristics as one's religion, country, race, or culture. In addition, different ethical standards can apply to different areas of one's life. For example, *personal ethics* guide an individual's personal behavior and *professional ethics* guide an individual's workplace behavior. Ethics with respect to the use of computers is referred to as **computer ethics**.

Computer ethics has taken on more significance in recent years because the proliferation of computers in the home and the workplace provides many more opportunities for unethical acts than in the past. The Internet also makes it easy to distribute information that some would view as unethical. For example, the Belgian teenaged virus writer known as "Gigabyte" does not release the viruses she writes, but she has been known to post the code for her viruses on her Web site, where others who are so inclined can access and release them. When asked about someone else taking her viruses and launching them on the public, Gigabyte has responded that it's certainly not her fault. Undoubtedly, many people would disagree and would view making viruses easily available to other individuals to release as a highly unethical act.

Whether at home, at work, or at school, individuals encounter ethical issues every day. For example, you may need to make such ethical decisions as whether or not to accept a relative's offer of a free copy of a CD or movie, whether or not to have a friend help you take an online exam, whether or not to print your child's birthday party invitations on the office color printer, or whether or not to forward the most recent e-mail warning about a new computer virus to everyone in your address book.

Businesses also deal with a variety of ethical issues in the course of normal business activities—from determining how many computers on which to install a particular software program, to deciding how customer information should be used, to developing new business practices. **Business ethics** is the term often used to cover the standards of conduct that guide a business' policies, decisions, and actions.

## Ethical Use of Copyrighted Material

Both businesses and individuals should be very careful when copying, sharing, or otherwise using copyrighted material to ensure that the material is used in both a legal and an ethical manner. Common types of copyrighted material encountered on a regular basis include software, books, and Web-based articles, music, and movies.

**ONLINE TUTORIAL**

For an online look at the basic classes of software and their ownership rights, go to www.course.com/morley2003/ch6

### Software

After a software program is developed, the developer is entitled to copyright protection and the ownership of all rights to that program. Whether or not the program can be sold, shared with others, or otherwise distributed is up to the copyright holder. When software is purchased, the buyer isn't actually buying the program. Instead, the buyer is acquiring a **software license** that permits him or her to use the program. This license specifies the conditions under which a buyer can use the program, such as whether or not the program may be shared with others and the number of computers on which the program may be installed (most commercial software licenses are *single-user licenses* that permit the software to be installed on just one PC). In addition to being included in printed form inside a software box, most programs display and require acceptance of the licensing agreement during the installation process (see Figure 6-4). There are four basic classes of software (*commercial software*, *shareware*, *freeware*, and *public-domain software*), each having different types of ownership rights.

**Commercial software** is usually available in packaged form, such as from a retail store, an online store, or the manufacturer. Some programs can also be downloaded from the Internet (see Figure 6-5). To purchase software in a downloadable format, usually the order is placed and the payment processed in the same manner as if the software was being purchased in a physical format, and then the buyer is provided with a link to download the purchased program. With a downloaded program, you typically do not receive a CD containing the program, although some vendors recommend that you back up a downloaded program onto a CD as soon as it is downloaded in case the program needs to be reinstalled sometime in the future.

When you buy a single-user license for a commercial software program (such as Microsoft Office, TurboTax, or The Sims) you cannot legally make copies of the CD to give to your friends, nor can you install the software on their computers using your CD. You usually cannot even install the software on a second PC that you own, unless allowed by the license. For example, some software licenses may state that the program can be installed on one desktop PC and one notebook PC; others may allow installation on both a home and work PC, as long as the two computers will never be used at the same time. Leasing your copy of a program is also typically forbidden, unless a specific licensing agreement for that is obtained. For many programs, *site licenses* and *network licenses* are available for schools or businesses that need to install the software on multiple computers or need to have the software available to multiple users over a network. To determine what activities are allowable for a particular piece of software, refer to the licensing agreement for that program.

**FIGURE 6-4**

**A typical software license displayed during program installation**

This statement points out that the program will not be installed unless you accept the terms of the license agreement.

A checkmark indicates that you accept the terms of the license agreement.

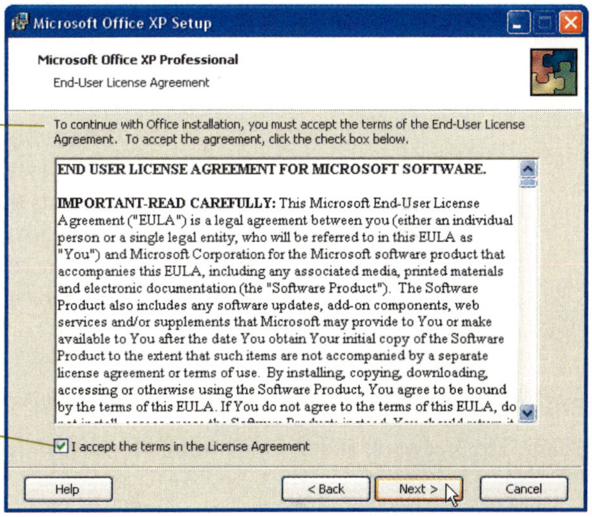


**FIGURE 6-5**

**Some commercial software programs can be downloaded from the Internet.**

Many commercial programs today can be purchased in a downloadable format, instead of in a physical package.

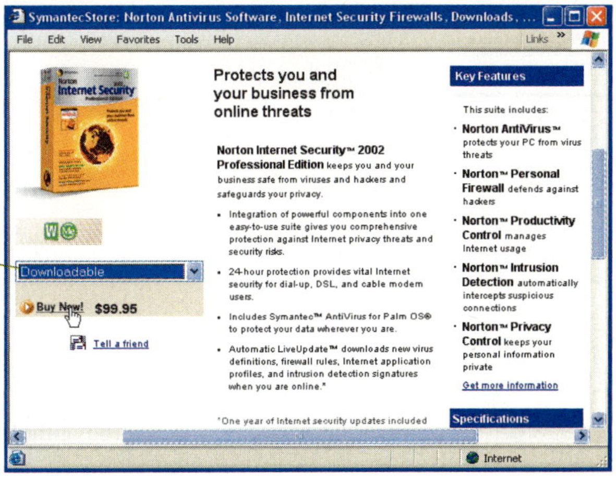

Many commercial software programs request that you register the program after purchase. If a software program has *mandatory registration*—such as with recent Microsoft products—you can only use the software before registering it for a certain number of times or for a certain period of time; once the program has been registered, that restriction is removed. Microsoft started mandatory registration with the introduction of Microsoft Office 2000 as one of its anti-piracy methods. Originally, Microsoft wanted the mandatory registration to include personally identifiable information about the user and PC, but that announcement resulted in a high level of outrage and Microsoft deciding to require only geographical information.

In addition to their full versions, some commercial software programs are available in *demo* or *trial versions*. Typically these versions can be used free of charge and distributed to others, but often they are missing some key abilities (such as the ability to save or print a document) or they will not run after the trial period expires. Since these programs are not designed as replacements for the fee-based versions, it is ethical to use them only to determine if you would like to buy the full program. If the decision is made against purchasing the product, the demo or trial version should be uninstalled from your PC.

**Shareware** programs are copyrighted programs that are distributed on the honor system. Most shareware programs are available to try free of charge, but the author usually requests that you pay a small fee if you intend to use the program regularly. By paying the requested shareware fee, you become a registered user and can typically receive product support, documentation, and updates. Shareware programs are widely available from a variety of download sites on the Internet, such as the one shown in Figure 6-6. You can copy shareware programs to pass along to friends and colleagues, but those individuals are expected to pay the shareware fee if they decide to keep the product. Most shareware programs have a specified trial period, such as one month. Although it is not illegal to use shareware past the specified trial period, it is unethical to do so. Ethical use of shareware dictates either paying for the program or uninstalling it from your PC at the end of the trial period. Shareware is typically much less expensive than commercial versions of similar software, because it is often developed by a single programmer and is usually sold directly to customers with little or no packaging or advertising expenses. Shareware authors stress that the ethical use of shareware helps to cultivate this type of affordable software distribution.

**FIGURE 6-6**

**Shareware, freeware, and demo software are frequently downloaded from the Internet.**

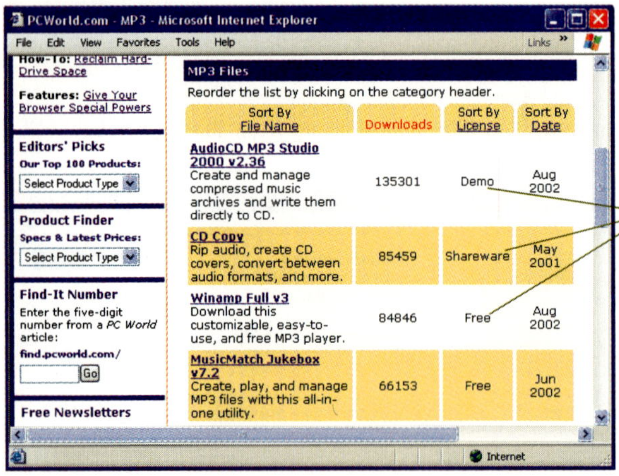


On most download sites, the license type and any registration fee will be specified prior to download.

**Freeware** programs are copyrighted programs that are given away for free by the author. Although freeware is available free of charge and can be shared with others, the author retains the copyright so you cannot do anything with it—such as sell it or modify it—that is not expressly allowed by the author. Freeware programs are frequently developed by students, professional programmers, and amateur programmers as a programming exercise or hobby; some commercial software programs are released as freeware as well, such as Internet Explorer, Netscape Navigator, and OpenOffice.org. Like shareware programs, freeware programs are widely available over the Internet.

**FIGURE 6-7**

Examples of common software types

| Type of Software | Examples | Most Commonly Obtained From |
|---|---|---|
| Commercial software | Microsoft Office (office suite)<br>Norton Antivirus (antivirus program)<br>Adobe PhotoShop (image-editing program)<br>Flight Simulator (game) | Manufacturer's Web site, online stores, and physical stores |
| Shareware | WinZip (file compression program)<br>MusicMatch Jukebox (MP3 player and CD ripper)<br>PaintShop Pro (image-editing program)<br>Quake (game) | Manufacturer/author's Web site and download sites, such as Shareware.com and ZDNet Downloads |
| Freeware | ZoneAlarm (firewall)<br>Netscape Navigator (Web browser)<br>Outlook Express (e-mail program)<br>South Park Space Invaders (game) | Manufacturer/author's Web site and download sites, such as Shareware.com and ZDNet Downloads |
| Public-domain software | Linux (operating system)<br>Lynx (text-based Web browser)<br>Pine (e-mail program) | Download, university, and government sites; open source and public-domain organizations |

**Public-domain software** is not copyrighted. Because it has been donated to the public domain, it is available for free and can be used, copied, modified, and distributed to others without restrictions. Sometimes just the executable program is in the public domain; other times—such as with non-copyrighted open source software—the source code is also public domain. Some examples of software programs falling into the four categories just discussed are shown in Figure 6-7.

### Books and Web-Based Articles

Print-based books, e-books, Web-based articles, and other types of literary material are all protected by copyright law. Consequently, they cannot be reproduced, presented as one's own original material, or otherwise used in an unauthorized manner. Students, researchers, authors, and other writers need to be especially careful when using literary material as a resource for papers, articles, books, and so forth to ensure the material is properly credited to the original author. To present someone else's work as your own is **plagiarism**, which is both a violation of copyright law and unethical. Some examples of what constitutes and what does not constitute a plagiaristic act are shown in Figure 6-8.

With the increased availability of online articles and fee-based online term paper services, some students might be tempted to create their papers by copying and pasting together excerpts of online content. But these students should realize that it is illegal and unethical, and instructors can usually tell when a paper is created in this manner. There are also online services instructors can use to test the originality of student papers; the results of one such test is shown in Figure 6-9. Many colleges and universities have strict consequences for plagiarism, such as automatically failing the assignment or course, or being expelled from the institution. For a review of how to cite online material properly, refer to the Chapter 3 How To box.

**Figure 6-8**

**Examples of what is and what is not considered plagiarism**

| Plagiarism | Not Plagiarism |
|---|---|
| A student copying or retyping a few sentences or a few paragraphs written by another author to include in his term paper without crediting the original author | A student copying or retyping a few sentences or a few paragraphs written by another author to include in his term paper, either indenting the quotation or placing it inside quotation marks, and crediting the original author with a citation in the text or with a footnote or endnote |
| A newspaper reporter changing a few words in a sentence or paragraph written by another author and including the revised text in an article without crediting the original author | A newspaper reporter paraphrasing a few sentences or paragraphs written by another author without changing the meaning of the text, including the revised text in an article, and crediting the original author with a proper citation |
| A student copying and pasting information from various online documents to create her research paper without crediting the original authors | A student copying and pasting information from various online documents and using those quotes in her research paper either indented or enclosed in quotation marks with the proper citations for each author |
| A teacher sharing a poem with a class, leading the class to believe the poem was his original work | A teacher sharing a poem with a class, clearly identifying the poet |

**FIGURE 6-9**

**An online originality test on a plagiarized essay**

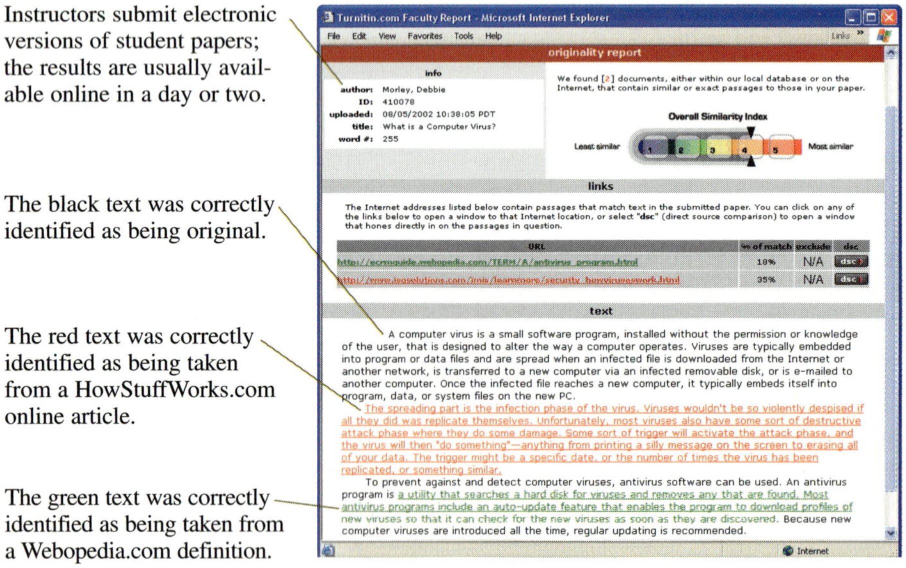


### Music

There have been several issues regarding the legal and ethical use of music over the past few years, fueled primarily by the emergence and wide-spread use of Napster, recordable and rewritable CD drives, and MP3 players. As a result of the Napster controversy, music downloads through most reputable Web sites are now limited to songs designated by the artist as free downloads or fee-based downloads in which a royalty system has been arranged with the copyright holder, although illegal distribution still exists. Once an MP3 file or audio CD has been legally obtained, however, most experts agree that it falls within the fair use concept for an individual to transfer those songs to a CD-R disc, PC, or an MP3 player, as long as it is for personal, noncommercial use (see the chapter How To box for a look at how this can be accomplished). In contrast, transferring songs to a CD to sell or give to a friend would be a violation of copyright laws and an unethical act.

To protect against piracy, new **copy-protection** methods are beginning to be used on some music CDs to prevent them from being copied, transferred to an MP3 player or PC, or even played in a computer's CD drive. There is also pending legislation regarding mandatory built-in copy protection in certain types of hardware. These copy-protection issues are discussed in more detail in the Closer Look box.

In response to what they view as a direct attack on their business, the music industry is testing various types of digital copy protection for music CDs. Typically, copy-protection schemes prevent the CD from being copied to another medium (such as to a hard drive, CD-R disc, or MP3 player) or played in any device other than an audio CD player (such as a computer CD-ROM or CD-R drive). While some consumer advocates argue that consumers should be able to copy legally-obtained music for their own use and play it on any device of their choosing, the copy protection movement is gaining ground.

Digitally locked CDs that cannot be copied or even played in a PC's CD drive are already on the market and the first lawsuit regarding them has recently been settled. A California woman (see Figure 6-10) filed a lawsuit in 2001 claiming that the "Charley Pride: A Tribute to Jim Reeves" CD—the first known copy-protected CD released in the U.S.—illegally violated consumer expectations by not including a disclaimer that it will not operate on computer CD players and required the purchaser to register personal information before being allowed to download the songs to a computer. The suit was settled in 2002 with the companies involved agreeing to stop collecting personally identifiable information of listeners, to purge their files of such information, and to warn consumers that the CD doesn't work in DVD players, MP3 players, or CD-ROM players. Although some view this settlement as a victory for consumers, the music industry is still backing legislation—such as the *Consumer Broadband and Digital Television Act* introduced by Senator Hollings in 2002—that would require mandatory copy protection to be built into future hardware such as CD, DVD, and MP3 players.

Other entertainment organizations—such as Disney, Sony, and the Motion Picture Association of America (MPAA)—are also backing the concept of mandatory copy protection. In addition to supporting the legislation introduced by Senator Hollings, the movie industry is pushing for a law or FCC regulation to implement a copy protection system for digital video and all devices (such as TV sets, PCs, and digital personal video recorders) that accept digital input to prevent the transfer of digital video over a TCP/IP network. Though intended to prevent transmission of pirated movies over the Internet, it would also prevent the transfer of digital movies over a home network that uses the TCP/IP protocol, as well as throw a monkey wrench into movie-on-demand services delivered via the Internet. One possible solution is technology that would allow a downloaded movie to be recorded one time to disc, but would prevent that disc from being copied. Another alternative being suggested is to extend the 3% royalty already in place for blank audio CD-R discs to all recordable media to reimburse the entertainment industry and artists for potential lost royalties due to piracy using that media.

Proponents of mandatory copy protection believe that it will reduce the potential for piracy, which, in turn, will reduce the reluctance of media companies to make entertainment content available through the Internet. Opponents counter that even sophisticated copy protection schemes can be cracked, and state as examples the instances of hackers rapidly breaking the *Content Scrambling System* used to protect DVDs and the anti-piracy system built into Windows XP—the Windows XP system was cracked within hours of its introduction. Opponents to mandatory copy protection add that while serious thieves will likely figure out a way to bypass any security measures adopted, copy-protection schemes will only prevent innocent consumers from exerting their fair use rights to use the music CDs and other digital content that they acquire legally.

The outcome of the push for mandatory copy protection is as of yet uncertain, but if any such legislation passes the *Digital Millennium Copyright Act* passed in 1997 makes it illegal to bypass those copyright protection methods—both for pirates that sell bootleg copies for a profit and for individuals trying to copy songs from CDs they have purchased to create a custom party CD. This may change in the future if one of the DMCA's original sponsors, Representative Rick Boucher, is able to pass his proposed amendment that would allow circumventing copy protection for an individual's fair use of the product. In the meantime, the debate over digital rights management continues.

**FIGURE 6-10**

**This copy-protected CD was the subject of a recent lawsuit.**

## Movies

In 1984 Disney and Universal sued Sony to stop producing the Betamax—the first personal VCR to come on the market. These movie companies were concerned about the ability of the Betamax product to record and copy movies and television shows. The entertainment industry considered this unauthorized copying and worried that Betamax and any other types of VCRs to come on the market would threaten their profits. The lawsuit was eventually decided in Sony's favor, and the Supreme Court upheld the consumers' rights to record shows for convenience and personal use. Interestingly, in direct contrast to the views held by the entertainment industry in 1984, videos have been credited with boosting Hollywood's revenues tremendously. Despite this positive financial impact, the entertainment industry remains concerned about consumers illegally making copies of movies—especially digital copies that can be duplicated an unlimited number of times without losing quality like a videotape. To address these concerns, copy protection has been built into many VHS, DVD, and pay-per-view movies to prevent individuals from making unauthorized copies of those items. Unfortunately, movie pirates have been able to circumvent the copy protection and the motion picture industry estimates that losses due to movie piracy exceed well over $3 billion per year.

Recently, new concerns for the entertainment industry have surfaced due to the increased availability of unauthorized copies of movies distributed through the Internet. The easy access to these unauthorized copies adds a new legal and ethical dilemma for individuals with broadband Internet connections. If one individual records a television show and then shares it with a friend via the Internet, does that go beyond the concept of fair use? If you run across a location where you can download a copy of a movie not yet out on video or DVD, are you legally at risk if you make the download? What if you watch the movie once and then delete it—are you still in the wrong?

While the answers to these questions have yet to be unequivocally decided, many people agree that distributing bootleg copies of movies via the Internet is both illegal and unethical. Some individuals must disagree, however, since a report by the Viant consulting firm estimates that between 300,000 and 500,000 feature movies are illegally downloaded from the Internet every day. Some downloads are facilitated by peer-to-peer file-swapping services; others take place via a central server sometimes with the owner's consent and sometimes without, such as in the recent case in which Stanford University students were using a school server to download pirated movies. (Upon notification, Stanford promptly deleted those movies from their servers.) To catch people who are illegally sharing movies on the Internet, the Motion Picture Association of America (MPAA) has recently begun using special software that monitors file-swapping networks to find copyrighted materials, hunt down the IP address of the person who is sharing the movie, and then discover that person's ISP. Under the Digital Millennium Copyright Act, ISPs must stop distribution of copyrighted materials when they are notified; to meet this mandate, ISPs typically threaten the user with cancellation of his or her Internet service.

Another strategy being used by the motion picture industry is offering Internet users the alternative of authorized movie downloads. Five of the seven major movie studios have started a joint venture, code-named *Moviefly* and expected to be available in the near future, to provide movie downloads on demand for an estimated $4 each. To protect against unauthorized distribution, the movies are expected to be encrypted and include timing software to render the movie file unusable 24 hours after downloading. A competing service called *Movies.com* has also been introduced by Disney and 20th Century Fox. Though an antitrust investigation into both of these proposed services from the Justice Department is under consideration, some type of Internet movie delivery is expected eventually to become a normal activity as Internet speeds increase and broadband access becomes more widespread.

## Ethical Use of Resources and Information

There are a variety of resources and types of information that can be used in an unethical manner, such as school computers, company computers and equipment, and customer or employee information. For example, some employees use company computers for personal use, some students perform dishonest acts while completing assignments or taking exams, and some job applicants provide erroneous or misleading information during the application or interview periods.

### Ethical Use of School or Company Resources

What is considered to be proper and ethical use of school or company resources may vary from school to school or company to company. To explain what is allowed at a particular organization, many schools and businesses have policies that specify which activities are allowed and which are forbidden. Often these policies—frequently called **codes of conduct**—are available as written documents; sometimes they are more informal. (To review an example of a code of conduct, refer back to Figure 4-2.) Because policies can vary so much from organization to organization—for example, one school may allow the use of school PCs to check personal e-mail and another school may not, and one business may allow limited use of the office photocopier or printer for personal use and another may forbid that activity—all students and employees should make a point to find out what is considered to be ethical use of resources at their school or place of business. (This information is often available in a student or employee handbook or on the organization's Web site or intranet.) The code of conduct should clearly identify what types of allowable computer and Internet activities, as well as what personal use (if any) of resources such as PCs, printers, photocopiers, telephones, and fax machines, are allowed.

In addition to or instead of a written code of conduct, some organizations use periodic letters or e-mails to inform individuals of new policies as they are implemented. For example, Microsoft recently sent an e-mail to more than 50,000 employees informing them that using a company PC or network to swap music, movies, software, or any other copyrighted material via a P2P network is against corporate policy. To enforce its policies, some businesses may use employee-monitoring techniques like those discussed in Chapter 5.

Another common type of code widely used by various industries and organizations is a **code of ethics**. Codes of ethics, such as the one shown in Figure 6-11, summarize the moral guidelines adopted by a particular organization (frequently a professional society) and typically address such issues as honesty, integrity, fairness, responsibility to others, proper use of intellectual property, confidentiality, and accountability. So, while codes of conduct usually address specific activities that can and cannot be performed, codes of ethics cover broader ethical standards of conduct.

**ONLINE RESOURCES**

For links to codes of ethics for a variety of industries, go to www.course.com/morley2003/ch6

In determining what actions they will or won't take at work, employees should give careful consideration to how they will use confidential or proprietary information they have access to. Although employees are typically forbidden from revealing this type of information to outsiders, a dilemma exists when the information an employee has access to is related to an illegal, unethical, or dangerous activity in which the business is involved. Employees who reveal wrongdoing within an organization to the public or to authorities are referred to as *whistleblowers.* These individuals have varying degrees of protection from retaliation, discharge, or other types of discrimination due to providing whistleblowing information. The type and extent of protection depends on the type of wrongdoing and organization involved, as well as the state in which the company and employee are located. The *Corporate Responsibility Act*, signed into law in mid-2002, provides protection for whistleblowers who provide information to a federal regulatory or law enforcement agency, a member of Congress or a Congressional committee, or a person with supervisory authority over the employee. At the time of this writing, federal whistleblowing legislation was being proposed to protect whistleblowing employees further.

**Figure 6-11**

A sample code of ethics

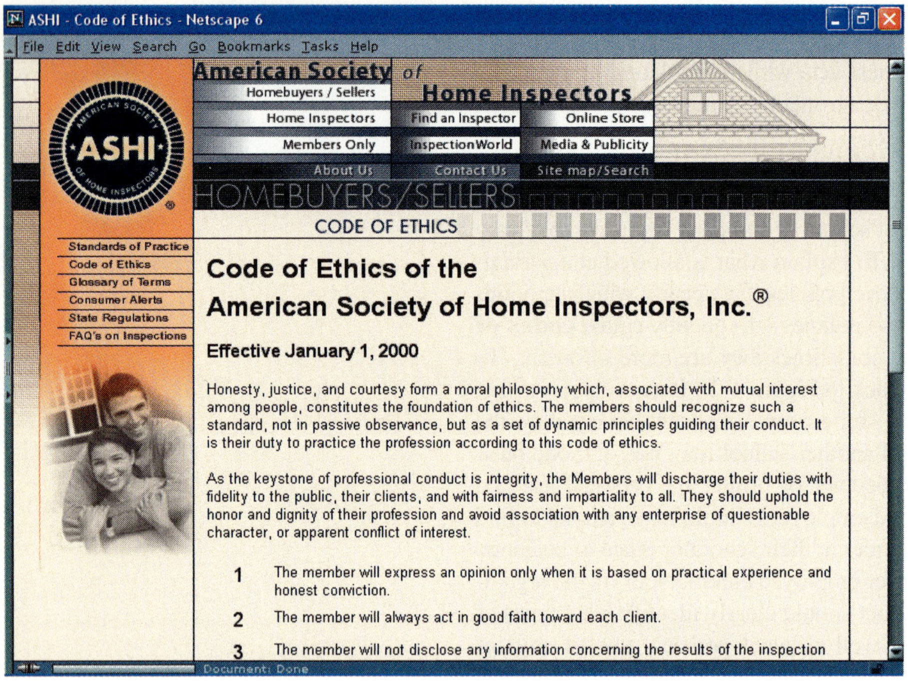


### Ethical Use of Employee and Customer Information

While a business may be legally bound by such restrictions as employee confidentiality laws, union contracts, and its customer privacy policy, there are gray areas inside which ethical decisions need to be made. For example, if it is legal for a business to share or sell customer information, should it do it? This is a decision that many businesses have struggled with in challenging economic times where a quick source of revenue gained from selling customer data may be tempting. Though some businesses have succumbed to the temptation of a quick infusion of cash and sold their customer lists, others believe that any short-term gains due to questionable ethical acts will adversely affect customer loyalty and will ultimately hurt the business in the long run.

To prepare future employees properly for these types of decisions, most business schools incorporate business ethics into their curriculum. However, the startling number of recently revealed corporate scandals and the perceived degrading moral climate today have caused some schools to reevaluate this curriculum to see if it is sufficient. According to George Brenkert, director of the Business Ethics Institute at Georgetown University, business schools have spread the message of maximizing profit at nearly any cost for too long. He believes that businesses have to derive a profit and a return on their investments, but they have to do it in the broader context of ethical considerations and social responsibility. Future business curricula for many schools will likely incorporate this new philosophy, at least to some extent. Corporate philosophies and employee training programs are also beginning to move in this direction. Some companies—such as Shell, Ford, and Nike—have made social responsibility a more central part of their corporate mission. Some organizations also have formal ethics training programs, such as the program at Lockheed Martin that requires its employees to complete ethics training every year.

### Cheating and Falsifying Information

Just as computers make it easier to plagiarize documents, computers and the Internet can also make it easier for those individuals who choose to cheat on assignments or online exams, falsify a resume, or perform similar unethical acts.

Unfortunately, cheating by students at both high school and college is rampant today. According to recent studies by Donald L. McCabe of Rutgers University, over 75% of students on most campuses admit to some cheating. In his 1999 survey, about one-third of the participating students admitted to cheating on tests and half admitted to one or more instances of cheating on written assignments. Although cheating can occur with noncomputerized assignments, the editing ability of a PC makes it fast and easy to share assignments created with a computer. To reduce the possibility of cheating on exams for distance learning courses, some colleges and universities require exams to be taken in person so that the identity of the exam-taker can be verified.

Most of the time, the in-person exams are taken at the campus through which the online course is offered, although some colleges allow exams to be taken at authorized testing centers for students not located close to the campus.

In addition to cheating themselves of an education, students who choose to cheat are being unfair to honest students by possibly altering the grading curve or even lessening the overall value of a diploma. Widespread cheating also has a negative impact on society if underprepared employees enter the workforce. How many of us would be comfortable having our taxes prepared by a CPA who cheated in his accounting classes, or having our surgery performed by a physician who cheated her way through medical school?

To explain to students what behavior is expected of them, many schools are developing *academic honor codes.* Sometimes these codes are published in the student handbook or on the school Web site; other times they are included in course syllabi. Research has shown that having an academic honor code effectively reduces cheating. For example, the McCabe studies found that cheating on tests on campuses with honor codes is typically one-third to one-half less than for campuses that do not have honor codes, and the level of cheating on written assignments is one-quarter to one-third lower. To bring attention to their honor codes, some schools encourage incoming students to sign an honor code upon admission. For instance, all incoming University of Denver students are asked to sign the school's honor code publicly (see Figure 6-12). Regardless of whether or not students chose to sign the honor code, they are required to abide by it. To remind students of this responsibility at the University of Denver, the honor code pledge "I affirm my commitment to the University of Denver Honor Code" appears on every exam blue book purchased through the university bookstore.

**FIGURE 6-12**

**The honor code at the University of Denver is signed by virtually all incoming students.**

Like academic cheating, lying on a job application or resume is more common than most of us would like to think it is. Sometimes referred to as *resume padding*, providing false information in an attempt to look more qualified for a job is both dishonest and unethical. But it is also widespread. Recent research conducted by the New York Times advertising department found that almost half of hiring managers and 84% of job seekers believe that resume padding is done by a significant number of candidates. Besides being unethical, providing false information to a potential employer can have grave consequences. The majority of the companies surveyed in the New York Times study have a policy that lists termination as the appropriate action for employees who were hired based on falsified resumes or applications. Being blacklisted from an industry or being sued for breach of contract are also possibilities. With background checks available so easily on the Web, many career guidance experts caution clients against embellishing their resumes or job applications to any extent.

In addition to employment documents, there are other times when some individuals may be tempted to provide inaccurate personal information, such as in personal advertisements, chat rooms, and similar situations where individuals may wish to appear different than they really are. There are differing opinions about how ethical these actions are, with some individuals of the opinion that it is a person's right to portray himself or herself in any way desired, and others believing that any type of dishonesty is unethical.

## Computer Hoaxes and Digital Manipulation

Most people realize that information in print media can at times be misleading and that photos can be manipulated. Information found on the Internet may also be inaccurate, misleading, or biased. Some of this information is published on Web pages; other information is passed on via e-mail. Two types of computer-oriented misinformation include *computer hoaxes* and *digital manipulation.*

**ONLINE RESOURCES**

For links to sites that list recent computer hoaxes, go to www.course.com/morley2003/ch6

## Computer Hoaxes

A **computer hoax** is an inaccurate statement or story—such as the "facts" that flesh-eating bacteria has been found in banana shipments and that antiperspirant use causes cancer—spread through the use of computers. These hoaxes are sometimes published on Web pages, but are more commonly spread via e-mail. Common hoax subjects include nonexistent computer viruses or impending legislation, serious health risks of a particular product, impending terrorist attacks, and chain letters. These hoaxes are written with the purpose of being circulated to as many people as possible. Some are started as experiments to see how fast and widespread information can travel via the Internet; others originate from a joke or desire to frighten people. Because hoaxes are so common, regardless of how realistic or frightening the information appears to be, it is a good idea to double check any warning you receive by e-mail or read on a Web site before passing that warning on to another person. One reliable source to use is the government's Hoaxbusters site shown in Figure 6-13.

## Digital Manipulation

Computers make it very easy to copy or modify text, images, photographs, music, and other digital content. In addition to being a copyright concern, **digital manipulation** can be used to misquote individuals, repeat comments out of context, retouch photographs—even to create completely false photographs. While there are some beneficial, ethical, noncontroversial applications of digital manipulation—such as aging photos of missing children to show what they may look like at the present time or altering photos of wanted criminals or suspects to show possible appearances for law enforcement purposes—the matter of altering photos to be published is the subject of much debate. Some publications and photographers see no harm in altering photographs to remove an offending item (such as a telephone pole behind someone's head), to make someone look a little more attractive, to illustrate a point, or to increase circulation; others view any change in content as unethical and a great disservice to both the general public and our history. For example, fifty years from now, will anyone know that a staged or altered photograph of a historical event wasn't an actual depiction of the event?

Although manipulation of photographs has occurred for quite some time in tabloids and other publications not known as being reputable news sources, there have been several incidents of more reputable publications using digitally altered photographs in recent years. Most of these became known because the unaltered photograph was used in another publication at about the same time. One of the most widely publicized cases occurred in 1994 just following

**FIGURE 6-13**

**The federal government's Hoaxbusters site (located at hoaxbusters.ciac.org) is a good resource for checking into the huge number of computer hoaxes being spread at any given time.**

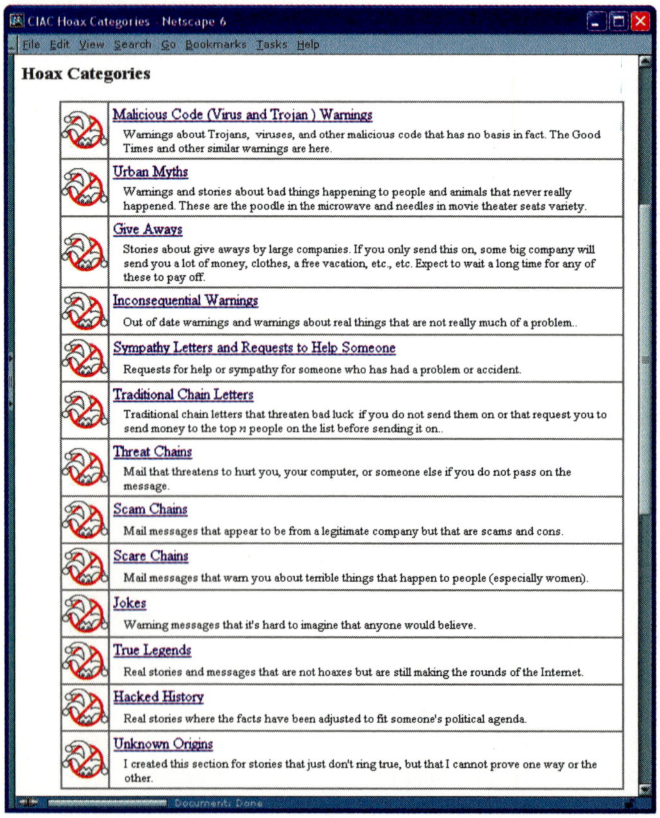

the arrest of O.J. Simpson. While *Newsweek* ran Simpson's mug shot unaltered, *TIME* magazine darkened the photograph, creating a more sinister look and making Simpson's skin color appear darker than it actually is. This photo drew hard criticism from Simpson supporters who felt the photograph made him appear guilty, the black community who viewed the alteration as an act of racial insensitivity, and news photographers who felt that the action damaged the credibility not only of that particular magazine, but also of all journalists.

**ONLINE TUTORIAL**

For an online look at digital photograph manipulation, go to www.course.com/morley2003/ch6

Another example occurred during the U.N. Millennium Summit in September 2000. A photo ran in the New York Daily News, showing then-President Clinton and Cuba's leader Fidel Castro extending their right hands towards each other, appearing that they were just about to shake hands (see Figure 6-14). What is significant about this photo is that the situation never occurred—it was a digitally created composite. Although Clinton and Castro reportedly did shake hands during the summit—something no other U.S. President has done since Castro took control of Cuba some 40 years ago—there are no known photographs of the event. Although the Daily News originally argued that the photograph was labeled a "photo illustration" and there wasn't any attempt at misrepresentation, they eventually admitted to a lapse in judgment.

**FIGURE 6-14**

**The digital manipulation of two photographs created this composite image which ran on the cover of the Daily News in 2000.**

Perhaps the most disturbing thing about known alterations such as this is that they may never have been noticed, and consequently been accepted as true representations. Adding to the problem of unethical digital manipulation is digital camera use by professional photographers, which virtually eliminates any concrete evidence—such as negatives—that can show what photographs actually looked like at the time they were taken.

## Ethical Business Practices and Decision-Making

Companies must make business decisions such as whether or not to sell a product or service that some may find offensive or disagree with, whether or not to install monitoring cameras in the workplace, whether or not to release potentially misleading information, and whether or not to perform controversial research. In addition, corporate integrity in terms of accounting practices and proper disclosure are business ethics topics that have received a great deal of attention lately with the recent rash of corporate scandals and bankruptcies.

### Fraudulent Reporting and Other Scandalous Activities

Perhaps business ethics has never been quite so much in the public eye as following the large number of corporate scandals occurring in 2002. The scandals, such as the ones surrounding Enron, Tyco International, Martha Stewart, and WorldCom, involved lies, fraud, deception, and other illegal and unethical behavior, which forced both Enron and WorldCom into bankruptcy proceedings and threatened many individuals with jail time. When asked to comment on the scandals, 3Com chief executive officer Bruce Claflin said on CNBC that "I would argue we don't have an accounting problem—we have an ethics problem."

As a result of these scandals, attention has become more focused on corporate integrity, as well as on the responsibility of executives to make sure illegal and fraudulent activity does not take place within the company. Before these scandals became public, a survey done for the Pew Research Center found that 66% of the public rated the heads of major companies as "low or very low" in terms of honesty and ethical standards. Since then, if the declining Dow Jones Industrial Average in 2002 is any indication, public confidence in corporate America has eroded even further.

**Figure 6-15**

In 2002, President Bush signed into law a package of corporate reforms aimed to deter and punish corporate corruption.

In reaction to the scandals, Congress passed the *Sarbanes-Oxley Act of 2002*, sometimes referred to as the Corporate Responsibility Act (see Figure 6-15). This act, signed into law in July 2002, includes provisions to improve the quality of financial reporting, independent audits, and accounting services for public companies; to increase penalties for corporate wrongdoing; to protect the objectivity and independence of securities analysts; and to require CEOs and chief financial officers personally to vouch for the truth and fairness of their company's disclosures.

### Ethically Questionable Products or Services

Another ethical issue a business may run into is whether or not to sell products or services that some people find objectionable. For example, the eBay Web site states that it will not allow auction listings for items that promote hate, violence, or racial intolerance. Consequently, it bans items that bear symbols of the Nazis or the Ku Klux Klan (KKK), crime scene and morgue photographs, and letters and belongings of notorious criminals, even though sellers may legally be able to sell such items elsewhere. Policies within a particular industry may vary from company to company. For instance, pornographic movies and other adult-oriented materials are not allowed to be sold via Yahoo! Auctions, but are permitted on eBay.

For businesses that offer products or services that are inappropriate for children, decisions need to be made about how much protection against access by children the company is legally and ethically required to provide. This is especially significant for businesses with an e-commerce presence. Although in a conventional store individuals can be asked to show an ID to prove they are of the required age before being allowed to buy tobacco products, alcohol, pornographic materials, and other products that cannot legally be sold to minors, it is much more difficult to verify that an online buyer is of the required age.

To try to protect themselves, some Web sites selling these types of products and services require visitors to click a statement declaring that they are of the required age or to enter a valid credit card number before accessing or purchasing adult-only content or products. However, these precautions can be easily overcome. For example, in a recent experiment by the San Francisco Department of Public Health, five underage volunteers attempted to buy tobacco products illegally via the Internet. Visiting approximately 20 different sites, the teenagers were able to place an order at each site. Although some sites did require use of a credit card, all orders were delivered without any verification of their age.

The decisions about which products or services to offer online and offline are important—and sometimes difficult—ethical decisions for businesses to make. Typically, these decisions are based on the company's overall corporate mission and desired public image. Consequently, some businesses may choose not to sell adult-only or other types of controversial products at all. Others may decide not to sell it via the Internet until the age of online buyers can be proven beyond a doubt. Still other businesses may feel that a warning statement or similar precaution on their Web sites is all that is needed, and that it is the parents' responsibility to make sure their children don't purchase illegal or inappropriate items or view adult-only content via the Internet.

### Vaporware and Other Ethically Questionable Misinformation

**Vaporware** is a term sometimes used to designate software and hardware products that have been announced and advertised, but are not yet—and may never be—available. Sometimes a premature announcement isn't intentional, such as when a delay in production or other last-minute problem results in a late introduction. At other times, it may be an intentional act, designed to convince customers to wait for the company's upcoming product instead of buying an existing competitive product.

### Workplace Monitoring

Although businesses have the right and responsibility to ensure that employees are productive and the company resources are not being abused, many believe that businesses also have an ethical responsibility to inform employees of any monitoring that will be taking place. Although not required by law, it does make good business sense to convey this information to employees.

### Cultural Considerations

With today's global economy, businesses need to be sensitive to the ethical differences that may exist between different businesses located in the same country, as well as between businesses located in different countries. Because ethics are fundamentally based on values, when beliefs, laws, customs, and traditions vary, ethics will likely differ as well. One example is the concept of *human cloning*. There are widely differing beliefs within the United States about the ethics of human cloning, such as support by some disabled Americans who look to cloning as a means of finding a medical cure to their ailment and opposition on the same topic by other citizens and groups on religious or ethical grounds. Despite disagreements among U.S. citizens, a legislative ban on human cloning has been proposed, which would prevent researchers in the U.S. from performing human cloning research—such bans currently exist in Germany, Australia and Japan. Even if such a ban passes in the U.S., researchers in other countries, such as the United Kingdom, are expected to continue human cloning research.

Ethical decisions need to be made whenever a business practice or product is legal or socially acceptable in one country, but not another. One example is copyright law. While the United States and many other countries have copyright laws, some countries do not. Although an individual may be able to purchase an unauthorized—bootleg—copy of a software program, music CD, or movie in such a country, import restrictions prevent these items from coming into the U.S. to be sold. With the Internet, however, U.S. citizens now have the capability of buying unauthorized copies of copyrighted materials from countries where those copies are legal. This raises the question of ethical responsibility. Is it the individual's responsibility not to make these types of unethical purchases, even if technology makes it possible? What role does the government have in preventing individuals from buying products that are illegal in their country? What legal and ethical responsibility do businesses have to ensure that customers do not have access to products or services that are illegal in their particular area?

One example that has brought these issues into the forefront is the November 2000 French court ruling ordering the Yahoo! Auction Web site to prevent people located in France from accessing pages on the U.S. auction site containing Nazi books, daggers, uniforms, badges, and other items for sale that are illegal under French law. Although the Yahoo! France auction site didn't list those items, the French court order required Yahoo! to block access to these pages on its U.S. auction site from French Web surfers. Yahoo! appealed in a U.S. court on the grounds that this order was not technologically possible without completely removing all Nazi materials from its U.S. auction site, which would violate its First Amendment rights. In a decision that may set an important precedent regarding how far foreign jurisdictions can go to impose regulations against Internet content originating within the United States, a

U.S. District Court in California ruled in May 2002 that the French order could not be enforced against Yahoo! in the U.S. Although Yahoo! had already implemented a new policy banning any items that promote, glorify, or are directly associated with hate groups (such as the Nazis or the Ku Klux Klan) based on criticism from the public and consumer watchdog groups, this ruling—and any additional rulings as this issue continues to move its way through the courts—may turn out to be a landmark ruling regarding the boundaries and jurisdictions of cyberspace.

In addition to legal differences, organizations conducting business in other countries should also take into consideration the ethical standards prominent in the countries with which they do business. Factors such as gender roles, religious beliefs, and cultural customs should be considered and respected when corresponding, negotiating, and otherwise interacting with businesses located in other countries. For example, some cultures may require a handshake or other ritual that is impossible to carry out online in order to close a deal. To properly prepare students, some business schools include diversity and cross-cultural training in their curriculum; some international organizations arrange for such training prior to their employees traveling out of the country to avoid offending their international business partners or clients.

## RELATED LEGISLATION

There have been several new laws over the past few years (see Figure 6-16) attempting to revise intellectual property laws to reflect digital content and the Internet. One such law, the *Copyright Term Extension Act* passed in 1998, has been challenged as unconstitutional and was being heard by the U.S. Supreme Court at the time of this writing. If it is overturned, copyright terms would revert back to 50 years and older works—such as Mickey Mouse cartoons and early films such as "The Wizard of Oz"—would enter the public domain.

Legislation regarding ethics has been difficult to pass—or to keep as law once it has been passed. For example, the *Communications Decency Act* was signed into law in 1996 and made it a criminal offense to distribute patently indecent or offensive material online. Although intended to protect children from being exposed to inappropriate Web content, in 1997 the Supreme Court declared this law unconstitutional on the basis of free speech. The courts so far have had difficulty defining what is "patently offensive" and "indecent" and finding a fair balance between protection and censorship. Consequently, very few ethically oriented laws have been passed in recent years. Two exceptions are the *Children's Online Privacy Protection Act of 1998*—which regulates how Web sites can collect information from minors and provides tax incentives for Web sites and ISPs that facilitate protecting minors from accessing materials deemed harmful to them—and the Corporate Responsibility Act passed in 2002.

**FIGURE 6-16**

Some federal laws regarding intellectual property rights and ethics

| Date | Name/Description |
|---|---|
| 2002 | **Sarbanes-Oxley Act of 2002 (Corporate Responsibility Act)**<br>Includes provisions to improve the quality of financial reporting and other accounting services for public companies, increases penalties for corporate wrongdoing, and requires CEOs and chief financial officers to vouch personally for the truth and fairness of their company's disclosures. |
| 1999 | **U.S. Anticybersquatting Consumer Protection Act of 1999**<br>Amends the Trademark Act of 1946 to forbid a person from registering or using a domain name that infringes on a distinctive trademark by being either identical or confusingly similar to that mark. |
| 1999 | **Digital Millennium Copyright Act (DMCA)**<br>Makes it illegal to circumvent anti-piracy measures built into commercial software, as well as outlawing the manufacturing or sale of devices used to copy software illegally. |
| 1999 | **Trademark Amendments Act of 1999**<br>Amends the Trademark Act of 1946 to give grant holders of famous trademarks the right to oppose or seek cancellation of a mark that would cause dilution of their marks. |
| 1999 | **Digital Theft Deterrence and Copyright Damages Improvement Act of 1999**<br>Amends federal copyright law to increase statutory and additional damages a court may award for copyright infringement. |
| 1998 | **Children's Online Privacy Protection Act**<br>Regulates how Web sites can collect information from minors and communicate with them; also provides an exception from Internet tax moratoriums for Web sites providing material that is harmful to minors (unless access to such material is restricted to those 18 or over), and for ISPs (unless they offer screening software that allows customers to limit access to Internet material that is harmful to minors). |
| 1998 | **Copyright Term Extension Act**<br>Extends the duration of copyright in a work created on or after January 1, 1978, from 50 years after the author's death to 70 years after the author's death; extends the duration of copyright in anonymous works or works for hire to 95 years from date of publication or 120 years from creation, whichever is sooner. |
| 1997 | **No Electronic Theft (NET) Act**<br>Expands computer piracy laws to include distribution of copyrighted material over the Internet, and set penalties for willfully infringing a copyright for purposes of commercial advantage or private financial gain (redefined as including the receipt of anything of value, including other copyrighted works), as well as reproducing or distributing electronically or in material form copyrighted products valued at over $1,000 within any 180-day period. |
| 1976 | **Copyright Act of 1976**<br>Gives the owner of a copyright the exclusive right to publish, reproduce, distribute, perform, or display the work. |
| 1946 | **Lanham Act (Trademark Act of 1946)**<br>Allows the registration of trademarks for commerce purposes and prohibits the use, reproduction, or imitation of registered trademarks. |

## HOW TO... CREATE LEGAL DATA OR MUSIC CDS

With the large size of many files today—particularly those containing photographs, video, music, or other multimedia content—it is becoming increasingly common to need to create or *burn* a CD to transport files to another computer or to send to another individual. Data CDs are also commonly used for backup purposes. Creating CDs of your own personal data is perfectly legal. As discussed in the chapter, creating custom music CDs from CDs that you purchased for personal use or MP3 files that you downloaded legally is also considered to be legal, as long as the custom CD will be used for personal use and you are not circumventing any copy protection built into the CDs from which you are obtaining songs. Custom music CDs can be played in most CD and DVD players; if desired, the collection can also be transferred to an MP3 player.

### Creating a Data CD

Data files can be stored on either CD-R or CD+RW discs, depending on whether or not you want to be able to reuse the disc or add files to the disc after it has been burned. CD-R discs are designed to be burned once, and all the files are copied to the disc at the same time. CD+RW discs can be formatted to be used similar to a floppy or hard disk (where files can be copied to and deleted from the disc as desired); typically you will be asked when you first use a new CD+RW disc if you would like to format it for rewritable use. Though specialized CD burning software is available, such as Easy CD Creator and Nero Burning, file management programs can be used instead (see Figure 6-17).

**FIGURE 6-17**

**Copying a folder to a formatted CD+RW disc using the Windows XP My Computer file management program**

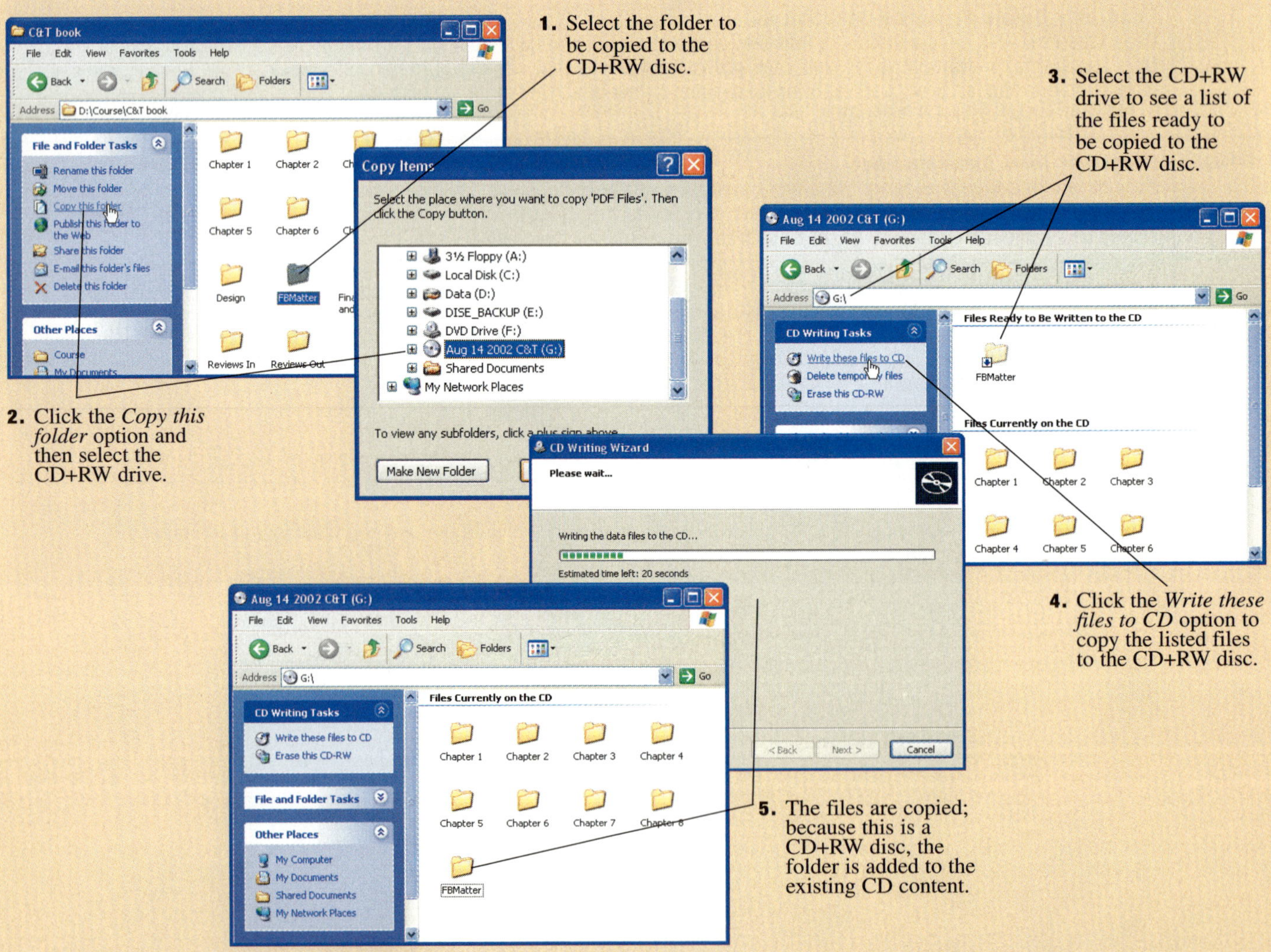

## Creating a Custom Music CD

At the present time, copying songs from a music CD you have legally obtained to your PC and custom music CDs is a legal activity. Songs located on a CD are stored in *WAV* format; when you transfer them to your PC, you typically can choose between storing them in WAV format or converting the songs to the more efficient *MP3* format to save room. Once the song is stored on your PC, it can be copied to a recordable or rewritable CD or transferred to an MP3 player. Transferring songs from a CD to a PC's hard drive in MP3 format using the MusicMatch program is shown in Figure 6-18. This process is sometimes referred to as *ripping* a CD.

Once all the desired songs have been transferred to the PC's hard drive, an appropriate program—such as MusicMatch or Windows Media Player—can be used to burn the desired songs onto a CD-R disc (see Figure 6-19). It is important to realize that many programs allow you to choose between storing the songs in WAV or MP3 format, as well as to select the desired quality and corresponding compression levels for MP3 files. WAV files take up much more storage space than MP3 files, so typically MP3 format is used, unless the CD player to be used doesn't support that format. The different compression levels also affect file size—usually near-CD quality (93 Kbps) or CD quality (128 Kbps) is selected to have good audio quality at a reasonable file size.

**FIGURE 6-18**

**Transferring songs from a CD to a PC's hard drive**

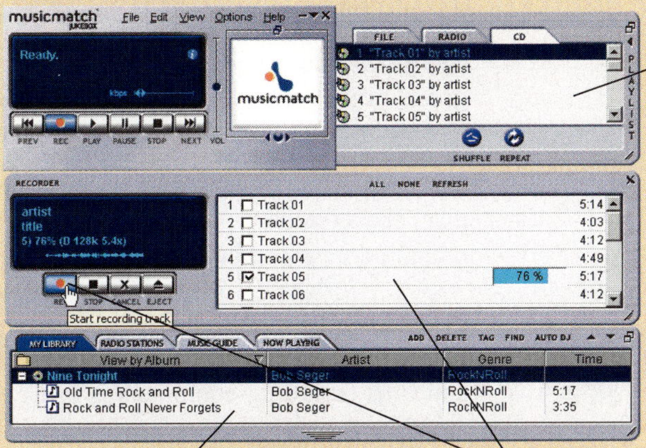

1. The CD to be used is inserted into the PC's CD drive and the appropriate software is opened.

2. The recorder controls are used to select the songs to be saved to the hard drive. Settings, such as where on the hard drive the files will be stored and the compression ratio to be used, are typically set up on an Options or Settings menu.

3. Once the songs have been ripped and decoded, they usually appear in some kind of playlist or music library accessible from within the software program being used. Then they can be played from the PC, transferred to an MP3 player, or burned onto a CD.

**FIGURE 6-19**

**Burning a custom music CD**

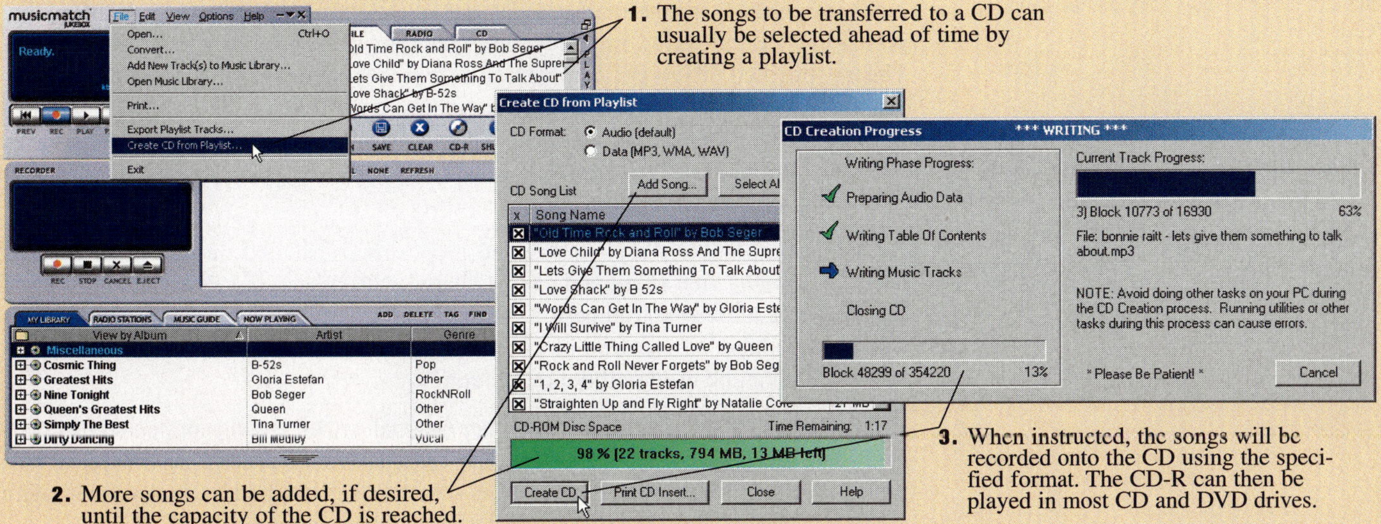

1. The songs to be transferred to a CD can usually be selected ahead of time by creating a playlist.

2. More songs can be added, if desired, until the capacity of the CD is reached.

3. When instructed, the songs will be recorded onto the CD using the specified format. The CD-R can then be played in most CD and DVD drives.

# SUMMARY

**CHAPTER OBJECTIVE 1**

Understand the concept of intellectual property rights and how they can be protected legally.

## What Are Intellectual Property Rights?

**Intellectual property rights** specify how *intellectual property*, such as original music compositions, drawings, essays, software programs, symbols, and designs, may be lawfully used. **Copyrights** protect the creator of original artistic or literary works and are automatically granted once the work exists in a physical medium. The copyright can be registered for further protection should infringement occur. The copyright symbol © can be used to remind others that content is copyrighted; **digital watermarks** can be incorporated into digital content so that the copyright information can be viewed, even if the work is altered. One timely debate over copyright infringement involves **peer-to-peer (P2P) file sharing**, where files are transferred directly from one user's PC to another's via the Internet.

**Trademarks** are words, phrases, symbols, or designs that identify an organization's goods or services and can be either claimed ™ or registered ®. In addition to logos and identifying text, domain names can be also protected by trademark law.

**Patents** grant an exclusive right to an invention for 20 years. In addition to products, processes and procedures may be patented as well, such as specific Internet or e-commerce procedures.

**CHAPTER OBJECTIVE 2**

Explain what ethics are and how they relate to computer use.

## What Are Ethics?

**Ethics** refers to standards of moral conduct. Today one of the most important ethical concerns regarding computers is using someone else's property in an improper way. Another is being dishonest with others when it works to one's advantage. *Personal ethics* guide one's personal life; **business ethics** provide the standards of conduct guiding business decisions, and **computer ethics** provide the standards of conduct in respect to computers and computer use. Computer ethics has taken on more significance in recent years because the abundance of computers in the home, in the workplace, and at school provides many more opportunities for unethical behavior than in the past.

**CHAPTER OBJECTIVE 3**

List several types of copyrighted materials and describe how they can be used ethically.

## Ethical Issues

Businesses and individuals should use caution when copying, sharing, or in any way using copyrighted materials, to ensure that they are used in an ethical and legal manner. A software program's **software license** specifies the conditions for use. Many software products on the market today are in the form of **commercial software**, which can be purchased in stores and, sometimes, downloaded from the Internet. Unless specified otherwise, commercial software is intended for use on a single PC. *Site licenses* and *network licenses* are sometimes available for schools and businesses that need to use a program on multiple computers. A commercial program might be available in a *demo* or *trial version*, which allows the consumer to try the program before buying it.

**Shareware** programs are copyrighted programs distributed on the honor system. They are usually free to try and can be shared with others, but should be paid for if used past the allowable trial period. **Freeware** programs are copyrighted programs that are available to use free of charge. **Public-domain software** is not copyrighted and can be used without restriction.

Literary material, such as books and other original works, are also protected by copyright law. Presenting someone else's work as your own is referred to as **plagiarism** and is illegal and unethical. Plagiarism is sometimes performed by students, although it can be detected and usually has grave academic consequences.

Music and movies also qualify for copyright protection and have been a main source of legal and ethical copyright debates due to individuals sharing songs and movies via the Internet. New **copy-protection** schemes have been proposed to try to prevent this.

Students and employees should refer to their organization's **code of conduct**, if one exists, when determining the specific ethical and allowable activities regarding the organization's resources, such as computers, copy machines, and telephones. Some organizations and industries publish **codes of ethics** listing overall standards of conduct, such as honesty, fairness, confidentiality, and more.

**CHAPTER OBJECTIVE 4**

State several ethical issues related to the use of school or business resources and information.

Businesses need to determine how they will use employee and customer information based on both legal and ethical guidelines. Because computers make it easier to plagiarize and cheat on assignments and exams, students need to make an ethical decision regarding their behavior. Some job applicants choose to supply erroneous or misleading information on their applications or resumes in hopes of gaining an advantage. This action is unethical and can result in job termination at many organizations if the applicant is found out.

A **computer hoax** is an inaccurate statement or story spread through the use of computers, often by e-mail. It is a good idea to check questionable information as a possible computer hoax before passing the information on to others. **Digital manipulation** is the use of computers to modify something in digital form, usually text or a photograph. While digitally altering photographs sometimes has a positive and an ethically acceptable use—such as aging photos of missing children—the use of digital manipulation on photographs published in newspapers and magazines is more controversial and is viewed as highly unethical by many.

**CHAPTER OBJECTIVE 5**

Explain what computer hoaxes and digital manipulation are and how they relate to computer ethics.

Ethics are highly intertwined with determining business practices and making business decisions. Decisions such as which financial information to publicize, which products or services to provide, which safeguards (if any) to take with products or services that are illegal for minors or objectionable to some individuals, and whether or not to promote potential **vaporware** products all require ethical consideration. Because ethics are fundamentally based on values, different types of businesses may have different ethics, and ethics and moral standards may vary from country to country, and from culture to culture. In addition to legal considerations, businesses with global connections should consider the prevailing ethical standards of all countries involved when making business decisions.

**CHAPTER OBJECTIVE 6**

Identify several ethical issues surrounding business practices and decisions.

## Privacy Legislation

The laws protecting intellectual property are fairly old, but have been periodically updated to reflect digital content and the Internet. For example, the *Digital Millennium Copyright Act* makes it illegal to circumvent anti-piracy measures built into commercial software, and also outlaws the manufacturing or sale of devices used to copy software illegally.

**CHAPTER OBJECTIVE 7**

Discuss the current status of legislation related to intellectual property rights and ethics.

Because moral and ethical standards are more difficult to agree on, ethical legislation is slower in coming. One attempt to protect children from access to inappropriate Internet content—the *Communications Decency Act*—was overturned by the U.S. Supreme Court. The *Corporate Responsibility Act* was implemented in 2002 in reaction to the numerous corporate scandals that took place in that year.

# BALANCING ACT

## GOVERNMENT PROTECTION VS. GOVERNMENT CENSORSHIP

There has always been a delicate balance between what is viewed as government protection and what is viewed as government censorship. *Censorship*, typically defined as restricting access to materials deemed objectionable or offensive, is performed at some level by every government. Even though the United States was founded on the concept of freedom and free speech, some government censorship exists and most of us would agree that it is necessary at a basic level. For example, public schools are not permitted to teach a particular religious viewpoint and network television must edit out certain levels of foul language and nudity in movies before they can be aired. Where the idea of censorship gets more tricky and controversial is when it is used to block access to materials or information that will offend or are inappropriate for some, but not all, citizens.

Among the most notable examples in recent years are the attempts by some groups and the government to limit access to online pornography and other Internet content that most people agree are not appropriate for children. As mentioned in the chapter, the Communications Decency Act passed in 1996 was overturned by the Supreme Court the following year. A more recent example is the Child Internet Protection Act (CIPA) that went into effect in 2001 and required public libraries and schools to use filtering software to block Internet access to certain materials in order to receive public funds. Though intended to protect children, it was fought strenuously by free speech advocacy groups and some library associations and was ruled unconstitutional by a federal court in 2002.

### YOUR TURN

Give some thought to the balance between government protection and government censorship with respect to the Internet, and then answer the following questions.

1. Do you think the courts were correct in overturning the Communications Decency and Child Internet Protection Acts? Why or why not?
2. One objection to mandatory library filtering by free speech advocates is the premise that filtering software is not perfect and its use may block access to valuable educational material. Another is that filtering would increase the digital divide because affluent individuals with home computers would have access to Internet content that poor citizens (who more often would need to use their library's free public Internet access) would not be able to access. Do you think these arguments are valid? Why or why not?
3. Is there any Internet content that you believe the government has the right or obligation to censor? If so, what? Do you believe the government should block access to this content originating from just U.S. computers or from computers located in any country?
4. Even if Internet filtering at schools isn't required, should individual schools have the right to block access to Web content they view as inappropriate for students using school PCs? Or do students have the right to use those computers to access any content they desire, on the basis that their fees, tuition, or parents' taxes paid for that access? What about the rights of other students who do not want to see content that they find offensive displayed on computer screens as they pass by computers that other students are using? Should the ability to filter be different for public schools versus private schools? Why or why not?

## KEY TERMS

**Instructions:** Match each key term on the left with the definition on the right that best describes it.

**a.** **business ethics**

**b.** **code of conduct**

**c.** **code of ethics**

**d.** **commercial software**

**e.** **computer ethics**

**f.** **computer hoax**

**g.** **copy protection**

**h.** **copyright**

**i.** **digital manipulation**

**j.** **digital watermark**

**k.** **ethics**

**l.** **freeware**

**m.** **intellectual property rights**

**n.** **patent**

**o.** **peer-to-peer (P2P) file sharing**

**p.** **plagiarism**

**q.** **public-domain software**

**r.** **shareware**

**s.** **trademark**

**t.** **vaporware**

**1.** ______ A method that prevents a disc from being copied or played in an unauthorized device.

**2.** ______ A policy, often for a school or business, that specifies allowable use of resources such as computers and other equipment.

**3.** ______ A policy, often for an organization or industry, that specifies overall moral guidelines adopted by that organization or industry.

**4.** ______ A form of protection that can be granted by the government for an invention; gives exclusive rights of an invention to its inventor for 20 years.

**5.** ______ A subtle alteration of digital content that isn't noticeable under normal use, but that identifies the copyright holder.

**6.** ______ A word, phrase, symbol, or design that identifies a good or service; can be either claimed or registered.

**7.** ______ An inaccurate statement or story spread through the use of computers.

**8.** ______ Copyrighted software that is developed, usually by a commercial company, for sale to others.

**9.** ______ Copyrighted software that is distributed on the honor system; should be either paid for or uninstalled after a trial period.

**10.** ______ Copyrighted software that may be ethically used free of charge forever.

**11.** ______ Overall standards of moral conduct.

**12.** ______ Presenting someone else's work as your own.

**13.** ______ Sharing files directly from one user to another over a network.

**14.** ______ Software or hardware products that are announced or advertised, but that are not yet available.

**15.** ______ Software that is not copyrighted and may be used without restriction.

**16.** ______ Standards of moral conduct in regards to computer use.

**17.** ______ Standards of moral conduct that guide a business' policies, decisions, and actions.

**18.** ______ The alteration of digital content, usually text or photographs.

**19.** ______ The legal right to sell, publish, or distribute an original artistic or literary work; is held by the creator of a work as soon as it exists in physical form.

**20.** ______ The rights to which creators of original creative works (artistic or literary works, inventions, corporate logos, etc.) are entitled.

# ✓ SELF-QUIZ

Answers for the self-quiz appear at the end of the book.

## True/False

**Instructions:** Circle **T** if the statement is true or **F** if the statement is false.

**T F 1.** All unethical acts are illegal.

**T F 2.** As long as a business purchases one legal copy of a software program, it can install it on as many computers as desired without fear of retribution.

**T F 3.** Copying a song from a CD you own to your computer to create a custom music CD for personal use is an example of fair use.

**T F 4.** Resume padding or lying on a job application would rarely result in termination if it was discovered.

**T F 5.** Changing the background behind a television newscaster to make it appear that he or she is reporting on location instead of from inside the television studio would be viewed by most people as an unethical use of digital manipulation.

## Completion

**Instructions:** Supply the missing words to complete the following statements.

**6.** A software program would be protected by ______________ law, while a corporate logo would be protected by ______________ law.

**7.** The symbol ® is used to indicate that the text or logo immediately preceding the symbol is a(n) ______________.

**8.** An individual's ______________ can vary from another's depending on his or her values, culture, etc.

**9.** To avoid having to purchase individual copies of a software program for each computer in the company, some commercial programs have ______________ or ______________ licenses available.

**10.** If you want to continue to use a(n) ______________ program after trying it out, you are ethically obligated to send in the requested payment to the creator of the program.

**11.** Turning in a copy of a poem you found on a Web site as an original composition for a poetry class assignment is an example of ______________.

**12.** Computer ______________, such as warnings about a nonexistent virus, are frequently spread via e-mail.

**13.** Digital ______________ of published photos, such as the darkening of O.J. Simpson's photograph in the 1994 *TIME* magazine cover, is viewed as unethical by many, including photojournalist organizations.

**14.** A microprocessor manufacturer that announces a new CPU that is supposedly faster than any other CPU on the market, but only releases 25 chips to be placed in PCs tested and reviewed by computer magazines, could be accused of releasing ______________.

**15.** The overturning of the ______________ Act, which made it illegal to distribute patently indecent or offensive material online, by the U.S. Supreme Court was considered to be a landmark decision for free speech advocates.

# PROJECTS

## 1. Digitally Locked Music

**YOUR OPINION**

The chapter Closer Look box discusses copy-protection schemes both used and proposed by the entertainment industry. Some types of protection—such as those that make any copies made from a copy-protected disc record in poor quality—are more straightforward piracy-prevention schemes than others—such as discs that can't be played in a computer's CD drive.

For this project, consider the issue of mandatory hardware-based copy protection and write a short essay expressing your opinion about this issue. Do you think that the high level of piracy today justifies forcing hardware manufacturers to alter their products' functionality? Which is ultimately more important: the copyright holder's right to protection or a manufacturer's freedom to offer the products of their choosing? If it becomes impossible to play purchased music CDs in a computer CD or DVD drive, or to copy songs from a purchased CD to an MP3 player, do you think a consumer's fair use rights will have been violated? Or, as some in the entertainment industry state, do you believe that this type of use exists at the moment because of technology, but is not a perpetual right? Can you think of any possible solutions that prevent piracy, don't impose additional restrictions on hardware manufacturers, and allow consumers fair use of end products? Submit your opinion on this issue, and any possible solutions you came up with, to your instructor in the form of a short paper, not more than two pages in length.

## 2. Internet Radio

**INDEPENDENT RESEARCH**

Internet radio—featuring songs broadcast over the Web—has been quickly gaining popularity in recent months. It is estimated that there are approximately 25 million listeners to the 10,000 or so different online stations. The Digital Millennium Copyright Act, however, included a clause granting record companies and artists the right to be paid an additional royalty whenever their recordings are played over the Internet. This fee is expected to drive many independent Internet radio sites out of business, such as the popular SomaFM.com station, which shut down in June 2002 to avoid paying approximately $15,000 per month in royalties (the site was supported by listener donations, which brought in approximately $3,000 per month revenue).

For this project, research the Internet radio royalty issue. The last proposed royalty rate at the time of this writing was 7/100ths of one cent per song per listener, but the issue had not been resolved. How does that royalty rate compare to traditional broadcast radio royalties? (You may need to call a local radio station to find this out.) Find several articles that discuss the Internet radio royalty issue in relation to the DMCA and determine the current status. Has any legislation regarding this issue made it into law? A back payment for royalties accrued since 1998 was scheduled to be paid by all Internet radio stations in late 2002. Was that payment enforced, delayed, or cancelled? What are the current (if any) royalty fees required for Internet radio stations? Has a fair settlement been reached? Have any of the Internet radio stations that went off the air due to these fees come back online? Summarize your findings in a two- to three-page paper.

## 3. Digitally Altered Photos

**HANDS-ON**

As mentioned in the chapter, computers make manipulation of images much easier than in the past. Artistic examples include recent photographs of New York that include some hint of the World Trade Center Towers added to them; beneficial uses include aging the photo of a runaway or kidnap victim for easier identification. Less noble examples include putting a celebrity's head on another person's nude body and altering prisoner photographs before posting them on a pen pal site so the convicts don't look like they are in prison.

For this project, look through magazines, newspapers, Web sites, or other media to locate two examples of digitally altered photographs. You may need to compare two photographs of the same person or location to notice subtle alterations, such as changing an individual's eye color, removing wrinkles, or erasing an offending tree or building from a photograph. You may also wish to visit Web sites that feature current examples of digital manipulation—use a search site to find them. Make a photocopy of each of your selected examples and indicate on each copy what manipulation you believe was performed. For each example, decide if you think the manipulation is ethical or unethical and why you think it was done. Was the photograph altered to mislead the public? For artistic purposes? To make a statement? To entertain us? Prepare a short summary of your findings to turn in to your instructor, along with your two photocopies containing your notations.

**4. Copyright Registration**

Think of a paper or poem that you have written, a photograph you have taken, a song or play you have written, or another original creation to which you believe you are entitled to copyright protection. As you know from reading the chapter, copyright protection begins as soon as the creation exists on some type of physical medium, but assume that you would like officially to register a copyright for your creation.

For this project, research how you would obtain a copyright for your chosen creation. Visit the U.S. Copyright Office Web site (search for it using your favorite search site) and determine the necessary procedure for registration, such as what paperwork you would need to submit and the necessary fee to secure your copyright. Use the information located on the site to make sure your creation is entitled to copyright protection, and then find the appropriate online registration form (if one is available online). If possible, open and print just one page of the form (you will likely need to have the Adobe Acrobat Reader plug-in installed in your browser to see the form). From the site, also determine what notice you will receive once your copyright claim has been recorded, and how long it will take to receive it. Prepare a short summary of your findings to turn into your instructor, stapled to the single page of the appropriate application if you were able to print it.

## GROUP PRESENTATION

**5. Consumer Hacks**

According to several published reports, Sony (the maker of the Aibo programmable dog) recently sent a cease-and-desist letter to the owner of a Web site that posted techniques that could be used to alter the software that controls Aibo's actions or personality. According to the complaint, the Web site violated the Digital Millennium Copyright Act, which prohibits breaking technological controls placed on any copyrighted work. The owner of the Web site acknowledged that he broke Sony's encryption to create his software, but states that users of his programs don't have to break it. Other consumer hacks include sites that instruct visitors how to alter their Internet appliances and game consoles to add additional capabilities.

For this project, form a group to research and discuss the provisions of the DMCA that prohibit circumventing copy protection schemes and how these provisions relate to consumer product use. Locate the text of the part of the act that mentions this restriction. Also find at least two articles (online or offline) that discuss how the act applies to circumventing copy protection schemes by individuals. Does your group feel that the restrictions in the act apply to all of the examples listed above? Why or why not? Does your research indicate that the law applies to those individuals who break through a copy protection scheme for their own use, or only to those individuals who share the circumvention process with others? What about those individuals who try to break a copyright or security technology just to prove it can be done? Should they be prosecuted, sued, or congratulated for uncovering a weakness in the existing technology?

Share your findings with the class in the form of a short presentation. The presentation should not exceed 10 minutes and should make use of one or more presentation aids such as the chalkboard, handouts, overhead transparencies, or a computer-based slide presentation (your instructor may provide additional requirements). Your group may also be asked to submit a summary of the presentation to your instructor.

**6. Online Term Papers**

There are Web sites from which term papers on a variety of subjects can be purchased and downloaded. Although many of these sites state that they provide the papers for research purposes only and do not support plagiarism, it is not surprising that some dishonest students turn in purchased term papers as their own work for assignments.

For this project, form a group to discuss the availability and ethical use of online term papers. Has anyone in the group ever visited one of these sites? If so, what services were offered through the site? Was it clear to the student that there was a way of utilizing the site's services without encountering plagiarism problems? Do the members of your group believe it is ethical to use online term papers for research? Are there any valuable (and legal) reasons for using these sites? If a term paper is purchased, instead of just downloading the information without permission from a Web site, does turning it in as an original term paper still constitute plagiarism? Why or why not? What responsibility, if any, does your group feel the Web site has if its papers are used in an illegal or unethical manner? By referring to your course syllabus, student handbook, or talking with your dean of students, determine what penalties are possible at your school if a student submits a plagiarized term paper. Share your findings with the class in the form of a short presentation. The presentation should not exceed 10 minutes and should make use of one or more presentation aids such as the chalkboard, handouts, overhead transparencies, or a computer-based slide presentation (your instructor may provide additional requirements). Your group may also be asked to submit a summary of the presentation to your instructor.

**7. DirecTV Pirates**

**VIDEO VIEWPOINT**

Stealing satellite TV service is becoming more common as hackers figure out ways of providing consumers with the means to steal the service. For example, with DirecTV, access cards are used to tell the system which programs each user is entitled to see. As discussed in the accompanying video, altered cards, which are widely available on the Internet and through newspaper ads, can be used to obtain free service.

After watching the video, think about the impact of the unauthorized use of services, such as satellite TV. The U.S. Justice Department is actively pursuing distributors of these altered cards, but not individual buyers at the moment. Periodically DirecTV sends out a signal that identifies altered access cards and destroys them. Is this procedure sufficient or should the users of altered cards be prosecuted? In Canada, DirecTV doesn't have a license to broadcast its signals. For those Canadians who live in an area where the U.S. signal spills over the border, the only way they can get DirecTV is to steal it, although it isn't illegal, according to the video. Is there an ethical difference between Canadians and U.S. citizens buying these altered cards? DirecTV estimates that their annual loss due to unauthorized use of service is in the millions of dollars, but they are not the only ones affected. What about the movie industry, advertising industry, sports teams, and others who profit from DirecTV subscribers? Are illegal users stealing from these individuals as well? What are the long-range implications if the use of altered cards continues to grow?

**ONLINE VIDEO**

To view the DirecTV Pirates video clip, go to www.course.com/morley2003/ch6

**Express your viewpoint:** What impact does stealing services, such as satellite TV, have on our society and it is ever ethical to do so?

Use the video clip and the questions previously asked as the foundation for your response. Your instructor will direct you to be prepared to discuss your position (either in class, via an online class discussion group, or in a class chat room), or to write a short paper stating and supporting your viewpoint on the issue. You may also be asked to do research and provide resources to support your point of view on this issue.

# HEALTH, ACCESS, AND THE ENVIRONMENT

## OUTLINE



## OBJECTIVES

**After completing this chapter, you will be able to:**

- Understand the concerns and potential risks regarding physical health and computer use.
- Describe some possible emotional health risks surrounding the use of computers.
- Explain what is meant by the "digital divide."
- Discuss the impact factors such as income, race, education, and physical disabilities may have on computer access and use.
- List some types of assistive hardware that can be used by individuals with physical disabilities.
- Suggest some ways computer users can practice "green computing" and properly dispose of obsolete computer equipment.

# CHAPTER 7

## OVERVIEW

Like any fast-paced revolution, the computer revolution has impacted our society in more ways than could have been imagined when it first began. Although computers now help many workers do their jobs more effectively and efficiently, when computers were first introduced in the workplace they cost some employees their jobs and required other employees to learn new skills. Even now, the increasing number of jobs that utilize a computer and the rapid pace at which technology is continuing to improve means that some positions may become eliminated as technology makes those jobs obsolete and many people need to learn new computer-oriented skills and techniques periodically to remain up-to-date. Another unexpected result of our increased computer use is the large impact it has had on the personal health of some users and on the environment. And, although computer use is becoming almost mandatory in our society, many believe that access to computers is not equally available to all individuals.

This chapter begins with a look at health-oriented concerns, including the impact computers may have on a user's physical and emotional health, as well as strategies individuals can use to lessen those risks. Next comes the issue of equal access. The digital divide is defined and discussed, along with how other factors—such as gender, age, and physical disabilities—may affect computer access and use. The chapter closes with a look at the potential impact of computers on our environment.

## STAYING HEALTHY AT HOME AND ON THE JOB

Computers, it has been said, pose a threat to a user's physical and mental well-being. *Repetitive stress injuries* and other injuries related to the workplace environment are estimated to account for one-third of all serious workplace injuries and cost employees, employers, and insurance companies approximately $50 billion each year. *Stress, burnout, Internet addiction*, and other emotional health problems are more difficult to quantify, although many experts believe computer-related emotional health problems are on the rise. Researchers are continuing to investigate the physical and emotional risks of computer use and develop strategies for minimizing those risks; in the meantime, all computer users should be aware of the major concerns raised about the possible effects of computers on their health and what they can do today to stay healthy while using a computer at home and on the job.

### Physical Health

**ONLINE RESOURCES**

For links to information about computer use injuries and how they can be prevented, go to www.course.com/morley2003/ch7

There are several factors to look at when considering how computer use may impact physical health. The workplace environment as a whole is one factor. Another is the design of the actual workspace—such as the desk, chair, and lighting—being used. Special computer hardware and office equipment can be used to prevent or ease the discomfort of physical injuries due to computer use. A proper work environment is important for anyone who works on a computer, including employees using a computer on the job, individuals using a PC at home, and children doing computer activities at home or at school.

Common physical conditions caused by computer use include eyestrain, blurred vision, fatigue, headaches, and backaches. A condition known as **carpal tunnel syndrome (CTS)**—a painful and crippling condition affecting the hands and wrists—has been traced to the repetitive finger movements made when using a keyboard, although it can be caused by non-computer-related activities as well. CTS is an example of a **repetitive stress injury (RSI)**, in which hand, wrist, shoulder, or neck pain can result from performing the same physical movements over and over again. Extensive mouse use has also been associated with disorders of the hand, wrist, forearm, and shoulder. Another physical condition stemming from the use of computers is **computer vision syndrome (CVS)**—a collection of eye and vision problems associated with computer use. According to experts, CVS affects about three-quarters of all computer users to some extent, and the most common symptoms are eyestrain or eye fatigue, dry eyes, burning eyes, light sensitivity, blurred vision, headaches, and pain in the shoulders, neck or back.

Many physical problems resulting from computer use can be prevented by using a proper work environment and good habits—a concept known as *ergonomics.*

#### What Is Ergonomics?

**Ergonomics** is the science of fitting a work environment to the people who work there. It typically focuses on making products and workspaces more comfortable and safe to use. With respect to computer use, it involves designing a safe and effective workspace, which includes properly adjusting furniture and hardware and using ergonomic hardware when needed. Due to increased computer use at home and in schools, the concept of ergonomics applies to those computing environments as well. But there is more to ergonomics than just hardware and other physical equipment—good user habits and procedures are important, too.

#### Workspace Design

The design of a safe and effective computer workspace—whether it is located at work, home, or school—includes the placement and adjustment of all the furniture and equipment involved, such as the user's desk, chair, keyboard, and monitor. Workspace lighting or glare from the sun also needs to be taken into consideration. Proper workspace design can result in fewer injuries, headaches, and general aches and pains for computer users. Businesses can reap economic benefits from proper workspace design, such as less employee absence, higher productivity, and lower insurance costs. For example, when one government department in New Jersey installed new ergonomically correct workstations in their new offices, computer-related health complaints fell by 40% and doctor visits dropped by 25% in less than one year.

Proper placement and adjustment of furniture is a good place to start when evaluating a workspace from an ergonomic perspective. The desk should be placed where the sun and other sources of light can't shine directly onto the screen or into the user's eyes. The monitor should be placed at an appropriate height (where the top of the screen is no higher than the user's eyes once the user's chair is adjusted) with the monitor directly in front of the user, and the desk chair should be adjusted so that the keyboard is either at, or slightly below, the height that results in the user's forearms being horizontal to the floor. A footrest should be used, if needed, to keep the user's feet flat on the floor once the chair height has been set. The monitor settings should be adjusted to make the screen brightness match the brightness of the room and to have a high amount of contrast, and the screen should be periodically wiped clean of dust. Proper posture can also reduce many types of discomfort. Some guidelines for designing an ergonomic workspace are shown in Figure 7-1.

**ONLINE TUTORIAL**

For an online look at creating an ergonomic computer workspace, go to www.course.com/morley2003/ch7

**FIGURE 7-1**

**Guidelines for designing an ergonomic workspace**

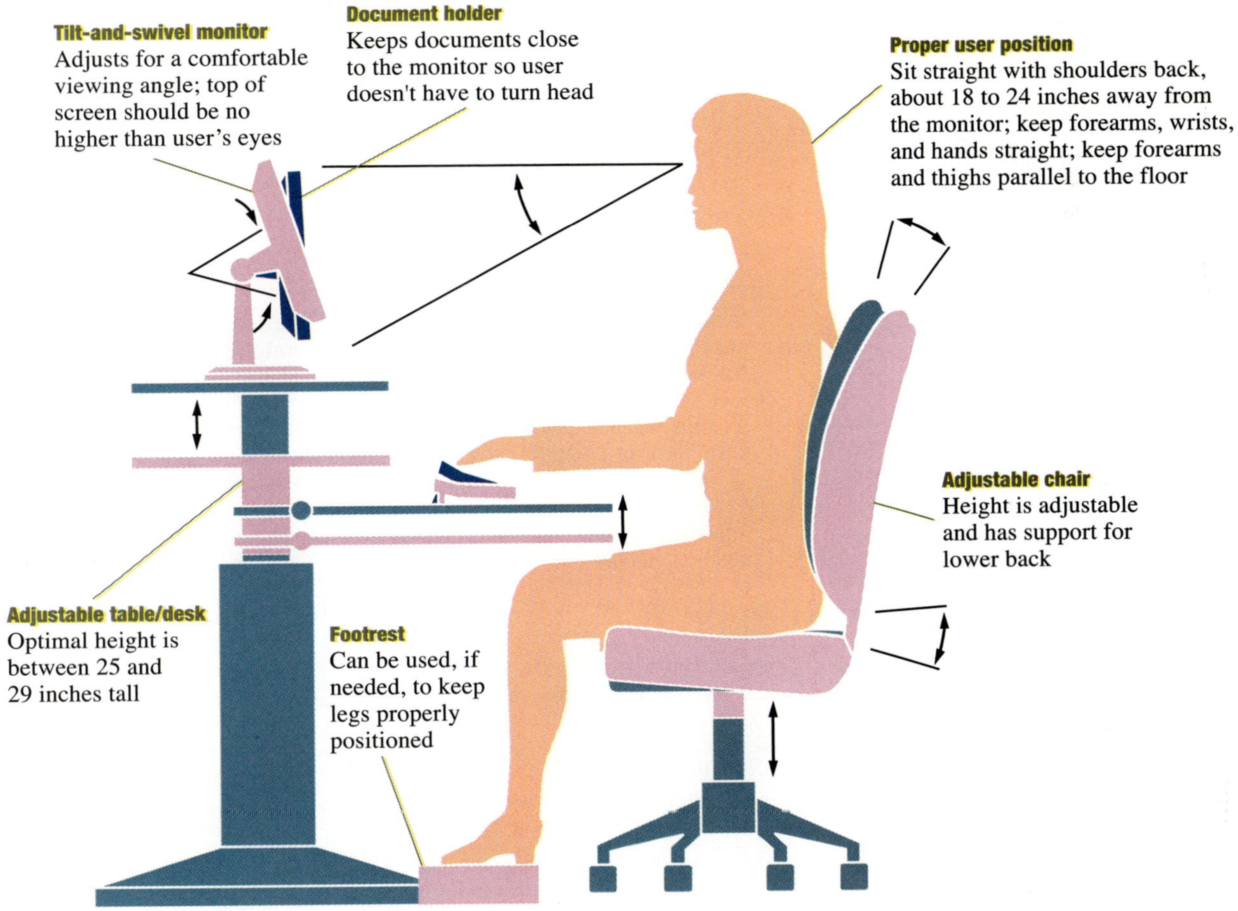

When designing or evaluating a computer workspace, the type of computer work to be performed should be considered. For example, people who refer to written documents while working on their PCs should use a *document holder* to keep their documents close to the monitor. Placing the document holder close to the monitor helps users avoid the repetitive motion of turning their heads to look between the document and the monitor—an action that can create or aggravate neck problems. These users should also place the keyboard directly in front of them for easy access. On the other hand, if Web surfing or other computer activities requiring a great deal of mouse work (such as computer-aided design or graphics design) will be performed, placement of the mouse for comfortable access should be given high priority.

Workspace design typically concentrates on fixed workspace setups with a desktop PC. However, notebook users and users of other types of portable PCs should also try to create an environment that allows them to work as safely and comfortably as possible. This is more difficult than in a fixed workspace because the current design of most portable devices doesn't meet basic ergonomic standards—such as having keyboards and monitors that can be positioned and adjusted separately to fit the user's needs—although some more ergonomically correct portable PCs are beginning to come on the market, such as notebook PCs that have a detachable screen. To overcome the current limitations, some notebook PC users choose to use a **docking station**, if there is a location—such as at home or in the office—where their notebook PC will be used on a regular basis. A docking station (shown in Figure 7-2) is a connector between a portable PC and conventional desktop PC hardware, such as a keyboard, mouse, monitor, and printer. The hardware is always connected to the docking station, although it can only be used when a PC is connected to the docking station. Once a PC is plugged into the docking station, the devices attached to the docking station can be used as input and output devices for the portable PC. Some additional ergonomic tips for notebook users are listed in Figure 7-2.

**FIGURE 7-2**

**Ergonomic tips for notebook PC users**

**Docking station**

Used to create an easy connection between a notebook PC and many standard pieces of hardware, such as a keyboard, mouse, monitor, and printer.

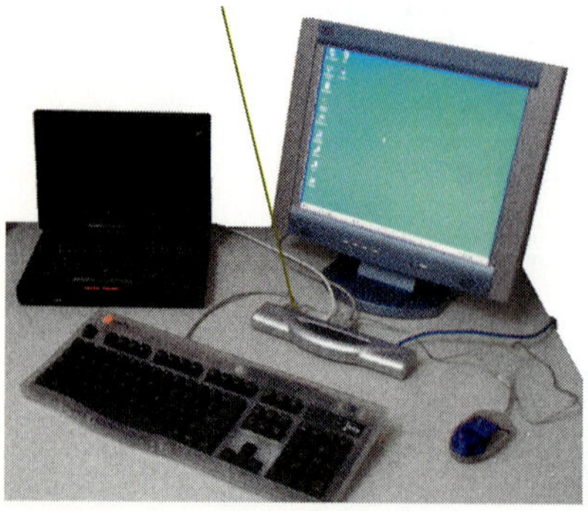

**Tips by Type of Notebook User**

| Occasional users (who use a notebook PC while on location, traveling, etc.) | Full-time users (who use a notebook PC full-time instead of desktop PC) |
|---|---|
| Sit with notebook in your lap and position it for comfortable wrist posture. | Use a separate keyboard and mouse, either attached directly to the PC or to a docking station. |
| Adjust the screen to a comfortable position, so you can see the screen as straight on as possible. | Place notebook on a desk or table; either elevate the notebook so the screen is the proper height or use a docking station to utilize a stand-alone monitor instead of the notebook's built-in monitor. |
| When purchasing a notebook, pay close attention to the total weight of the system (PC, batteries, power supply, additional drives, etc.) to avoid neck and shoulder injuries when carrying the notebook from one location to another. | When purchasing a notebook, pay close attention to the size and clarity of the monitor, unless you will be using a docking station with a separate stand-alone monitor attached. |

## Ergonomic Hardware

To avoid physical problems due to extensive PC use, or to help alleviate discomfort of an already existing condition, a variety of **ergonomic devices** are available (see Figure 7-3).

**FIGURE 7-3**

Examples of ergonomic devices

^ Ergonomic keyboard

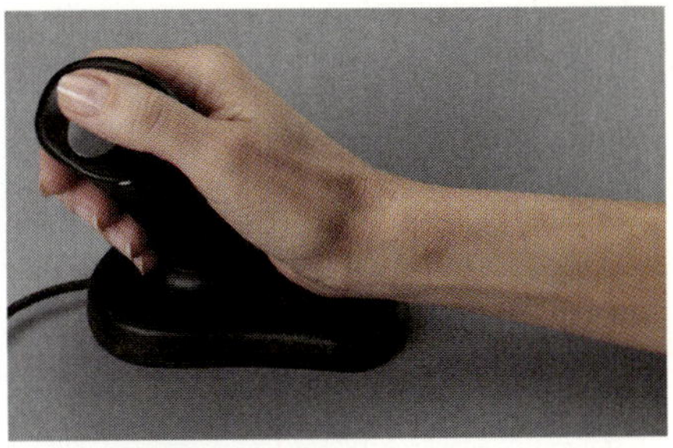

^ Ergonomic mouse

^ Keyboard drawer

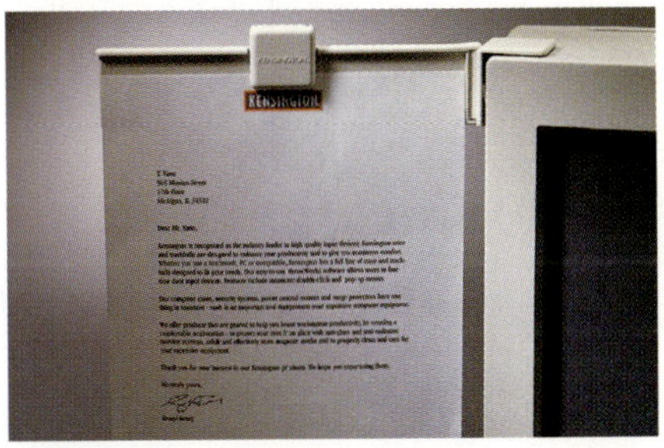

^ Document holder

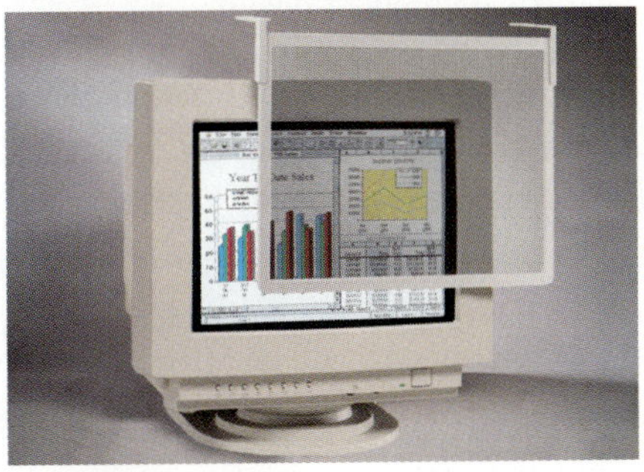

^ Antiglare screen

^ Wrist rest

- **Ergonomic keyboards** are designed in a shape and arrangement to lessen the strain on the hands and wrists. To fit a child's hand size better, a child's keyboard—which is smaller than a regular keyboard—can be used in homes, schools, and other locations where children may use a computer frequently.
- **Ergonomic mice** typically look more like joysticks than mice and are designed for more comfortable use by extensive mouse users. Just like keyboards, child-sized mice are also available. Some users find other types of pointing devices (such as a trackball) more comfortable than a mouse for extensive use.
- **Keyboard drawers** lower the keyboard, enabling the user to more easily keep his or her forearms parallel to the floor.
- **Document holders**—sometimes called *copy holders*—can be used to keep documents close to the monitor, enabling the user to see both the document and the monitor without turning his or her head. Document holders are available for both desktop and portable PCs.
- **Antiglare screens** or *shields* that fit over the monitor screen can be used to lessen glare and resulting eyestrain. Some manufacturers claim antiglare screens reduce the amount of radiation emitted from a monitor, although many experts believe that today's monitors—particularly those that adhere to the *MPR II* standards of acceptable levels of radiation—are not a significant health hazard.
- **Wrist rests** designed to be placed next to the mouse or keyboard can be used to help keep wrists straight while those devices are being used, as well as to support and minimize the pressure points on the wrists and forearms when resting.

### Good User Habits and Precautions

In addition to utilizing an ergonomic workspace, there are a number of preventive measures computer users can adhere to. Finger and wrist exercises and frequent breaks in typing are good precautions for helping to prevent repetitive hand and finger injuries. Using good posture and periodically taking a break to relax or stretch the body can help reduce or prevent back and neck strain. For locations where some glare from a nearby window is unavoidable at certain times of the day, closing the curtains or blinds can help to avoid eyestrain. Eyeglass wearers should discuss any eye fatigue or blurriness during computer use with their optometrist—sometimes a different eyeglass prescription or special *computer glasses* can be used to reduce eyestrain while working on a PC.

A number of studies point to a break in activity as one of the most effective precautions for many computer ailments. Consequently, taking short breaks from computer use at regular intervals, such as alternating between computer work, telephone work, and paperwork every 15 minutes or so, is a good idea—both on the job and at home. Some additional common sense precautions are listed in Figure 7-4.

**FIGURE 7-4**

**Preventative measures users can take while working on a PC**

| Condition | Prevention |
|---|---|
| Wrist/arm soreness and injury | Use a light touch on the keyboard<br>Rest and gently stretch your fingers and arms every 15 minutes or so<br>Keep your wrists and arms relaxed and parallel to the floor when using the keyboard |
| Eyestrain | Cover windows or adjust lighting to eliminate glare<br>Concentrate on blinking your eyes more often<br>Rest your eyes every 15 minutes or so by focusing on an object in the distance (at least 20 feet away) for one minute and then closing your eyes for an additional minute<br>Make sure your monitor's brightness and contrast settings are at an appropriate level<br>Use a larger text size or overall lower screen resolution, if needed (if the text is large enough, you should be able to read what is displayed on your monitor from three times the distance that you normally sit) |
| Sore or stiff neck | Use good posture<br>Locate the monitor and any documents you need to refer to while using your PC directly in front of you<br>Adjust your monitor to a comfortable viewing angle with the top of the screen no higher than your eyes |
| Backache; general fatigue | Use good posture<br>Adjust your chair properly to support your lower back<br>Use a footrest, if needed, to keep your feet flat on the floor<br>Walk around or stretch briefly at least once every hour<br>Alternate between activities frequently |

## Emotional Health

The extensive use of computers and related technology in the home and office in recent years has raised new concerns about emotional health. Factors such as financial worries, feelings of being overworked, being unable to relax, and information overload often produce emotional *stress.* For many individuals, computer use or computer-related events are the cause of, or at least partially contribute to, the stress that they experience. Another emotional health concern related to computer use is *computer* or *Internet addiction.*

### Stress of Ever-Changing Technology

When computers were first introduced into the workplace, workers who found that their jobs required computer use needed to learn the appropriate skills. Airline agents, for example, had to learn to use computer databases. Secretaries and other office employees needed to learn word processing and other office-related software. Today, many people entering the workforce are aware of the computer skills they will need to perform their chosen professions. However, as computers become continually more integrated into our society, jobs that didn't require the use of a computer in the recent past may very well require it today (see Figure 7-5). At the rapid pace that technology keeps changing, many workers must regularly learn new skills to keep up-to-date; for example, to switch to and become accustomed to using a newer version of software or to learn how to use a new piece of hardware. Although some find this exciting, the on-going battle to stay current with changing technology creates stress for many individuals.

Another related problem is the tenuous nature of many technology- and Internet-related companies at the present time. As discussed in the Closer Look box, layoffs and losses due to the recent failure of many companies in the technology sector are an added stress for the people—such as workers, management, and investors—who are emotionally or financially invested in the failing organizations.

**FIGURE 7-5**

**Many jobs that used to be non-computer-related require computer use today.**

^ **Auto technician**

^ **Casino worker**

^ **Telecommunications technician**

^ **Law enforcement officer**

## A CLOSER LOOK AT... THE DOT COM FALLOUT

Since the beginning of the technology boom, some technology companies have done very well financially. One of the most dramatic is Microsoft Corporation, whose stock rose by a factor of approximately 750 from the time in went public in 1986 until the tech sector high in 2000. Put another way, an investment of $1,000 in Microsoft made in March 1986 would have been worth about three-quarters of a million dollars 14 years later.

Towards the end of this period, *dot coms* began to emerge. Unlike traditional stores, such as Wal-Mart and Macy's, which added a Web component to their businesses after the Internet began to be viewed as a viable business opportunity, dot coms are Internet-only businesses with no traditional physical presence. Despite the fact that many dot coms and other new technology companies had little or no history, assets, or profits and were viewed as highly speculative by some investors, stock prices in the technology sector soared. As illustrated in Figure 7-6, the composite value of the NASDAQ (the exchange on which many technology stocks are listed) almost doubled in the six month period from September 10, 1999 to March 10, 2000, rising from 2,887 to an astounding 5,048. Some attribute this boom to investors looking for the "next Microsoft" to make them rich in a short period of time. But companies that don't make any money have trouble staying in business. And resources such as domain names and customer lists—the only assets of some dot coms—are hard to put a dollar value on or use as collateral. As seems obvious in hindsight, it was inevitable that the tech sector was ready for a fall.

The tech bust came in March 2000. With the subsequent record declines in the stock market—particularly technology oriented stocks—enormous losses, and consequential layoffs and bankruptcies, abounded. At least 862 dot com companies have failed since January 2000, according to Webmergers.com. Even dot com giants were affected, such as Amazon.com, which announced plans in January 2001 to cut 1,300 jobs—15% of its total workforce. Overall, U.S. unemployment rose to 8.3 million in December 2001 and was holding steady at the time of this writing, according to the U.S. Bureau of Labor Statistics. Although dot coms can't be blamed entirely for the bleak economic picture of late, they certainly helped to contribute to it. Down from the peak layoff months of the dot com shakeout—such as April 2001, which saw more than 17,000 dot com jobs eliminated—tech layoffs were still averaging about 1,000 per month in mid-2002. Investors were also extremely affected by the bankruptcies and overall stock market decline. Many suffered enough losses to affect their lives significantly, such as having to delay their retirement. Another group affected by the dot com fallout is impending or recent college graduates who are just entering the professional workforce and now have to compete for jobs with the seasoned professionals who were recently laid off.

To survive the fallout, remaining dot com and tech companies have tightened their belts—particularly when it comes to marketing expenses. The 2001 Super Bowl was enlightening. Instead of the seventeen dot com companies that were willing and able to shell out millions of dollars for Super Bowl ads just the year before, only three purchased Super Bowl ads in 2001. In addition to reevaluating their marketing strategies, dot com companies have reorganized their business plans. As a result of revamped operations, some companies are rebounding—such as Amazon.com, whose stock rose 47% in the first nine months of 2002. Some view the loss of the weakest members of the e-commerce community—while devastating for them and their shareholders—to be good for the industry as a whole.

There are signs that the shakeout may be nearing its end. While the NASDAQ was still hovering around the 1300 mark at the time of this writing and may take a long time to return to the 4,000 and 5,000 marks of the recent past, bankruptcies of dot coms have fallen significantly. According to Webmergers.com data, fewer than 100 Internet companies went out of business or filed for bankruptcy protection in the first six months of 2002, down from the 345 cases during the same period one year before. Once things level off, hopefully the dot coms and traditional businesses in the tech sector that are able to remain in business will have a stronger base, streamlined operations, and the experience necessary to survive the next economic rollercoaster.

**FIGURE 7-6**

**The NASDAQ's recent rollercoaster ride (composite value shown here for the four year period from October 1998 through September 2002)**

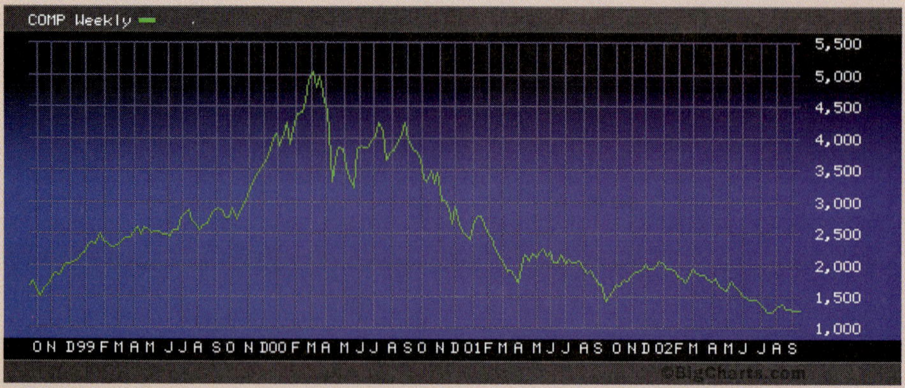

## Impact of Our 24/7 Society

One benefit of our communications-oriented society is that one never has to be out of touch. With the use of personal cell phones and pagers, as well as the ability to access e-mail and company networks from virtually anywhere, individuals can be available around the clock, if needed (see Figure 7-7). Although the ability to be in touch constantly is an advantage for some people under certain conditions, it can also be a source of great stress. For example, employees who feel that they are "on call" 24/7 and can't ever get away from work may find it difficult to relax on their downtime. Others who are used to being in touch constantly may not be able to relax when they are on vacation and supposed to be unavailable because they are afraid of missing something important that may affect their careers. In either case, these individuals may lose the distinction between personal time and work time and end up being always on the job. This can affect their personal lives, emotional health, and well-being. Finding a balance between work time and personal time is important for good emotional health.

**FIGURE 7-7**

**With mobile phones, pagers, and portable PCs, many individuals are available 24/7.**

## Information Overload

Although the amount of information available through the Internet is a great asset, it can also overwhelm all of us at times. Combined with TV and radio news broadcasts; newspaper, journal, and magazine articles; and telephone calls, voicemail messages, and faxes, some Americans today are practically drowning in information. For some individuals and organizations, the amount of e-mail received each day is almost unfathomable. For example, the U.S. Senate receives between 1 million and 2 million e-mail messages each day, and it has been estimated that some employees spend half their workday reading and responding to work-related e-mail messages. Several strategies can be used to avoid becoming completely overwhelmed by information overload.

For efficiently extracting the information you need from the vast amount of information available over the Internet, good search techniques are essential. (Refer to the How To box in Chapter 3 for a review of search techniques, if needed.) Perhaps the most important thing to keep in mind when dealing with information overload is that you can't possibly read everything ever written on a particular subject. Just like the law of diminishing returns for economics and production, at some point in time when performing Internet research, the value of additional information decreases and is eventually not worth your time to pursue it. Knowing when to quit a search, or when to try another research approach, is an important skill in avoiding information overload.

*Clipping services* that can locate and deliver appropriate newspaper and Web site content to you on a daily basis based on your specified interests are another way to reduce information overload. *Intelligent agents*—software programs that do specified jobs based on your instructions—can also gather information for you on a regular basis, as well as perform other helpful tasks, such as notifying you when a particular Web page has been updated or a certain stock hits a specified price. Still other software programs can suppress those annoying pop-up ads, speed up downloads, or otherwise help you have a more efficient and pleasant Internet experience.

Efficiently managing your incoming e-mail is another way to help avoid information overload. Tools for managing e-mail can help alleviate the stress of an overflowing Inbox, as well as speed up the amount of time you spend dealing with your online correspondence. E-mail filters can be used to route messages automatically into particular folders based on your stated criteria, such as suspected spam, work messages, and personal e-mail. This allows you to concentrate on the messages most important to you first and leave the others—such as the possible spam—to be sorted through and dealt with at your convenience.

### Burnout

Our heavy use of computers, combined with information overload and 24/7 accessibility via technology, can lead to **burnout**—a state of fatigue or frustration brought about by overwork. Burnout is often born from good intentions, such as when hard-working people try to reach goals that, for one reason or another, become unrealistic. Early signs of burnout include a feeling of emotional and physical exhaustion, no longer caring about a project that used to be interesting or exciting, irritability, feelings of resentment about the amount of work that needs to be done, and feeling pulled in many directions at once.

When you begin to notice the symptoms of burnout, experts recommend reevaluating your schedule, priorities, and lifestyle. Sometimes, just admitting that you are feeling overwhelmed and need some help is a good start to solving the problem. Taking a break or getting away for a day can help put the situation in perspective. Saying no to additional commitments and making sure you eat properly, exercise regularly, and otherwise take good care of yourself are also important strategies for coping with and alleviating both stress and burnout.

### Computer and Internet Addiction

Although experts disagree about whether it should be called an *addiction* or a *compulsion*, the problem of not being able to stop using a computer or the Internet—or the overuse of computers or the Internet creating problems in your personal or professional life—definitely exists. Officially referred to as *computer addiction disorder (CAD)* or *Internet addiction disorder (IAD)*, depending on whether or not the use is focused on the Internet, these conditions are increasingly being viewed by mental health professionals as true psychophysiological disorders. According to Maressa Hecht Orzack, a Harvard University psychologist and the founder and director of Computer Addiction Services at McLean Hospital in Massachusetts, computer addiction is "...an emerging disorder suffered by people who find the virtual reality on computer screens more attractive than everyday reality."

Computer addiction can affect people of any age and can take a variety of forms. Some individuals become addicted to e-mail or instant messaging. Others become compulsive online shoppers or become addicted to chat room activities. Still others can't stop playing Internet or computer games. The most common forms of addiction at the present time include online chatting/instant messaging and online multiplayer games. One example is a 17-year-old high school student located in Washington who was addicted to instant messaging. This young woman found herself coming home from school and immediately getting online because she was afraid of missing something. During summer vacation, she stayed online all day. When people didn't respond immediately to her messages, she took it personally and became depressed and, eventually, suicidal. After breaking her addiction cold turkey with counseling and antidepressants, she now spends much less time at her computer and has a healthy balance between the Internet and other activities. Another case of IAD is of the divorced mother of two who used the Internet as an escape. Because of her habit of spending 10 hours or more online each day and neglecting her children, this woman lost custody of her children. An additional example involved one manager who was recently fired from two different computer companies—he lost both jobs because he couldn't stop playing computer games at work.

Like other addictions, computer or Internet addiction can cause problems at home and on the job, lead to depression, result in increasing amounts of time and money spent on computers, and other serious problems. A list of Dr. Orzack's symptoms of computer addiction are shown in Figure 7-8. Like Dr. Orzack, many experts believe computer addiction is a growing problem, but it can be treated—typically by such methods as therapy, support groups, and, sometimes, medication.

**FIGURE 7-8**

**Symptoms of computer addiction***

| |
|---|
| You need to use the computer in order to experience pleasure, excitement, or relief. |
| You lose control when not on the computer, becoming anxious, angry, or depressed. |
| You have overwhelming thoughts about the computer before you turn it on, while it is on, and after you have turned it off. |
| You crave the newest hardware or software, never satisfied with what you have. |
| You need to spend increasing amounts of time or money on computer activities in order to get the same effect. |
| You lie to everybody about the amount of time spent on the computer and where you are spending that time. |
| You risk the loss of relationships with your family and friends because of your compulsive computer use. |
| You face financial ruin because of excessive computer use. |
| You repeatedly fail at efforts to stop your compulsive computer use. |
| Your physical health suffers because you miss meals, don't exercise, and neglect personal hygiene. |
| You experience repetitive stress injuries, backaches, dry eyes, migraines, and changes in sleep patterns as a result of excessive computer use. |
| *According to Dr. Orzack, you are addicted to or dependent on your computer if you experience at least five of these symptoms, and your behavior is not the result of either bipolar or obsessive-compulsive disorder. |

## IS THERE EQUAL ACCESS TO TECHNOLOGY?

A major concern about the increased integration of computers and technology in our society for many is whether or not technology is accessible to all individuals. Some believe there is a distinct line dividing those who have access and those who don't. Factors such as one's age, gender, race, income, education, and physical challenges can all impact one's access to technology and how it is used.

### The Digital Divide

The **digital divide** refers to the gap between those who have access to information and communications technology and those who do not—often referred to as the "haves" and "have nots." Its status is typically assessed based on physical access to computers and other types of related technology. Some individuals, however, believe that the definition of digital divide goes deeper than just access. For example, they classify those individuals who have physical access to technology but who don't understand how to use it or are discouraged from using it in the "have not" category. Groups and individuals trying to eliminate the digital divide are working toward providing real access to technology (including access to up-to-date hardware, software, and training) so that it can be used to improve people's lives.

The digital divide can refer to the differences between individuals within a particular country, as well as between one country and another. Within a country, use of computers and related technology can vary based on such factors as age, race, education, and income.

### The U.S. Digital Divide

Although there is disagreement among experts about the current status of the digital divide within the U.S., there is indication that it has begun to shrink in the last few years. The digital divide involves more than just Internet use—it involves the use of any type of technology necessary to succeed in our society—but the increased Internet use noted in the past few years is an encouraging sign. For example, a report from the U.S. Department of Commerce published in February 2002 and titled "A Nation Online" states that more than half the population of the United States is now online, using the Internet at work, schools, libraries, or home—an increase of 26 million people in 13 months (an estimated additional 31 million people use a computer, but not the Internet). While individuals living in low-income households or having little education still trail the national average, the report shows that Internet use is continuing to increase for everyone regardless of income, education, age, race, ethnicity, or gender. In fact, many of the groups that have historically been low Internet users have grown faster than other groups. For instance, between December 1998 and September 2001, Internet use by individuals in the lowest income households (those earning less than $15,000 per year) increased significantly each year—in 2001, a total of 25% of the people in this group were online. The increase may be explained in part by low-priced computers and free dial-up access making Internet access more feasible for low-income families, as well as increased opportunities for free public Internet access, such as in public schools, libraries, and neighborhood clubs. Figure 7-9 shows some key findings from that study, based on September 2001 data.

In addition to access differences based on factors such as income, age, education, and race, there are also differences in the types of Internet activities performed based on these factors. For instance, the Department of Commerce report includes the following use information about U.S. users:

- *Income*—There is a pattern of broader Internet use (more activities) as income increases.
- *Age*—Online shopping is particularly common among 25- to 44-year-old Internet users; Internet users in the 25-34 age group are the most likely to bank online; and those 55 and older are more likely to check health information online.
- *Children*—Family households with children under age 18 are more likely to have computers than families without children.
- *Education*—Among 18- to 24-year-olds, Internet use is heavily affected by whether or not they attend school or college (85% of those in school or college use the Internet, compared to 51.5% of those who are not in school).
- *Gender*—More men than women use the Internet to check news, weather, and sports, but more women go online to find information on health services or practices.
- *Race*—Compared to other races, a smaller proportion of Black and Hispanic Internet users exchange e-mail, search for news, conduct searches for product information, or make online purchases.

Because the U.S. is such a technologically advanced society, many believe reducing—and trying to eliminate—the digital divide is extremely important to ensure that all citizens have an equal chance to be successful in this country. Although there has been lots of progress in that direction, more work still remains ahead. However, it is important to realize that not all individuals want to use computers or get online. Some people—rich or poor—choose not to have a PC, voice mail, call waiting, or even a television. Sometimes this is a religious decision; other times it is simply a lifestyle choice.

**FIGURE 7-9**

**Key U.S. Internet use statistics (percent of individuals in each category using the Internet)**

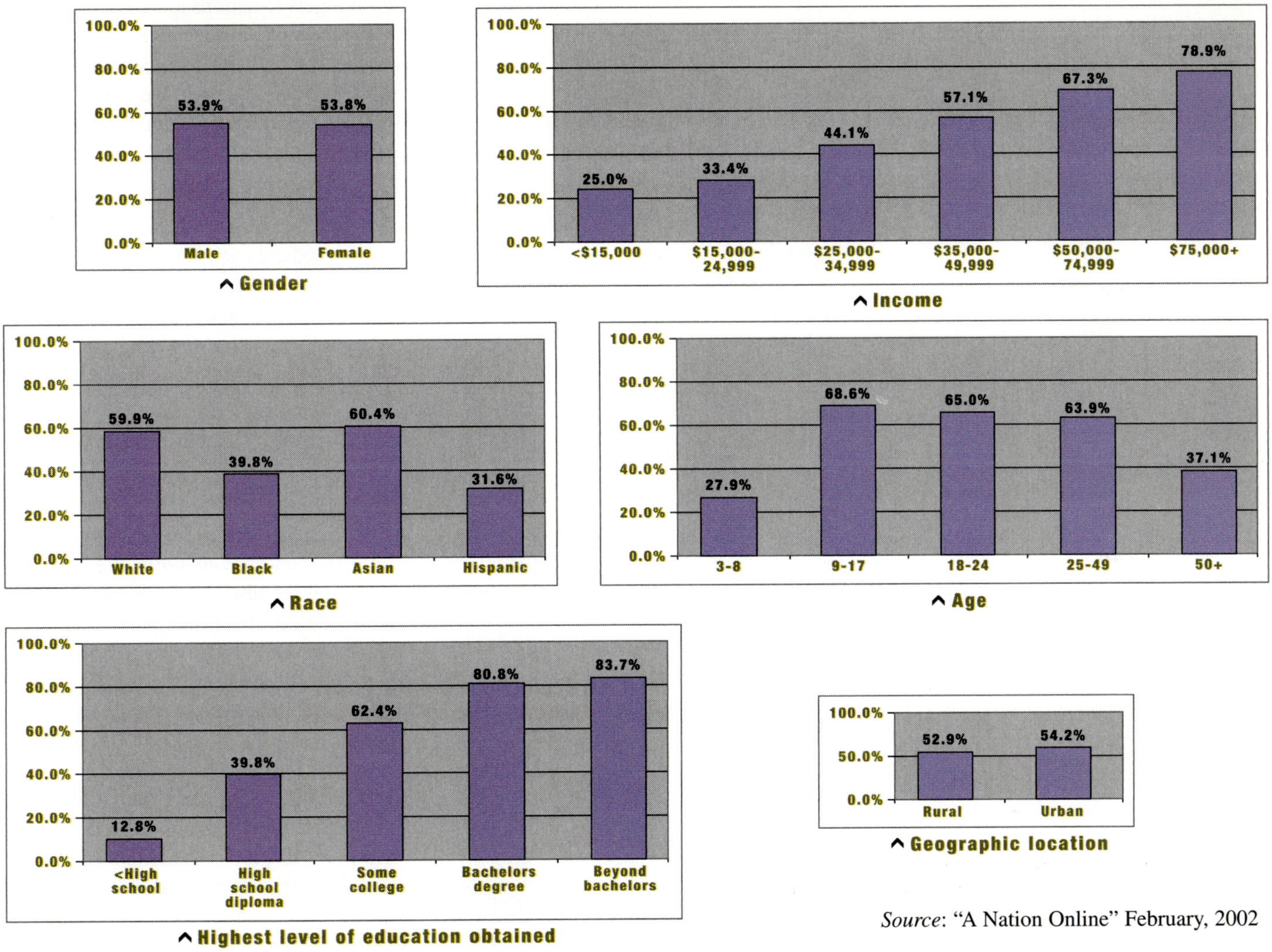


*Source*: "A Nation Online" February, 2002

## The Global Digital Divide

The global digital divide is perhaps more dramatic than the U.S. digital divide. An estimated 429 million people are online globally—only about 6% of the world's population. Worldwide computer use is highly dominated by the United States, which, according to Neilsen/Netratings, has more computers than the rest of the world combined. Part of this can be attributed to the use of technology in general and the sophisticated technological infrastructure that exists and is continually being upgraded in the U.S. Another factor is income versus cost. For example, research indicates that the typical U.S. consumer spends just 1% to 2% of their average monthly income on Internet access, compared to the 191% of monthly income that the average citizen in Bangladesh would spend on Internet access.

For some, it is difficult to imagine how computers and the Internet can benefit the world's hungry or the 2 billion people without access to reliable electricity. For others, like Carleton Fiorina (CEO of Hewlett-Packard) who echoes the sentiment of many world leaders when she states that "the Internet and related technologies hold the promise of rapid, sustainable economic growth that directly benefits everyone on the planet," the need for bridging the global digital divide is real. Over the past few years, world leaders have been working on a new development aid framework that aims to address the global digital divide. Private programs also exist, such as the *CEO Charter for Digital Development* started in 2002 that consists of CEOs who target at least 20% of their annual corporate philanthropy budgets to actions aimed at promoting social, economic, and educational progress in developing countries and disadvantaged communities throughout the world through information and communication technologies. Fiorina, Steven Ballmer (CEO of Microsoft Corporation), and several CEOs from other countries were among the first to sign the CEO Charter for Digital Development.

Some technological applications for developing countries include mobile phones with solar-rechargeable batteries, and computers to be used for telemedicine and distance learning. For instance, a telemedicine project in Siliguri, India, a remote town in the foothills of the eastern Himalayas, aims to provide medical care via computer to local residents. Currently, residents have to travel overnight to Calcutta to see a specialist; with telemedicine, residents could often be diagnosed and treated without leaving their village.

For personal computer use, new products are emerging that could help alleviate the global digital divide. For example, the *Simputer* (see Figure 7-10) was developed to bring low-cost computer use first to India, and then to other countries. Developed by a Bangalore-based group of seven professors and engineers, the Simputer uses a simple user interface based on sight, touch, and audio. With the help of built-in text-to-speech capabilities, literacy is not essential for its use. Although it looks like a handheld PC, the Simputer is not called a PDA; instead it is referred to as a *community digital assistant (CDA)*—a device designed to be shared by several members of a community. This is facilitated by an integrated smart card reader/writer. Each villager stores all personal information on an inexpensive rewritable smart card, which he or she keeps. When a villager wants to use a Simputer, he or she inserts this card into any Simputer; the individual's profile is then read from the smart card and the Simputer display is personalized for that person. Data can be read from and written to the card, until the card is removed.

**FIGURE 7-10**

**The Simputer, recently introduced in India, costs around $200 and is designed to be shared by several individuals.**

The Simputer device is currently being tested in several locations in India. Because the units are expensive relative to personal income (depending on its configuration, the cost of the Simputer is expected to be between $200 and $400 in U.S. dollars—approximately one-half of one year's income for the average Indian), it is hoped that the Indian government will provide each community with several CDAs, but that had not been decided at the time of this writing. If a unit is available in the village either to rent or to borrow, such as through the local school or a village shop, villagers would need to buy only a smart card to be able to use a Simputer. Current applications include farmers being able to check the latest crop prices, fishermen being able to get accurate weather reports, and rural health workers having access to reliable medical data. Expected future applications include long-distance medical diagnostics, basic literacy training, banking and commodity trading, communications, voting, and GPS navigation.

While the digital divide within a country is more about some individuals within a country having access to technology and others not, the global digital divide affects one country versus another. It is becoming increasingly important for all countries to have real access to information and communications technology in order to be able to compete successfully in our global economy.

## Assistive Technology

Research has found that people with disabilities tend to use computers and the Internet at rates below the average for a given population. Part of the reason may be because some physical conditions—such as visual impairment, deafness, or limited dexterity—make it difficult to use a conventional computer system. That's where **assistive technology**—hardware and software specifically designed for use by individuals with physical disabilities—fits in. There has been much improvement in the area of assistive hardware and software in recent years. This may be due in part to the *Americans with Disabilities Act (ADA)* that requires companies with 15 or more employees to make reasonable accommodations for known physical or mental limitations of otherwise qualified individuals with disabilities, unless it results in undue hardship. Consequently, assistive input and output devices—such as *Braille keyboards*, specialized mice, large monitors, and *screen readers*—and wheelchair-compatible workspaces have become more commonplace in businesses, as well as in homes and schools.

### Assistive Input Devices

*Assistive input devices* allow for input in a nontraditional manner (see Figure 7-11). For example, **Braille keyboards**, large key keyboards, or conventional keyboards with Braille or large-print key overlays are available for visually impaired computer users. *Keyguards*—metal or plastic plates that fit over conventional keyboards—enable users with limited hand mobility to press the keys on a keyboard with fingers or a special device without accidentally pressing other keys. *One-handed keyboards* are available for users that have the use of only one hand, and **voice-recognition systems**—which use special software and a microphone—can be used to input data and give commands to the PC hands-free. *Switches*—hardware devices that can be turned on or off with hand, foot, finger, or face movement or with sips and puffs of air—can be used in conjunction with a keyboard, mouse, or other input device to perform a preprogrammed set of actions, such as opening the Windows menu or performing a left mouse click. Some conventional input devices can also be used for assistive purposes, such as scanners which—if they have **optical character recognition (OCR)** capabilities—can input printed documents into the computer as editable text.

For mouse alternatives, there are assistive pointing devices that can be used—sometimes in conjunction with a switch—to move and select items with an onscreen pointer; used in conjunction with an onscreen keyboard they can also be used to enter text-based data. There are also *feet mice,* which are controlled by the feet, and *head-pointing systems* or *head mice,* which control the onscreen pointer using head movement. For example, the head-pointing systems shown in Figure 7-11 use a headset containing sensors (bottom left image) or a reflective dot placed on the forehead or eyeglasses (bottom right image) in conjunction with a tracking camera to move an onscreen pointer based on the user's head movement.

In addition to their use by disabled computer users, assistive hardware can also be used by the general population. For example, one-handed keyboards are sometimes used by people who wish to keep one hand on their mouse and one hand on their keyboard at all times; voice-input systems are used by individuals who would prefer to speak input instead of type it; and head-pointing systems are available for gaming and VR applications.

**FIGURE 7-11**

Examples of assistive input devices

**Braille keyboard**

The keys on this keyboard contain Braille overlays.

**One-handed keyboard**

All keys can be reached with either the left or right hand, depending on which version of the keyboard is being used.

**Head-pointing system with puff switch**

With this system, head movement controls the pointer movement and puffs of air into the tube are used to "click" on objects.

**Head-pointing system without a switch**

With this system, head movement controls the pointer movement and pointing to an object for a specified period of time "clicks" that object.

## Assistive Output Devices

Once data has been input into the computer, a variety of *assistive output devices* can be used (see Figure 7-12). For blind and other visually impaired individuals, **screen readers** (software that reads aloud all information displayed on the computer screen, such as instructions, menu options, documents, and Web pages), **Braille displays** (which convert screen output on an ongoing basis into Braille form on the Braille display device attached to the keyboard), and **Braille printers** (which print embossed dots in Braille format on paper) are available. Some operating systems—such as Windows—also have settings that can be used to magnify the screen, change text size and color, convert audio cues into written text, and otherwise make the computer more accessible to individuals, as discussed in the chapter How To box.

**FIGURE 7-12**

Examples of assistive output devices

**Screen reader software**

**Braille display**

**Braille printer**

### Impact on Web Page Design

In 1998, Congress amended the Rehabilitation Act to require federal agencies to make their electronic and information technology accessible to people with disabilities. The law—often referred to as *Section 508*, for the section number in the U.S. Code—applies to all federal agencies and, consequentially, all federal Web sites. It was also hoped that passing this requirement would lead other companies to expand their Web content to make it more available to people with disabilities. As Tim Berners-Lee, the inventor of the World Wide Web, once said, "The power of the Web is in its universality. Access by everyone regardless of disability is an essential aspect."

**ONLINE TUTORIAL**

For an online look at how to create an accessible Web page, go to www.course.com/morley2003/ch7

Assistive technology affects Web page design because some assistive hardware and software isn't compatible with all types of Web content. For example, screen reading devices can typically only read text-based data. In order for navigational images or other graphics to be understandable to visitors using screen reading software, the images must be identified with an *alternative text description*. This description can easily be added to an image when the Web page is developed, but it is not always done. In addition to being read by screen readers, alternative text descriptions are displayed when the image is pointed to with the mouse or other pointing device, as well as in text-only browsers and when images are turned off in a regular Web browser. Other features that make a Web page accessible include having meaningful text-based hyperlinks—such as *How to Contact Us* instead of *Click Here*—and providing alternative content for Flash, JavaScript, or other animated components that may be incompatible with assistive technology. When some features included on a Web page make it simply not possible for users with screen readers to understand the content, an alternate text-based page can be made available for those users. Some characteristics of an accessible Web page are shown in Figure 7-13.

**FIGURE 7-13**

**Some characteristics of an accessible Web page**

Hyperlinks make sense when read aloud because they are descriptive instead of saying only "Click here."

There is a high degree of contrast between the text and the background colors.

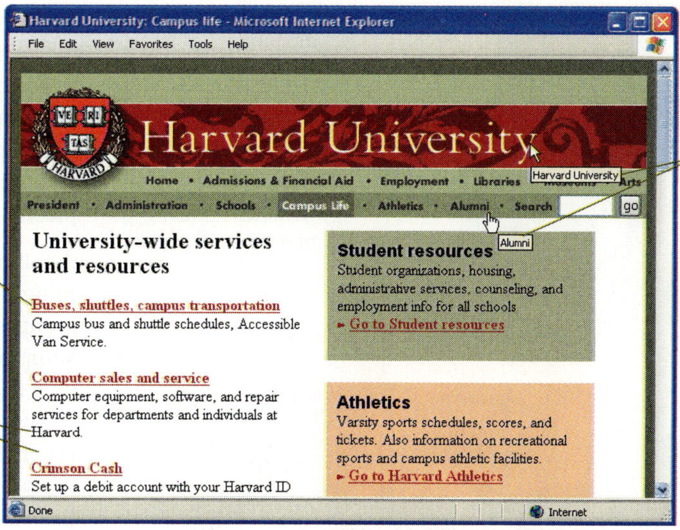


Images have alternative text descriptions. (Even though the images shown here have text included on them, they are still seen as images by the browser and so are ignored by screen reading software, unless alternative text is included.)

In general, multimedia is avoided unless it is absolutely necessary. When it is used, text transcripts and descriptions of the visual effects are included so screen readers can be used to understand the multimedia content being portrayed.

# ENVIRONMENTAL CONCERNS

The increasing use of computers in our society has caused a variety of environmental concerns. The amount of energy used to power PCs and other computer components, for example, is one concern. Another is our extensive use of paper and how much of it ends up as trash in landfills. The hazardous materials contained in computer equipment or generated by the production of computers and related technology, and the disposal of used and obsolete computing products, are additional concerns.

**FIGURE 7-14**

**Examples of eco-labels**

^ **United States** "ENERGY STAR"

> **European Union** "Flower Eco-label"

^ **Korea** "Environmental Label"

^ **Brazil** "Ecolabel"

## Green Computing

The term **green computing** refers to the use of computers in an environmentally friendly manner. Minimizing the use of natural resources, such as energy and paper, is one aspect of green computing. To encourage the development of energy-saving devices, the U.S. Department of Energy and the Environmental Protection Agency (EPA) developed the **ENERGY STAR** program. Hardware that is ENERGY STAR compliant exceeds the minimum federal standards for reduced energy consumption. To see if a device produced in the U.S. is ENERGY STAR compliant, look for the ENERGY STAR label shown in Figure 7-14; this figure also shows other **eco-labels**—environmental performance certifications—used in a variety of other countries. Some energy-saving features found on computer equipment today include hardware (such as computers and printers) that can go into low-power sleep mode when not in use, low-power-consumptive chips and boards, and flat-panel displays.

Green computing products currently in development include solar-powered PDAs and cell phones, as well as notebooks that run on *hydrogen-powered fuel cells*. The world's first environmentally-friendly desktop PC was released by NEC in 2002 (see Figure 7-15). This PC consumes much less power than conventional desktop PCs. It radiates less heat than a conventional computer, reducing the amount of waste heat generated that would need to be eliminated by air conditioning. Moreover, the system requires no internal fans and has a quiet hard drive to help reduce noise pollution, uses a lead-free motherboard, and has a case made out of recyclable plastic.

**FIGURE 7-15**

**The NEC PowerMate Eco is the world's first environmentally friendly personal computer.**

Another environmental concern stemming from the use of computers and computing equipment is paper consumption and refuse. It now appears that the so-called *paperless office* that many visionaries predicted for the computer age is largely a myth. Instead, research indicates that global paper use has grown more than six-fold since 1950 and one-fifth of all wood harvested in the world today ends up as paper. According to a Gartner study,

Web users alone print an average of 28 pages per day. The estimated number of pages generated by computer printers each year worldwide is almost one-half billion a year—an amount that would stack more than 25,000 miles high. The chapter Trends In box takes a look at a possible solution for the future—*electronic paper*.

**ONLINE RESOURCES**

For links to information about green computing, go to www.course.com/morley2003/ch7

## Recycling and Disposal of Computing Equipment

Another environmental concern is the amount of trash—and sometimes toxic trash—generated by computer use. In addition to paper-based trash, computing refuse includes used toner cartridges and obsolete or broken hardware. Compounding the problem of the amount of electronic waste (called *e-trash*) generated today is the fact that conventional PC hardware contains a variety of toxic and hazardous materials. For instance, the average CRT monitor alone contains about eight pounds of lead and a single computer may contain up to 700 different chemical elements and compounds, many of which (such as arsenic, lead, mercury, and cadmium) are hazardous and expensive to dispose of properly. Conventional computers may also be constructed out of material that is difficult to recycle. It is likely that PCs in the near future will follow the trend of the NEC PowerMate Eco and be comprised of more environmentally friendly components. Unlike most computer cases, which can't be fully recycled and give off toxic fumes when burned in an incinerator, the PowerMate Eco system unit is made of a special type of plastic called *NuCycle*, which was developed by NEC, is fully recyclable, and contains no toxic flame-retardant coatings. The PowerMate Eco system also uses lead-free solder on the motherboard, making recycling of the PC easier and less hazardous.

A global concern regarding obsolete computer equipment is where it all eventually ends up. The majority of all discarded computer equipment ends up in landfills (see Figure 7-16); a study by the Silicon Valley Toxics Coalition and the Basel Action Network revealed that 50% to 80% of America's technology trash that is sent for recycling ends up as trash in other countries, such as China, India, and Pakistan. Activists say they believe unchecked dumping by the U.S. and other countries—such as England, Japan, Australia, and Singapore—has been going on for as long as 10 years. The primary reason for exporting e-trash is monetary—proper disposal of a computer in the U. S. normally costs between $5 and $10, compared to $1 or less in third-world countries. Much of the e-trash exported to these countries is simply dumped into fields and other informal dumping areas. Unaware of the potential danger of these components, villagers often sort through and dismantle discarded electronics parts looking for precious metals and other sources of revenue—potentially endangering their health as well as polluting nearby rivers, ponds, and other water sources.

**FIGURE 7-16**

**The vast majority of the 40 million or so computers that become obsolete each year end up as e-trash in landfills, which creates a threat to the environment.**

## TRENDS IN... ELECTRONIC PAPER

Similar to *e-books,* which display the contents of books in an electronic format on a special book-sized device, **electronic paper (e-paper)** displays written content in electronic form, but on thinner, more paper-like plastic displays. Still in the early stages of development at a number of companies, such as Gyricon Media, Xerox, and E Ink, electronic paper is expected eventually to become a viable replacement for some traditional paper and ink applications. Practical applications from an environmental standpoint include any documents that only need to be kept for a short period of time, such as newspapers, retail display signs, and some e-mail messages; using e-paper, these documents could be erased and the e-paper reused, instead of having to be physically exchanged for new ones and then the old ones disposed of.

So how does e-paper work? One product (currently in the testing stage) consists of two sheets of very thin transparent plastic with millions of very small beads—each smaller than a grain of sand and sealed inside a tiny pocket surrounded by liquid (these beads and their liquid are sometimes referred to as *electronic ink*). Each bead has two colors—such as half white and half black—and can rotate within its pocket only when an electrical signal is received. To change the text or images displayed on the "paper," electronic signals—usually sent to the paper through a wireless transmission—instruct the beads to rotate appropriately to display either their black sides or white sides to form the proper text and images, similar to the way pixels are used to display images on a monitor. The content remains displayed until another transmission changes the pattern, such as changing all the beads to display their white sides to "erase" the paper. Current e-paper products can be written to and erased electronically thousands of times, but in the near future that number is expected to increase to several million times.

One of the first areas in which e-paper has been applied is retail signs, such as those found in department stores and other retail establishments (large stores often spend thousands of dollars on printed paper signs each week, and Target has reported that it delivers three planeloads of signs each week from the company's production center for distribution to individual stores). These *e-signs* look like ordinary paper signs, but their text can be changed wirelessly (see Figure 7-17). Consequently, instead of continually having to print new paper signs, e-signs can be changed electronically, which saves the time and expenses of printing, delivering, and setting up new signs, as well as disposing of the old ones. Other retail applications currently in development include e-paper shelf price tags that continually display the price entered in the store's database and newspaper boxes that are updated periodically during the day to reflect the latest headlines or a featured section of the newspaper.

As e-paper technology improves, it is expected that the paper will more easily support the smaller text conducive to personal printouts. Future configurations include regular-sized e-paper that can be inserted into a special computer printer to be printed electronically and then reused over and over again; regular and newspaper-sized e-papers that can wirelessly download new content from the Internet; and e-books that look and feel like real paper books, but whose content can be rewritten to display the content of a different book when directed by the user.

Improvements that need to be made before e-paper becomes more commonplace include lower cost, an increased life span, and thinner and more flexible paper. Future possibilities for electronic ink applications include its use on billboards, T-shirts, and even wallpaper and paint for easy redecorating.

**FIGURE 7-17**
**Electronic paper**

^ E-paper is thin and flexible.

^ E-paper products, such as the e-sign shown here, are rewritten electronically and can be reused over and over again.

While it is difficult—or, perhaps, impossible—to correct the damage that has already occurred from e-waste, many organizations are working on ways to protect people and the environment from future contamination. For instance, the *National Electronics Product Stewardship Initiative*—a coalition of computer companies, government agencies, and recycling centers—is working to develop a plan that would accept old computers, recycle what is possible, and safely dispose of the rest. The initiative is based on the concept of *product stewardship*, in which all parties who have a role in producing, selling, or using a product also have a role in managing it at the end of its useful life. The plan is expected to be financed through a fee added to the cost of new computers beginning in late 2002 and taking effect gradually over the next few years.

Even though recycling computer equipment is difficult because of the materials currently being used, proper disposal is essential to avoid pollution and health hazards. Older equipment that is still functioning can be donated to schools and nonprofit groups. Some organizations accept and repair donated equipment and then distribute it to disadvantaged groups. For example, the organization Computers for Africa refurbishes used computers, networks them, and then ships ready-to-set-up labs to non-profit organizations in Africa.

Equipment that is not worth refurbishing should be properly recycled. Some recycling centers will accept computer equipment, but many charge a fee for this service. Another option is a manufacturer's program, such as the ones offered by IBM and Hewlett-Packard. If the manufacturer of your obsolete or broken computer equipment has such a program, typically you send the equipment—along with a processing fee—to the company and the company makes sure your equipment gets to a recycling facility. Expired toner cartridges and ink cartridges can sometimes be returned to the manufacturer (using the supplied shipping label included with some cartridges) or exchanged when ordering new cartridges; the cartridges are then *recharged* (refilled) and resold. (Cartridges that cannot be refilled can be sent to a recycling facility.) In addition to helping to reduce e-trash in landfills, using recharged printer cartridges saves the consumer money, since they are less expensive than new cartridges. Other computer components—such as CDs, DVDs, and computer disks—can also be recycled through some organizations, such as the Green Disk group which accepts shipments of these items free of charge and then uses the components to make new disks and other products.

Consumers and companies alike are recognizing the need for green computing. A growing number of computing equipment manufacturers are announcing that they are committed to environmental responsibility. Support for a nationwide recycling program, such as the National Electronics Product Stewardship Initiative, is growing. New classifications from the EPA are expected to encourage recycling of an even greater number of computer components. So, even though computer manufacturing and recycling has a long way to go before computing equipment stops being an environmental and health hazard, it is encouraging that the trend is moving towards creating a safer and less wasteful environment.

# HOW TO... USE THE WINDOWS ACCESSIBILITY OPTIONS

Many operating systems include the capability to change a variety of display settings, such as the desktop color, background picture, text size and color, and so forth. What is not widely known is that many also include *accessibility options* to change the appearance and behavior of operating system components to enhance accessibility for some vision-impaired, hearing-impaired, or mobility-impaired users without requiring the use of additional software or hardware. An example of a desktop with a variety of settings changed to improve readability for a visually-impaired user is shown in Figure 7-18.

Some Windows XP options are as follows:

- *Magnifier program*—enlarges a portion of the screen for easier viewing
- *Narrator program*—uses text-to-speech technology to read the contents of the screen aloud
- *Onscreen keyboard*—provides users with limited mobility the ability to type onscreen using a pointing device (see Figure 7-19)
- *StickyKeys*—enables the use of Shift, Control, and Alternate keys without having to press two keys at once
- *SoundSentry*—generates visual warnings when the system makes a sound
- *ShowSounds*—displays text-based captions for the speech and sounds programs make
- *MouseKeys*—allows the user to control the mouse pointer with the keyboard's numeric keypad
- *High contrast*—changes the screen background and text colors to high-contrast combinations, such as black and white
- *Text size*—allows the user to change the display text to large or extra-large as needed
- *Screen resolution*—allows the user to display all screen content larger or smaller

The accessibility tools that ship with Windows are available through the Control Panel, as shown in Figure 7-20. They can be used to provide increased functionality for users with special needs, although they are not designed to replace assistive hardware or software. Other, non-assistive, uses of the Windows Control Panel include adjusting network or modem settings, uninstalling programs, adding a printer or other piece of hardware, changing the Start menu or taskbar options, and changing the settings for the keyboard, mouse, scanner, digital camera, or other installed input devices.

**FIGURE 7-18**

**Examples of the accessibility features for visually-impaired users that are built into Windows XP**

**Magnifer**
Enlarges the portion of the screen the mouse is pointing to

**High contrast**
Changes the screen and text colors to high contrast black and white for easier reading

**Large text**
Enlarges all text displayed on menus, toolbars, desktop, etc.

**FIGURE 7-19**

**An onscreen keyboard allows the use of a pointing device to enter text input.**

## FIGURE 7-20

**Changing the Windows accessibility options**

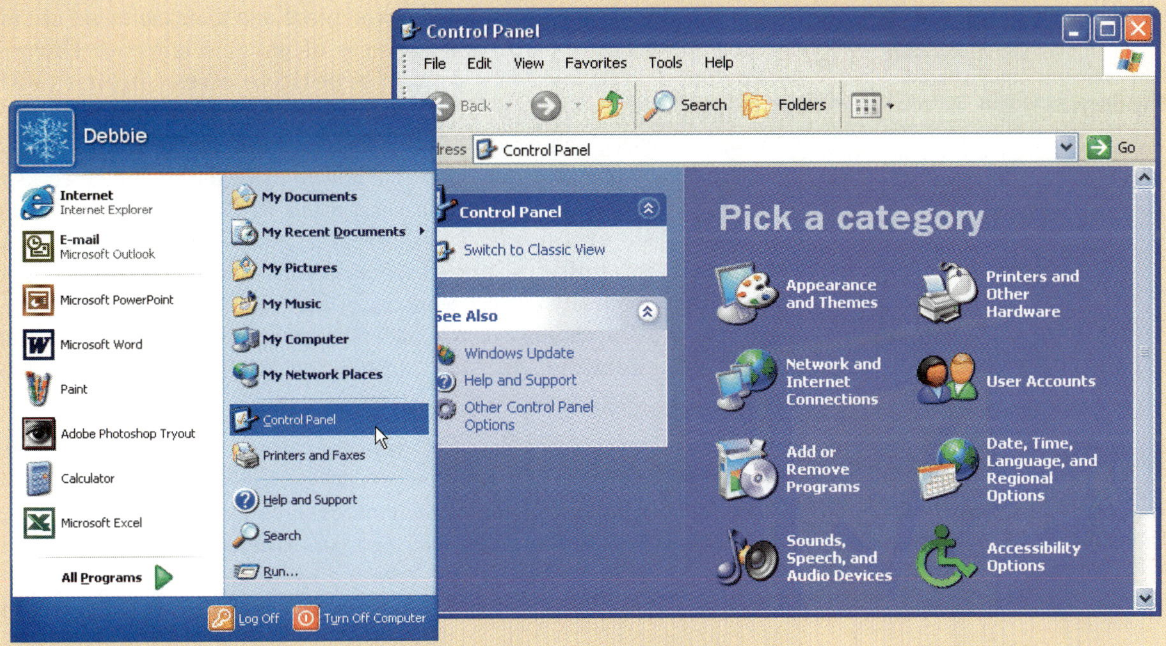


**^Control Panel**

Contains virtually all computer setting options, such as the Display Properties and Accessibility Options dialog boxes shown below

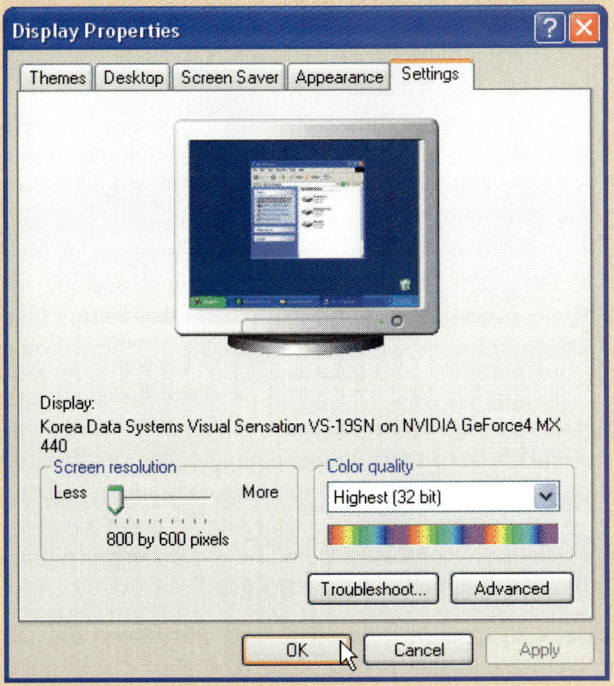


**^Display Properties**

Include changing text size and color, background colors, and screen resolution

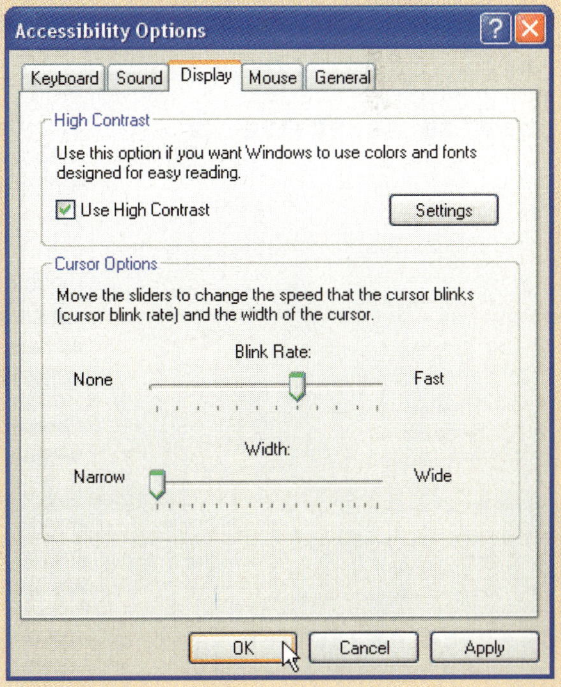


**^Accessibility Options**

Include StickyKeys, SoundSentry, High Contrast, MouseKeys, and more

# SUMMARY

**CHAPTER OBJECTIVE 1**

Understand the concerns and potential risks regarding physical health and computer use.

## Staying Healthy at Home and On the Job

Since the entry of computers into the workplace and their increased use in our society, they have been blamed for a variety of physical ailments. **Carpal tunnel syndrome (CTS)** and other types of **repetitive stress injuries (RSIs)** have been linked to high computer use. **Computer vision syndrome (CVS)**, eyestrain, fatigue, backaches, and headaches are other possible physical risks related to computer use. **Ergonomics** is the science of how to make the computer workspace, hardware, and environment fit the individual using it. Common types of **ergonomic devices** include **ergonomic keyboards**, **ergonomic mice**, **keyboard drawers**, **document holders**, **antiglare screens**, and **wrist rests**. In addition to using an ergonomically correct workspace, users should use good posture, take frequent rest breaks, alternate tasks, and take other common-sense precautions. For portable PCs, **docking stations** can be used to allow easy connections to more ergonomically correct hardware.

**CHAPTER OBJECTIVE 2**

Describe some possible emotional health risks surrounding the use of computers.

In addition to physical health issues, the extensive use of computers and related technology in the home and office has raised concerns about emotional health. The *stress* of keeping up with ever-changing technology, layoffs, always being in touch, fear of being out of touch, information overload, and **burnout** are all possible emotional problems related to computer use. Taking a break, reevaluating your schedule, and taking good care of yourself can help to avoid or reduce the stress that these problems may cause.

Computer or Internet *addiction* or *compulsion*, sometimes referred to as *computer addiction disorder (CAD)* or *Internet addiction disorder (IAD)*, refers to not being able to stop using computers or the Internet, or to the problems that their use creates in a user's personal or professional life. It can affect users of any age and is treated similarly to other addictions.

**CHAPTER OBJECTIVE 3**

Explain what is meant by the "digital divide."

## Is There Equal Access to Technology?

The **digital divide** refers to the gap between those who have access to computers and communications technology and those who do not. There can be a digital divide within a country or between countries. In the U.S., studies show that the digital divide may be lessening as people of every income, education, age, race, ethnicity, and gender continue to go online at increased rates. However, individuals living in low-income households or having little education still trail the national average for computer use. In addition to having access at all, research indicates that factors such as race, income, age, and education influence the types of activities performed on a computer.

Globally, the digital divide separates countries with access to technology from those without access to technology. The U.S. has a much higher computer use rate than the rest of the world. There are programs in place to try to bring computers, Internet access, and basic technology to developing countries. One example is the *Simputer* recently introduced in India. In addition, corporations and non-profit organizations are sponsoring a variety of programs designed to bridge the gap.

**CHAPTER OBJECTIVE 4**

Discuss the impact factors such as income, race, education, and physical disabilities may have on computer access and use.

Research suggests that people with disabilities tend to use computers and the Internet at rates less than the average population. Part of the reason may be because some types of conventional hardware—such as keyboards and monitors—are difficult to use with some types of physical conditions. **Assistive technology** includes hardware and software that makes conventional PC systems easier for users with disabilities to use.

Examples of *assistive input devices* include **Braille keyboards**, *keyguards*, *one-handed keyboards*, **voice-recognition systems**, and scanners with **optical character recognition (OCR)** capabilities built in. *Switches* can be used to perform some keyboard and mouse functions, and alternate pointing devices—such as *head-pointing systems*—can be used instead of a mouse. *Assistive output devices* include **screen readers**, **Braille displays**, and **Braille printers**. In order to be compatible with screen readers, Web pages need to use features such as *alternative text descriptions* for graphics and descriptive hyperlinks.

**CHAPTER OBJECTIVE 5**

List some types of assistive hardware that can be used by individuals with physical disabilities.

## Environmental Concerns

Many people also worry about environmental issues related to computer use, such as high energy usage and the massive amounts of paper computer use generates. **Green computing** refers to using computers in an environmentally friendly manner. It can include using hardware approved by an **eco-label** system, such as **ENERGY STAR** in the U.S. Environmentally friendly computers are just starting to come on the market, and alternate-powered hardware is expected to be introduced sometime in the future. **Electronic paper (e-paper)** is another developing product, which uses *electronic ink* to display text and images on plastic sheets of "paper" that can be erased and reused.

**CHAPTER OBJECTIVE 6**

Suggest some ways computer users can practice "green computing" and properly dispose of obsolete computer equipment.

In addition to practicing green computing when buying and using computer equipment, obsolete equipment should be reused whenever possible. Computer equipment that is still functioning may be able to be donated and refurbished for additional use, and toner and ink cartridges can often be refilled and reused. Hardware that cannot be reused should be recycled, if possible, or properly disposed of if not, so it does not end up as hazardous e-trash in landfills in this or another country.

## BALANCING ACT

### INTERNET ACCESS: LUXURY OR NECESSITY?

A *luxury* can be defined as something that is an indulgence, rather than a necessity. Most people in the world would view such items as food, shelter, and water as necessities. In the U.S., many would likely add electricity, indoor plumbing, and, possibly, telephone service to that list. But about 2.5 billion people in the world have no access to electricity, let alone indoor plumbing or telephone service. This opens up an interesting question: How can one item—such as electricity—be a luxury for some and a necessity for others? The answer lies in the fact that what we view as a necessity tends to evolve over time as access to that item improves. For example, think of telephone use in the U.S. One century ago, it was rare to have a telephone. Fifty years ago, many people had party lines. A decade or two ago it was uncommon to meet someone who did not have a telephone. Now it is quite rare.

Some of the reason for these types of transitions is access—when an item becomes available at an affordable cost. Another contributing factor seems to be the way an item is integrated into society. If an item becomes critical to the daily tasks of the general public, then it changes from being viewed as a luxury item to being thought of as a necessity. For instance, many individuals are beginning to view cell phones, pagers, and Internet connections as necessities. Internet use has expanded dramatically in the United States in recent years, with over half of the population now online. But while most people would agree that the Internet offers many conveniences, the question remains: Is it a necessity—that is, essential for existence? For instance, are there activities that must be performed online? If so, what about the other half of the population that doesn't have Internet access? How does this lack of Internet access affect them?

**YOUR TURN**

Give some thought to whether or not Internet access is a luxury or necessity in the United States, and then answer the following questions.

1. What products or services do you view as necessities? Did you include computers or Internet access? If not, do you think you might list these as necessities five years from now? Why or why not?
2. In order to be viewed as a necessity, must Internet access involve some activity that can only be performed online? Or can Internet access be viewed as a necessity even if there is an alternative method for accomplishing the same tasks you might accomplish using the Internet? Why or why not?
3. Common marketing wisdom is to position your products or services as necessities and not as luxury purchases. In other words, they should be marketed as very necessary solutions to very real problems. Have computers and Internet access been marketed in the U.S. as luxuries or necessities?
4. Research indicates that people with low incomes, low levels of education, of Hispanic or African descent, or with disabilities are less likely to have Internet access. If Internet access eventually becomes mandatory for certain activities—such as voting or taking college classes—whose responsibility is it to get the rest of the nation online? Should the government subsidize Internet access, or is it each American's responsibility to gain access to products deemed necessary in our country? Explain.
5. There will likely always be some individuals who will never use a computer or the Internet, just as there are some individuals in this country who choose to live without electricity or indoor plumbing. How is the necessity status of a product or service affected if some individuals choose to live without it?

## KEY TERMS

**Instructions:** Match each key term on the left with the definition on the right that best describes it.

**a. assistive technology**

**b. Braille display**

**c. Braille keyboard**

**d. burnout**

**e. carpal tunnel syndrome**

**f. digital divide**

**g. docking station**

**h. document holder**

**i. eco-label**

**j. electronic paper (e-paper)**

**k. ENERGY STAR**

**l. ergonomic keyboard**

**m. ergonomic mouse**

**n. ergonomics**

**o. green computing**

**p. keyboard drawer**

**q. optical character recognition (OCR)**

**r. repetitive stress injury**

**s. screen reader**

**t. voice-recognition system**

**1.** ______ A certification, often by a government agency, that identifies a device as meeting minimal environmental performance specifications.

**2.** ______ A clamp or other device, commonly attached to a monitor or resting on a desk, that holds documents used for computer input.

**3.** ______ A device that connects a portable PC to conventional hardware, such as a keyboard, mouse, monitor, and printer.

**4.** ______ A drawer attached to a desk onto which a keyboard can be placed.

**5.** ______ A keyboard consisting of Braille letters and symbols.

**6.** ______ A keyboard that is designed to lessen the strain on the user's hands and wrists.

**7.** ______ A mouse that is designed for more comfortable use by extensive mouse users.

**8.** ______ A painful and crippling condition affecting the hands and wrist that can be caused by computer use.

**9.** ______ A program developed by the U.S. Department of Energy and Environmental Protection Agency to encourage the development of energy-saving devices.

**10.** ______ A device that usually attaches to a computer and transfers all output displayed on the computer monitor to Braille form.

**11.** ______ A state of fatigue or frustration usually brought on by overwork.

**12.** ______ A system, typically consisting of software and a microphone, that enables a computer to recognize spoken input.

**13.** ______ A type of injury, such as carpal tunnel syndrome, that is caused by performing the same physical movements over and over again.

**14.** ______ Hardware and software specifically designed for use by individuals with physical disabilities.

**15.** ______ Reusable, erasable "paper," typically comprised of thin plastic.

**16.** ______ Software that reads aloud what is displayed on a computer screen.

**17.** ______ The ability of a scanning device to recognize written or typed characters on a paper-based document and convert it to electronic form as text, not an image.

**18.** ______ The gap between those who have access to technology and those who don't.

**19.** ______ The science of fitting a work environment to the people who work there.

**20.** ______ The use of computers in an environmentally friendly manner.

## SELF-QUIZ

Answers for the self-quiz appear at the end of the book.

### True/False

Instructions: Circle **T** if the statement is true or **F** if the statement is false.

**T F 1.** Carpal tunnel syndrome can be caused by using a computer keyboard.

**T F 2.** An antiglare screen fits over a monitor to enlarge the text for easier reading.

**T F 3.** As computer use has become more common in this country, the potential for stress related to computer use has decreased.

**T F 4.** Assistive technology is hardware and software designed to help all beginning computer users learn how to use a computer.

**T F 5.** Many computer components today contain potentially dangerous materials.

### Completion

**Instructions:** Supply the missing words to complete the following statements.

**6.** If a hardware product is described as being ______________, it is designed to be more comfortable and safe to use than conventional hardware.

**7.** To keep documents close to a monitor for more comfortable reference when word processing, a(n) ______________ can be used.

**8.** Overwork or trying to reach unrealistic goals can result in an extreme state of stress called ______________.

**9.** Craving more and more time at the computer can be an indicator of computer ______________.

**10.** The ______________ can be used to describe discrepancies in access to technology by individuals within a country, as well as to compare access from country to country.

**11.** The ______________ Act requires companies with 15 or more employees to make reasonable accommodations for individuals with disabilities.

**12.** ______________ keyboards, displays, and printers allow blind computer users to input data and understand output using their fingers.

**13.** If an image on a Web page doesn't have a(n) ______________ description assigned to it, screen reader software won't be able to understand it.

**14.** Products in the U.S. that are ______________ compliant meet or exceed the minimum federal guidelines for reduced energy consumption.

**15.** Erasable, reusable material used to display computer output in a mobile format is called ______________.

## PROJECTS

### 1. E-paper

YOUR OPINION

The chapter Trends In box discussed electronic paper (e-paper)—an erasable, reusable alternative to traditional paper and ink for computer output. Although currently in its early stages, some experts predict that it will become a viable product for many personal applications in the very near future. One of the first widespread applications is expected to be newspapers, followed shortly by office printouts. The obvious benefit of e-paper is reducing the use of traditional paper and ink and the resources needed to create and dispose of paper. Two disadvantages at the current time are limited life and expense.

For this project, consider the issue of environmentally friendly products, such as e-paper and green computers, and write a short essay expressing your opinion regarding whether these types of products will become widely used by the general public anytime in the near future. Often, these environmentally friendly products are more expensive than their less-friendly counterparts. Do you think businesses or individuals will choose to use these types of products if the only incentive is a cleaner environment? Or will there need to be an economic incentive, such as savings on the cost of paper and ink surpassing the cost of using e-paper? Submit your opinion on this issue to your instructor in the form of a short paper, not more than two pages in length.

### 2. Recycle or Trash?

INDEPENDENT RESEARCH

As mentioned in the chapter, most obsolete computer equipment eventually ends up in a landfill somewhere, although there may be alternative actions that could be taken instead.

For this project, research what options would be available to you to discard the following: 1) a 10-year old computer that is no longer functioning; 2) a 4-year old computer that still works but is too slow for your needs; 3) a used-up toner cartridge for a laser printer. Check with your local schools and charitable organizations to see if they accept any of these items as donations. Contact your trash disposal company or local dump to see what their regulations are for accepting computer equipment. Also, check with two computer manufacturers to see if they have a trade-in or recycling program, and with vendors selling recharged toner cartridges to see if they accept a trade-in with an order. Summarize your findings in a two- to three-page paper. Be sure to include any costs associated with the disposal options you found, as well as your recommendations for getting rid of each of these three items.

### 3. Ergonomic Workspaces

HANDS-ON

Some aspects of an ergonomic workspace, such as a comfortable chair and nonglaring light, may feel good right from the beginning. Others, such as using an ergonomic keyboard or wrist rest, may take a little getting used to.

For this project, find at least one local store that has some type of ergonomic equipment—such as adjustable office chairs, desks with keyboard drawers or ergonomic keyboards—on display that you can try out. Test each piece of available equipment, adjusting it as needed, and evaluate how comfortable the equipment seems. Next, go to your usual computer workspace and use the equipment and hardware located there. Do you notice any difference between the ergonomic equipment and your usual equipment? Are there any adjustments you should make or any new equipment you would need to buy to make your workspace more comfortable and healthy? Make a note of any changes you could make for free (such as adjusting the furniture, moving the computer components or desk, and changing the lighting), as well as a list of anything you would need to purchase and the estimated cost. Prepare a short summary of your findings to turn in to your instructor.

### 4. Green Computing

There are several easy things any computer user can do to practice green computing. For instance, most operating systems have energy-saving options that can be enabled, such as turning off the monitor and hard drive when the PC has been idle for a specified period of time—called putting the computer into sleep mode. To save paper, many programs have a print preview option that can be used before printing to make sure the document will print as expected and to determine the pages to be printed.

For this project, first explore the power-saving features of the computer that you use most often. In Windows, open the Control Panel using the Start menu and look for a *Power Management* option. Select that option to find where you can specify when the monitor and hard drive will be turned off and record the current settings. Next, open any word processing program (such as Word or WordPerfect) available on your PC. Either open an existing document that is at least two pages long or enter enough text to fill up two pages (the text doesn't have to make sense, just fill up two pages). Find the *Print Preview* option on the File menu to see what the document will look like when printed. Are there any changes you would make to the document before printing, such as changing the margin size or adjusting a page break?

Close your word processing program (don't save your file) and open your Web browser. Go to a news site (such as CNN.com or MSNBC.com) and click on a hyperlink to a news story. Assuming that you would want to print the story for future reference, use your browser's File menu to see if it has a *Print Preview* feature. If so, preview the document to see if all the pages would need to be printed (sometimes the last page of a Web page printout doesn't contain any useful information) or if the page looks strange (Web pages that are organized using *frames* sometimes just print the frame that is currently selected—such as just the navigation bar on the left edge of the screen). Close the preview screen and select *Print* from your browser's File menu (don't use the Print toolbar button). If the Web page will print on more than one page, find the appropriate option on the Print dialog box that prints just selected pages of the document. If the page is divided into frames, see if the Print dialog box has an option to print the entire page as it appears on the screen (if not, you'll need to close the Print dialog box, click in the desired frame, and then return to the Print dialog box before continuing). Use the Print dialog box to print just the first page of the Web page. Prepare a short summary of your work to turn in to your instructor along with the first page of the news article you printed, describing what you discovered and which, if any, of these techniques you plan to use on a regular basis.

**GROUP PRESENTATION**

### 5. Internet Addiction

Computer and Internet addiction can happen to computer users of all ages, races, income levels, and occupations. As with other addictions, computer or Internet use is said to be a problem when it adversely affects your life, such as causing problems with your health, your family, or your job.

For this project, form a group to research and discuss Internet addiction. Locate at least two organizations that have information about Internet addiction, including its typical causes, symptoms, and treatment. Do the organizations agree? Designate one member of your group to contact your local mental health organization or school health center and see if Internet addiction is considered an actual mental health condition and, if so, what types of counseling and other treatment are available in your area. Do the members of your group believe this condition should be referred to as an addiction? Have any of the members in your group noticed behavior exhibited by a friend or relative that might suggest the beginnings of an addiction to any type of technology? Are there precautions individuals can take to avoid becoming addicted to the Internet? Do you think the possibility of addiction will increase or decrease in the future?

Share your findings with the class in the form of a short presentation. The presentation should not exceed 10 minutes and should make use of one or more presentation aids such as the chalkboard, handouts, overhead transparencies, or a computer-based slide presentation (your instructor may provide additional requirements). Your group may also be asked to submit a summary of the presentation to your instructor.

### 6. Assistive Computing

As discussed in the chapter, there are a variety of assistive devices that physically challenged individuals can use to make computing easier and more efficient.

For this project, form a group to research assistive technology. As a group, select one type of disability, such as being blind, deaf, paraplegic, quadriplegic, or having the use of only one arm or hand. Research the hardware and software options that could be used with a new PC for someone with the selected disability. Make a list of potential limitations of any standard PC hardware and the assistive hardware and software that would be appropriate for this individual to use. Research each possibility, comparing such factors as ease of use, cost, and availability. As a group, determine the best computer system for this hypothetical situation.

Share your findings with the class in the form of a short presentation. The presentation should not exceed 10 minutes and should make use of one or more presentation aids such as the chalkboard, handouts, overhead transparencies, or a computer-based slide presentation (your instructor may provide additional requirements). Your group may also be asked to submit a summary of the presentation to your instructor.

### 7. Rural Broadband

Citizens who live in rural areas typically have less access to broadband Internet than those in more highly populated areas. Maryland's Speaker of the House Casper R. Taylor views this as the real digital divide. Without broadband, he believes that "our kids are not going to have the advantage of urbanized society going into the future if we're disconnected from the rest of the world...If we don't accomplish this, we are clearly creating a second-class society." The accompanying video clip discusses bringing broadband Internet access to his small rural home town of Cumberland.

After watching the video, think about the importance of broadband Internet and whose responsibility it is to provide it. If a region has only 56K dial-up service, does that really put it at a disadvantage? Is the digital divide more about separating those who have access to technology such as the Internet and those who don't, or is it about the quality of that technology? What about the government's role—should the government provide the necessary infrastructure (as in Cumberland) to ensure an appropriate level of Internet access to all U.S. citizens? If not, how will the digital divide within the U.S. be eliminated? Will it ever be eliminated?

**Express your viewpoint:** What impact does access or lack of access to broadband Internet have on individuals, and is it the government's responsibility to make sure it is available to all?

Use the video clip and the questions previously asked as the foundation for your response. Your instructor will direct you to be prepared to discuss your position (either in class, via an online class discussion group, or in a class chat room), or to write a short paper stating and supporting your viewpoint on the issue. You may also be asked to do research and provide resources to support your point of view.

**VIDEO VIEWPOINT**

**ONLINE VIDEO**

To view the Rural Broadband video clip, go to www.course.com/morley2003/ch7

# EMERGING TECHNOLOGIES

## OUTLINE

**Overview**

**The PC of the Future**

- Nanotechnology
- Quantum and Optical Computers
- Holographic and Multilayer Storage
- Greener Hardware

**Artificial Intelligence (AI)**

- What Is Artificial Intelligence?
- AI Applications

**Virtual Reality (VR)**

- What Is Virtual Reality?
- VR Applications

**Technological Advances in Medicine**

- Electronic Implants
- Robot-Assisted Surgery
- Telemedicine

**Technological Advances in the Military**

- Smart Guns, Bullets, and Bombs
- Surveillance Tools
- Improved Uniforms and Gear

**Societal Implications of Emerging Technology**

## OBJECTIVES

**After completing this chapter, you will be able to:**

- Discuss some emerging PC technologies—such as nanotechnology, quantum and optical computers, and holographic and multilayer storage—and speculate as to the makeup and appearance of the PC of the future.
- Explain what is meant by the term artificial intelligence (AI) and list some AI applications.
- Discuss the concept of and some applications for virtual reality (VR).
- List some new and upcoming technological advances in medicine.
- Name some new and upcoming technological advances in the military.
- Discuss some potential societal implications of emerging technologies.

# CHAPTER 8

## OVERVIEW

No study of computers would be complete without a look to the future. The rapid technological advancements that we've seen in the last few decades have been extraordinary, but some believe the best is yet to come. New advances are being made all the time in areas such as computer hardware and software, consumer and business applications, medicine, the military, and the environment. In general, technology is getting friendlier and more integrated into our daily lives. For instance, imagine the following scenario: You walk up to your front door and gain access simply by your presence. When you enter a room, the lights, stereo system, and digital artwork on the walls are changed automatically to reflect your preferences. Your refrigerator and pantry keep up-to-the-moment inventories of their content, and your closet automatically selects outfits for you based on the weather and your schedule for the day. Sounds like something out of a science fiction movie? Actually all the technologies just mentioned are either available or in development at the present time.

While many of us are excited to see what new applications and technological improvements the future will bring and what computers, the Internet, and other technologies evolve into next, we shouldn't lose sight of the possibility that some future applications may not turn out the way we expect or may actually have a negative impact on our society. One of the biggest challenges in an era of rapidly changing technologies is evaluating the potential impact of new technology and trying to ensure that new products and services don't adversely affect our security, privacy, and safety.

This chapter focuses on a few selected emerging technologies that may impact our lives in the future. Topics include what the PC of the future may be like, artificial intelligence (AI), virtual reality (VR), and technological advances in medicine and in the military.

# THE PC OF THE FUTURE

While the exact makeup of future PCs is anyone's guess, it is expected that they will keep getting smaller, smarter, faster, more powerful, more user-friendly and, eventually, be driven primarily by a voice-input interface. Tomorrow's PCs will likely not even look like today's PCs—instead they may be built into walls, desks, appliances, clothing, and jewelry. Some examples of characteristics expected for the PCs of the future are illustrated in Figure 8-1; the Trends In box takes a look at another type of PC expected to become more commonplace soon—the *wearable PC*.

In addition to their changing appearance, computers and other devices are expected to continue to converge and take on multiple roles—such as being able to use a television screen to access a PC, make video telephone calls, control home systems, and watch downloaded TV shows and movies. Computers in the future may also be able to detect gestures and offer multisensory output, such as enabling users to see, hear, feel, taste, and smell output—a logical next step for e-commerce applications. Areas of expected growth in the more distant future are *nanotechnology*, *quantum* and *optical computers*, and *holographic* and *multilayer storage*. Computers will also likely become more environmentally friendly—*green*—in upcoming years.

**FIGURE 8-1**

**Examples of expected characteristics for PCs in the future**

**< Small and wearable PCs**

Computer size will continue to shrink and wearable PCs, such as the watch PC shown here, are likely to be more prominent in the future.

**> Flexible materials**

Computers and related components (such as the soft cell phone shown here) will likely be made out of flexible materials for easier portability and additional functionality.

**< Integrated PCs**

PCs are expected eventually to become integrated into a wide variety of appliances and furniture, such as the computer display built into this kitchen countertop.

## Nanotechnology

Today's process of forming integrated circuits (ICs) by imprinting patterns on semiconductor materials—called *lithography*—allows for circuits smaller than one micron (1,000 nanometers or one-millionth of a meter). A newer field of science—called **nanotechnology**—is working at the individual atomic and molecular levels to create computer chips and other components that are thousands of times smaller than conventional technologies permit. Researchers at several organizations—such as IBM, Motorola, Dow Chemical, Xerox, and Hewlett-Packard—are working to create nanometer-sized products and materials. Some prototypes include a miniscule device (about one-fiftieth the width of a human hair) that can measure small amounts of electric charge; a single switch that can be turned on and off like a transistor, but is made out of a single organic molecule; and a miniature hard drive that holds 20 GB of data and is read by heads only a few nanometers thick.

Future implications of nanotechnology breakthroughs include microscopic robots that can enter the bloodstream and perform tests or irradiate cancerous tumors, molecular circuits that can function similar to today's silicon-based

## TRENDS IN... WEARABLE PCS

Like most other electronic devices, computing devices are shrinking. For example, the same computing power that used to require an entire room of electronics and machinery now fits into a computer that can be held in the palm of a hand. As computer components get smaller, the possibility of creating PCs that can be worn on the body or embedded in clothing becomes more plausible. Already we have watches that can perform some of the functions found on handheld PCs, such as view Web pages, check e-mail, give GPS navigational readings, take digital photos, or play MP3 files. Smart mobile phones and portable PCs that fit into a pocket can provide full Internet service.

Going a step further is the truly **wearable PC**. In a work-oriented wearable PC, the CPU and hard drive are contained in a small unit, which is typically worn on a belt. A *microdisplay*—a tiny display screen often fitted into glasses or goggles—is used to display images close to the eye, which simulates viewing them on a large monitor. Instructions can be entered into the PC by using a wrist-worn keyboard or through a voice-input system. Wearable PCs are currently used by workers in a variety of industries—such as warehouse and construction workers, police and fire personnel, delivery and other types of service workers, telephone repair personnel, and other positions where hands-free computing and communications is an advantage (see Figure 8-2). For business travelers, a wearable PC is much easier to carry around and use on a cramped airplane than a notebook PC; the eyepiece screen also allows one to work privately on documents in public places.

Wearable PCs designed for consumer use have been introduced recently. One unit, about the size of a Sony Walkman, is designed to slip into a coat pocket or be worn on a belt and contains a 128 MHz processor, 32 megabytes of RAM, a compact flash slot, and a USB port. The PC uses the Windows CE operating system software and comes with versions of Pocket Word, Pocket Outlook, Internet Explorer, and Windows Media Player.

Some of the limitations of wearable PCs at the current time are limited battery life; corded connections between the system unit, eyepiece, and other components; unfamiliar appearance; and less-than-perfect voice-input systems. However, as PC components and related technology continue to shrink and as technology improves, we all may end up with a ready-to-wear PC.

**FIGURE 8-2**

A wearable PC gives workers hands-free access to data and communications.

circuits but that are much, much smaller and much more efficient, and memory and storage media significantly smaller and denser than is currently possible. Nanotechnology is also expected to eventually lead to computers that are small enough to be woven into the fibers of clothing or embedded into paint and other materials. In addition, nanotechnology may eventually solve much of the toxic waste problem associated with e-trash by being able to rearrange dangerous components at the atomic level to become inert substances.

## Quantum and Optical Computers

Computers a few decades from now will likely use technology very different from the silicon chips and electrical bits and bytes we're accustomed to today. In addition to being miniature—based on nanotechnology—two other viable possibilities for the future include *quantum computers* and *optical computers.*

### Quantum Computers

The idea of **quantum computing** emerged in the 1970s when scientists were pondering the fundamental limits of computation and *Moore's Law*—a prediction made by Gordon Moore, the cofounder of Intel, in 1965 that the number of transistors per square inch on a chip would continue to double every year or so for the foreseeable future. Still applicable today—transistor density now doubles about

**FIGURE 8-3**

The vial of liquid shown here contains the seven-qubit computer used by IBM researchers in 2001 to perform the most complicated quantum computation to date—factoring the number 15.

every 18 months—Moore's Law has been expanded to describe the amount of time it takes computer components to double in capacity or speed. Looking towards the future, some scientists envision that the amount of circuitry packed onto silicon chips will eventually reach a point where individual elements will be no larger than a few atoms. Consequently, scientists have begun working on applying the principles of quantum physics and quantum mechanics to computers, going beyond traditional physics to work at the subatomic level.

Quantum computers differ from conventional computers in that they utilize atoms or nuclei working together as quantum bits or *qubits*; qubits function simultaneously as both the computer's processor and memory. Each qubit can represent much more than just the two states (0 and 1) available to today's electronic bits. A qubit can even represent many states at one time. Theoretically quantum computers will able to perform calculations exponentially faster than conventional computers and perform operations on multiple numbers in parallel in one step.

At the present time quantum computers are in the pioneering stage, but working quantum computers do exist. For instance, the researchers at IBM's Almaden Research Center in San Jose, California created a seven-qubit quantum computer (comprised of the nuclei of seven atoms, which can interact with each other and be programmed by radio frequency pulses) that can successfully factor the number 15 (see Figure 8-3). Although this is not a complicated computation for a conventional computer, the fact that it was possible for a person to supply a quantum computer with the problem and have it compute the correct answer is viewed as a highly significant event in the area of quantum computer research. Quantum computers in the future may consist of a thimbleful of liquid whose atoms are used to perform calculations as instructed by an external device. A primary application area for quantum computers is expected to be encryption and code-breaking.

### Optical Computers

*Optical* components, such as the fiber optic cables commonly used as Internet and communications backbone cables, use light waves to transmit data. *Optical chips*, which emit less heat and can move data much more quickly than conventional chips, are in development. A possibility for the future is the **optical computer**—a computer that uses light, such as from laser beams or infrared beams—to perform digital computations. Because light beams don't interfere with each other, optical computers could be much smaller than electronic PCs.

Currently being researched by NASA and other organizations, the biggest expected advantage is increased computation speed. According to Hossin Abduldayem, a senior research scientist at NASA's Marshall Space Flight Center in Huntsville, Alabama, an optical computer could solve a problem in one hour that would take an electronic computer 11 years to solve. While some researchers are working on developing an all-optical computer, others believe that a mix of optical and electronic components—or an *opto-electronic computer*—may be the best bet for the future.

## Holographic and Multilayer Storage

Storing information in three dimensions (3D) is far from a new idea. For example, today's DVDs use two layers to store more data on the same size disc as a CD (which uses only one layer). However, two emerging storage technologies go even further.

Currently in its first generation, the *fluorescent multilayer disc (FMD)* is an optical disc with many fluorescent layers. Today's FMD discs use between 5 and 21 layers and hold up to 140 GB of data; future discs are expected to use up to 100 layers and hold somewhere between 450 GB and 1 TB of data. Instead of using a reflective coating like CDs and DVDs, FMD discs are transparent and are coated with fluorescent dye. When read by an *FMD drive*, the fluorescent light is emitted at a different wavelength than the source light and the data can be retrieved. One of the first commercial applications expected for FMD discs is for high definition movies and other multimedia content.

A promising new storage technology being researched by companies such as IBM, Lucent Technologies, and Imation is *holographic storage* (see Figure 8-4). Unlike conventional storage methods that record data only on the surface of a disc, holographic data storage records through the entire thickness of the material; in fact, thousands of holograms can be stored in the same location throughout the entire depth of the medium. Similar to other optical discs, lasers are used to record the data, but data is stored much more densely and can be stored and retrieved very rapidly (up to 1 million bits can be written or read in a single flash of light). Some predictions include a future capacity of 1 TB of data—the equivalent of over 1,000 of today's CDs—on a crystal the size of a sugar cube.  Potential applications for holographic data storage systems include satellite communications, military operations, high-speed digital libraries, and image processing for medical, video, and military purposes.

**FIGURE 8-4**

**Scientists are working to develop and market high-capacity storage solutions; shown here is a lab test of a holographic drive system.**

## Greener Hardware

It is expected that the PC of the future will include *greener*—more environmentally friendly—hardware than today. The NEC PowerMate Eco, which became available in 2002, was the first green PC designed for general use; if it's successful, other manufacturers are sure to follow suit. As discussed in Chapter 7, this PC uses a low power CPU and flat-panel monitor for reduced power consumption, has no internal fan and a quiet hard drive to reduce noise pollution, uses a lead-free motherboard, and has a case made out of recyclable plastic. Some other future trends for greener hardware are listed next and shown in Figure 8-5.

- *Smaller and thinner display devices*—use less power than conventional CRTs and will eventually become the norm. For portable applications, displays similar to the prototype *flexible organic light-emitting diode (FOLED)* display shown in Figure 8-5 may be used.
- *Smaller and more energy-efficient PCs*—tend to use less power than larger PCs. If tiny devices (such as smart phones, watch PCs, and wearable PCs) become more commonly used as conventional PC alternatives, energy consumption due to PC use may be reduced.
- *Alternate powered devices*—include solar powered PCs and other devices that can be powered by the sun or hand power are used currently where dependable electricity isn't available, such as in developing countries and while outdoors. Before alternative power sources become the norm for everyday use, they must become more stable, dependable, and capable of producing sustainable power.

**ONLINE TUTORIAL**

For an online look at how solar power can be used with computers, go to www.course.com/morley2003/ch8

**FIGURE 8-5**

**Green hardware for the future**

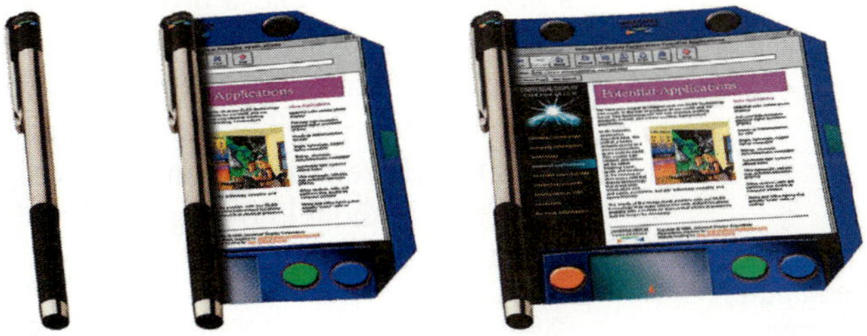

**< Small displays**

The roll-up FOLED screen shown here is an example of a thin, energy-efficient portable display.

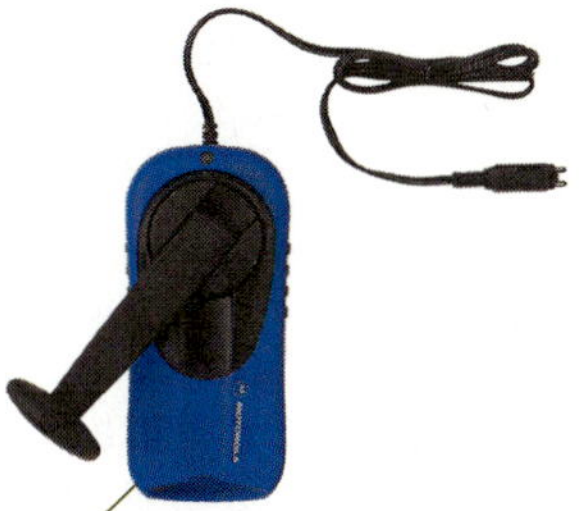

Hand-powered charger

Solar-powered charger

**> Alternate power**

Hand-powered or solar-powered chargers can be used to power a cell phone, GPS device, or portable PC when electricity isn't available or for consumers who would prefer to use an alternative source of power.

# ARTIFICIAL INTELLIGENCE (AI)

Computers are continually becoming faster and smarter. Although they can't yet think completely on their own, computers and software have become more sophisticated and are being programmed to act in an increasingly intelligent manner.

## What Is Artificial Intelligence?

According to John McCarthy, who coined the term in 1956 and is considered by many to be one of the fathers of **artificial intelligence (AI)**, AI is "the science and engineering of making intelligent machines." In other words, AI is concerned with creating intelligent devices controlled by intelligent software programs—in other words, machines that think and act like humans. Researchers have been working in the field of artificial intelligence for decades; one of the first researchers, English mathematician Alan Turing, gave a lecture on it in 1947.

While some believe that no machine could ever be considered intelligent and true AI will never be reached, many experts disagree. Alan Turing argued in a 1950 article that if a machine could successfully pretend to be human to a knowledgeable observer then it should be considered intelligent. To illustrate this idea, Turing developed a test—later called the *Turing Test*—in which one observer interacts with both a computer and a human being electronically (originally by teletype and later by computer). During the test, the observer asks both the computer and the human questions in writing, evaluates their written responses, and tries to identify which answers came from the computer and which came from the human. Turing argued that if the computer could repeatedly fool the observer into thinking it was human, then it should be viewed as intelligent. Many Turing Test contests have been held over the years, but so far no computer has passed the test because none have come close to fooling the judges consistently.

In 1990 Dr. Hugh Loebner initiated the Loebner Prize, pledging a grand prize of $100,000 and a solid gold medal for the first computer whose responses to a Turing Test were indistinguishable from a human's. A contest is held every year, awarding a prize of $2,000 and a bronze medal to the most human computer, but so far the gold medal has not been awarded. Although the Turing Test is interesting and is still providing grounds for research today, most experts agree that the Turing Test provides only one possible test of computer intelligence. These experts argue that there could be different definitions of intelligence and a machine could still be considered intelligent without knowing enough about humans to imitate a human.

**FIGURE 8-6**

**In 1997, IBM's Deep Blue computer (operated here by IBM Research Scientist Murray Campbell, right) beat chess master Garry Kasparov in a chess match.**

Some of the initial advances in AI were made in the area of game playing. Chess, for example, has been a popular challenge for computer programmers—probably because chess is a complicated game that takes strategic planning on the part of both players. Many believed a computer could never play chess as well as a human; this idea was supported by the fact that early chess-playing programs were easily defeated by amateur chess players. Eventually, as computers became more powerful and AI software became more sophisticated, chess-playing programs began to be able to play chess at the Master level. In 1996, IBM's Deep Blue computer won 2 of 6 games in a chess match with World Chess Champion Garry Kasparov. A landmark moment in AI history occurred in 1997 when Deep Blue beat Kasparov in a rematch (see Figure 8-6), winning the match 3½ to 2½ (three of the six games ended in a draw).

## AI Applications

Today's AI applications contain some aspect of artificial intelligence, although they tend to mimic human intelligence instead of display pure intelligence. Technological advances will undoubtedly help these AI applications continue to evolve and become more intelligent and sophisticated in the future. While many welcome the idea of more intelligent computers to help humans, some foresee a future where humans and computers may eventually merge together. Not surprisingly, there are many others that find that scenario frightening and very objectionable. Just as the debate about what constitutes intelligence in non-humans continues, so will the debate about how far we as a society should go into the area of artificial intelligence. AI applications that exist in some form today include *intelligent agents*, *natural language systems*, *expert systems*, *neural networks*, *and robotics*.

### Intelligent Agents

**Intelligent agents** are small programs that perform specific tasks, such as retrieving and delivering information as specified by the user, automating repetitive tasks, and helping to make a user's work environment more efficient or entertaining. Put another way, intelligent agents are *virtual assistants*. Intelligent agents typically can modify their behavior based on the user's actions, and are used extensively on the Web in addition to being built into operating systems, e-mail programs, Web browsers, application programs, and other products.

Some specific types of intelligent agents include the following:

- *Application assistants*—provide help or assistance for a particular application program, such as Microsoft Office's Office Assistant shown in Figure 8-7.
- *Search agents*—search for the information that you specify, gathering and compiling results from a variety of Web sources; can be used for general searching; finding people, music, or images; gathering news articles on specified subjects; etc.
- *Shopping bots*—search through thousands of online stores to find the best prices on the product that you specify; some can gather shipping costs and delivery information, as well (see the PriceGrabber.com shopping bot in Figure 8-7).
- *Entertainment bots*—can take a variety of forms; two of the most popular at the moment are in the form of a virtual pet or plant that you care for online, or in the form of an animated character that reads you your e-mail or plays a game with you. Because these programs are AI applications, they respond to your actions, such as a virtual pet or plant thriving or dying depending on your care, and an AI game opponent learning and adapting its game strategy based on previous games played (see the 20 questions game in Figure 8-7).

The potential wide-spread use of intelligent agents brings up some important social concerns. Will we rely on and trust intelligent agents too much and forget to use common sense to evaluate results? Will the use of intelligent agents by online stores to adjust product pricing according to the prices at competitors' Web sites lead to price fixing? Should software agents be used to carry out critical tasks, such as supplying intravenous medicine to hospital patients? Questions like these are sure to merit serious debate as the use of intelligent agents continues to grow.

**ONLINE TUTORIAL**

For an online look at various types of intelligent agents and how they can be used, go to www.course.com/morley2003/ch8

### Natural Language Systems

One of the greatest challenges that scientists in the field of AI face is finding a way for computer systems to communicate in *natural languages*—such as English, Spanish, French, and Japanese. This challenge is not easy to meet, because people have personalized ways of communicating and because the meanings of words vary according to the contexts in which they are used. Different people may pronounce the same word differently because of accents, personal styles of speech, and the unique quality of each person's voice. And even the same person may pronounce words differently at various times, such as when eating or suffering from a cold. Despite these roadblocks, researchers have made major strides toward designing computer programs that listen to and respond in natural languages—whether in spoken or in written context. **Natural language systems** are systems that enable the computer to understand natural language input.

**FIGURE 8-7**

**Examples of intelligent agents**

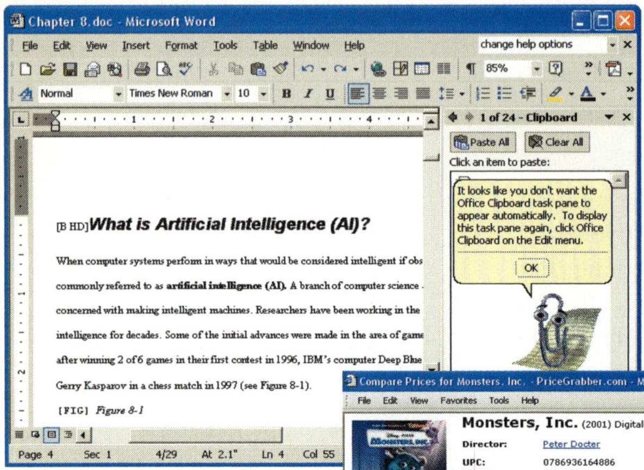


**❮ Application assistants**

The Office XP Office Assistant shown here makes suggestions based on the user's actions, in addition to being available to answer specific questions about how to use the program.

**❯ Shopping bots**

A shopping bot is used to gather price, tax, shipping, availability, and seller information for the product and ZIP code specified.

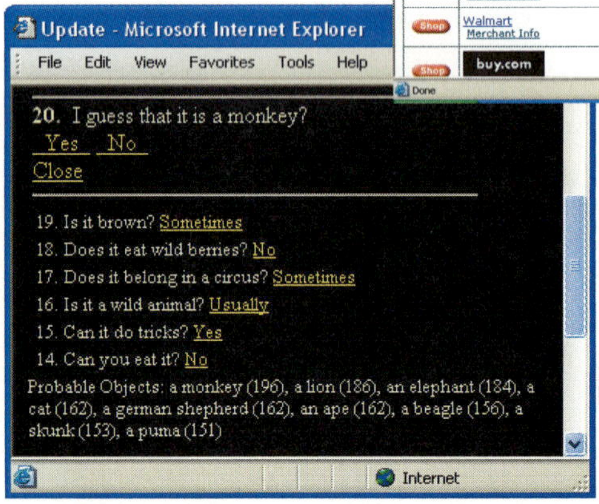


**❮ Entertainment bots**

This AI game of 20 questions is updated after each game to learn from the responses. Here, the program correctly identified the selected animal as a monkey after the 19th question, based on the user's responses.

One of the first commercial advances in natural language systems was in the form of the **voice-input system**—software (such as Dragon NaturallySpeaking and IBM ViaVoice) that, in conjunction with a microphone, can convert a user's spoken words into digital data. Early voice-input systems were used solely for dictation and the software required significant training, with users repeating supplied text until the system became able to recognize the patterns in their voices consistently. Some voice-input systems today can be used to issue commands to the computer, such as to open a particular program or save a document. Voice-input systems are also used in some telephone menu systems, in which users can select options and answer questions verbally, instead of having to press the telephone keypad. Specialty voice-input systems are even becoming available to assist in surgical procedures, such as to control robots, microscopes, and other electronic equipment. Although voice-input systems are still not perfect, they have come a long way and some people use them consistently as an alternative to the mouse and keyboard.

On the Web, natural language systems can be found on some search sites—such as Ask Jeeves—where users can type search requests in natural language sentences instead of using key terms and search operators. Some Web agents use natural language input to accept questions from visitors and provide them with customer service. As shown in Figure 8-8, sometimes these agents—called **chatterbots** when they also respond in natural languages—utilize animated characters that respond both verbally and with appropriate physical gestures to try to create the illusion that the exchange is taking place between two thinking, living entities. In addition to being used as Web site assistants, animated digital characters are also beginning to be used to deliver Web-based news and entertainment, as discussed in the Closer Look box.

## Expert Systems

**Expert systems** are software programs that perform tasks that would otherwise be performed by a human expert. For example, there are expert systems that can diagnose human illnesses, provide situational training for employees, make financial forecasts, schedule routes for delivery vehicles, and perform credit authorizations. Figure 8-9 shows a simplified example of how an expert system might work.

Some expert systems are designed to take the place of human experts, while others are designed to assist them. For instance, medical expert systems, which incorporate the knowledge and decision-making guidelines of some of the world's best physicians, are used to assist physicians when diagnosing their patients. To use such a system, the symptoms exhibited by a patient would be entered into the expert system. The program may then ask the attending health provider questions to obtain more specific information. By asking questions and comparing the responses to a large database of successfully diagnosed cases, the program can offer one or more possible diagnoses—possibly the same as the ones concluded by the attending physician, but perhaps also including other possibilities that the physician may not have thought of because the expert system has access to a wider base of knowledge.

Most expert systems consist of two main components: a database and a software program. The database part is commonly called a **knowledge base** and contains specific facts about the expert area and any rules that the expert system should use to make decisions based on those facts. For instance, an expert system used to authorize credit for credit card customers would have in its knowledge base facts about customers as well as rules, such as "Do not automatically authorize purchase if the customer has already made three purchases today." Generally, the knowledge base is jointly developed by a human expert and a specialized computer professional. The software program—called the **inference engine**—is used to apply the rules to the data stored in the knowledge base to reach decisions.

Expert systems can be built from scratch or by use of an *expert system shell*—a skeletal system that needs to be supplied with the expert knowledge and rules to be used with the system. Regardless of how an expert system is created, it is important to realize that its conclusions are based on the data and rules stored in its knowledge base, as well as the information provided by the users. If the data in the knowledge base is correct, the inference engine program is written correctly, and the user supplies honest, correct information in response to the questions posed or information requested by the expert system, the system will draw correct conclusions; if the knowledge base is wrong, the inference engine is faulty, or the user provides incorrect input, the system won't work properly.

**FIGURE 8-8**

Example of interacting with a Web-based chatterbot

**FIGURE 8-9**

How an expert system might work

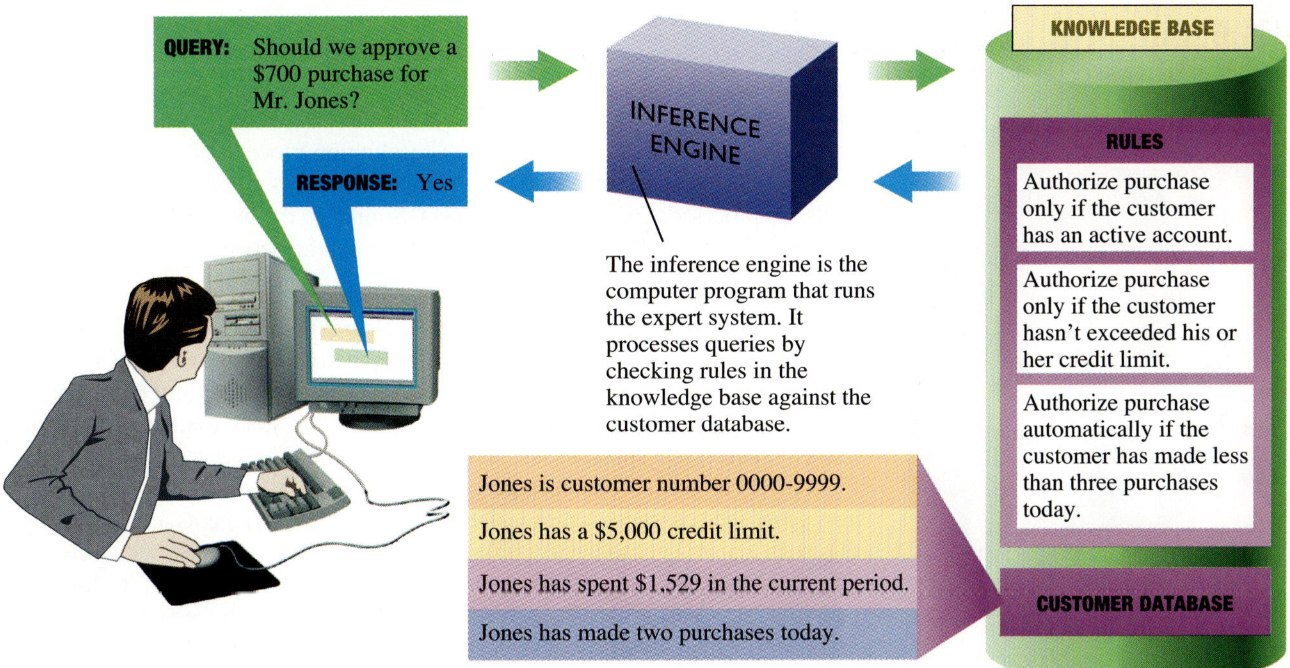

## A CLOSER LOOK AT... ANIMATED ANCHORS

Ananova, a digital character, made her debut as the world's first *virtual newscaster* on the Internet on April 19, 2000 with the words "Hello World! Here is the news and this time it's personal!" Since then, the use of animated digital characters to deliver Web content has begun to catch on. They are increasingly being found on news and entertainment Web sites to deliver information with a more "human" feel.

Over the last few years, virtual newscasters—also called *animated anchors*—have become very life-like. Typically, through the use of a sophisticated animation model and software, their faces and voices can change throughout a story to express emotion. For example, to prepare a news story for Ananova to deliver, editors mark up articles with the general emotion of the story, as well as any particular parts of the story that require a specific emotion. When the story is run, the software makes Ananova behave as directed by the marked up text, and generates speech (with Ananova displaying appropriate lip synching and facial animations) from the text. The result? A realistic humanoid delivering of the news.

Ananova isn't the only game in town, however. The animated anchors on the 1KTV Web site are photorealistic and difficult to discern from real humans (see Figure 8-10). 1KTV programs are designed to deliver news, information, and entertainment to portable PCs and mobile phones on demand.

Although animated news anchors have their limitations (virtually everyone would rather hear about airplane crashes, bombings, and other such tragedies from a real human rather than from an animated character), their ability to deliver news live or on demand on devices ranging from a PC to a cell phone make them an appealing option for those individuals who prefer to see and hear Web-based news, rather than read it. Other uses for digital characters are expected in the future, such as the sign language interpreter system currently being tested at post offices in the UK. This system inputs the postal worker's spoken English and converts it in real-time to text, and then the digital character signs the meaning of the text on the display screen—essentially becoming a digital interpreter for deaf and hard-of-hearing post office patrons.

**FIGURE 8-10**

1KTV's virtual newscaster

**FIGURE 8-11**

A neural network system in use.

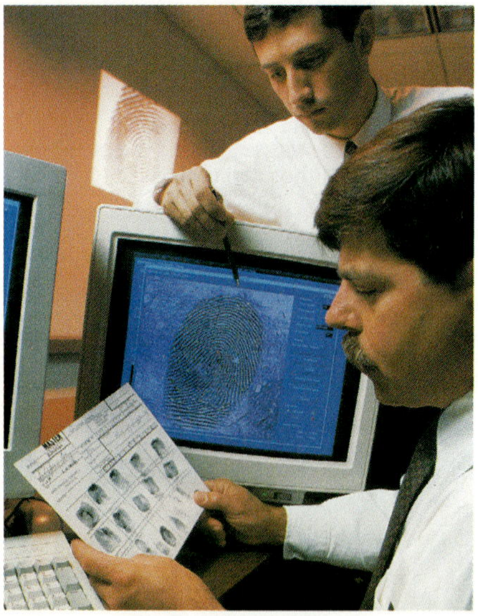

### Neural Networks

Artificial intelligence systems that attempt to imitate the way a human brain works are called **neural networks**. Neural networks use connections between processing elements, similar to the way neurons in the human brain are connected, to try to enable the computer to emulate the brain's pattern-recognition process. Neural network systems (also called *neural nets*) are similar to computer networks, only the networked components are processors, not entire computers. Similar to the human brain and a computer network, if parts of a neural network are damaged, the network can still function.

Neural networks are designed to learn by observation and by trial and error, and are typically used to recognize patterns in data. Neural network systems specialize in recognizing and analyzing patterns and, in conjunction with large databases, are used often in areas such as handwriting, speech, and image recognition; biometric identification; geographical mapping; credit-risk assessment; stock market analysis; medical imaging; aerospace applications; and crime analysis. The neural net system shown in Figure 8-11 is used to match fingerprints with the ones in a database. Neural nets are also being increasingly used in *vision systems*, in which cameras are used in conjunction with a neural net to inspect objects and make determinations, such as the systems that check products for defects at manufacturing plants, try to identify known criminals in a crowd using face recognition technology, or recognize stamps during postal processing. Other applications in development include systems that can read a person's lips or interpret sign language.

## Robotics

**Robotics** is the field devoted to the study of **robot** technology. Robots are devices, controlled by a human operator or a computer, that can move and react to sensory input. Robots are currently used in factories to perform high-precision, but monotonous, jobs such as welding, riveting, and painting. They are also used in situations that are dangerous or impossible for humans, such as mining coal, defusing bombs, exploring the bottom of the ocean, repairing oil rigs, locating land mines, finding survivors in collapsed mines and buildings, and photographing the surface of Mars. *Personal robots* are available for performing specific tasks, such as mowing the lawn and vacuuming, as well as for entertainment purposes.

**ONLINE RESOURCES**

For links to information about robotics and examples of robotic products, go to www.course.com/morley2003/ch8

Two of the first personal robots were *AIBO* and *PaPeRo* (see Figure 8-12). Sony's AIBO robot dog, introduced in 1999, can recognize up to 75 voice commands, sing and dance, take pictures, and change its behavior based on its treatment and training. NEC's Personal Robot PaPeRo (not yet available for consumer use) can perform such activities as making small talk (it recognizes human faces and remembers information about family members and previous interactions to facilitate this), playing games, recording and delivering audio and video messages exchanged between family members, acting as a TV remote control, and accessing messaging via the Internet. Both robots use multiple cameras, microphones, and touch sensors for input. In addition to being used for entertainment and general household tasks, future personal robotic applications include assisting the disabled and the elderly.

The appearance of robots used for business purposes varies widely, as shown in the bottom part of Figure 8-12. While many robots don't resemble humans, some researchers are working to develop humanoid robots that can walk on two legs. One of the most advanced at the current time is *ASIMO* built by Honda. ASIMO is child-sized to allow it to operate freely in a human living space, but still reach needed fixtures such as light switches and doorknobs, and can successfully avoid obstacles and navigate stairs. It can recognize about 50 spoken phrases and is beginning to be rented out to businesses, such as Japan's National Museum of Emerging Science and Innovation and IBM Corporation, as a

**FIGURE 8-12**

Examples of robots

**‹ Personal robots**

Personal robots are available to do specific household tasks, such as mow the lawn (left); entertainment robots (below) can be used for play and for performing small tasks.

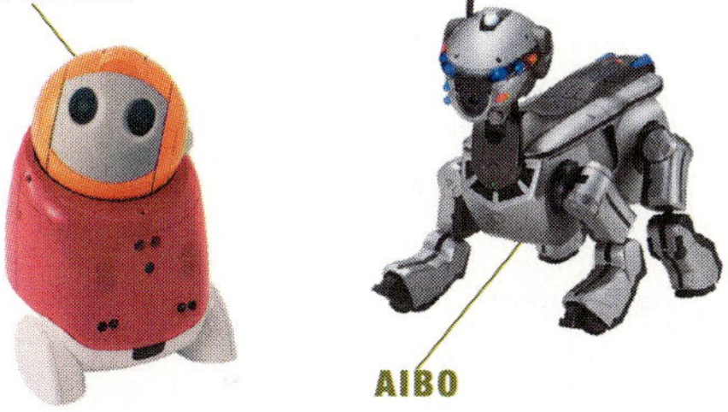

**^ Business robots**

Humanoid robots like ASIMO (above) can be used for business tasks such as greeting customers and taking them on tours; the CyberGuard robot (right) patrols offices and other facilities looking for intruders, smoke, gas leaks, and more.

greeter and tour guide. In addition to business applications, Honda also envisions personal applications for ASIMO, such as bringing food to a sick person, carrying groceries up a flight of stairs, and other household tasks.

As new robotic applications are developed and as the prices come down, more robots are expected to be used in both homes and businesses. Newer robots will likely have improved vision and sensor systems, which will allow for better navigation and more accurate assessments of the hardness and temperature of objects. Artificial intelligence and facial emotions will make humanoid robots even more life-like, and their communications systems will continue to improve. In fact, robots are already available for business videoconferences. While the use of robots has many benefits to society—such as adding convenience to our lives and replacing humans in dangerous situations—some individuals are concerned that, as true artificial intelligence becomes closer to a reality, we may eventually create a class of robots that has the potential for great harm. While others disagree, it is an area that should receive a great deal of consideration and debate as the future unfolds.

## VIRTUAL REALITY (VR)

One limitation of traditional computer applications is their use of two dimensions instead of three. Although you can play computer games or look at photographs of products, vacation destinations, and other items on Web pages, the experience is somewhat limited. Three-dimensional (3D) games and other applications were developed to give the illusion of three dimensions for a more realistic experience, but they were still viewed in two dimensions. To bring an even greater sense of reality to games, simulations, and Web page content, *virtual reality* was developed.

### What Is Virtual Reality?

**Virtual reality (VR)** is the use of a computer to create environments that look like they do in the real world. VR can be used in conjunction with objects, people, locations, or simulated situations. Through VR, it is possible to participate in activities such as taking "tours" of buildings, museums, vacation destinations, and homes for sale; viewing products from all angles before purchasing them; and receiving training in and practicing a new sport, skill, or technique.

At its simplest level, VR computer programs or Web page components use no special hardware. More complex VR applications may require special goggles (which enable the user to see computer-generated images up close), gloves (containing built-in sensors that change the visual images accordingly when the hands are moved), or other VR hardware. VR training applications, such as practicing new surgical techniques, learning how to fly an airplane, or performing repairs on expensive aircraft, may require specialized VR hardware for that particular application—some even require a complete simulator, such as those resembling a cockpit or driver's seat.

### VR Applications

VR can be used for a wide variety of purposes. Applications can be stand-alone, networked, or Web-based. Stand-alone and networked applications are more common for entertainment and training purposes; Web-based VR applications—although not widespread at the current time—have enormous consumer potential. Some examples of VR applications are shown in Figure 8-13. To explore virtual components contained on Web pages, you typically need a browser or plug-in that supports **virtual-reality modeling language (VRML)**. For example, the e-commerce application shown in Figure 8-13 is displayed using the *QuickTime* program. One of the biggest limitations of Web-based VR has been high bandwidth requirements. As the speeds

**ONLINE RESOURCES**

For links to information about Web-based virtual reality, go to www.course.com/morley2003/ch8

**FIGURE 8-13**

**Virtual reality applications**

**^ Entertainment**

In this VR game, participants experience a journey through outer space to discover an enemy alien outpost that threatens Earth. A 3D motion simulator, high resolution VR goggles, and surround sound add to the realism of the experience.

**^ Training**

This VR commercial pilot training simulator with monitors in the shape and size of a windshield allows pilots to practice flying in a variety of different conditions as many times as needed to achieve the needed level of competence.

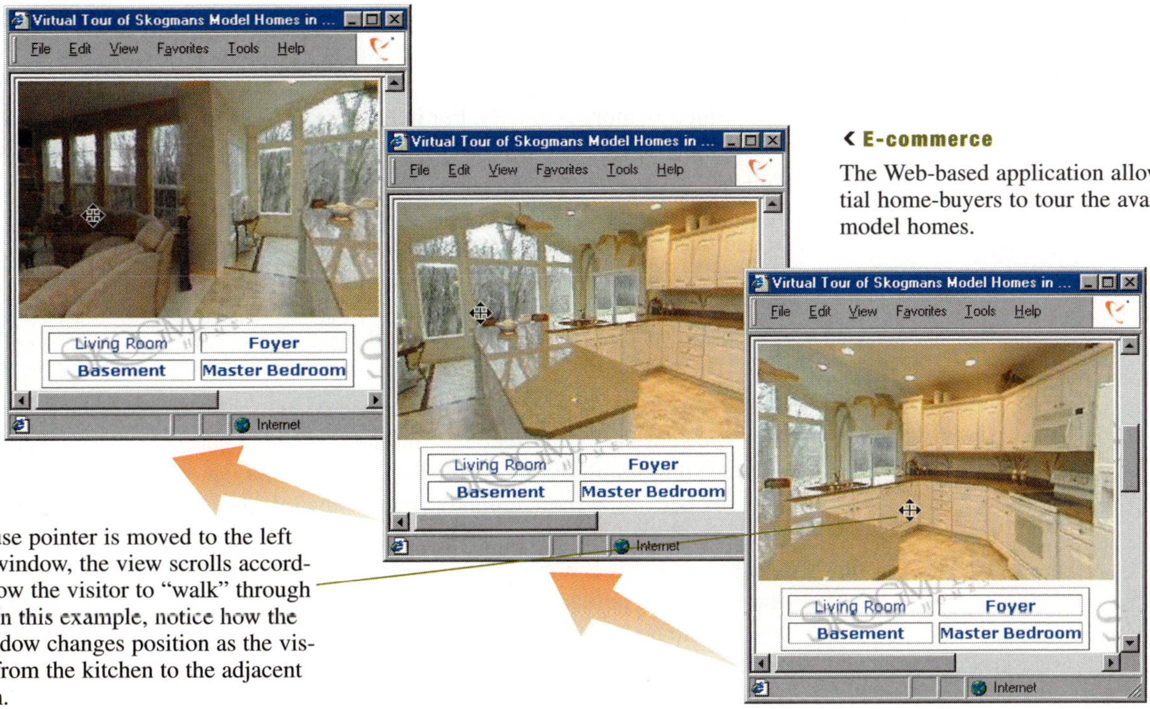


**< E-commerce**

The Web-based application allows potential home-buyers to tour the available model homes.

As the mouse pointer is moved to the left of the VR window, the view scrolls accordingly to allow the visitor to "walk" through the home. In this example, notice how the picture window changes position as the visitor walks from the kitchen to the adjacent living room.

of computers and use of broadband continue to increase, Web-based VR applications are expected to grow accordingly. VR possibilities include the following:

- *Entertainment*—enables individuals to experience activities such as exploring ancient civilizations, touring museums, battling enemies in games, and parachuting out of an airplane.
- *Design and engineering*—permits clients to perform activities such as previewing buildings before construction or previewing and selecting from various interior or landscape designs.
- *Education and training*—allows students to participate in activities such as exploring and taking part in an historical event, or safely practicing how to drive a bus, fly an airplane, or repair expensive equipment; can also be used to overlay virtual images over real objects to show trainees what to do next.
- *E-commerce*—enables consumers to experience activities such as touring homes for sale, customizing and viewing products before purchasing them, and previewing clothing on virtual models of themselves.
- *Medicine*—allows physicians to practice activities such as simulating the effect of medical treatment or trying out new surgical techniques; also been with cancer patients to distract them from their discomfort during chemotherapy, such as by "visiting" an art museum during treatments.

## TECHNOLOGICAL ADVANCES IN MEDICINE

New technological advances in the area of medicine include computers that can analyze mammogram results to identify precancerous cells too small for a human to see, implanted devices to assist in the functioning of the heart or other biological organs, and digital cameras the size of a pill that are swallowed to photograph the patient's colon. In addition, computers are being integrated into prosthetic devices to make them function more normally. For instance, Curtis Grimsley, a computer analyst who worked on the 70th floor of the Twin Towers before it collapsed on 9/11, was able to walk down all 70 flights of stairs using his computerized artificial leg—something he says he would never have been able to do using other artificial legs he has used. In addition to these medical advancements, other topics in the forefront of medical technology research include electronic implants, *robot-assisted surgery*, and *telemedicine*. Some of these are *remote* applications, meaning the patient and physician are in two different physical locations.

### Electronic Implants

Some current electronic medical implants, such as cardiac devices that can keep a heart beating regularly and *cochlear implants* that can restore hearing, are remarkable, but becoming more commonplace. Other electronic medical implants, however, are just emerging and are somewhat more controversial. For example, the *VeriChip* (see Figure 8-14) is a miniaturized RFID chip about the size of a grain of rice that is designed to be implanted under the skin, such as on the forearm. Each VeriChip contains a unique verification number that can be read when a proprietary scanner is passed over the implanted chip. Although the VeriChip doesn't contain any personal data at the present time, it can be used in conjunction with a database to access needed data, such as to provide hospital emergency room personnel with health information about an unconscious patient. According to the company that invented VeriChip, future applications could include access control for secure facilities, personal computers, cars, and homes, as well as to authenticate users for ATM and credit card transactions—a possible replacement for applications that use possessed objects today. Versions of the VeriChip with GPS capabilities could also be used to find missing individuals, such as kidnap victims and lost Alzheimer's patients, similar to the clip-on and wristwatch monitoring systems available today that allow for continuous location information about the person wearing the monitor to be broadcast to a proprietary receiver. After months of heated debate, a Florida family became the first humans implanted with the VeriChip in 2002. Although privacy-rights advocates worry that a chip like this could someday be used by the government to track citizens, others view the chip no differently than a medical ID bracelet and aren't concerned because it is available on a purely voluntary basis.

**FIGURE 8-14**

**The tiny implantable VeriChip contains an ID number that can be used to access personal identity and medical information in an emergency.**

Another controversial implant issue is implanting electrodes directly into the brain. Because of the vast possibilities, such as enabling severely disabled individuals to communicate with others via a computer or being able to restore some movement to paralyzed patients, brain implants are receiving a great deal of research and attention. Nearly 15,000 people with Parkinson's disease currently use implanted electronic devices connected to electrodes implanted in the brain to try to prevent tremors. One company, Neural Signals, has had some success in creating systems that enable patients to move a computer cursor using just their thoughts. Similar experiments that were conducted with monkeys were successful in getting the monkeys to control both a cursor and a robotic arm with their thoughts—raising the possibility for paralyzed individuals to control robot assistants with their thoughts sometime in the future. Some brain-implant products—such as Neural Signals' Brain Communicator—are available today for use by humans.

Despite the potential benefits of brain implants, there is the concern that this technology could be misused. Medical ethicists are currently working on setting up standards and criteria to ensure that brain implant devices allow, according to medical ethicist Joseph Fins of Cornell University, "...patients to have control, not be under control." Currently the focus of brain implants and thought-controlled computers is bringing communications capabilities to the severely disabled. Some researchers, however, foresee the technology becoming mainstream sometime in the future—viewing brain wave input as the next step in the evolution of the human-computer input interface.

## Robot-Assisted Surgery

True *robotic surgery*—where robots perform surgery on their own—isn't likely to happen soon, if ever. But **robot-assisted surgery** is an emerging application that shows a lot of potential. With robot-assisted surgery, the robot device actually operates on the patient, but it is controlled by a surgeon either physically (from a control console, as shown in Figure 8-15) or verbally (by using voice commands). Robotic surgery systems usually use cameras to give the human surgeon an extremely close view of the surgery area and typically can work within much smaller incisions than are possible by human surgeons. These smaller incisions allow for less invasive surgery (for example, not having to crack through the rib cage to access the heart), resulting in less pain for the patient, a faster recovery time, and fewer potential complications.

## Telemedicine

**Telemedicine** is the use of communications technology to provide medical information and services. It exists today in the form of telephone consultations and videoconferences, remote monitoring and diagnosis of patients, and similar activities. Remote robot-assisted surgery where surgeons control the robotic surgery hardware remotely, such as over the Internet from a computer at another physical location, is an emerging telemedicine application. Telemedicine has enormous potential for providing quality long-distance medical care to individuals who live in areas without sufficient medical services or personnel. It will also be necessary for future long-term space exploration—such as a trip to Mars and back that may take three years or more—since astronauts will undoubtedly need medical care while on the journey. Some current and future telemedicine applications include the following (see Figure 8-16):

- *Remote monitoring*—allows individuals wearing a continuous-monitoring system to have their vital statistics accessed remotely by healthcare professionals for diagnostic purposes; can also be used for monitoring the health of individuals involved in dangerous situations, such as race car drivers, firefighters, and soldiers.
- *Remote diagnosis*—enables local healthcare workers at rural locations, child-care facilities, and other locations with telemedicine equipment to use video cameras, stethoscopes, otoscopes, and other tools to send images and vital statistics of a patient to a physician located at a medical facility. If remote diagnosis and treatment is possible, the sick individual need not go to a hospital or doctor's office.
- *Professional consultations*—permits physicians to use videoconferencing technology for activities such as conferring on a diagnosis or contacting a specialist for an emergency consultation during surgery; can also involve research collaboration between doctors located in different states or countries.
- *Follow up/pre-visit care*—enables healthcare professionals to use remote monitoring, teleconferencing, e-mail, and other technologies to follow up on a patient's recovery status. Some physicians also offer online consultations via e-mail to determine if a patient needs to be seen in the office.
- *Medical education*—includes videoconferencing, distance learning, and other Internet applications which provide up-to-date professional training to physicians and other

**Figure 8-15**

**A robot-assisted surgery in action**

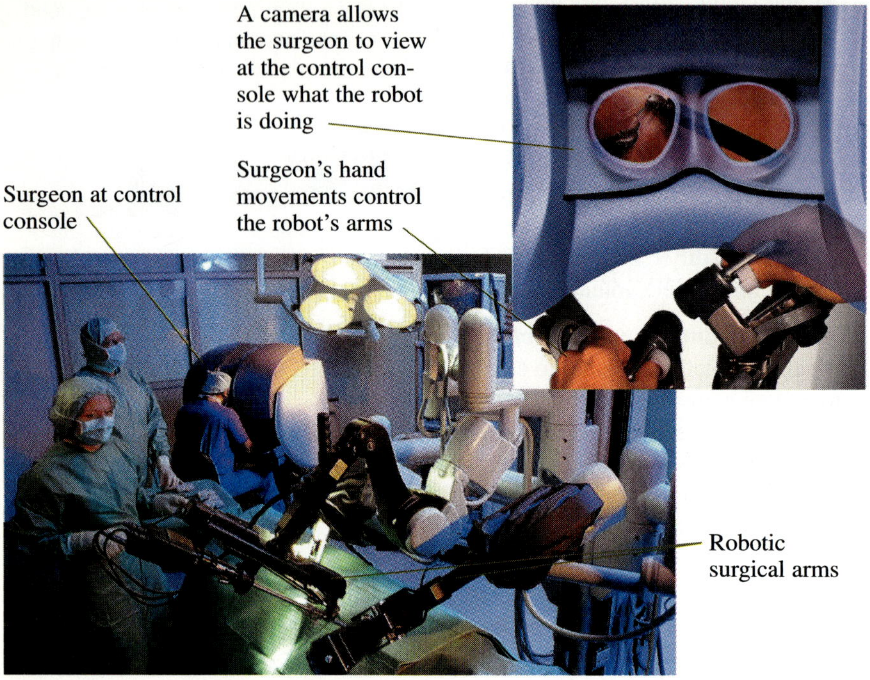


**Figure 8-16**

**Telemedicine applications**

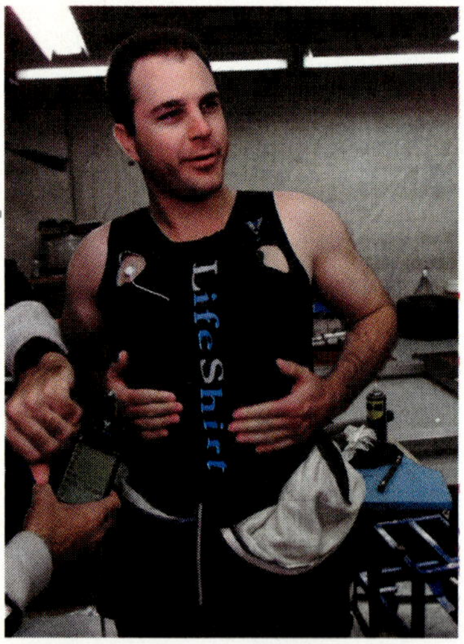


**‹ Remote monitoring**

The LifeShirt shown here continually records vital signs that can be sent to an attending physician for analysis. It can be used both for diagnostic purposes and to monitor the health of individuals in dangerous situations, such as Indy race car driver Jon Herb shown here.

**⌄ Remote diagnosis**

At remote locations, such as the New York child care center shown here, trained employees provide physicians with the real-time data (sent via the Internet) they need for diagnosis.

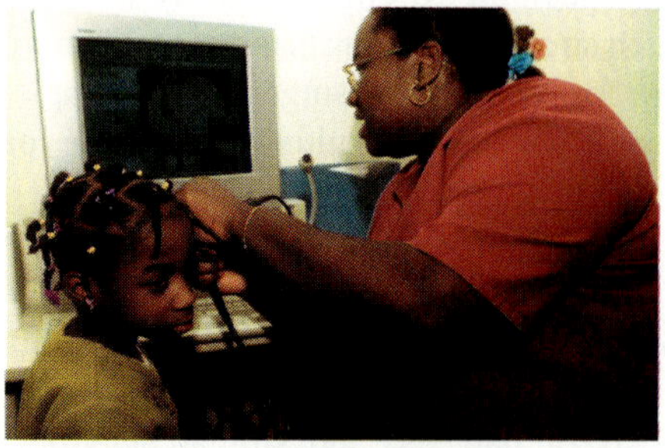

**‹ Professional consultations**

Physicians can confer with patients and other physicians via the Internet, sharing patient data, test results, and more.

healthcare professionals located in rural communities, enabling them to stay current with the latest medical research and techniques. A great deal of medical information is also available to consumers online.

As with other sensitive information sent via the Internet, the security of private medical information sent via telemedicine applications is a crucial consideration—some privacy advocates would call it a grave concern. Research has shown that security is one of the key reasons most doctors resist conferring with patients online; other factors include lack of PCs and Internet access by patients. But many physicians using Web-based consultations believe that the online visits benefit both doctors and patients alike. For instance, doctors who use Web-based consultations say that handling routine matters over the Internet frees up more time for complicated cases and allows them to spend more time with critically ill patients. The use of online visits and other types of telemedicine are bound to increase as physicians and patients become more familiar and comfortable with the technology, the technology continues to improve, and online security measures continue to be strengthened.

## TECHNOLOGICAL ADVANCES IN THE MILITARY

The U.S. military works on a continual basis with technological and research organizations to improve military equipment, as well as to outfit soldiers with more protective gear. *Smart bombs*, *smart bullets*, and improved surveillance tools, uniforms, and gear are all on-going areas of military advancement. The military is also involved in researching many of the other emerging technologies already discussed, such as nanotechnology and artificial intelligence.

### Smart Guns, Bullets, and Bombs

In the first major update to the Army's M-16 rifle since 1967, a new infantry rifle system—called the *XM29*—is currently in development. According to the rifle's manufacturer, ATK, the XM29 is five times more effective at over twice the range than existing rifle systems. Instead of relying on a soldier's perfect aim, this new gun uses a laser and *smart bullets* to hit its mark. Once the soldier marks the desired target with a red dot in his or her laser sights, microprocessors located inside the bullet determine how many times the bullet must revolve in flight to reach the marked destination. In addition to increased accuracy, the gun has the advantage of being able to be fired from up to 1,000 meters away.

Another smart technology is the **smart bomb**—a bomb that can be guided to its target. One common way of implementing smart bombs involves the use of a *Joint Direct Attack Munition (JDAM)* kit that fits over the tail of a regular dumb bomb to give it satellite-guidance capabilities. Unlike the Gulf War, where fewer than 10% of the bombs were smart bombs, approximately 60% of bombs dropped on Afghanistan at the time of this writing have been smart bombs, and Pentagon officials have said that they would aim for 100% smart bombs in the opening days of any war with Iraq. Smart bombs are much more accurate than their dumb-bomb counterparts—according to preliminary Navy data, overall about 90% of all smart bombs dropped over Afghanistan have hit their specified targets. Smart bombs offer the military several advantages, such as cost-savings and increased safety by requiring fewer planes and bombs, posing less risk of inadvertently killing civilians, and causing less pollution and other types of collateral damage. However, smart bombs are only as accurate as their hardware and supplied directional information. For instance, problems such as faulty coordinates, bad weather, and guidance systems failure have resulted in very serious accidents—such as two incidents in Afghanistan in 2001 in which civilians were killed by off-target U.S. missiles and the accidental U.S. bombing in 1999 of the Chinese Embassy in Belgrade.

## Surveillance Tools

While the existence of new military surveillance tools is not always public knowledge, information about two new tools and their use in the war on terrorism has been recently released. Unmanned surveillance planes—such as the *Predator* aircraft shown in Figure 8-17—are currently being used for surveillance and reconnaissance missions. These planes can transmit surveillance images and other information in real-time to front line soldiers, commanders, and other appropriate individuals via satellite communications links.

Another new surveillance tool is the **battlefield robot**—a robot used to check out trails, buildings, caves, and other structures before soldiers enter them. These remote controlled robots, such as the *PackBot* model shown in Figure 8-17 entering a cave on its first mission in Kandahar, Afghanistan, act as a point-man and transmit images back to the unit so the unit leader knows if it's safe to proceed. Although now just a reconnaissance tool to reduce the risk to soldiers on the ground, future applications may include outfitting battlefield robots with guns, grenades, chemical-agent testing capabilities, and additional cameras, such as ones on swivel arms.

**FIGURE 8-17**

**Examples of advances in military technology**

**< Smart guns**

Smart guns, such as the XM29 shown here, are more accurate than conventional weapons.

**> Surveillance tools**

Unmanned surveillance aircraft (right) and battlefield robots (below) are helping fight the war in Afghanistan.

**> Improved gear**

Gear such as the Land Warrior shirt shown here are being developed to keep soldiers safer and give them additional physical and communications capabilities when they are used in actual combat in the future.

## Improved Uniforms and Gear

The Pentagon has announced that it is redesigning the U.S. military uniform completely to become safer and more high-tech. One such option is the *Land Warrior* system currently in development and shown in Figure 8-17. Plans include a helmet with features such as built-in GPS navigation and night vision capabilities, video and infrared cameras, a visor with a flip-down eyepiece to view transmitted images, chemical and biological weapons detectors, and a gas mask. The uniform is expected to be constructed out of *e-fabric*—a special fabric created specifically for the military. E-fabric is designed to conduct heat and electricity, to double as a radio antenna, and to power and connect the soldier's digital equipment so that it all works together, as well as is networked with the devices belonging to others in the soldier's unit. Recent prototypes of e-fabrics have been made with thread consisting of actual metals, such as steel. Bulletproof capabilities, body sensors that send the wearer's vital signs to medics, and an internal climate control system are all additional possibilities for these future uniform systems.

Another possibility for the future is the **exoskeleton** suit. Currently being researched and developed by several organizations—such as MIT and Sarcos—under grants from the *Defense Advanced Research Projects Agency (DARPA)*, exoskeleton suits are wearable robotic systems designed to give soldiers additional physical capabilities and protection. For instance, an exoskeleton suit would give a soldier the ability to run faster, lift and carry heavier items, and leap over large obstacles. MIT is using nanotechnology to create exoskeleton suit material that could solidify on demand, such as to form a shield or to turn into a medical cast if a soldier gets injured. Other possibilities include the suit being able to change color automatically for camouflage purposes; relay information via sensors about a soldier's health, injuries, and location to field headquarters; and administer painkillers or apply pressure to a wound when directed by a physician.

As is often the case with new technology developed for the military or NASA, there are expected to be consumer benefits based on the research being done in the areas of e-fabric and exoskeleton suits. For example, exoskeleton technology may eventually lead to stronger and safer search and rescue workers, give the elderly back their youthful physical abilities, or provide paralyzed people with a means of mobility.

Although there are some distinct foreseeable benefits from new and emerging military technologies, some wonder if this research will ultimately benefit us in the end. Will war become so sterile with surgical strikes and robots fighting robots that we forget how horrific it really is? Would the money going into these types of developments be better spent on medical and agricultural research, education, or other programs? These questions will need to be addressed as we contemplate the directions in which we want our military and government to go.

## SOCIETAL IMPLICATIONS OF EMERGING TECHNOLOGY

There are usually many benefits of a new computing technology, since it normally wouldn't become widely available for consumers if it wasn't suppose to solve a problem or add convenience to our lives. Some individuals who welcome emerging technologies look forward to advances in computing technology, medicine, and the military. Others envision a "Star Trek life" of instant food and product replicators, space travel, voice-controlled computers, and digital transporters "beaming" us places in just an instant.

However, not all advances are embraced by all individuals. For instance, security and privacy issues are continual areas of concern with emerging technologies. Potential implications include trusting "intelligent" computers and robots so much so that they become a personal safety hazard; losing ourselves in virtual reality to the extent that we lose touch with our real reality; allowing medical technology to enable humans to be controlled by others; and spending resources on some areas of research and development that might be better spent elsewhere. Some people also worry that technology is advancing at such a rapid pace that we can't possibly envision all the potential repercussions until it's too late.

## HOW TO... DOWNLOAD AND INSTALL NEW BROWSER PLUG-INS

As emerging technologies are made available via the Web, many will require a special *browser plug-in*—a program that updates your browser with features that it currently lacks—to view or experience that new technology. For instance, one widely used plug-in package, *Adobe Acrobat Reader*, enables your browser to view pages that have been formatted as Adobe Acrobat *PDF files* (formatted electronic documents often used for financial statements, applications, government forms, and other published documents because they look very close to the way they appear in print). The popular *Shockwave* plug-in is needed to view some types of Web animation, and QuickTime or some other type of plug-in that supports virtual reality is needed to experience Web-based VR. As new capabilities, such as VR and new types of animation, are introduced to Web pages, typically new plug-ins are required to use them.

When you visit a Web page that requires a plug-in your browser lacks, a message is usually displayed containing the option to download the plug-in file (see Figure 8-18). To download the file, click the link. When you encounter a link to a plug-in application, it is a good idea to be sure you understand what the plug-in will be used for before actually downloading and installing it. Just as with other types of Web activity and downloaded files, security and privacy risks or scams are possible.

To download a plug-in before viewing a Web page that requires it, you can go to the Web site of the publisher of the plug-in or otherwise find a Web page containing a link to download the file (such as a "Get QuickTime Player now" button); it will either start downloading the file directly or bring you to a Web page where you can download the file. In addition to plug-ins, other types of files that you may want to download in a similar manner include:

- *Zipped (.zip) files*—are compressed for faster downloading and are opened with a decompression program, such as WinZip.
- *PDF (.pdf) files*—are opened using the Adobe Acrobat Reader program or plug-in.
- *Image (.gif, .jpg, .jpe, .tif, .bmp,* etc.*) files*—are opened with a browser, image viewer, or image editor, depending on the type of file and the programs available on your computer.
- *Music (.wav, .mp3,* etc.*) files*—are opened with an appropriate media player, such as Windows Media Player, or an appropriate plug-in, such as RealPlayer or WinAmp.
- *Video (.avi, .mov,* etc.*) files*—are opened with an appropriate media player, such as Windows Media Player or MusicMatch, or an appropriate plug-in, such as RealPlayer or QuickTime.
- *Executable (.exe) files*—automatically execute (run) when opened. They usually either start the program or start the installation process for the downloaded program.
- *Application (.doc, .xls,* etc.*) files*—are files in a common application format, such as Microsoft Word (*.doc*) or Microsoft Excel (*.xls*) and are opened in their respective programs.

After giving the command to download a file, you are usually prompted to indicate where you would like the file to be stored (usually it's downloaded to your desktop or an easy-to-find folder, such as My Documents or My Download Files, on your hard drive). Depending on the size of the file and the speed of your computer and Internet connection, downloading a file can take anywhere from a few seconds to several hours. After the file has finished downloading, unless the installation automatically takes place after the download has been completed (as in Figure 8-19), you will need to find the file and open it using your file management program. Opening the downloaded file usually begins the process of installing the program onto your computer. Once the plug-in has been installed, your browser will be able to display that type of content (as shown in Figure 8-19).

**FIGURE 8-18**

**If a new plug-in is needed, a message will typically be displayed.**

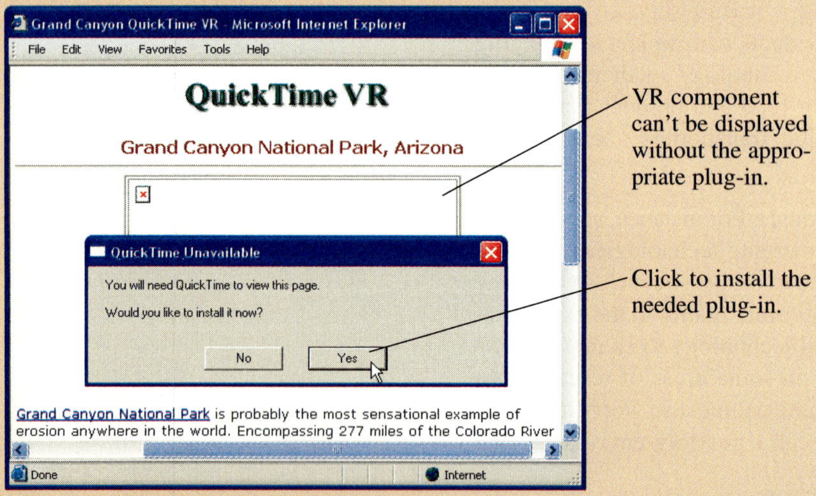

**FIGURE 8-19**

**Downloading and installing a plug-in**

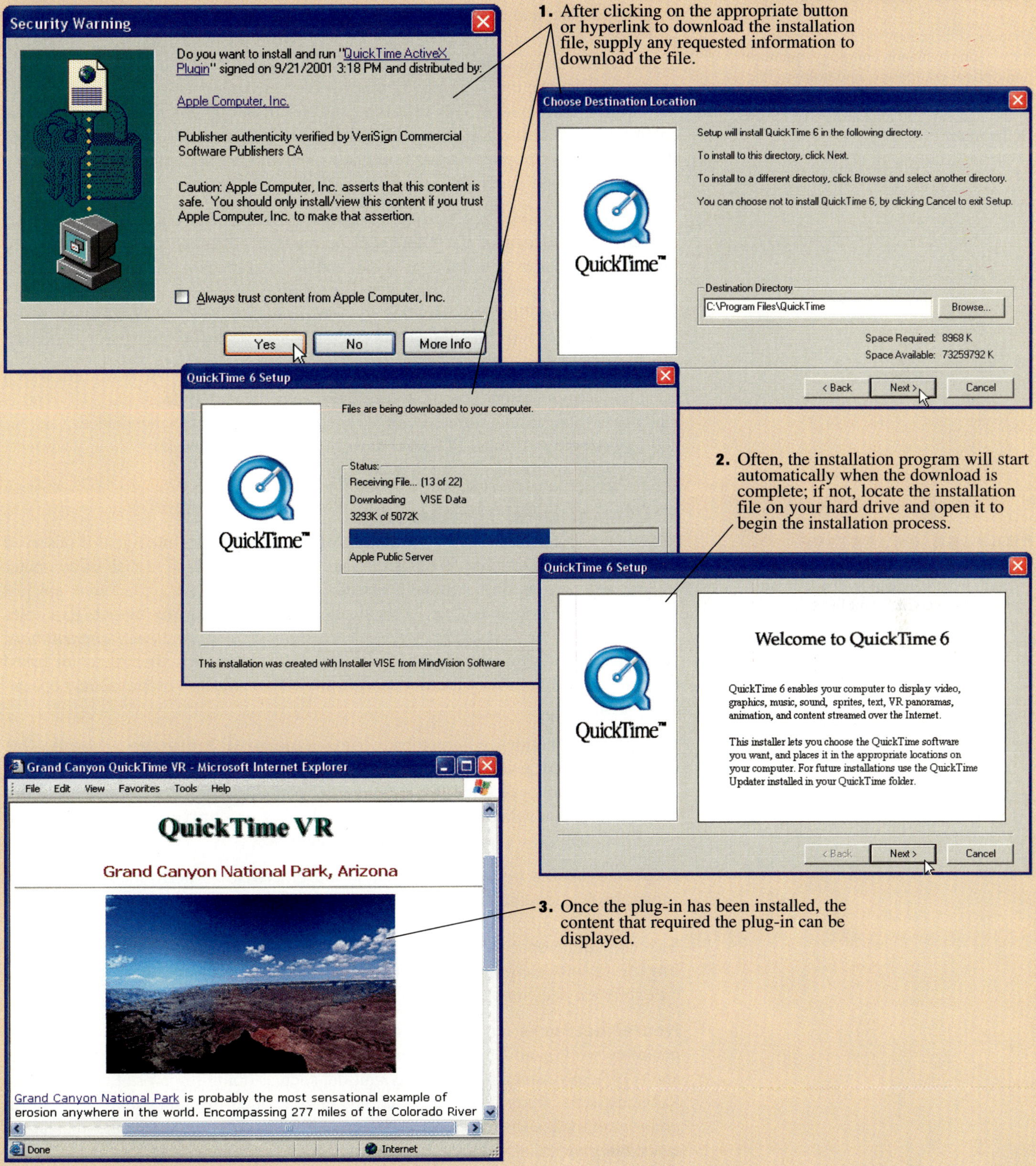


1. After clicking on the appropriate button or hyperlink to download the installation file, supply any requested information to download the file.

2. Often, the installation program will start automatically when the download is complete; if not, locate the installation file on your hard drive and open it to begin the installation process.

3. Once the plug-in has been installed, the content that required the plug-in can be displayed.

# SUMMARY

**CHAPTER OBJECTIVE 1**

Discuss some emerging PC technologies—such as nanotechnology, quantum and optical computers, and holographic and multilayer storage—and speculate as to the makeup and appearance of the PC of the future.

## The PC of the Future

While the exact makeup of future PCs isn't certain, they will likely continue to get smaller, smarter, and more user-friendly. Computers that we keep with us on a regular basis—such as small PCs we carry or **wearable PCs**—are expected eventually to become the norm. The science of **nanotechnology** is working at the atomic and molecular levels to create computer chips and other components that are just a fraction of their current size. This research could result in tiny computers or robots that could be injected into a patient's bloodstream to perform tests or administer treatment, as well as components that could be woven into fiber or embedded in paint and other conventional materials.

Instead of using today's electronic components and silicon chips, **quantum** and **optical computers** of the future will be made of different materials altogether. Quantum computers use atoms or nuclei and will likely exist as some sort of liquid state; optical computers perform operations using light instead of electrical current. Future storage applications—such as *fluorescent multilayer discs (FMDs)* and *holographic storage*—have the potential to increase data storage capacity tremendously.

There has been a push in recent years to create *greener* computer hardware, which is more energy-efficient and otherwise more environmentally correct. This trend is likely to continue in the future. Look for smaller and thinner display devices, smaller and more energy-efficient PCs, and devices powered by alternative energy sources, such as solar and hand-generated power.

**CHAPTER OBJECTIVE 2**

Explain what is meant by the term artificial intelligence (AI) and list some AI applications.

## Artificial Intelligence (AI)

When a computer performs in ways that would be considered intelligent if observed in humans, it is referred to as **artificial intelligence (AI)**, a branch of computer science and engineering. Although discussed for decades, AI applications are just beginning to be available. One AI application is the **intelligent agent**. Examples include *application assistants*, *search agents*, *shopping bots*, and *entertainment bots*. Intelligent agents typically act as *virtual assistants* and modify their behavior based on the user's actions. They are frequently built into application programs and operating systems.

Some AI applications communicate using a **natural language system**. One example is a **voice-input system** that can be used to input spoken data into the computer, either as dictated text or as verbal commands for the computer to carry out. Some Web applications—such as search sites or **chatterbots** used for customer service—also use a natural language interface.

**Expert systems** perform tasks that would otherwise be performed by a human expert, such as diagnosing medical conditions, making financial forecasts, and performing credit authorizations. Most expert systems use a **knowledge base** (a database containing specific facts and rules about the expert area) and an **inference engine** (a software program used to apply rules to the data stored in the knowledge base to reach decisions).

**Neural networks** and **robotics** are two other areas of artificial intelligence. A neural network is an AI system that tries to imitate the way the human brain works and is typically used for pattern recognition, such as doing fingerprint comparisons. Robotics is the study of **robots**—computer-controlled machines that can perform preprogrammed tasks. Robots are commonly used for repetitive and dangerous tasks; but they are also appearing as toys and as entertainment devices.

## Virtual Reality (VR)

The use of a computer to create environments that appear to be three-dimensional—that is, like they do in the real world—is called **virtual reality (VR)**. A wide variety of VR applications exist; some require special hardware, such as goggles or gloves, to get the full VR experience. VR applications can be used for entertainment purposes, as well as for design and engineering, education and training, e-commerce, and medicine. Web-based VR typically is based on **virtual-reality modeling language (VRML)**.

**CHAPTER OBJECTIVE 3**

Discuss the concept of and some applications for virtual reality (VR).

## Technological Advances in Medicine

Technological advances in recent years include using computers to analyze test results, implanting devices to assist an organ's functioning, and digital cameras that can be ingested to record images of a person's digestive tract. Some electronic implant applications—such as the *VeriChip* identification chip and electrodes implanted in the brain—are embraced by some, but are not without controversy.

**Robot-assisted surgery** occurs when a robot—controlled by a human surgeon via voice commands or equipment located at a control console—operates on a patient. Because robots can use smaller incisions in some types of surgeries, this results in less pain for the patient and a faster recovery period. **Telemedicine** can be defined as the use of communications technology to provide medical information and services. Many forms of telemedicine—such as *remote monitoring*, *remote diagnosis*, *professional consultations* via telephone or videoconference, *follow up* or *pre-visit care*, *medical education*, and remote robot-assisted surgery—exist at some level today, but are expected to become more prevalent as concerns about privacy and security on the Internet are alleviated and computer and Internet use becomes even more widespread.

**CHAPTER OBJECTIVE 4**

List some new and upcoming technological advances in medicine.

## Technological Advances in the Military

Recent and expected future technological advances in the military include newly designed rifles that can use *smart bullets* for increased accuracy, the **smart bomb**, and improved surveillance tools and personnel gear.

Unmanned aircraft, such as the *Predator* drone, are currently being used for surveillance and reconnaissance missions. **Battlefield robots**, used for the first time in combat in Afghanistan, can explore buildings, caves, and other locations prior to humans entering for increased safety. Future robots may be armed with more than just cameras. New high-tech uniforms are being designed and are expected to be fully implemented before the end of the decade. They will likely be created out of special *e-fabric* that has special capabilities, such as component and communications connectivity and antennas, woven into the fabric. Uniforms may also include bulletproof shields, body sensors for medical purposes, and other useful features. Going beyond the high-tech uniform is the **exoskeleton**—a wearable robotic system that not only protects the user, but gives him or her additional physical capabilities.

**CHAPTER OBJECTIVE 5**

Name some new and upcoming technological advances in the military.

## Potential Societal Implications of Emerging Technology

There are many potential societal implications of emerging technologies, such as unexpected results, trusting "intelligent" computers and robots so much that they become a personal safety hazard, losing ourselves in virtual reality to the extent that we lose touch with our real reality, and allowing medical technology to enable humans to be controlled by others. Since virtually any new technology could be used for both good and evil, we need to weigh the societal risks and benefits of emerging technologies in order to make educated and informed decisions about what we'd like our lives and society to be like.

**CHAPTER OBJECTIVE 6**

Discuss some potential societal implications of emerging technologies.

# BALANCING ACT

## UBIQUITOUS COMPUTING VS. BIG BROTHER

Ubiquitous computing—also known as pervasive computing—suggests a future in which few aspects of daily life will remain untouched by computers and computer technology. Computers and related technology will become embedded into more and more devices, and people will depend on computing technology for an ever increasing number of everyday activities. All of the devices in our lives are expected eventually to communicate wirelessly with each other and to do their jobs so invisibly that we don't even pay attention to them anymore.

That's the part that really bothers some people. If all electronic devices in our lives can communicate with one another automatically, how can we control what they say and who they say it to? Will these devices be used to track our movements so the government will always know where we are? Will there really become a "Big Brother" computer that knows everything about everybody? What about personal privacy? How will it be protected?

The big challenge for ubiquitous computing is making it work while still giving us control over what it does. That is difficult to accomplish, since the idea is that the computing devices in our lives will become invisible. If we don't need to instruct these devices on a regular basis and if we can just forget about them, it becomes much more difficult for us to realize what the devices are doing, which device is controlling what function, where information about us is going and how it is being used, which systems are not functioning, and what the consequences of any given action (such as walking into a room, making a telephone call, or placing an order over the Internet) might be. Balancing simplicity and control is one of the biggest issues facing ubiquitous computing research.

**YOUR TURN**

Give some thought to the potential implications of ubiquitous computing and then answer the following questions.

1. Does the idea of ubiquitous computing concern you or interest you? Is it something that you would like to see become a reality in the near future? Why or why not?
2. If ubiquitous computing makes it possible, should the government have the right to track individuals' movements? If so, under what conditions? Name some advantages and disadvantages of the government always knowing where you are.
3. Some aspects of ubiquitous computing at work are intriguing. For example, as you move from place to place within your office building, devices would recognize you and adjust to reflect your settings automatically. As you approach any computer not being used by someone else, it would display the exact desktop currently displayed on your regular PC to allow you to use the computer as if it was your own—such as recording an idea that just popped into your head or showing a coworker a project you are working on. List some other advantages and some disadvantages of ubiquitous computing at work.
4. When ubiquitous computing becomes the norm, how easy do you think it will be for an individual who strongly objects to the concept to choose not to participate? Do you think people should have the right to make that decision? If someone opts out of participating, what might be the consequences for them and for the rest of society?

## KEY TERMS

**Instructions:** Match each key term on the left with the definition on the right that best describes it.

a. **artificial intelligence (AI)**

b. **battlefield robot**

c. **chatterbot**

d. **exoskeleton**

e. **expert system**

f. **inference engine**

g. **intelligent agent**

h. **knowledge base**

i. **nanotechnology**

j. **natural language system**

k. **neural network**

l. **optical computer**

m. **robot**

n. **robot-assisted surgery**

o. **robotics**

p. **smart bomb**

q. **telemedicine**

r. **virtual reality (VR)**

s. **voice-input system**

t. **wearable PC**

**1.** ______ A bomb that can be guided towards its target, usually by GPS.

**2.** ______ A computer system that provides the type of advice that would be expected from a human expert.

**3.** ______ A computer that can be worn on the body, such as an accessory or built into clothing.

**4.** ______ A device, controlled by a human operator or a computer, that can move, react to sensory input, and perform the tasks it is programmed to do.

**5.** ______ A computer that performs digital computations using light.

**6.** ______ A robot used by the military to ensure that locations are safe prior to sending in human soldiers.

**7.** ______ A small program that performs specific tasks for a computer user and that typically modifies its behavior based on the user's actions.

**8.** ______ A software program, often accessed from a Web page, that can respond to natural language input to appear to converse with humans.

**9.** ______ A surgical process in which robots, controlled by human surgeons, operate on actual patients.

**10.** ______ A system that enables a computer to receive spoken or written input in English, French, Chinese, or some other natural language.

**11.** ______ A system that enables a computer to recognize the human voice, either for data input or for providing verbal commands to the PC.

**12.** ______ A wearable robotic system designed to give the wearer additional physical capabilities and protection.

**13.** ______ An artificial intelligence system that links processing elements together in an attempt to imitate the way the neurons in the human brain are connected, in order to emulate the brain's pattern-recognition process.

**14.** ______ The field of study devoted to studying robots.

**15.** ______ The part of an expert system that contains specific facts and rules regarding the expert area.

**16.** ______ The part of an expert system that is used with the system's knowledge base to apply rules to the data to reach decisions.

**17.** ______ The science of creating tiny computers and components by working at the individual atomic and molecular levels.

**18.** ______ The use of a computer to create three-dimensional environments that look like they do in the real world.

**19.** ______ The use of communications technology to provide medical information or services.

**20.** ______ When a computer performs in ways that would be considered intelligent if those same ways were observed in humans.

# ✓ SELF-QUIZ

Answers for the self-quiz appear at the end of the book.

## True/False

**Instructions:** Circle **T** if the statement is true or **F** if the statement is false.

T F **1.** An example of an intelligent agent is a program that allows you to practice flying a fighter jet in what feels like a real-life environment.

T F **2.** Voice-input systems today can be used to dictate documents to a computer application, but not to issue commands to the PC.

T F **3.** Your browser typically needs a plug-in program to display Web-based VR applications.

T F **4.** One advantage of robot-assisted surgery is faster recovery time.

T F **5.** Currently, it is not possible to power a portable PC or mobile communications device with solar electricity.

## Completion

**Instructions:** Supply the missing words to complete the following statements.

**6.** ______________ is the science of building components at the atomic or molecular level, building computer chips and components thousands of times smaller than is possible with conventional technologies.

**7.** In quantum computing, ______________—which can represent more than two possible states—are used instead of electronic bits.

**8.** The most widely used test for artificial intelligence, in which an observer tries to determine if written responses to questions came from a person or a computer, is the ______________.

**9.** An intelligent agent that searches online stores to find the best prices for the products you specify is called a(n) ______________.

**10.** Sony's AIBO dog is an example of a personal ______________.

**11.** Being able to "walk through" a museum online is an example of a(n) ______________ application.

**12.** The ______________ was the first RFID chip approved to be implanted under a person's skin for identification purposes.

**13.** Diagnosing a patient via input received over the Internet or performing remote robot-assisted surgery are examples of ______________ applications.

**14.** A(n) ______________ is a bomb that is electronically guided to its target, such as by the use of satellites.

**15.** One expected advantage of a(n) ______________ suit, currently being designed for soldiers, is the ability to run faster, jump higher, and lift more weight than possible without wearing the suit.

# PROJECTS

### 1. Wearable PCs

**YOUR OPINION**

The chapter Trends In box takes a look at wearable computers. Although they have been available in some form for commercial applications for several years, their entry into the consumer market is just beginning. Some current features of wearable PCs, such as corded components and using an eyepiece display device that some individuals view as unattractive, may make today's wearable PCs undesirable to some.

For this project, write a short essay expressing your opinion about wearable computers. Take another look at the wearable computer shown in Figure 8-2. Would you be willing to wear one in public today? Why or why not? If not, how (if at all) would wearable computers need to be changed in order for you to be willing to wear one? As they become smaller, wireless, and voice-controlled, do you think their use by consumers will increase? Will their use be looked at any differently than wearing a portable radio, CD player, or MP3 player in public? Think about your chosen profession—is wearable or portable computer use needed or useful today in that field? What advantages and disadvantages do you see regarding wearable computer use in that profession? Submit your opinion on this issue to your instructor in the form of a short paper, not more than two pages in length.

### 2. Today's Robots

**INDEPENDENT RESEARCH**

As discussed in the chapter, robots are used today for a variety of activities, such as for industrial tasks and dangerous activities, and in toys and personal devices.

For this project, select one type of robotic device available on the market today—for instance, a robot toy, vacuum cleaner, or lawn mower—and research it. Find out what the product does, what types of hardware it contains, how it is powered, how it is controlled, if it can be reprogrammed, what it costs, and more. Are there any competing robotic products on the market? If so, compare the different alternatives.

After you have completed your research, summarize your findings in a two- to three-page paper. Be sure to include to whom the product is designed and marketed, and your opinion about whether or not you think the product is worthwhile.

### 3. Virtual Reality Web Sites

**HANDS-ON**

Many Web sites feature virtual reality panoramas to enable visitors to move around a particular location (such as an historical monument, a park, a home, or a museum) to explore the location at will. To view these programs, many of them require a special browser plug-in, such as QuickTime.

For this project, visit any Web site containing a VR tour (refer to the list of possible sites below) and see if the browser you are using is capable of viewing the VR component. If it's not and you are using a school computer, ask your instructor for additional directions. If you are missing the required plug-in and you are working on your home PC, follow the instructions on the Web site to download and install the necessary plug-in.

- *Virtual Visitor* (virtualvisitor.com)—tests your browser for QuickTime VR capabilities in the introductory part of the site; available VR tours include towns, restaurants, universities, resorts, ball parks, boats, museums, and more.
- *Desert USA* (www.desertusa.com)—after clicking the *QuickTime VR* link, this site provides you with a list of national parks to choose from.

- *VR Seattle* (www.vrseattle.com)—includes VR tours of a variety of Washington locations, such as the Space Needle, parks, zoos, museums, colleges, churches, and restaurants.

If you are able to view a VR component on a Web page on any site, follow the directions on that site to navigate through the virtual tour (usually you will place your mouse cursor inside the VR window and click and drag a particular direction to move the display). Feel free to try more than one site or VR tour until you find one that you like. At the end of your exploration, prepare a one-page summary of your experience to turn in to your instructor. Be sure to include the steps you had to take in order to get the VR components to work on your PC, whether or not you actually were able to take a VR tour, how easy or difficult you found the experience, and whether you would like to take more VR tours in the future.

**4. Chatterbots**

As discussed in the chapter, chatterbots are beginning to be used on Web pages to automate customer service in a friendlier manner. There are several Web sites that allow you to try out the chatterbots they are developing, such as the Virtual Personalities (www.verbots.com) and AgentLand (www.agentland.com) Web sites.

For this project, find a Web page containing a chatterbot that you can converse with. You can visit either of the sites above (you may need to log on as a guest at Virtual Personalities before being able to talk with their *Verbot)* or find a different site altogether. Ask the chatterbot some general questions about itself or the site and read the responses. Did the chatterbot answer your questions correctly? Do you think it responded in a human-like manner? Would you prefer to chat in real-time with a customer service chatterbot if it could answer your questions correctly, or would you rather wait for an e-mail reply from a human customer service representative? Prepare a one-page summary of your experience to turn in to your instructor.

GROUP PRESENTATION

**5. Emotion-Recognition Systems**

An application currently in development is *emotion-recognition technology*, which tries to read people's emotions. Similar to face-recognition technology, emotion-reading systems use a camera and software to analyze individuals' faces, but instead of trying to identify the individual, the system attempts to recognize their current emotion. The first expected application of such a system is for ATM machines, which already have the necessary hardware. By reading a customer's emotional response to displayed advertising, the advertising could be targeted more specifically to that individual. Even more helpful applications would include rephrasing instructions if the customer appeared confused or enlarging the screen text if the customer appeared to be squinting. Other applications for the future could include using this type of system to help therapists understand a patient's emotional state. Privacy advocates are concerned about the emotions of citizens being read in public locations without their consent. However, proponents of the technology argue that it's no different than when human tellers or store clerks interpret customers' emotions and modify their treatment of the customer accordingly.

For this project, form a group to discuss emotion-recognition systems. Do you think it is a worthy new technology or just a potential invasion of privacy? Create a list of the pros and cons of such a system from a business point of view, and then from a customer point of view. Can your group think of safeguards that could be implemented or specific ways of using an emotion-recognition system that would alleviate many of your listed disadvantages? Can your group think of other potential uses for such a system than the ones mentioned in this project?

Share your findings with the class in the form of a short presentation. The presentation should not exceed 10 minutes and should make use of one or more presentation aids such as the chalkboard, handouts, overhead transparencies, or a computer-based slide presentation (your instructor may provide additional requirements). Your group may also be asked to submit a summary of the presentation to your instructor.

### 6. Emerging Technologies

Many new and emerging technologies were discussed in this chapter, and more are announced virtually every day.

For this project, form a group to identify and research one type of emerging technology. It could be one that was mentioned in this chapter or a brand new product or technology just announced. After your group selects one technology, work together to investigate it, including how it works, what it is used for, and if alternate products or technologies are available. Try to locate a photo or illustration of your chosen technology to share with the class. Be sure to find out when the product or service is expected to become commercially available, who will use it, and how much it is expected to cost. Form an opinion about the usefulness of your selected technology.

Share your findings with the class in the form of a short presentation. The presentation should not exceed 10 minutes and should make use of one or more presentation aids such as the chalkboard, handouts, overhead transparencies, or a computer-based slide presentation (your instructor may provide additional requirements). Your group may also be asked to submit a summary of the presentation to your instructor.

### 7. NASA Robot Crews

**VIDEO VIEWPOINT**

Robotics research is continuing to make smarter and more capable robots. NASA researchers have even developed a way to make a crew of robots work together to grasp, lift, and move heavy loads across rough, varied terrain. The accompanying video clip takes a look at these new robots and some expected future uses.

After watching the video, think about the impact of continuing to make smarter and more capable robots. According to the video, the difference between the new NASA robot crews and other robots is special software that allows the robots to "share a brain," so that each robot knows what the rest are doing and can compensate or react accordingly. This technology enables the robots to work together to develop plans, such as how to maneuver around a rock or other obstacle the crew may encounter. Some might worry that this technology also provides the potential for a "super robot" in the future, such as the Borg enemy portrayed in the "Star Trek: The Next Generation" television show. Can robots get too smart? What steps should our society take to ensure that robots cannot become physically dangerous? What is the potential implication of replacing human laborers with robots? Currently robots are used mainly for monotonous or dangerous tasks, but what if the range of jobs given to robots continues to expand? Will it adversely affect our economy or will human workers automatically be able to evolve to more advanced positions?

**ONLINE VIDEO**

To view the NASA Robot Crews video clip, go to www.course.com/morley2003/ch8

**Express your viewpoint:** What is the potential impact of continuing to make smarter and more capable robots?

Use the video clip and the questions previously asked as the foundation for your response. Your instructor will direct you to be prepared to discuss your position (either in class, via an online class discussion group, or in a class chat room), or to write a short paper stating and supporting your viewpoint on the issue. You may also be asked to do research and provide resources to support your point of view.

# ANSWERS TO SELF-QUIZ

**CHAPTER 1**

1. F 2. T 3. F 4. T 5. F 6. Input 7. storage 8. vacuum tubes 9. programming; markup 10. network 11. tower 12. personal computer or PC 13. notebook or laptop 14. network computer (NC) or thin client 15. supercomputers

**CHAPTER 2**

1. F 2. T 3. F 4. F 5. T 6. Data; information 7. 250 million 8. pen, electronic pen, or stylus 9. scanner or flatbed scanner 10. central processing unit (CPU), microprocessor, or processor 11. pixels 12. output 13. hard drive 14. modem or communications device 15. file management

**CHAPTER 3**

1. F 2. T 3. F 4. F 5. T 6. Internet 7. servers 8. user; domain 9. billg@microsoft.com 10. online auction 11. DSL or digital subscriber line 12. telecommuting 13. bookmarks or favorites 14. spam 15. computer virus

**CHAPTER 4**

1. T 2. F 3. F 4. T 5. F 6. hacker 7. digital counterfeiting 8. attachments 9. Trojan horse 10. secure 11. public key 12. universal power supply (UPS) 13. Face recognition 14. digital certificate 15. disaster-recovery plan

**CHAPTER 5**

1. T 2. F 3. F 4. F 5. T 6. cookie 7. spyware 8. Electronic profiling 9. instant messaging (IM) 10. Proximity cards 11. Third-party 12. filter 13. encryption 14. opt out 15. filtering

**CHAPTER 6**

1. F 2. F 3. T 4. F 5. T 6. copyright; trademark 7. registered trademark 8. ethics 9. site; network 10. shareware 11. plagiarism 12. hoaxes 13. manipulation 14. vaporware 15. Communications Decency

**CHAPTER 7**

1. T 2. F 3. F 4. F 5. T 6. ergonomic 7. document holder or copy holder 8. burnout 9. addiction or compulsion 10. digital divide 11. Americans with Disabilities 12. Braille 13. alternative text 14. ENERGY STAR 15. e-paper or electronic paper

**CHAPTER 8**

1. F 2. F 3. T 4. T 5. F 6. Nanotechnology 7. qubits 8. Turing Test 9. shopping bot 10. robot 11. virtual reality (VR) 12. VeriChip 13. telemedicine 14. smart bomb 15. exoskeleton

# CREDITS

Throughout the chapters: Screenshots of Microsoft Access®, Excel®, Internet Explorer®, Paint®, PowerPoint®, Word®, and Windows® reprinted with permission from Microsoft Corporation.

## Chapter 1

**Figure 1-1a**, Courtesy of Hewlett-Packard Company; **Figure 1-1b**, © Comstock Photography; **Figure 1-1c**, © Comstock Photography; **Figure 1-1d**, Courtesy of The Electrolux Group; **Figure 1-2a**, © Eyewire; **Figure 1-2b**, Courtesy David Young-Wolff; **Figure 1-2c**, Courtesy Gettysburg College; **Figure 1-2d**, © Comstock Photography; **Figure 1-3a**, Courtesy of IBM Corporation; **Figure 1-3b**, Courtesy of Intel Corporation; **Figure 1-3c**, InFocus LP650 digital projector used with permission from InFocus; **Figure 1-3d**, Courtesy of 3M, Inc.; **Figure 1-4a**, Courtesy of Symbol Technologies, Inc.; **Figure 1-4b**, Courtesy of Ceiva Logic, Inc.; **Figure 1-4c**, Courtesy of Kiosk Information Systems; **Figure 1-4d**, Courtesy of Garmin Ltd. or its subsidiaries; **Figure 1-4e**, Courtesy of Garmin Ltd. or its subsidiaries; **Figure 1-6a**, Courtesy of IBM Archives; **Figure 1-6b**, Courtesy U.S. Army; **Figure 1-6c**, Courtesy of IBM Archives; **Figure 1-6d**, Courtesy of IBM Archives; **Figure 1-6e**, Courtesy of IBM Archives; **Figure 1-7a**, Courtesy of Gateway, Inc.; **Figure 1-7b**, Courtesy of Hewlett-Packard Company; **Figure 1-7c**, Courtesy of Telex Communications, Inc.; **Figure 1-8**, Courtesy of VeriFone, Inc.; **Figure 1-11a**, MUSICMATCH(tm) Jukebox Deluxe v7 by MUSICMATCH Inc.; **Figure 1-11b**, Courtesy of Microsoft Corporation; **Figure 1-13**, Courtesy Acer America and Courtesy of IBM Corporation; **Figure 1-14**, Courtesy CNAV Systems, Inc.; **Figure 1-16a**, Photo courtesy of Nokia. Copyright © 2002 Nokia. All rights reserved. Nokia and Nokia Connecting People are registered trademarks of Nokia Corporation.; **Figure 1-16b**, Courtesy of Research in Motion; **Figure 1-17a**, Courtesy of Xi Computer Corporation; **Figure 1-17b**, Courtesy Acer America; **Figure 1-17c**, Don Couch Photography; **Figure 1-17d**, Courtesy of MicronPC; **Figure 1-17e**, Courtesy of Palm, Inc.; **Figure 1-17f**, Courtesy of ViewSonic Corporation; **Figure 1-18a**, Courtesy of Sun Microsystems; **Figure 1-18b**, Courtesy of EarthLink; **Figure 1-19**, © Comstock Photography; **Figure 1-20**, © Corbis; **Figure 1-21**, Courtesy of Japan Marine Science and Technology Center; **Figure 1-22a**, Courtesy Kensington and Courtesy© Rodney Collins Photography; **Figure 1-22b**, © Rodney Collins Photography; **Figure 1-22d**, © Rodney Collins Photography; **Figure-1 22e**, Courtesy Kensington

## Chapter 2

**Figure 2-2**, Courtesy of Belkin Components; **Figure 2-3a**, Photo courtesy Targus, Inc.; **Figure 2-3b**, Photo courtesy Targus, Inc.; **Figure 2-3c**, Courtesy of Seiko Instruments Austin, Inc.; **Figure 2-4a**, Courtesy of Belkin Components; **Figure 2-5a**, Copyright © 2002 Eclipsys Corporation. All rights reserved. Used with permission.; **Figure 2-5b**, Courtesy of Symbol Technologies, Inc.; **Figure 2-5c**, Courtesy of Sony Electronics, Inc.; **Figure 2-6**, Courtesy of Symbol Technologies, Inc.; **Figure 2-7a**, Courtesy of Micron PC; **Figure 2-7b**, Courtesy of Toshiba; **Figure 2-7c**, Courtesy of Kensington Technology Group; **Figure 2-7d**, Courtesy of Kensington Technology Group; **Figure 2-7e**, Courtesy of 3M Inc.; **Figure 2-8a**, Courtesy of C Technologies AB/Anoto Group AB (publ); **Figure 2-8b**, Courtesy of Hewlett-Packard Company; **Figure 2-8c**, Courtesy of NCR Corporation; **Figure 2-8d**, Courtesy of Intermec Technologies Corporation; **Figure 2-9**, Courtesy of Texas Instruments RFID Systems; **Figure 2-10**, Courtesy of Lexar Media; **Figure 2-12**, Courtesy Acer Inc.; **Figure 2-13a**, Courtesy of Intel Corporation; **Figure 2-13c**, AMD Athlon(TM) processor (Courtesy of AMD); **Figure 2-14**, Courtesy of ViewSonic; **Figure 2-15a**, Image Courtesy of SGI. Screen image courtesy of 2000 American Museum of Natural History. Photo by Denis Finnin.; **Figure 2-15b**, Courtesy of Casio, Inc.; **Figure 2-15c**, Photo courtesy of Nokia. Copyright © 2002 Nokia. All rights reserved. Nokia and Nokia Connecting People are registered trademarks of Nokia Corporation.; **Figure 2-15d**, Photography by Hunter Freeman; **Figure 2-16**, Courtesy of Acer, Inc.; **Figure 2-17b**, Courtesy of Hewlett-Packard Company; **Figure 2-18b**, Courtesy of Hewlett-Packard Company; **Figure 2-18c**, Courtesy of Hewlett-Packard Company; **Figure 2-19**, Courtesy Acer Inc.; **Figure 2-22b**, Courtesy of Imation; **Figure 2-22c**, Courtesy of Maxell Corporation of America; **Figure 2-22d**, Courtesy of DataPlay, Inc.; **Figure 2-23**, Copyright © Iomega Corporation. All Rights Reserved. Iomega, the stylized "i" logo and all product images are property of Iomega Corporation in the United States and/or other countries.; **Figure 2-24a**, Courtesy of Sony Electronics, Inc.; **Figure 2-24b**, Courtesy of Sony Electronics, Inc.; **Figure 2-24c**, Courtesy of Agate Technologies, Inc.; **Figure 2-24d**, Courtesy of Lexar Media; **Figure 2-24e**, Courtesy of Lexar Media; **Figure 2-24f**, Courtesy of Lexar Media; **Figure 2-25**, Courtesy of Visa USA Inc.; **Figure 2-26**, Courtesy of Seagate Technology LLC; **Figure 2-27a**, Courtesy of International Business Machines Corporation. Unauthorized use not permitted.; **Figure 2-27b**, Copyright © Iomega Corporation. All Rights Reserved. Iomega, the stylized "i" logo and all product images are property of Iomega Corporation in the United States and/or other countries.

## Chapter 3

**Figure 3-6c**, © Zigy Kaluzny/Getty Images; **Figure 3-11a**, Courtesy of Acer, Inc.; **Figure 3-11b**, Courtesy of CorAccess; **Figure 3-11c**, Courtesy of Novatel; **Figure 3-11d**, Photo courtesy of Nokia. Copyright © 2002 Nokia. All rights reserved. Nokia and Nokia Connecting People are registered trademarks of Nokia Corporation.; **Figure 3-12a**, Courtesy of The Internet Exchange; **Figure 3-12b**, Courtesy of

Yahoo! Inc.; **Figure 3-13a**, Courtesy of U.S. Robotics; **Figure 3-13b**, Courtesy StarBand Communications, Inc.; **Figure 3-13c**, Courtesy of Novatel; **Figure 3-13d**, Courtesy of Intel Corporation, Inc.; **Figure 3-14**, © Reuters NewMedia Inc./CORBIS; **Figure 3-16**, AOL screenshot © 2002 America Online, Inc. used with permission; **Figure 3-24a**, Courtesy of AT&T Wireless

## Chapter 4

**Figure 4-1**, Courtesy Verizon Communications; **Figure 4-4b**, Courtesy Acer Inc.; **Figure 4-5b**, Courtesy of Iplex Marin; **Figure 4-6**, Courtesy of Social Security Administration; **Figure 4-7**, Courtesy of Microsoft Corporation; **Figure 4-8**, Photos courtesy of United States Secret Service; **Figure 4-9a**, Courtesy of Kensington Technology Group; **Figure 4-9b**, Courtesy of Kensington Technology Group; **Figure 4-10**, Courtesy of Kensington Technology Group; **Figure 4-13**, Courtesy Diebold, Inc.; **Figure 4-14**, Courtesy Diebold, Inc.; **Figure 4-15a**, Courtesy Digital Persona; **Figure 4-15b**, Courtesy Recognition Systems; **Figure 4-15c**, © AP Wide World Photos; **Figure 4-15d**, Courtesy Diebold, Inc.; **Figure 4-17**, Courtesy Identix Inc. Minnetonka, MN, USA; **Figure 4-25**, Courtesy U.S. Treasury Department

## Chapter 5

**Figure 5-9**, Courtesy of Ascentive.com; **Figure 5-11**, Courtesy HID Corporation; **Figure 5-12a**, © 2002 Cédric Laurant; **Figure 5-12b**, Alan Chin/The New York Times; **Figure 5-13**, Courtesy of Bantu. Inc.; **Figure 5-17**, Courtesy TRUSTe; **Figure 5-24a**, Courtesy of www.PeepLock.com; **Figure 5-24b**, Courtesy www.PeepLock.com

## Chapter 6

**Figure 6-1b**, Courtesy of NBC, Inc.; **Figure 6-1c**, Courtesy of LEGO Company; **Figure 6-1d**, Courtesy of Microsoft Corporation; **Figure 6-1e**, Courtesy of Coca-Cola Company; **Figure 6-1f**, [eBay Mark] is a trademark of eBay Inc.; **Figure 6-2**, © Ken Krauss/AP World Wide Photos; **Figure 6-3**, Courtesy of United States Patent and Trademark Office; **Figure 6-10**, © AP Wide World Photos; **Figure 6-12**, Courtesy of University of Denver; **Figure 6-14**, © AP Wide World Photos; **Figure 6-15**, © AP Wide World Photos

## Chapter 7

**Figure 7-2a**, Courtesy of DataPro Inc.; **Figure 7-3a**, Courtesy of Datadesk Technologies; **Figure 7-3b**, Courtesy of 3M; **Figure 7-3c**, Courtesy of Kensington Technology Group; **Figure 7-3d**, Courtesy of Kensington Technology Group; **Figure 7-3e**, Courtesy of Kensington Technology Group; **Figure 7-3f**, Courtesy of Kensington Technology Group; **Figure 7-5a**, Courtesy of FastPoint Technologies, Inc. (http://www.fastpoint.com); **Figure 7-5b**, Courtesy of Symbol Technologies; **Figure 7-5c**, Photo courtesy Xybernaut® Corporation; **Figure 7-5d**, Photo courtesy of Nokia. Copyright © 2002 Nokia. All rights reserved. Nokia and Nokia Connecting People are registered trademarks of Nokia Corporation; **Figure 7-7**, Courtesy of Motorola; **Figure 7-8**, Courtesy of Maressa Hecht Orzack, Ph.D.; **Figure 7-10a**, Photo of "Encore Simputer" courtesy of Encore Software Limited, Bangalore; **Figure 7-10b**, Photo of "Encore Simputer" courtesy of Encore Software Limited, Bangalore; **Figure 7-11a**, Hooleon Corporation; **Figure 7-11b**, Courtesy of Maltron; **Figure 7-11c**, Courtesy of Prenke Romich; **Figure 7-11d**, Courtesy of NaturalPoint, Inc.; **Figure 7-12a**, Courtesy of Freedom Scientific, Inc.; **Figure 7-12b**, Courtesy of Freedom Scientific, Inc.; **Figure 7-12c**, Courtesy of Freedom Scientific, Inc.; **Figure 7-12d**, Courtesy of NanoPac, Inc. www.nanopac.com; **Figure 7-14a**, Courtesy of U.S. Environmental Protection Agency; **Figure 7-14b**, Courtesy of European Commission, Environment Directorate-General; **Figure 7-14c**, Courtesy of Korea Environmental Labelling Association(KELA); **Figure 7-14d**, Courtesy of ABNT - ASSOCIAÇÃO BRASILEIRA DE NORMAS TÉCNICAS; **Figure 7-15**, Courtesy of NEC Solutions (America), Inc.; **Figure 7-16**, Courtesy of Silicon Valley Toxics Coalition; **Figure 7-17a**, Courtesy of E Ink; **Figure 7-17b**, Courtesy of Gyricon Media

## Chapter 8

**Figure 8-1a**, Courtesy of Matsucom, Inc.; **Figure 8-1b**, Courtesy of Marcus Rose and ElekSen; **Figure 8-1c**, Courtesy of Microsoft Corporation; **Figure 8-2**, Courtesy of Xybernaut® Corporation; **Figure 8-3**, Courtesy: IBM Research, Almaden Research Center; **Figure 8-4**, Courtesy of InPhase Technologies; **Figure 8-5a**, Courtesy of Universal Display Corporation; **Figure 8-5b**, Courtesy of Motorola; **Figure 8-5c**, Courtesy of iSun; **Figure 8-6**, Courtesy of IBM Corporation; **Figure 8-10**, Courtesy of V-Star 1KTV; **Figure 8-11**, Courtesy of TRW, Inc.; **Figure 8-12a**, Courtesy of Friendly Robotics, Inc.; **Figure 8-12b**, Courtesy of NEC Corporation; **Figure 8-12c**, Courtesy of Sony Electronics, Inc.; **Figure 8-12d**, Courtesy of American Honda Motor Co., Inc.; **Figure 8-12e**, Courtesy of CyberMotion; **Figure 8-13a**, Courtesy of KRAMER ENTERTAINMENT - www.kramerintl.com; **Figure 8-13b**, Courtesy Evans & Sutherland Computer Corporation; **Figure 8-14**, Courtesy of Applied Digital Solutions, Inc.; **Figure 8-15a**, Courtesy of Intuitive Surgical; **Figure 8-15b**, Courtesy of Intuitive Surgical; **Figure 8-16a**, © Corbis; **Figure 8-16b**, Courtesy of University of Rochester; **Figure 8-16c**, © Corbis; **Figure 8-17a**, Courtesy of ATK; **Figure 8-17b**, Courtesy of NASA; **Figure 8-17c**, Courtesy of iRobot Corporation; **Figure 8-17d**, Courtesy of iRobot Corporation; **Figure 8-17e**, Courtesy of U.S. Army

# GLOSSARY/INDEX

Notes: Page numbers in *italics* indicate references to figures that are located outside the page ranges specified for that key term. **Boldface** key terms include definitions.

# C

## E

# I

## N



## O

# P

# Q



# R



# S

## W



## X



## Y



## Z